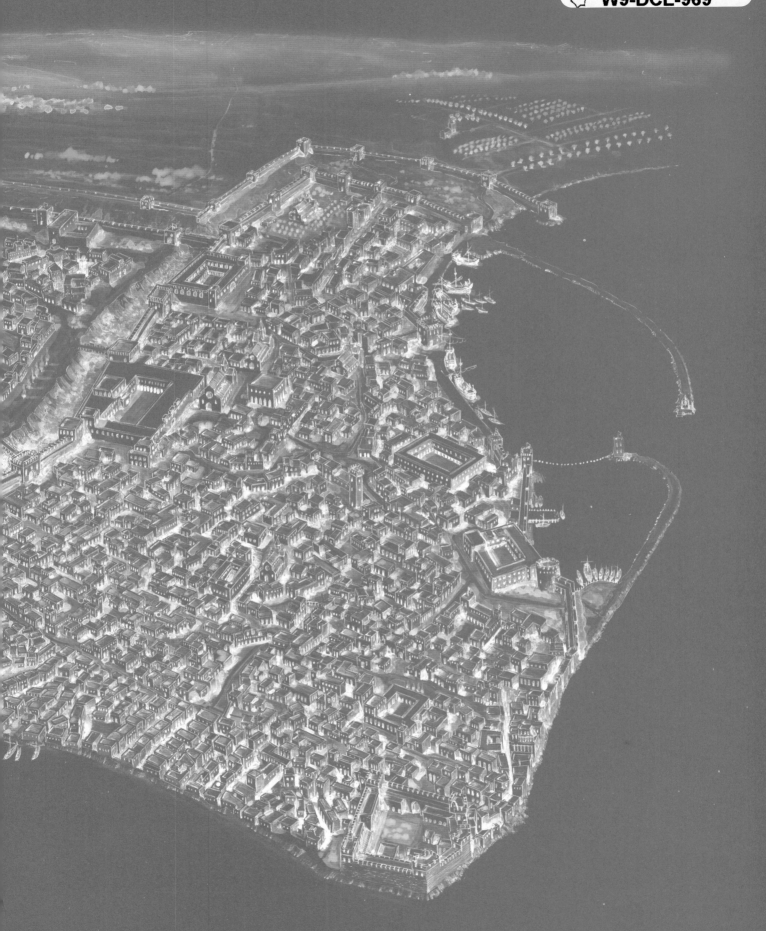

THE ATLAS OF THE
CRUSADES

THE ATLAS OF THE
CRUSADES

Edited by
Jonathan Riley-Smith

Times Books

First published in 1991 by
Times Books,
16 Golden Square,
London W1R 4BN

Cartographic director: Malcolm Swanston

Editorial director: Anne Benewick
Editor: Chris Schüler
Place names consultant and Index: P.J.M. Geelan
Picture research: Suzanne O'Farrell
Design: Ian Cockburn

Maps, illustrations and typesetting by
Swanston Graphics, Derby

Isabelle Verpeaux, Jacqueline Land, Ralph Orme,
Graham Malkin, Adrian Van Weerdenburg,
James Mills-Hicks, Melvyn Pickering,
Irene Hopkins, Cheryl Wilbraham,
Andrew Bright, Virginia MacFadyen

For Times Books:
Andrew Heritage

British Library Cataloguing in Publication Data
The Atlas of the Crusades.
  1. Crusades
  I. Riley-Smith, Jonathan
  909.070223

Printed and bound in Hong Kong by
Mandarin Offset International (HK) Ltd.

ISBN 0-7230-0361-0

CONTENTS

FOREWORD

The crusades is a field of scholarship in which British historians are playing a leading part. The existence of so much local talent stems from a long tradition of eastern Mediterranean scholarship, supplemented by the growing interest in the crusades that followed the establishment of the British Mandate in Palestine after the First World War. One of the most distinguished upholders of that tradition is Sir Steven Runciman, whose three-volume *History of the Crusades*, appearing in the early 1950s, was an inspiration to young historians at a time when by coincidence several scholars in mid-career were teaching the crusades at postgraduate level, among them Professor L. H. Butler, who is represented by four pupils among the contributors to this Atlas, and Dr R. C. Smail, who is represented by two. At any rate, a very strong team of British historians was assembled to contribute to the Atlas. It was divided into five groups, each concentrating on one of the following: Crusading to the East; Crusading in Europe; the Military Orders; the Latin East and Seapower; and Muslims and Mongols. The groups met for short conferences to discuss and change if necessary a draft synopsis and to allot the map spreads.

The Atlas reflects the way the subject has been developing over the last twenty years. Most historians now agree that the study of crusading should not be confined to the expeditions to the East, but should also encompass the campaigns in Spain, the Baltic region, North Africa and sometimes in the interior of western Europe. There is also general agreement that the crusading movement reached its high point in the thirteenth century, remained appealing in the fourteenth and retained its popularity, at least among certain classes, to the end of the sixteenth century and beyond. Very large numbers of men and women were involved directly and indirectly in expeditions in many different theatres of war, thousands of miles apart, but the experiences of the crusaders were on the whole unpleasant and expensive: there was little compensation to be gained in financial terms, and their long absences from home on campaign threatened disruption to their estates and families, quite apart from the discomfort and danger they endured. Many historians are convinced that most crusaders must have been so strongly motivated that they were prepared to make great sacrifices for what was, in spite of the violence and cruelty associated with it, a genuinely popular movement, and a religious one at that.

An atlas ranging so widely in space and time poses special editorial problems, and we have tried to resolve these pragmatically. For instance, it is well known that even when the course of a frontier can be accurately plotted - and that is rare for the Middle Ages - it meant less then than it does now, being more often than not simply the boundary between the lands of two villages which owed returns to lords who were the subjects of different powers. In some regions, indeed, frontiers were characterized by broad belts of *condominia*, in which lords of different nationalities, and in Palestine and Syria of different religions, shared the ownership of great swathes of villages. Customs posts were sometimes to be found - there was one on the road from Damascus into the kingdom of Jerusalem - but they were often not on the border itself, but some way within it, perhaps at the first town.

It is a convention among English-speaking historians of the central Middle Ages to anglicize the Christian names and prepositions of European names (Godfrey of Bouillon rather than Godefroid de Bouillon). On the other hand English-speaking historians of late medieval and early modern Europe are accustomed to leave the names in their native forms (Jacques de Molay). We have sacrificed consistency to the conventions. In the same way we have opted for the historical integrity and 'feel' of each map spread when choosing the form of place names, so that, for example, Adrianople in the early maps becomes Edirne in the later ones. All place-names are cross-referenced in the index.

When distinguishing countries or regions by religion or denomination, clarity and the historical demands of the subject have forced us to portray the religious beliefs of the governments in power, rather than those of the majority of the inhabitants. For instance, the Latin East has been given a 'Catholic' colour, while sixteenth-century Ireland has been given a 'Protestant' one. We have made three exceptions. First, Cilician Armenia was technically uniate Catholic from the 1190s, when the ruler submitted to Rome. But that submission was never a reality and the Armenians played so distinctive a part in the story that we considered that it would be misleading if we did not give Cilicia a distinctive 'Armenian' colour throughout. Secondly on the map describing the Catholic missions in the East the religion of the majority in any region was more relevant than religious control, and thirdly, the very last map of all, which describes conditions in 1990, in the case of atheist Communist governments.

In all histories of the crusades the brothers of the Order of the Hospital of St John of Jerusalem appear in a bewildering range of guises, as brothers of St John, Hospitallers, Knights of St John or Knights of Malta. We have tried to keep the variety of names used for the Hospitallers to a minimum, but have found it impossible to adhere strictly to one form.

The Atlas consists of 64 double-page map spreads, divided into four parts. Each part is preceded by an introduction. A good deal of attention is paid to Islamic history in the map spreads, but readers who view the crusades primarily as wars between Christians and Muslims may be surprised by the fact that the introductions concern themselves almost entirely with internal Christian developments. Two points should be made here. The first is that crusades were launched against a variety of enemies, of which the Muslims were one, although the most important: the nature of the enemies was less significant to contemporaries than the perceived injury done to Christendom by them. The second is that the crusades grew out of developments within Christianity itself. It was pointed out long ago that crusading emerged from internal Christian wars engendered by an eleventh-century movement for 'liberation', linked to Church reform. The attention of the reformers was bound sooner or later to turn from the oppression suffered, as they saw it, by the western Church from the practices of European kings and lords to the plight of eastern Christians living under infidel yoke. The crusades were so much a Christian development that it is almost as if Muslim foes would have to have been invented had they not already existed.

Whatever scale of measurement one uses, the crusading movement was one of the great forces in European history. Nothing can really do justice to the emotions poured out, the cash expended, the pain suffered, and inflicted, by the crusaders, the worry of the families they left behind, the disturbance caused by the regular departure of large bodies of men from western Europe and by the efforts to preserve the settlements established in the East, the Baltic region and Spain. But this Atlas illustrates better than words alone could the distances involved, the range of options available to crusaders and the variety of their experiences.

Jonathan Riley-Smith

CONTRIBUTORS

General Editor
PROFESSOR JONATHAN RILEY-SMITH
Department of History, Royal Holloway and New Bedford
College, University of London

CRUSADING TO THE EAST

DR WENDY BRACEWELL
Department of History, School of Slavonic and East
European Studies, University of London

DR NORMAN HOUSLEY
Department of History, University of Leicester

DR SIMON LLOYD
Department of History, University of Newcastle

DR DENYS PRINGLE
Principal Inspector of Ancient Monuments, Scotland

DR CHRISTOPHER TYERMAN
Hertford College, University of Oxford

CRUSADING IN EUROPE

DR MALCOLM BARBER
Department of History, University of Reading

DR NORMAN HOUSLEY
(see Crusading to the East)

PROFESSOR DEREK LOMAX
School of Modern Languages, University of Birmingham

DR ELIZABETH SIBERRY
Surbiton

THE MILITARY ORDERS

DR MALCOLM BARBER
(see Crusading in Europe)

DR MICHAEL BURLEIGH
Department of International History, London School
of Economics, University of London

DR ALAN FOREY
Department of History, University of Durham

PROFESSOR DEREK LOMAX
(see Crusading in Europe)

DR ANTHONY LUTTRELL
Bath

THE LATIN EAST AND SEAPOWER

DR DAVID ABULAFIA
Gonville and Gaius College, University of Cambridge

DR PETER EDBURY
Department of History, University of Wales, Cardiff

DR ANTHONY LUTTRELL
(see The Military Orders)

MUSLIMS AND MONGOLS

DR MICHAEL BRETT
Department of History, School of Oriental and African
Studies, University of London

DR COLIN HEYWOOD
Department of History, School of Oriental and African
Studies, University of London

DR DAVID MORGAN
Department of History, School of Oriental and African
Studies, University of London

ROBERT IRWIN
Formerly of Department of Mediaeval History,
University of St Andrews

Chronology

CRUSADES IN THE EAST

1095 July 1095-Sept 1096: Pope Urban II's journey through France. Nov: Council of Clermont. 27 Nov : Crusade first preached by Pope Urban II. Dec 1095-July 1096: 'The First Holocaust' - persecution of Jews in Europe by crusaders.

1096 Mar: First departures of first wave of crusaders. Jun-Aug: Three first wave armies defeated in Hungary. Sept-Oct: Peter the Hermit's crusade defeated in Asia Minor.

1097 19 June: Surrender of Nicaea to the Byzantines. 1 July: Battle of Dorylaeum. 21 Oct-3 June 1098: Siege of Antioch.

1098 10 Mar: Baldwin of Boulogne establishes county of Edessa. 28 June: Battle of Antioch.

1099 15 July: Crusaders capture Jerusalem. 22 July: Godfrey of Bouillon elected ruler of Jerusalem. 12 Aug: Battle of Ascalon.

1100 18 July: Death of Godfrey of Bouillon. Sept: First departures of third wave of crusaders.

1100-1118 Baldwin of Boulogne king of Jerusalem.

1101 Aug-Sept: Crusade armies defeated by Turks in Asia Minor.

1106 Bohemond of Taranto on recruiting drive in France.

1107 Sigurd of Norway's crusade departs. Oct: Bohemond of Taranto's crusade musters in Apulia.

1108 Sept: Bohemond of Taranto surrenders to Byzantines.

1110 4 Dec: Sidon falls to forces of Jerusalem and Norwegian crusaders.

1113 Pope Paschal II recognizes Hospital of St John in Jerusalem.

1118 Knights Templar founded.

1118-1131 Baldwin II king of Jerusalem.

1122 Pope Calixtus II proclaims crusade to be fought in East and in Spain.

1123 Mar-Apr: First Lateran Council issues privileges for crusaders.

1124 7 July: Tyre falls to forces of Jerusalem and crusaders.

1128 Preaching of new crusade by Hugh of Payns, Grand Master of Templars and others. Crusaders depart.

1129 Nov: Forces of Jerusalem and crusaders attack Damascus.

1131-1143 Fulk (V) of Anjou king of Jerusalem.

1131-1152 Melisende queen of Jerusalem.

1136 Castle of Bethgibelin granted to Hospitallers. March on Amanus Mountains granted to Templars.

1144 24 Dec: Edessa falls to Zangi.

1145 1 Dec: Pope Eugenius II issues letter *Quantum praedecessores*, proclaiming Second Crusade.

CRUSADES IN EUROPE AND NORTH AFRICA

1096 Pope Urban II extends crusading to Spain.

1097 Aragonese take Huesca.

1114 Crusade of Count Berenguer of Barcelona against Balearic Islands and down mainland coast.

1118 Pope Gelasius II proclaims crusade. 19 Dec Saragossa falls to crusaders.

1120 Restoration of Tarragona.

1122 Crusade proclaimed in Spain.

1123 Privileges used for crusaders in Spain.

1125-1126 Alfonso I of Aragon raids southern Spain.

1135 May: Council of Pisa. Pope Innocent III offers crusade indulgences in war against Normans in southern Italy and anti-pope Anacletus.

BACKGROUND EVENTS

1095 Mar: Council of Piacenza. Byzantine empire appeals to West for help.

1127 Zangi appointed governor of Mosul.

1128 Jan: Council of Troyes recognizes Order of Knights Templar. 18 June: Zangi occupies Aleppo.

CRUSADES IN THE EAST

1146 Persecution of Jews in Rhineland.

1146-1147 May: St Bernard of Clairvaux preaches Cross.

1147 May: First departures of crusade forces for East. Oct: Conrad III defeated near Dorylaeum in Asia Minor.

1148 20 Jan: Louis VII reaches Antalya. 24-28 July: Second Crusade defeated outside Damascus.

1149 15 July: Dedication of new church of Holy Sepulchre in Jerusalem.

1151 12 July: Last fortress in county of Edessa surrenders to Nur al-Din.

1152-1163 Baldwin III king of Jerusalem.

1153 22 Aug: Christians take Ascalon.

1157-1184 Seven papal crusade proclamations elicit little response.

1163-1174 Amalric king of Jerusalem.

1163 Sept: Amalric's first expedition to Egypt.

1164 Aug-Oct: Amalric's second expedition to Egypt.

1167 Jan-Aug: Amalric's third expedition to Egypt.

1168 Oct-Jan 1169: Amalric's fourth expedition to Egypt.

1169 Oct-Dec: Amalric's fifth expedition to Egypt.

1174-1186 Baldwin IV king of Jerusalem.

1177 Crusade of Philip of Flanders. 25 Nov: Christians defeat Saladin at Mont Gisard.

1183 Reynald of Châtillon launches attack aimed at Mecca.

1185-1186 Baldwin V king of Jerusalem.

1186-1192 Guy of Lusignan king of Jerusalem.

1186-1190 Sybilla queen of Jerusalem.

1187 4 July: Saladin annihilates Christians at Battle of Hattin. 2 Oct: Saladin takes Jerusalem. 29 Oct: Pope Gregory VIII proclaims Third Crusade in letter *Audita tremendi*. Nov: Richard of England takes Cross.

1188 Jan: Henry II of England and Philip II of France take Cross. Saladin Tithe imposed. Mar: Emperor Frederick I takes Cross. Spring: Archbishop Baldwin of Canterbury's preaching tour.

1189 May: Frederick I sets off from Regensburg. 27 Aug: King Guy of Jerusalem opens siege of Acre.

1190-1205 Isabella I queen of Jerusalem.

CRUSADES IN EUROPE AND NORTH AFRICA

1147 Pope extends crusade to Spain. 13 Apr: Papal letter *Divina dispensatione* authorizes German crusade against the Wends. July-Sept: German campaigns against the Wends. 17 Oct: Crusaders take Almería. 24 Oct: Portuguese and North European crusaders take Lisbon.

1149 24 Oct: Lérida falls to Christian forces from Barcelona.

1153 Crusade authorized in Spain.

1157 Crusade authorized in Spain.

1158 Order of Calatrava founded.

c.1166 Order of Avis founded (as order of Evora).

1170 Order of Santiago founded.

1171 Crusade in Baltic region authorized.

1172 Defence of Huete.

c.1173 Order of Montegaudio founded.

1175 Crusade authorized in Spain.

c.1175 Order of Alcántara founded (as Order of San Julián del Peirero).

1177 Cuenca captured by Christians.

1189 3 Sept: Silves captured by Christians.

BACKGROUND EVENTS

1146 14 Sept: Zangi assassinated. Succeeded in Aleppo by Nur al-Din.

1154 25 Apr: Nur al-Din occupies Damascus.

1169 23 Mar: Saladin in control of Egypt for Nur al-Din.

1171 23 Jan: Mosul recognizes overlordship of Nur al-Din.

1172 10 Sept: 'Abbasid caliphate proclaimed by Saladin in Egypt.

1174 15 May: Death of Nur al-Din. 28 Oct: Saladin occupies Damascus.

1176 17 Sept: Defeat of the Byzantines by the Seljuks at Myriokephalon.

1183 11 June: Aleppo recognizes Saladin's overlordship.

1186 3 Mar: Mosul recognizes Saladin's overlordship.

CRUSADES IN THE EAST

1190 10 June: Frederick I drowns. July: Richard I of England and Philip II of France set off from Vézelay.

1191 Richard I conquers Cyprus. Crusaders capture Acre. 7 Sept: Battle of Arsur.

1192-1194 Guy of Lusignan ruler of Cyprus after acquiring island from Richard I.

1192 Jan: Richard I within a few miles of Jersusalem. June: Richard I again within a few miles of Jerusalem. Aug: Richard defends Jaffa. 2 Sept:Richard 's treaty with Saladin.

1194-1205 Aimery of Lusignan ruler of Cyprus.

1195 Emperor Henry VI takes Cross.

1197-1205 Aimery of Lusignan king of Jerusalem and Cyprus.

1197-1198 German crusade.

1198 6 Jan: Cilician Armenia becomes a kingdom. German field-hospitallers reconstituted as Teutonic Knights. Aug: Fourth Crusade proclaimed.

1199 28 Nov: Tournament at Écry. Many nobles take Cross. Dec: First direct taxation of Church for crusades.

1201 Feb: Venice agrees to ship Fourth Crusade to East.

1202 Oct: Fourth Crusade sails from Venice. 24 Nov: Crusaders capture Zara.

1203 17 July: Crusaders attack Constantinople. Isaac II Angelus and Alexius IV replace Alexius III on Byzantine throne.

1204 1 Feb: *Coup d'état* puts Alexius on Byzantine throne. 12-15 April: Crusaders sack Constantinople. 9 May: Count Baldwin of Flanders elected Latin emperor of Constantinople. Winter 1204-1205: Conquest of Morea by Geoffrey of Villehardouin and William of Champlitte.

1205-1218 Hugh I king of Cyprus.

1208 Crusade proclaimed by Pope. Little response.

1210-1225 John of Brienne king of Jerusalem.

1210-1212 Maria queen of Jerusalem.

1212 Spring: Children's Crusade.

1213 April: Pope Innocent III in letter *Quia major* proclaims Fifth Crusade.

1215 Nov-Dec: Fourth Lateran Council. 14 Dec: *Ad liberandam* constitution agreed. Taxation of Church formalized.

1217 Aug: First departures of Fifth Crusade. Autumn-winter: Crusaders in Palestine.

CRUSADES IN EUROPE AND NORTH AFRICA

1191 Danes attack Finland.

1193 Pope authorizes indulgences for defenders of Church in Livonia. Crusade proclaimed in Spain.

1194 Danes attack Estonia.

1195 19 July: Muslim victory at Alarcos.

1197 Pope renews indulgences for Livonia. Danes attack Estonia. Crusade proclaimed in Spain.

1199 5 Oct: Livonian crusade proclaimed. 24 Nov: Crusade proclaimed against Markward of Anwelier.

1202 Sword Brothers established in Livonia.

1204 Pope permits Bishop Albert of Riga to recruit for the Livonian crusade on regular basis.

1206 Danes crusade to Ösel.

1208 14 Jan: Papal legate Peter of Castelnau assassinated. Crusade proclaimed against Cathars.

1209 First campaign in crusade against Cathars. 22 July: Béziers sacked.

1210 Danes attack Prussia.

1211 Sept: Muslims take Salvatierra.

1212 Crusade proclaimed in Spain. 17 July: Christian victory in Battle of Las Navas de Tolosa.

1213 Crusades in Spain and against Cathars downgraded in favour of Fifth Crusade. 12 Sept: Simon of Montfort defeats Peter of Aragon and Raymond of Toulouse in the Battle of Muret.

1216 28 Oct: Child-king Henry III of England takes Cross against English rebels.

BACKGROUND EVENTS

1193 4 Mar: Death of Saladin.

1195 8 Apr: Byzantine emperor Isaac II Angelus deposed and blinded by his brother Alexius III.

1211-12 Mongols conquer northern China.

1211 Teutonic Knights given march in Transylvania by king of Hungary.

CRUSADES IN THE EAST

1218-1253 Henry I king of Cyprus.

1218 27 May: Fifth Crusade lands in Egypt.

1219 5 Nov: Crusaders occupy Damietta.

1221 17 July: Fifth Crusade advances into Egyptian interior. 30 Aug: Crusaders defeated at Mansurah. 8 Sept: Crusaders leave Egypt.

1225-1243 Emperor Frederick II ruler of Jerusalem.

1225-1228 Yolande (Isabella II) queen of Jerusalem.

1229-1233 Civil war in Cyprus.

1229 14 July: Battle of Nicosia.

1231-1242 Commune of Acre embodies resistance to Frederick II in Palestine.

1232 15 June: Battle of Agridi (Cyprus).

1235 John of Brienne saves Constantinople. Defeat of Byzantines and Bulgarians.

1243-1254 Conrad king of Jerusalem.

1244 Kingdom of Jerusalem enters into alliance with Damascus and Transjordan against Egypt. 11 July-23 Aug: Jerusalem falls to Khwarizmians. 17 Oct: Christians defeated in Battle of La Forbie.

1250-1254 Louis IX in Palestine.

1253-1267 Hugh II king of Cyprus.

1254-1268 Conradin king of Jerusalem.

1254 French regiment established in Acre.

CRUSADES IN EUROPE AND NORTH AFRICA

1218 25 June: Simon of Montfort killed outside Toulouse.

1219 Danes invade northern Estonia.

1225 Teutonic Knights invited to Prussia.

1226 Golden Bull of Rimini gives Grand Master of Teutonic Knights status of imperial prince. Jan: King Louis VIII of France vows to undertake the crusade against the Cathars. 9 Sept: Avignon falls to crusaders. 8 Nov: King Louis VIII dies.

1227 Crusade proclaimed against heretics in Bosnia (renewed 1234).

1229-1231 Crusade to Majorca of James I of Aragon.

1229 Teutonic Knights begin conquest of Prussia. New crusade proclaimed in Spain. Crusade against the Cathars.

1231 John of Brienne's crusade to Constantinople. Crusade of Ferdinand III of Castile.

1232-1234 Crusade against the Stedinger peasants.

1232-1253 James I of Aragon conquers Valencia.

1233 Inquisition established in Toulouse.

1234 Prussia becomes papal fief.

1236 Crusade proclaimed in support of Constantinople against Byzantines and Bulgarians. 29 June: Ferdinand III of Castile takes Córdoba.

1237 Teutonic Knights take over Sword Brothers in Livonia.

1239 Summer: Crusade departs for Constantinople.

1240 Pope Gregory IX proclaims crusade against Emperor Frederick II (renewed 1244).

1241 Crusade proclaimed against Mongols (renewed 1243, 1249).

1242 First Prussian revolt against Teutonic Knights. 5 Apr: Prince Alexander Nevsky of Novgorod defeats Teutonic Knights in Battle on Lake Peipus.

1245 Teutonic Knights empowered to wage permanent crusade against Prussians.

1248 Oct: Crusaders against Frederick II capture Aachen. 23 Nov: Ferdinand III of Castile takes Seville.

1252 Memel founded.

1254 Crusade to Prussia of King Ottokar II of Bohemia, Rudolf of Hapsburg and Otto of Brandenburg. Königsberg founded.

BACKGROUND EVENTS

1219-1220 Central Asia falls to Mongols.

1228-1230 Papal invasion of Emperor Frederick II's territory in southern Italy.

1237-1239 Central Russia falls to Mongols.

1240 Ukraine falls to Mongols.

1241 Mogols invade Poland and Hungary. Apr: Battle of Liegnitz.

1243 2 July: Defeat of Seljuks by Mongols at Köse Dagh.

1245 June-July: First Council of Lyon. Crusade against Mongols discussed; Emperor Frederick II deposed.

1249 22 Nov: Death of as-Salih Ayub of Egypt.

1250 2 May: Assassination of Turan-Shah. Rule of Shajar al-Durr and Aybeg in Egypt.

CRUSADES IN THE EAST

1256-1258 Civil war in Acre (War of St Sabas).

1259 Latins of Achaea defeated by Byzantines in Battle of Pelagonia.

1260 Antioch and Cilician Armenia ally with Mongols.

1261 25 July: Byzantines reoccupy Constantinople. Latins surrender Monemvasia, Mistra and Maina to Byzantines.

1263 Baybars destroys Nazareth.

1265 Baybars takes Caesarea and Arsur.

1266 Baybars takes Saphet.

1267-1284 Hugh III king of Cyprus.

1267 24 Mar: Louis IX takes Cross. 24 May: Achaea ceded to Charles of Anjou.

1268 Baybars takes Jaffa, Belfort and Antioch. June: Edward of England takes Cross.

1269-1284 Hugh III king of Jerusalem.

1269 Dec: Aragonese crusade arrives in Acre.

1270 2 July: French crusade leaves France. 18 July: French land in Tunisia. Aug: Edward leaves England. 25 Aug: Death of Louis IX in Tunisia. 11 Nov: Crusaders leave Tunisia.

1271 Baybars takes Chastel Blanc, Krak des Chevaliers and Montfort. Charles of Anjou recognized as king in Albania. 9 May: Edward of England reaches Acre. Nov: Edward launches attack on Caco.

1272 22 Sept: Edward of England leaves for home.

1274 Second Council of Lyon. 18 May: Crusade decree *Constitutiones pro zelo fidei*.

1276 Oct: King Hugh of Jerusalem leaves for Cyprus.

1277 Maria of Antioch sells Crown of Jerusalem to Charles of Anjou. Sept: Charles of Anjou's vicar arrives in Acre. Kingdom divided into those lords who will or will not recognize Charles of Anjou.

1277-1283 Civil war in county of Tripoli.

1278 1 May: Death of William of Villehardouin. Charles of Anjou takes over government of Achaea.

1284-1285 John I king of Jerusalem and Cyprus.

1285-1324 Henry II king of Cyprus.

1285 Kalavun takes Margat.

1286 4 June: Kingdom of Jerusalem reunited under Henry of Cyprus. 15 Aug: Henry crowned king of Jerusalem.

CRUSADES IN EUROPE AND NORTH AFRICA

1255 Crusade preached against Manfred. Crusade preached against Ezzelino and Alberic of Romana.

1260 Livonian Teutonic Knights defeated by Lithuanians at Durben. Second Prussian revolt. Castilian crusade temporarily occupies Salé in Morocco.

1265 Oct: Crusade of Charles of Anjou leaves France.

1266 Jan: Charles of Anjou crowned king of Sicily. 26 Feb: Manfred defeated and killed by crusaders in Battle of Benevento.

1268 23 Aug: Crusaders defeat Conradin in Battle of Tagliacozzo. 29 Oct: Conradin executed.

1283 13 Jan: Crusade against Sicilians proclaimed. Crusade proclaimed against Aragon.

1284 June: Charles of Anjou's heir, Charles of Salerno captured by Aragonese.

1285 Spring French launch crusade against Aragon. Oct: French retreat. Death of Philip III of France.

BACKGROUND EVENTS

1256 20 Dec: Destruction of Assassins at Alamut by Mongols.

1257 11 Apr: Assassination of Aybeg.

1258 Feb: Mongols sack Baghdad.

1259 12 Nov: Kutuz proclaimed sultan of Egypt.

1260 Mongol invasion of Syria. 3 Sept: Mongols defeated at Battle of 'Ayn Jalut. 23 Oct: Assassination of Kutuz. Baybars becomes sultan of Egypt.

1261 15 Aug: Byzantine emperor Michael VIII crowned at Constantinople.

1277 1 July: Death of Baybars

1279 Dec: Accession of Kalavun to sultanate of Egypt.

1282 30 Mar: Sicilian Vespers. 30 Aug: Peter of Aragon lands in Sicily.

1285 7 Jan: Death of Charles of Anjou.

CRUSADES IN THE EAST

1287 Muslims take Latakia. 18 June: Crusade of Alice of Blois lands in Acre.

1288 Crusade of John of Grailly.

1289 26 April: Kalavun takes Tripoli.

1290 Crusades of Odo of Grandson and North Italians.

1291 5 April: Siege of Acre begins. 18 May: Acre falls to al-Ashraf Khalil. July: Sidon and Beirut fall. Aug: Christians evacuate Tortosa and Château Pélerin.

1300 Rumours of Mongol advance on Palestine leads to revival of crusading fervour in West.

1302 Muslims take Ruad Island. Probable end of Latin rule in Gibelet.

1306 April-May: Government of Cyprus taken from King Henry and entrusted to his brother Amalric of Lusignan. 23 June: Hospitallers begin invasion of Rhodes.

1309 Large groups of popular crusaders muster in Western Europe. Hospitallers move their headquarters to Rhodes.

1310 Crusade under the Hospitallers consolidates the Hospitallers hold on Rhodes. June-July: Amalric of Lusignan assassinated. King Henry restored to power in Cyprus.

1311 15 Mar: Latins in Greece defeated by Catalan Company at Battle of Halmyros. Catalans take over government of Athens and Thebes.

1313 June: Philip IV of France, his sons and Edward II of England take Cross.

1316 5 July: Battle of Manolada: Ferdinand of Majorca, pretender to principality of Achaea, killed.

1320 Shepherds' Crusade.

1324-1359 Hugh IV king of Cyprus.

1331 New crusade to the East preached.

1332 Sept: Agreement between Venice, Hospitallers on Rhodes and Byzantine empire leads to formation of the first crusade league.

1333 1 Oct: Philip VI of France takes Cross. Papacy and France join crusade league.

CRUSADES IN EUROPE AND NORTH AFRICA

1299 Battle of Cape Orlando. Angevin naval victory over Aragonese.

1302 31 Aug: Treaty of Caltabellotta recognizes Aragonese rule over Sicily.

1306-1307 Crusade against followers of Fra Dolcino in Piedmont.

1307 Crusade proclaimed in support of Charles of Valois's claims to Constantinople.

1308-1309 Teutonic Knights acquire Eastern Pomerania and Danzig.

1309-1310 Castilian and Aragonese crusade against Muslims in Spain. Crusade against Venice.

1309 Sept: Teutonic Knights move their headquarters to Marienburg. They launch perpetual crusade against Lithuanians.

1310 Pope Clement V orders investigation of behaviour of Teutonic Knights in Livonia.

1314 Crusade proclaimed in Hungary (renewed 1325, 1332, 1335, 1352, 1354).

1321 Crusade against Ferrara, Milan and the Ghibellines in the march of Ancona and duchy of Spoleto.

1323 Norwegian crusade against Russians in Finland.

1324 Crusade in Italy extended to cover Mantua.

1325 Crusade proclaimed in Poland (renewed 1340, 1343, 1351, 1354, 1355, 1363, 1369).

1327 Crusade planned against Cathars in Hungary.

1328 Crusade proclaimed against King Louis IV of Germany. Crusading revives in Spain.

1330 Crusade planned against Catalan Athens.

BACKGROUND EVENTS

1290 4 Nov: Death of Kalavun. Accession of al-Ashraf Khalil to sultanate of Egypt.

1299 22 Dec: Mongols defeat Mamluks near Homs.

1307 13 Oct: Arrest of Templars in France. Nov: Pope Clement V orders arrest of all Templars throughout Christendom.

1309 Clement V moves seat of papacy to Avignon.

1311-1312 Council of Vienne.

1312 3 Apr: Order of Knights Templar suppressed. 2 May: Clement V grants most Templar properties to Hospitallers.

1314 18 Mar: Jacques de Molay, Grand Master of the Templars, and Geoffroi de Charney burnt at stake.

1326 Ottomans take Bursa.

1327 Descent of King Louis IV of Germany on Rome.

1331 Ottomans take Nicaea.

CRUSADES IN THE EAST

1334 League ships defeat Turks in Gulf of Adramyttium.

1337 Mamluks take Ayas.

1344 28 Oct: Crusade league takes Smyrna.

1345-1347 Crusade of Humbert, dauphin of Viennois.

1345 Genoese granted crusade indulgences to defend Kaffa against Mongols.

1346 Genoese seize Chios and Foça.

1354 Lesbos granted to Genoese.

1358-1369 Peter I king of Cyprus.

1359 Crusade league wins naval victory over Turks at Lampsacus.

1360 Cypriots occupy Corycus.

1361 Cypriots occupy Adalia.

1362-1365 King Peter I of Cyprus in the West promoting a new crusade.

1365 27 June: Peter I of Cyprus's crusade leaves Venice. 10 Oct: Alexandria taken by crusade and held for six days.

1366 Aug-Dec: Crusade of Amadeus of Savoy in Thrace and Bulgaria.

1367 Peter I of Cyprus raids Cilicia and Syria.

1369 Byzantine emperor John V travels to the West to appeal for help against Turks. 17 Jan: Peter I of Cyprus assassinated.

1369-1382 Peter II king of Cyprus.

1373-1374 War between Cyprus and Genoa.

1374 Hospitallers take over defence of Smyrna.

1376 Achaea leased to Hospitallers for five years. This leads to rule of Navarrese Company.

1378 Hospitaller Master Juan Fernandez d'Heredia captured by Turks at Arta.

1379 Navarrese Company takes Thebes.

1382-1398 James I king of Cyprus.

1388 End of Catalan rule in Athens.

1390 Proclamation of new crusade. July: Crusade lands in North Africa and unsuccessfully besieges Mahdia.

1394 New crusade proclaimed.

CRUSADES IN EUROPE AND NORTH AFRICA

1340 Crusade against heretics in Bohemia. 30 Oct: Marinids defeated at Battle of Salado.

1342-1344 Siege of Algeciras.

1344 Crusade planned to Canary Islands.

1348 King Magnus of Sweden's crusade to Finland (renewed 1350, 1351).

1349-1350 Siege of Gibraltar.

1353-1357 Crusade to regain control of papal state in Italy.

1354 Peter I of Castile proposes crusade to Africa. Crusade against Cesena and Faenza.

1360 Crusade against Milan (renewed 1363, 1368).

1383 Bishop Henry Despenser of Norwich's crusade against Clementists in Flanders.

1386 John of Gaunt's crusade against Castile.

BACKGROUND EVENTS

1337 Ottomans take Nicomedia. Outbreak of Hundred Years' War between France and England.

1348 Ottomans begin to establish themselves in Europe.

1348-1350 Black Death.

1354 Ottomans occupy Gallipoli.

1363 Ottomans take Philippopolis.

1369 Ottomans take Adrianople.

1371 Ottoman victory at Battle of Maritsa gives them most of Bulgaria and Serbian Macedonia.

1378-1417 Great Schism divides Catholic Church.

1386 Union of Lithuania and Poland. Conversion of Lithuania to Christianity begins.

1389 15 June: First Battle of Kosovo: Serbs crushed by the Ottomans.

CRUSADES IN THE EAST

1396 Peter Bordo of St Superan, leader of Navarrese Company, becomes prince of Achaea. 25 Sept: Crusade destroyed by Ottomans at Battle of Nicopolis.

1398-1432 Janus king of Cyprus.

1398 Crusade proclaimed to defend Constantinople, (renewed)1399, 1400.

1399 John Boucicaut's crusade in eastern Mediterranean.

1402 Dec: Timur takes Smyrna from Hospitallers.

1403 John Boucicaut and Hospitallers raid coasts of Asia Minor and Syria.

1406-1407 Hospitallers start to build castle at Bodrum.

1425 Mamluks attack Cyprus.

1426 Mamluks attack Cyprus. 7 July: King Janus taken prisoner by Mamluks at Battle of Khirokitia.

1432 Thomas Palaeologus, despot of Morea, takes over principality of Achaea.

1432-1458 John II king of Cyprus.

1440 Mamluks attack Rhodes.

1443 1 Jan: New crusade proclaimed.

1444 Mamluks attack Rhodes and besiege it for 40 days. 10 Nov: Ottomans defeat crusaders at Varna.

1453 30 Sept: New crusade proclaimed.

1454 17 Feb: Feast of the Pheasant in Lille.

1455 Crusade indulgences granted to Genoese defenders of Chios. 15 May: Renewal of the crusade.

1456 14 Feb: St John of Capistrano takes the Cross at Buda. 4 June: Ottomans occupy Athens. 22 July: Successful defence of Belgrade by crusaders under Janos Hunyadi and St John of Capistrano.

1457 Papal fleet raids Aegean and occupies Samothrace, Thasos and Lemnos.

1458-1485 Charlotte queen of Cyprus

1459-1460 Crusade congress at Mantua.

1460-1473 James II king of Cyprus.

1460 14 Jan: New crusade proclaimed.

CRUSADES IN EUROPE AND NORTH AFRICA

1410 15 July: Battle of Tannenberg. Poles and Lithuanians defeat Teutonic Knights.

1411 1 Feb: First Peace of Thorn.

1415-1418 Council of Constance debates role of Teutonic Knights.

1415 Portuguese take Ceuta in Morocco.

1420 1 Mar: Crusade proclaimed against Hussites. May-Nov: First Hussite Crusade.

1421 Summer, Autumn and Winter: Second Hussite crusade.

1422 Autumn: Third Hussite crusade.

1427 July-Aug: Fourth Hussite crusade.

1431 June-Aug: Fifth Hussite crusade.

BACKGROUND EVENTS

1402 28 July: Mongols under Timur defeat Ottomans at Ankara.

1422 Ottomans besiege Constantinople.

1430 Ottomans take Thessalonica.

1448 17-19 Oct: Second Battle of Kosovo: Ottomans defeat Hungarians.

1453 End of Hundred Years' War between France and England. 29 May: Constantinople falls to Ottomans.

1461 Ottomans take Trebizond.

CRUSADES IN THE EAST

1462 Ottomans take Lesbos.
1464 18 June: Pope Pius II takes Cross. 15 Aug: Pope Pius II dies waiting for crusade to muster at Ancona.

1470 Ottomans take Negroponte.

1471 31 Dec: New crusade proclaimed.

1472 Summer Crusade league attacks Adalia and Smyrna.

1473-1474 James III king of Cyprus.

1474-1489 Catherine Cornaro queen of Cyprus.

1480 23 May-late Aug: Ottomans besiege Rhodes. 11 Aug: Ottomans take Otranto.

1481 8 Apr: New crusade proclaimed. 10 Sept: Ottomans in Otranto surrender.

1489 26 Feb: Venice takes over government of Cyprus.

1490 Mar: Congress in Rome plans new crusade.

1493 Crusade indulgences for defenders of Hungary.

1500 1 June: New crusade proclaimed.

1512-1517 Fifth Lateran Council discusses crusading.

1513 Crusade proclaimed in eastern Europe against Ottomans.

1517 11 Nov: New crusade proclaimed and planned.

1522 July: Ottoman siege of Rhodes begins. 18 Dec: Surrender of Rhodes to the Ottomans.

1523 1 Jan: Hospitallers leave Rhodes.

1526 Treaty of Madrid: Emperor Charles V and King Francis I of France express their desire for a 'general crusade'.

1530 2 Feb: New crusade proclaimed.

CRUSADES IN EUROPE AND NORTH AFRICA

1466 19 Oct: Second Peace of Thorn ends Thirteen Year War between Teutonic Knights and Poland.

1482 Spanish Reconquest renewed.

1487 Spanish take Málaga.

1489 Spanish take Baza, Almería and Guadix.

1490 Apr: Siege of Granada begins.

1492 2 Jan: Granada surrenders to the Spanish.

1497 Spanish occupy Melilla.

1499 Ottomans take Lepanto.

1500 Ottomans take Coron and Modon.

1505 Spanish take Mers el-Kebir.

1508 Spanish occupy Canary Islands.

1509 Spanish take Oran.

1510 Spanish take Rock of Algiers, Bougie and Tripoli.

1521 30 Aug: Ottomans take Belgrade.

1525 Albert of Brandenburg, Grand Master of the Teutonic Knights, adopts Lutheranism.

1526 29 Aug: Ottomans destroy Hungarians in Battle of Mohács.

1529 26 Sept-Oct: Ottomans besiege Vienna.

1530 23 Mar: Hospitallers given Malta and Tripoli (North Africa) by Emperor Charles V.

BACKGROUND EVENTS

1479 Aragon and Castile united.

1494-1495 King Charles VIII of France invades Italy.

1516 Ottomans conquer Syria and Egypt.

1517 Dec: Martin Luther denounced: start of Reformation.

1520 June: Field of the Cloth of Gold: Kings of France and England meet in context of preparations for new crusade.

1534 Henry VIII of England breaks with Rome.

CRUSADES IN THE EAST

1537 New crusade league formed, comprising the papacy, Venice and (after 1538) Spain and the Holy Roman empire.

1538 27 Sept: Defeat of league fleet off Prevéza.

1544 Summons of Council of Trent links reform of Church and crusading.

1570 25 May: Holy League, comprising the papacy, Spain and Venice, formed. 1 July: Ottomans land on Cyprus. 9 Sept: Ottomans take Nicosia.

1571 5 Aug: Famagusta surrenders; Cyprus in Ottoman hands. 9 Aug: Fleet of Holy League assembled at Naples. 7 Oct: Victory of League fleet over Ottomans at Battle of Lepanto.

1572 10 Feb: Holy League renewed. Late Summer League fleet operates in eastern Mediterranean.

1645-1669 Ottomans invade Crete.

1669 26 Sept: Surrender of Candia; Crete falls to Ottomans.

1685-1687 Venetians occupy Peloponnese.

1715 Ottomans reoccupy Peloponnese.

1722-1741 Hospitallers still active in naval operations.

CRUSADES IN EUROPE AND NORTH AFRICA

1535 16 June: Charles V's crusade lands in Tunisia. 14 July: La Goulette taken. 21 July: Tunis sacked.

1540 Nauplia and Monemvasia surrendered to Ottomans.

1541 Oct-Nov: Charles V's crusade to Algiers.

1550 8 Sept: Christian forces take Mahdia.

1551 14 Aug: Hospitallers surrender Tripoli (North Africa) to the Ottomans.

1562 Gotthard Kettler, Master of Teutonic Knights in Livonia, becomes a Lutheran duke.

1565 19 May-8 Sept: Siege of Malta by Ottomans.

1566 Ottomans take Chios.

1573 11 Oct: Don John of Austria takes Tunis.

1574 25 Aug: La Goulette falls to Ottomans. 13 Sept: Ottomans recapture Tunis.

1578 Crusade of King Sebastian of Portugal to Morocco. 4 Aug: Sebastian defeated and killed at Alcazarquivir.

1588 The Armada.

1601-1603 Hospitallers raid Greek and Tunisian coasts.

1607 Hospitaller Grand Master made prince of the empire.

1614 Ottoman raid on Malta.

1664 Hospitallers attack Algiers.

1683 14 July-12 Sept: Ottomans besiege Vienna.

1684 Mar: Formation of Holy League comprising the papacy, the Holy Roman empire, Poland and Venice.

1686 Christian forces take Buda.

1707 Hospitallers help to defend Oran.

1716-1717 Prince Eugene of Savoy commands Christian advance in the Balkans.

1741-1773 Hospitaller Grand Master Manoel Pinto adopts full attributes of sovereignty.

1792 Hospitaller properties in France seized.

1798 13 June Malta surrenders to Napoleon.

BACKGROUND EVENTS

1618 Outbreak of Thirty Years War in Germany.

1648 Peace of Westphalia ends Thirty Years War.

1789 French Revolution begins.

Part 1
THE WAY OF GOD

In March 1095 an embassy from the Byzantine emperor Alexius I asked Pope Urban II for help against the Seljuk Turks who had overrun most of the eastern provinces of the Byzantine empire and were within striking distance of the capital, Constantinople. Urban had already decided that during a visit to France he was planning he would appeal to western European knights to come to the aid of the Christians in the East. He had hit on the idea of summoning them to take part in a war which was also a pilgrimage to Jerusalem. This was to be the First Crusade. The idea of launching a crusade may not have been Pope Urban's own – it could have been around in papal circles for over twenty years. But Urban was the man who put it into effect and with his proclamation of the crusade he launched a movement which only petered out in the late 18th century and encompassed more than the crusades themselves, since it also expressed itself in the military defence of the Holy Land and other crusade settlements, the actions of the Military Orders and, from the 14th century onwards, crusading leagues.

One of those who answered Urban's call was the young lord of Amboise, Hugh of Chaumont-sur-Loire. In March 1096, at a ceremony in the presence of the pope in the abbey of Marmoutier just outside Tours, he vowed to take part in the crusade. Hugh's life was to be spent mostly on family matters and on the consolidation of his estates. He was prepared to act outside the law when it was in his interest: he even arranged the abduction of one of his cousins, who had been married to someone unsuitable. But he had a good crusade. During one night in the second week of June 1098, when there was such a panic in the Christian army that there was the danger of a mass break-out and flight from the city of Antioch

in Syria, he was one of those thought trustworthy enough by the leaders to guard the city gates. But he was a sick man when he returned to France at Eastertime 1100.

Two 12th-century pilgrims (below), a man and wife, from the cloister of the Priory of Belval in Lorraine. The tradition of couples making pilgrimage is one of the reasons why it was so hard for the Church to limit crusading to young healthy male warriors.

Twenty-eight years later, Hugh made over all his lands to his eldest son and went on crusade again, this time with his feudal lord and brother-in-law Count Fulk V of Anjou, who was going to marry the heiress to the crusader kingdom of Jerusalem. Hugh must have intended never to go back to the West. He fought before Damascus in 1129 and, after falling mortally ill on his return to Jerusalem, was buried on the Mount of Olives. One of his sons, another Hugh, was for a time castellan of Hebron, the supposed site of the tomb of Abraham.

The army of the First Crusade which gathered outside Nicaea in June 1097 may have consisted of rather more than 40,000 persons, of whom no more than 4,500 were nobles like Hugh, or knights. Most crusaders were, and for centuries were to be, artisans, townspeople and peasants. The presence of so many untrained men and non-combatants worried contemporaries, but little could be done about it because crusades were also pilgrimages on which ordinary men and women were accustomed to go, and it made the crusade leaders anxious because the poor had to be fed.

Pilgrimages

A crusade was a special kind of armed pilgrimage. The term 'pilgrim' originally meant 'stranger' or 'traveller'. In the Christian tradition life on earth is itself a pilgrimage, since Christians are estranged from this world and are far from their homeland in heaven. But as early as the 2nd century devout men and women also began to travel to locations which were associated with Christ's earthly career and to other places which were believed to be sanctified by Christian martyrdom or by the tombs of saints. The early pilgrims to Jerusalem began a tradition which continued even after Palestine fell to the Muslims in the 7th century, but at that time the character of pilgrimages changed; from being almost entirely devotional they became in part penitential and were prescribed as penances for sin. In the 10th and 11th centuries the number of pilgrims making for Jerusalem and other shrines greatly increased, and pilgrims gained a recognizable status in society. They seem to have been already taking vows. They had come to enjoy the official protection of the Church and the right to hospitality at the religious houses they visited on their journeys; and they had become exempted from tolls and taxes and immune from arrest.

Since they represented the vast majority in most armies, the masses could have a powerful voice, particularly when they organized themselves: one body on the First Crusade, called the Tafurs, was led by a 'king', a Norman knight who had been reduced through impoverishment to the ranks but who passed into legend as a major figure on the expedition. When the First Crusade was bogged down in northern Syria in the autumn of 1098, it was the demands of the people and their threat of revolt that forced the leaders to resume the march for Jerusalem. But very little evidence

about the masses survives and their ideas and aspirations are almost entirely lost to us, although it is clear that some of them were caught up in hysterical religious movements that were sweeping western Europe in the central Middle Ages: one party on the First Crusade followed a goose which they believed was filled with the Holy Spirit.

We know much more about a man like Hugh of Chaumont-sur-Loire and it is worth asking why he should have decided to go on crusade again when he was elderly. Fighting had taken up only a fraction of the time of the first crusaders and the appalling conditions on the march had been made bearable for them only through ritualization – they had been caught up in a continual round of processions, prayers and fasting, which had helped to bind them together and to alleviate their sense of isolation – by religious elation at the liberation of Jerusalem and by the respect they discovered they had earned back home. Hugh's abiding memories of his first crusade would have been of fear, danger, homesickness, illness and hunger.

Crusading was never to be a pleasant occupation; and it was always an expensive one. There were very few material rewards to be won. Taking part in a crusade to the East possibly entailed costs in the region of four or five times a knight's income, which, unless he was lucky enough to find a patron, could only be met by the disposal of land through sale or mortgage. At the time of the First Crusade, the problems of raising finance were made worse by the fact that France, the chief recruiting ground, was in the grip of a short but severe agricultural depression, caused by a succession of dry years and bad harvests, but even at the best of times a crusader and his family had to cope with a very heavy outlay.

So Hugh of Chaumont-sur-Loire must have left again in 1128 with no illusions. To understand why he was prepared to sacrifice a comfortable and respected old age on his estates in order to end his days 2,000 miles from home, we must look at the society in which he lived.

In the late 11th and 12th centuries most men spent most of their time in the neighbourhoods in which they had been born and raised and their lives naturally focused on their locality. A crusade, involving long journeys far from home, was bound to disorientate them and on it neighbours tended to stick together. When Guy of Bré, a castellan from the Limousin, lay dying in Latakia in Syria in 1099, he made two wills, leaving a lot of property to local religious communities back home, including a family foundation, and these were witnessed by seven men, all from the Limousin and including another castellan who was also a relative by marriage. When Bertrand of Bas, a canon of Le Puy, fell ill at sea returning from the First Crusade and renounced tithes he had held illegally at a place called Bauzac, his deed of renunciation was witnessed by six companions, all of them neighbours at home and on board ship with him. When Herbert II, viscount of Thouars, had what seems to have been a stroke or heart attack at Jaffa in Palestine in May 1102, his last words were about the community at the family foundation of Chaise-le-Vicomte, which he wished to enlarge through endowment, and they were witnessed by five men, of whom one was a member of his household, two were local Poitevin knights, a fourth was a knight whose home was not very distant and the fifth was a doctor from Nantes who must have been treating him.

Central to the daily lives of these men were the relationships imposed by feudal and family bonds. A feudal tie was embodied in the contractual relationship between a lord and each of his vassals, who owed him services, including military service, in return for being his tenant, holding a fief in land or money from him. Although family ties were stronger than feudal ones in the 11th and 12th centuries, the two types of bond would reinforce one another when benevolent lords helped their vassals to arrange good marriages for their kin. To compensate for the narrowness of local feudal interests, a straggling chain of family relationships stretched over large areas of western Europe. Families seem to have been greatly extended in the central Middle Ages, and there was a growing interest in genealogy. Of course blood relationships fuelled the social violence which was still endemic, and they could turn sour, but they were also positive forces: they provided channels for the transmission of ideas and enthusiasms, including a responsiveness to the evangelization which the Church had undertaken in the

Crusades

Crusades were holy wars fought against those who were perceived to be the external or internal foes of Christendom, for the recovery of Christian property or in defence of the Church or Christian people. Enemies included Muslims, pagan Slavs, Mongols, Orthodox Christians (Greeks and Russians), heretics (Cathars, Bogomils and Hussites) and political opponents of the papacy. Crusades were believed to be directly authorized by Christ himself through his mouthpiece the pope. Their cause was related to that of Christendom as a whole and a crusading army was considered to be international, even when it was actually composed of men from only one region. At least some of the participants took special vows which originated in those of pilgrims, and pilgrimage terminology was often used of them and their campaigns. And the privileges these crusaders enjoyed, particularly the protection in their absence of themselves, their families and properties, were based on those given to pilgrims. They were also granted indulgences. It was the vow and consequent indulgence that identified a man or woman as a crusader.

Crusades were waged in the Near East, Spain, North Africa, the Baltic region, eastern Europe and even within western Europe. But the crusades to liberate or defend Jerusalem were held in special esteem. All the others were measured against them, and often the sign that a crusade was being preached elsewhere was that the indulgence granted to the participants was directly equated with that given to crusaders going to Jerusalem. Crusades to the East moreover, were associated with territory which was regarded as Christ's own. Other crusades tried to reproduce the image of a feudal lord's estate threatened or usurped by an invading enemy: Spain was regarded the patrimony of St Peter and was also under the patronage of St James; Livonia (approximately modern Latvia) was by an extraordinary fiction treated as the dower land of Our Lady. But they could never rival the special position held by Jerusalem and the Holy Land in the minds of the people.

It took about a century for crusading to reach maturity and for much of the 12th century many elements existed only in embryo.

11th century. This manifested itself in a remarkable programme of parish church building and in the phenomenal growth of monasticism, which had to be fuelled by the entry gifts of those who were presented by their families to monasteries or wanted to become monks and by the endowments of lay men and women. By the 1090s this evangelization was having definite effects on the lower reaches of noble society: in Burgundy, for instance, the petty nobles were beginning to be noticeable for their endowment of religious communities.

Women played a significant part in the growth of monasticism by carrying traditions of support for particular communities from the families into which they had been born to the families into which they married. There are signs that women played a similar role in predetermining the response to crusade appeals by predisposing their families in favour of the movement. In spite of the universal treatment of them as inhibiters in commentaries and songs, they seem often to have been the agents who inspired their male relatives to take the cross: like the traditions of endowing particular religious communities, the impulse to crusade can be seen being carried from one family to another through the marriage of sisters and daughters.

Some women, of course, were to be found on crusade themselves. They included those who were committed to the movement, the wives and sisters of crusaders, at least one doctor (in the 13th century), and also prostitutes, who, together perhaps with some of those who fell on hard times, became attached to the brothels which were as much a feature of crusader camps as they were of any army encampments. Churchmen were appalled at the presence of women, particularly since pilgrims, as penitents, were supposed to practise sexual abstinence: at times of crisis on the First Crusade all women, respectable and unrespectable, were segregated into camps of their own. As non-combatants, most women fetched and carried water and projectiles to front-line troops and helped with menial and labouring tasks. But a few actually fought: during the Third Crusade the Muslims killed a Christian female sniper who had caused casualties with her arrows.

A feature of society in the late 11th and 12th centuries was that it was perceived to be sinful, not only because it was violent and because secular standards and paths to preferment in the world were conditioned by a martial class, but also because the Church, increasingly under the influence of monks, was setting standards of behaviour which were out of the reach even of faithful husbands and wives, who, for example, were expected to refrain from sexual relations for what must have amounted to at least half the year. Many of the laity were becoming profoundly anxious about a sinfulness from which they felt they could never escape. This explains their outstanding generosity to the Church and their enthusiasm for pilgrimages. A society in which there was no privacy, little literacy and no cheap books could never have coped with private devotions. In a public society piety was public, through attendance at Mass and participation in pilgrimages.

This is the context in which we should consider events like the response to the preaching of the early crusades, those acts of public penance and devotion, those pilgrimages on which knights could achieve grace exercising the skills in which they had been brought up to take a pride. This is well illustrated by the first surviving description of a crusader taking the cross. On 22 May 1096 Fulk Doon, the lord of Châteaurenard near Avignon, went through a ceremony at the abbey of Lerins in which he handed property over to the monks. In return the abbot gave him a mule, a napkin and a staff and 'enjoined on him the way to Jerusalem as a penance'.

The Theology of Sacred Violence

The theory of holy Christian violence was worked out by Christian thinkers of the 4th and 5th centuries and was available in the central Middle Ages in anthologies of theological texts. Its starting point was that violence was not evil but was morally neutral and drew moral colouring from the *intention* of the perpetrator, which could be loving. For instance, the surgeon who strapped a man to a table and amputated a gangrenous leg against the patient's will – an act of violence which could well lead to death – had the intention of healing a man who would otherwise have certainly died.

Like the surgeon, any perpetrator of Christian violence had to have a *right intention*. He also needed a *just cause*, because violence could only be resorted to in response to previous *injury* in the forms, for instance, of aggression, menaces, tyranny, or the invasion and occupation of land that rightly belonged to an earlier possessor. Moreover, since no Christian had any right even to defend himself as an individual against assault, acts of violence had to be authorized by a *legitimate authority*, who could be a minister of God such as the pope or the emperor, but could also be God himself. Christian sacred violence, in fact, whether medieval or modern, posits a 'political' God or Christ, whose intentions for mankind are believed to be reflected in some existing political structure or course of political events. If this structure or course of events comes under threat, Christ's intentions for mankind are believed to be at risk and his support for military counter-measures is assumed.

The Christianity of many nobles and knights was real, but it was a long way from the cool abstractions of intellectual theologians or even the nuanced religion of educated clergy. It was transformed by adaptation to a society which set great store by feudal lordship, honour, family solidarity, revealing itself in feuding, and extravagant social generosity. Lay men and women envisaged God as a father, king or lord: words which had specific resonances for them. In their minds God or Christ was the father of a noble household, Christians were his sons and daughters (and brothers and sisters of each other) and the Holy Land was his patrimony; or he was a king, the Holy Land was his royal domain and the rest of Christendom his kingdom. His 'sons' or 'vassals' had a duty to counter any threat to the territorial integrity of his kingdom, to the freedom of his subjects or to his own estates. In an age when vendettas were rampant it is not surprising that the crusade tended to degenerate into an act of vengeance, sometimes with the encouragement of the clergy. The commentator Baldric of Bourgueil made a First Crusade preacher declare:

'I address fathers and sons and brothers and nephews. If an outsider were to strike any of your kin down would you not avenge your blood-relative? How much more ought you to avenge your God, your father, your brother, whom you see reproached, banished from his estates, crucified!'

In this respect the theological concept of violence as an act of Christian charity was transformed at the time of the First Crusade into a commitment to a blood-feud, an expression of family love with which most crusaders would have been thoroughly familiar. And it is not surprising that the view of Islam expressed in early crusade writings was utterly negative, with the Muslims portrayed as depraved and barbarous blasphemers, enemies of God and servants of the devil.

Hugh of Chaumont-sur-Loire decided to end his days in Jerusalem. In the 12th century many noblemen dedicated themselves to spending their last days defending the Holy Land. As a goal of pilgrims, Jerusalem had never been a healing shrine; like Rome and Compostella it was associated particularly with absolution from sins at the end of a penitential pilgrimage, and it was a place in which to die because as the focus of God's interventions in this world it was considered to be closer to heaven than elsewhere. It was also itself a relic, since its ground had been trod by Christ and had soaked up his blood as it had streamed from the cross.

It is almost impossible to exaggerate the obsessive interest which Europeans took in Jerusalem, and by extension the Holy Land. The news of the success of the First Crusade swept through Christendom, and religious establishments associated with the holy places found themselves showered with endowments in Europe, while the ambitious building programme undertaken by the early western settlers in Palestine must have been funded by a stream of cash flowing across the Mediterranean.

The western Europeans came to occupy the length of the Levantine coast, their territory comprising a strip of land, nearly 600 miles from north to south, bounded by mountain ranges. Every now and then they also held salients into the interior, the deepest being in the north: Edessa was 160 miles north-east of Antioch and 45 miles east of the river Euphrates. They were, of course, isolated and their hold on the country was from the middle of the 12th century increasingly precarious. As the new Military Orders grew they were able to contribute more to the defence of the Latin settlements, but they were never strong enough to counter-balance the settlers' chief weakness: there were never enough permanent colonists. And, in spite of the settlers' appeals for help, the failure of the Second Crusade demoralized the West so much that for nearly 40 years there was comparatively little crusading.

The loss of the city of Jerusalem to Saladin in 1187 created as much dismay as there had been euphoria 90 years before. The Church ascribed this catastrophe to the sinfulness of Christendom. Pope Gregory VIII, launching the Third Crusade, pointed out:

'It is ... incumbent upon all of us to consider and to choose to amend our sins by voluntary chastisement and to turn to the Lord our God with penance and works of piety; and we should first amend in ourselves what we have done wrong and then turn our attention to the treachery and malice of the enemy.'

Thus began a long association of crusading with Church reform, without which, it was believed, crusades would never succeed. But there was also a revival of crusading. The Third Crusade ushered in a long period in which there was hardly a year in which a crusade was not being waged in some theatre of war.

Islam Divided

In 1095, Jerusalem, the goal of the First Crusade, had been in Muslim hands for over 400 years. But the Islamic Near East was in crisis.

The Muslim civilization of the Near East arose out of a great wave of expansion from the Arabian peninsula that began in the 7th century. It was ruled by an Arabic-speaking elite which, with great mosques and universities and a settled agriculture, had made itself the heir to the classical Mediterranean.

The caliphs were regarded as the direct successors of the prophet Muhammad. In reality, no caliph had wielded universal power since the 9th century when the 'Abbasid dynasty was in its prime. After that, the Muslim world fragmented. The 'Abbasids belonged to the majority, Sunni form of Islam, but in 969 a rival caliphate was established at Cairo by the Fatimid dynasty, who espoused the Isma'ili variety of the minority, Shi'i form of Islam. While the Fatimids extended their power into Palestine and Syria, the 'Abbasid caliphs at Baghdad became the virtual prisoners of a Persian Shi'i dynasty, the Buyids.

In 1040 a new force appeared on the scene. The Seljuks, Turkish nomads who had recently converted to Sunni Islam, conquered Afghanistan and eastern Persia; in 1055 they entered Baghdad where they were welcomed by the 'Abbasid caliph. The Great Seljuk empire reached its zenith in the 1070s, when the sultan Alp Arslan defeated the Byzantine empire at Manzikert, and his son Malikshah took Syria and much of Palestine from the Fatimids. After Malikshah's death, however, the Great Seljuk empire was riven by civil war.

Many Turcoman tribesmen crossed into Asia Minor, and members of the Seljuk family established themselves as sultans, with their capital at Nicaea, where they remained independent of their relatives to the east. In the centre and north of the peninsula the predominant power was the martial, nomadic Danishmends, inspired by the idea of *ghaza*, holy war against the Christians.

In Egypt, real power had passed from the caliphs to military chief ministers, or *wazirs*. In 1094, dissenters split and formed a schismatic Isma'ili sect, the Nizaris or (in the West) the Assassins. Their chief centre was the mountains of northern Iran, from where they expanded into Syria. In 1098 the Fatimids regained Jerusalem from the Seljuks, who by then had other worries: the armies of the First Crusade had crossed Asia Minor and taken Antioch. Such was the disunity of the Muslim world that even a threat of this magnitude could not produce a collective response.

> **A**s many of you have already been told, the Turks, a Persian race, have overrun the eastern Christians right up to the Mediterranean Sea. Occupying more and more of the land of the Christians on the borders of Romania [the Byzantine empire], they have conquered them ... slaughtering and capturing many, destroying churches and laying waste the kingdom of God. So, if you leave them alone much longer they will further grind under their heels the faithful of God.
>
> **Pope Urban II at the Council of Clermont, 27 November 1095**

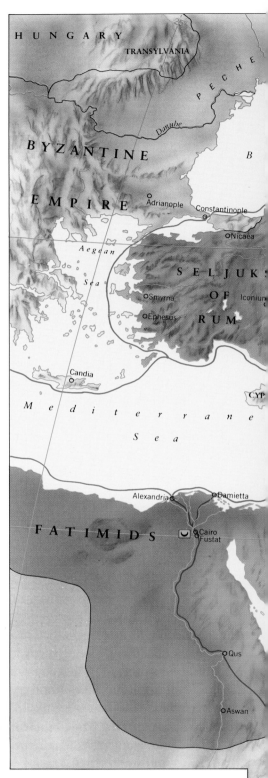

The Friday Mosque, the great mosque of Isfahan, a capital of the Great Seljuk empire. Although it has elements from most periods of Iranian Islamic architecture, its most important features are two brick dome chambers of the 1080s, built by the Seljuk *wazir* Nizam al-Mulk and his rival Taj al-Mulk. The mosque is perhaps the finest in Iran.

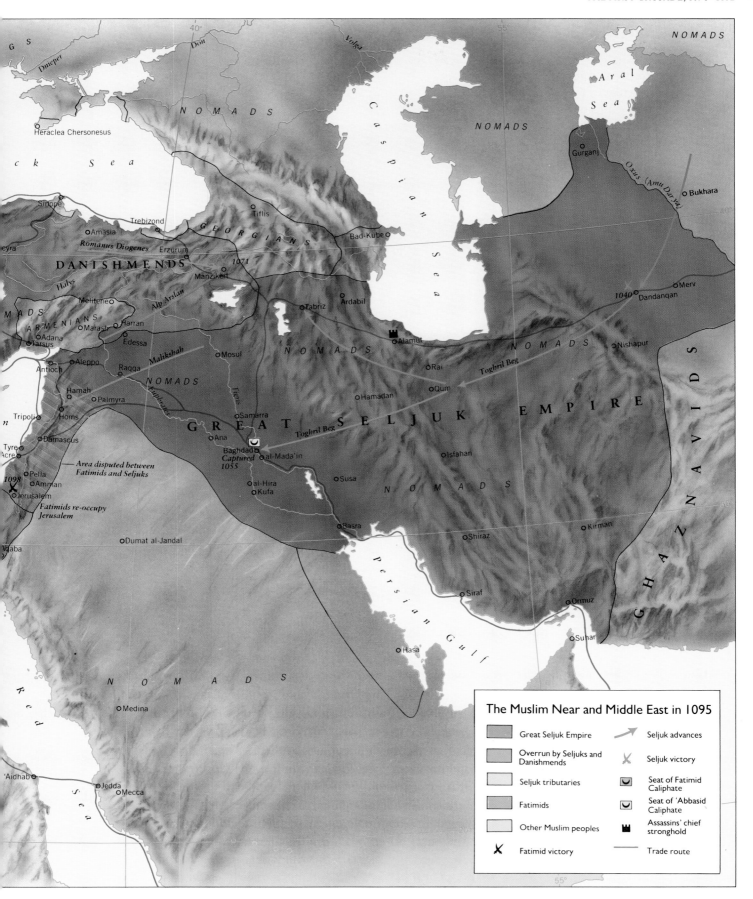

NOMADS

Dnieper

Don

Volga

A r a l S e a

GS

Heraclea Chersonesus

C a s p i a n S e a

NOMADS

NOMADS

Gurganj

Oxus (Amu Dar'ya)

Bukhara

ck S e a

Sinope

Trebizond

Tiflis

GEORGIANS

Bad-Kube

DANISHMENDS

Amasia

Romanus Diogenes

Erzurum

1071

Manzikert

Alp Arslan

1040 Dandanqan

Merv

eyra

Melitene

Tabriz

Ardabil

Nishapur

Harran

MADS

ARMENIANS

Marash

NOMADS

Alamut

Adana

Tarsus

Edessa

Rai

Toghril Beg

NOMADS

Aleppo

Raqqa

Malikshah

Mosul

Qum

Antioch

Euphrates

Tigris

Hamah

NOMADS

Hamadan

G R E A T   S E L J U K   E M P I R E

Palmyra

Toghril Beg

Tripoli

Homs

Samarra

Ana

Isfahan

G H A Z N A V I D S

n

Damascus

Baghdad

al-Mada'in

Tyre

Captured

1055

Acre

Pella

Area disputed between

Fatimids and Seljuks

al-Hira

Kufa

Susa

1098

Jerusalem

Fatimids re-occupy

Jerusalem

Basra

NOMADS

Shiraz

Kirman

qaba

Dumat al-Jandal

R e d

Siraf

Ormuz

P e r s i a n   G u l f

NOMADS

Hasa

Suhar

'Aidhab

Medina

Jedda

Mecca

S e a

The Muslim Near and Middle East in 1095

Great Seljuk Empire	Seljuk advances
Overrun by Seljuks and Danishmends	Seljuk victory
Seljuk tributaries	Seat of Fatimid Caliphate
Fatimids	Seat of 'Abbasid Caliphate
Other Muslim peoples	Assassins' chief stronghold
Fatimid victory	Trade route

The Call to Arms

The charismatic preaching of Pope Urban II inspired tens of thousands of people from all walks of life to join the First Crusade.

Pope Urban II proclaimed the First Crusade at the Council of Clermont on 27 November 1095, calling on western knights to liberate Jerusalem. His year-long preaching tour of France (1095-1096) was clearly important in generating support. The old French pope played on the emotions of his audience in scenes of extraordinary theatricality, and a large number of crusaders came from regions close to his itinerary.

Over the next six years, perhaps as many as 130,000 men and women joined the armies that left for the East (▶*page 30*). Several thousand more travelled independently in small parties. Most of these crusaders were peasants or townspeople, caught up on a wave of popular enthusiasm.

Nobles and knights comprised no more than 10 per cent of the total, although they provided leadership. In addition, the marriage ties that existed between the noble families of western Europe provided an international network through which the crusading tradition was spread. The family of the lords of Aalst, for example, produced five First Crusaders and another crusader in 1107. Their expenses, which had to cover food, animals and equipment for themselves and their followers, were heavy; many nobles were forced to sell or mortgage land. With France in the throes of an agricultural depression, it was hard to get a good price, and the fact that so many were prepared to make such a sacrifice demonstrated that the Church's appeal had struck a deep chord.

Crusading unleashed other, violent emotions. To the Church, the justification for the First Crusade was the Muslim occupation of Jerusalem; but many crusaders, before they had even left for the Holy Land, began a vendetta against the Jews, holding them responsible for the Crucifixion. There were anti-Jewish riots at Rouen in France, in Bavaria and Bohemia. By far the worst outbreaks of anti-semitism occurred in the Rhineland, where the Jewish community at Mainz, one of the largest in Europe, was annihilated. Churchmen tried, with varying degrees of success, to stop these outbreaks, but every major crusading appeal during the 12th century was to set off fresh attacks on the Jews.

Pope Urban II consecrates a new abbey church at the great monastic centre of Cluny a month before addressing the Council of Clermont in 1095. The pope had himself been Grand Prior of Cluny.

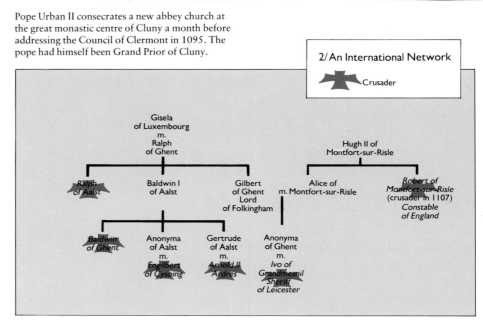

2/ An International Network

✠ Crusader

Gisela of Luxembourg m. Ralph of Ghent

Hugh II of Montfort-sur-Risle

Ralph of Aalst · Baldwin I of Aalst · Gilbert of Ghent Lord of Folkingham

Alice of m. Montfort-sur-Risle · Robert of Montfort-sur-Risle (crusader in 1107) Constable of England

Baldwin of Ghent · Anonyma of Aalst m. Engilbert of Cysoing · Gertrude of Aalst m. Arnold II Ardres · Anonyma of Ghent m. Ivo of Grandmesnil Sheriff of Leicester

I   Nivelo, raised in a nobility of birth which produces in many people an ignobility of mind, for the redemption of my soul and in exchange for a great sum of money given me for this, renounce for ever in favour of St Peter the oppressive behaviour resulting from a certain bad custom... I had harshly worn down the land of St Peter, that is to say Emprainville and the places around it, in the way that had become customary, by seizing the goods of the inhabitants there. Whenever the onset of knightly ferocity stirred me up, I used to descend on the aforesaid village, taking with me a troop of my knights and a crowd of my attendants, and against nature I would make over the goods of the men of St Peter for food for my knights.

And so since, in order to obtain the pardon for my crimes which God can give me, I am going on pilgrimage to Jerusalem which until now has been enslaved with her sons, the monks have given me 10 pounds in *denarii* towards the expenses of the appointed journey, in return for giving up this oppression.

The crusader Nivelo of Fréteval in a charter to the abbey of St Peter of Chartres, 1096

I/Recruitment for the First Crusade, 1095–1096

Major recruiting

Significant recruiting

Some recruiting

Centre of recruiting

Pope Urban II's preaching tour, 1095–1096

Persecution of Jews

NORWAY
Oslo
Uppsala

SWEDEN

SCOTLAND

IRELAND
Dublin

WALES
York

ENGLAND
London
Winchester
Thames

Aarhus
DENMARK
Lund
Kalmar
Baltic Sea

North Sea

Hamburg
Bremen
Elbe
SAXONY
Brandenburg

POMERANIA

POLAND
Breslau
Oder
Vistula

English Channel

FLANDERS
Ghent
Boulogne
Lille
Arras
Aachen
Cologne
Liège
Xanten

Atlantic Ocean

NORMANDY
Rouen
Beauvais
Rheims
Bouillon
LORRAINE
Mainz
Trier
Mosel
Metz
Speyer
Strasburg

Rhine
FRANCONIA
WESTERN

Wessili
Prague
BOHEMIA

BRITTANY
Rennes
Nantes
Le Mans
Chartres
Paris
Étampes
CHAMPAGNE
Angers
Tours
Vendôme
BLOIS
Loire
Seine
DUCHY OF BURGUNDY
Nevers
Dijon

Main
SWABIA
Ulm
Regensburg
Passau
BAVARIA
Danube

POITOU
Poitiers
Maillezais

AQUITAINE
Limoges
Clermont
Autun
Cluny
Lyon
Besançon
Constance

EMPIRE

Vienna
Salzburg

CARINTHIA

HUNGARY

Bay of Biscay

FRANCE

Bordeaux
GASCONY
Cahors
Garonne
Le Puy
COUNTY OF BURGUNDY
Valence
Gap
Asti
Milan
Brescia
Po
Piacenza
Verona
Venice
Aquileia
Trieste

Sava
Belgrade

OVIEDO
Oviedo

LEON AND CASTILE

NAVARRE
ARAGON
Toulouse
Carcassonne
Narbonne
Nîmes
St Gilles
Rhône
Forcalquier
PROVENCE
Marseille
Genoa
Bologna
Pisa
Florence

Adriatic Sea

Zara

Ragusa (Dubrovnik)

BARCELONA
Saragossa
Tortosa
Barcelona
Ebro

Corsica
Rome

Dyrrachium

Tagus

ALMORAVID EMPIRE

Valencia
Alicante
Almeria

Balearic Islands

Sardinia

Mediterranean
Cagliari

Naples
Amalfi
Salerno
Benevento
Bari
DUCHY OF APULIA
Taranto
Brindisi

Algiers

HAMMADID DOMINION

Sea

Palermo
COUNTY OF SICILY
Reggio

Tunis

The First Crusade

In 1099 against all odds, the First Crusaders succeeded in capturing Jerusalem and establishing Christian states in the Holy Land.

The task facing the First Crusaders was daunting. After marching across Europe they had to pass through the Byzantine empire, where they received a lukewarm welcome. Grudgingly provided with a minimum of provisions by the government, and exposed to the hostility of the inhabitants, they crossed the Bosporus into Asia Minor. Once they had entered Muslim territory, they were in a totally hostile environment, far from any regular supply points. With provisions arriving by ship only occasionally, they were forced to live off a land which, almost as far as Syria, was a devastated wilderness.

The crusade left in three waves. Most of the armies of the first, which started their march too early in 1096, before the good harvest of that year, never reached Asia; only that led by Peter the Hermit reached Asia Minor, where they were massacred by the combined forces of the Seljuks and Danishmends. The armies of the third wave met a similiar fate.

The success of the crusade was down to the second wave. In June 1097 it captured Nicaea, the first major city under Muslim control. By the following autumn, when the main army made a great loop north to avoid the mountain pass known as the Syrian Gates, nearly all the pack-animals had died and four out of every five knights were horseless.

The seven-and-a-half-month siege of Antioch must have been remembered above all for hunger and the constant search for food. The countryside around was stripped bare, and bands of crusaders travelled as far as 50 miles from the siege camps to establish foraging centres. A paralysis of will set in: none of the crusade leaders had a firm enough base to impose his will on the others.

In March 1098, Baldwin of Boulogne captured the county of Edessa, establishing the first crusader state. This provided the crusade with a strategic buffer and a desperately-needed source of material and funds for the later stages of the march. Without any real assistance from the Byzantine emperor, whom they had expected to take command, the crusaders liberated Jerusalem on 15 July 1099 and defeated a large Egyptian army of relief near Ascalon on the following 11 August. In the two years they had spent in Muslim territory, their numbers were reduced by two-thirds through death, desertion and settlement in northern Syria.

The crusaders' achievement astonished them as much as it did their contemporaries; in fact they could only ascribe it to divine intervention. Their isolation, alienation and fear help to explain the brutality they showed when they took centres of military or religious significance to them: Tell Bashir, Ravendan, Antioch, Ma'arrat-an-Nu'man and Jerusalem. They seem to have been determined to expel, or by acts of terror to frighten away, Muslims and Jews, leaving the indigenous Christian population to be supplemented, they hoped, by western settlers, a policy they pursued for another decade.

> **I**n all the ... streets and squares of the city, mounds of heads, hands and feet were to be seen. People were walking quite openly over dead men and horses. But I have as yet described only the minor horrors ... If I described what I actually saw you would not believe me ... What an apt punishment! The very place that had endured for so long blasphemies against God was now masked in the blood of the blasphemers ... Once the city had been captured it was most rewarding to see the devotion of the pilgrims before the Holy Sepulchre; how they clapped in exultation, singing *a new song to the Lord.*
>
> **Eye-witness, Raymond of Aguilers, describes the fall of Jerusalem in 1099**

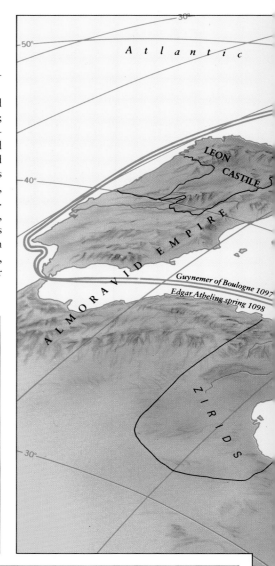

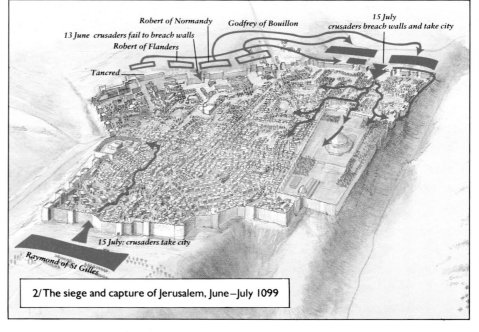

2/ The siege and capture of Jerusalem, June–July 1099

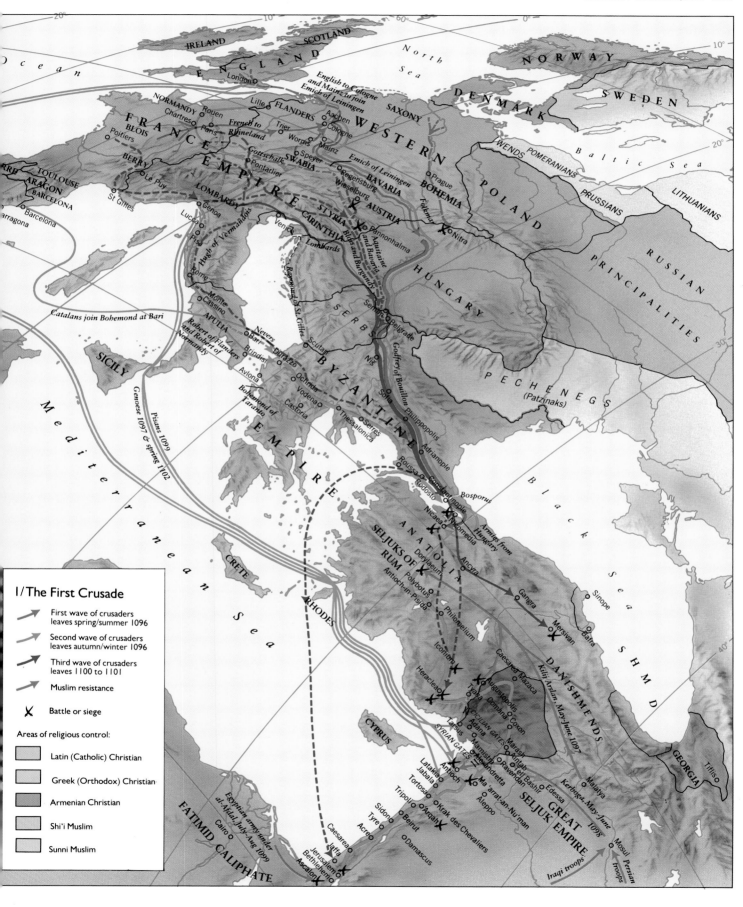

1/The First Crusade

First wave of crusaders
leaves spring/summer 1096

Second wave of crusaders
leaves autumn/winter 1096

Third wave of crusaders
leaves 1100 to 1101

Muslim resistance

✗ Battle or siege

Areas of religious control:

Latin (Catholic) Christian

Greek (Orthodox) Christian

Armenian Christian

Shi'i Muslim

Sunni Muslim

Spain: The Reconquest Begins

When the First Crusade was preached, Spain had already been a scene of conflict between Christians and Muslims for centuries.

Although Pope Urban II wanted to mobilize Christian Europe against the Muslims in the Near East (▶ page 28), he also wished to maintain the war against the Muslims in Spain, and treated it as a crusade.

In the 8th century Muslim armies had conquered the Visigothic kingdom of Spain. Christian resistance had begun almost immediately in Asturias, and after the Muslim defeat at Covadonga in 722 an independent Christian kingdom was established under King Pelayo. His descendants annexed Cantabria and Galicia, and ravaged the Duero valley to create a no-go area between Christians and the Muslims. Other centres of resistance arose in Pamplona and Aragon, while the Carolingians of France captured Gerona (785) and Barcelona (801).

Muslim Spain was an independent state ruled by the emir at Córdoba; after 929 he assumed the title of caliph. The first great Christian advance took place after 850, when the Christians resettled the Duero valley. The new frontier was defended for a century by fortresses like Simancas and by warrior-settlers organized from abbeys like Sahagún.

The second leap forward took place after 1002, when the caliphate of Córdoba collapsed into some 30 petty states known as *taifa* kingdoms. Too weak to resist the Christians, they paid them tribute until in 1085, Alfonso VI of León took Toledo and seemed ready to conquer them all. The Muslims begged for help from the Almoravid rulers of north-west Africa, who defeated Alfonso at Sagrajas in 1086 and annexed Muslim Spain to their own empire.

Meanwhile, in Aragon, there was an extraordinary foretaste of crusading. With papal help, King Sancho Ramírez recruited thousands of Frenchmen, stirred by religious motives as well as land hunger. He and his descendants conquered the Muslim kingdom of Saragossa, and by uniting it with Aragon and Catalonia created a new state to rival León. To the south, Rodrigo Diaz de Bivar – 'el Cid' – held Valencia from the Almoravids from 1094 to 1099.

Most Almoravid attacks were directed against Toledo, and it was Toledo's resistance which broke their strength. With the assis-

tance of the papacy and an enthusiastic policy of Europeanization, Kings Alfonso VI and VII of León built up the military, demographic and spiritual resources of their kingdoms. When the Almoravid empire collapsed after 1140, Alfonso VII was able to extend Christian power to the Tagus valley, leaving the Muslims confined to the southern third of the peninsula.

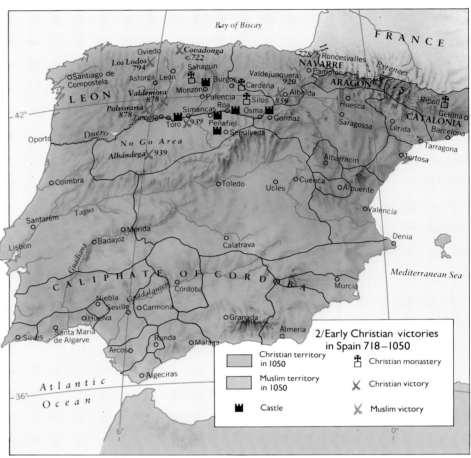

2/Early Christian victories in Spain 718–1050

Christian territory in 1050
Muslim territory in 1050
Castle
Christian monastery
Christian victory
Muslim victory

The Great Mosque of Córdoba was built in 786 by the Emir Abd al-Rahman I. Later rulers of Muslim Spain, especially al-Mansur, quadrupled the mosque in size and adorned it with the spoils of Christian churches. For centuries it symbolized the overwhelming power of the Islamic state.

Once you know that the Spanish Church is being continually worn down by such a succession of disasters and by so many deaths of the sons of God as a result of the oppression of the pagans, we believe that not one of you will lie low. We urge you ... to do your utmost to defend your brothers and to liberate the churches. With apostolic authority and the power divinely bestowed on us we graciously grant to all those fighting firmly on this expedition the same remission of sins that we conceded to the defenders of the eastern Church.

Pope Calixtus II proclaiming a crusade in Spain, 2 April 1123

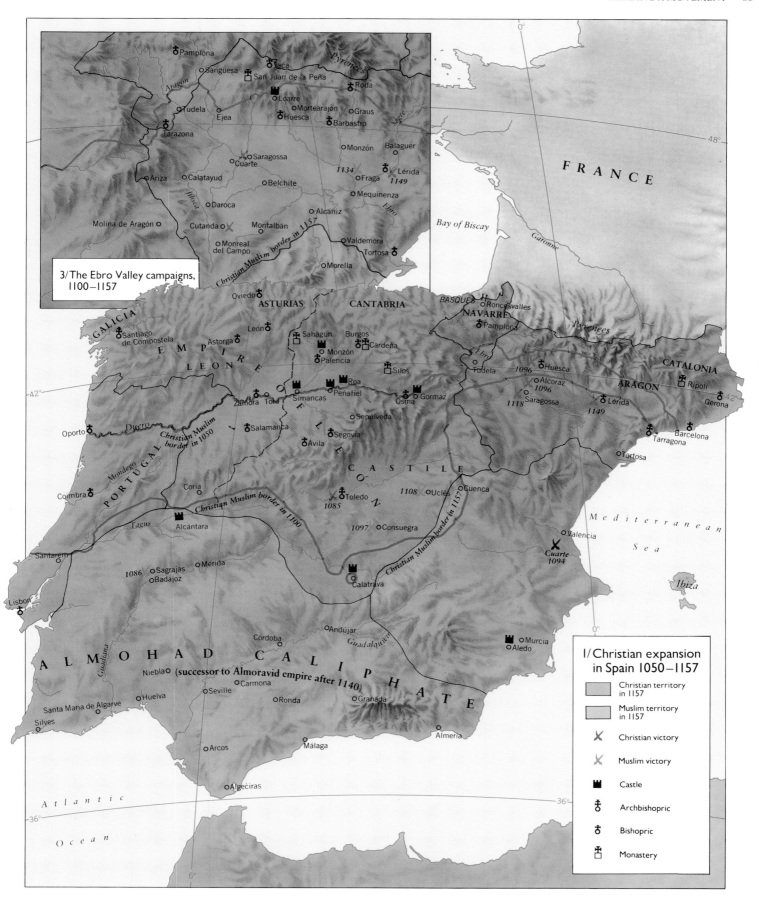

3/ The Ebro Valley campaigns, 1100–1157

Pamplona
Sangüesa
Jaca
San Juan de la Peña
Roda
Loarre
Tudela
Montearajón
Graus
Huesca
Barbastro
Tarazona
Ejea
Monzón
Balaguer
Saragossa
Cuarte
1134
Lérida
1149
Ariza
Calatayud
Belchite
Fraga
Mequinenza
Daroca
Alcañiz
Molina de Aragón
Cutanda
Montalbán
Valdemora
Monreal
del Campo
Tortosa
Morella

FRANCE

Bay of Biscay
Garonne

48°

42°

GALICIA
Santiago
de Compostela
Oviedo
ASTURIAS
CANTABRIA
BASQUES
Roncesvalles
NAVARRE
Pamplona
Pyrenees
CATALONIA
Ripoll

Astorga
León
EMPIRE
LEON
Sahagún
Burgos
Cardeña
Monzón
Palencia
Silos
Tudela
1096
Huesca
Alcoraz
1096
ARAGON
Lérida
1149
Gerona
42°

Zamora
Toro
Simancas
Peñafiel
Roa
Osma
Gormaz
Saragossa
1118

Oporto
Duero
Christian Muslim
border in 1050
PORTUGAL
Mondego
Coimbra
Salamanca
Ávila
Sepúlveda
Segovia
CASTILE
Barcelona
Tarragona
Tortosa

Coria
Christian Muslim border in 1100
Tagus
Alcántara
Toledo
1085
1108
Uclés
Cuenca
Christian Muslim border in 1157
Mediterranean
Sea

Santarem
1097
Consuegra
Cuarte
1094
Valencia

Lisbon
1086
Sagrajas
Badajoz
Mérida
Calatrava
Murcia
Aledo
Ibiza

ALMOHAD
CALIPHATE
(successor to Almoravid empire after 1140)
Guadiana
Andújar
Córdoba
Guadalquivir
Nieblaa
Huelva
Seville
Carmona
Ronda
Granada
Almería
Santa María de Algarve
Silves
Arcos
Málaga

Atlantic
Ocean
Algeciras
36°
36°

6°
0°

I/ Christian expansion
in Spain 1050–1157

	Christian territory in 1157
	Muslim territory in 1157
☓	Christian victory
☓	Muslim victory
♜	Castle
⚔	Archbishopric
♰	Bishopric
⌂	Monastery

The Struggle for Christian Control

The crusading expeditions of the early 12th century secured the coast for the Latin settlers and developed the ideology of the movement.

In 1100 the crusaders who had chosen to settle held isolated enclaves of territory. They needed more help from the west, and between 1101 and 1147 there were a number of expeditions to the Holy Land. As yet there was no developed crusade terminology, and it is not always clear how they should be treated. Sigurd of Norway's crusade of 1107, for example, may simply have been an armed pilgrimage. But several others were widely preached as crusades: Bohemond of Taranto's crusade of 1107-1108; the crusade of 1122-1126 proclaimed by Pope Calixtus II; and the crusade of 1128-1129 which attacked Damascus. The term 'Second Crusade', generally used to describe the campaigns of 1147-1148 (▶pages 48-51) is therefore a misnomer. The crusade of Pope Calixtus II, indeed, foreshadowed the Second Crusade. It was waged concurrently in the east where Tyre was taken in 1124, and in Spain, where Alfonso I of Aragon raided as far as Málaga in 1125, (▶page 32).

With western help, the settlers in Palestine and Syria systematically took the coastal ports. The fall of Tyre in 1124 deprived the Egyptian fleet of any watering place north of Ascalon, which itself was taken in 1153. This so reduced the fleet's range that it could not operate effectively against the main trade routes in the north-eastern Mediterranean

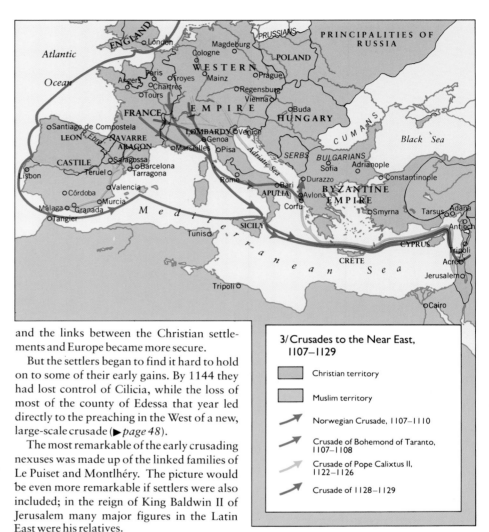

and the links between the Christian settlements and Europe became more secure.

But the settlers began to find it hard to hold on to some of their early gains. By 1144 they had lost control of Cilicia, while the loss of most of the county of Edessa that year led directly to the preaching in the West of a new, large-scale crusade (▶page 48).

The most remarkable of the early crusading nexuses was made up of the linked families of Le Puiset and Montlhéry. The picture would be even more remarkable if settlers were also included; in the reign of King Baldwin II of Jerusalem many major figures in the Latin East were his relatives.

3/ Crusades to the Near East, 1107–1129

- Christian territory
- Muslim territory
- → Norwegian Crusade, 1107–1110
- → Crusade of Bohemond of Taranto, 1107–1108
- → Crusade of Pope Calixtus II, 1122–1126
- → Crusade of 1128–1129

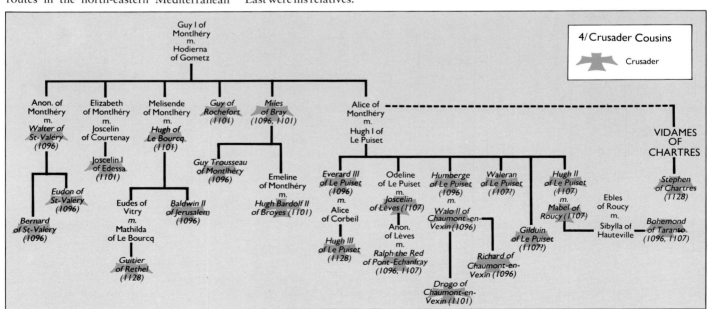

4/ Crusader Cousins
✠ Crusader

Guy I of Montlhéry m. Hodierna of Gometz

Anon. of Montlhéry m. *Walter of St-Valéry (1096)*

Elizabeth of Montlhéry m. Joscelin of Courtenay

Melisende of Montlhéry m. *Hugh of Le Bourcq (1101)*

Guy of Rochefort (1101)

Miles of Bray (1096, 1101)

Alice of Montlhéry m. Hugh I of Le Puiset

VIDAMES OF CHARTRES

Joscelin I of Edessa (1101)

Guy Trousseau of Montlhéry (1096)

Eudon of St-Valéry (1096)

Eudes of Vitry m. Mathilda of Le Bourcq

Baldwin II of Jerusalem (1096)

Emeline of Montlhéry m. *Hugh Bardolf II of Broyes (1101)*

Everard III of Le Puiset (1096) m. Alice of Corbeil

Odeline of Le Puiset m. Joscelin of Lèves (1107)

Humberge of Le Puiset (1096) m. *Walo II of Chaumont-en-Vexin (1096)*

Waleran of Le Puiset (1107?)

Hugh II of Le Puiset (1107) m. Mabel of Roucy (1107)

Ebles of Roucy m. Sibylla of Hauteville

Stephen of Chartres (1128)

Bernard of St-Valéry (1096)

Guitier of Rethel (1128)

Hugh III of Le Puiset (1128)

Anon. of Lèves m. Ralph the Red of Pont-Echanfray (1096, 1107)

Richard of Chaumont-en-Vexin (1096)

Gilduin of Le Puiset (1107?)

Bohemond of Taranto (1096, 1107)

Drogo of Chaumont-en-Vexin (1101)

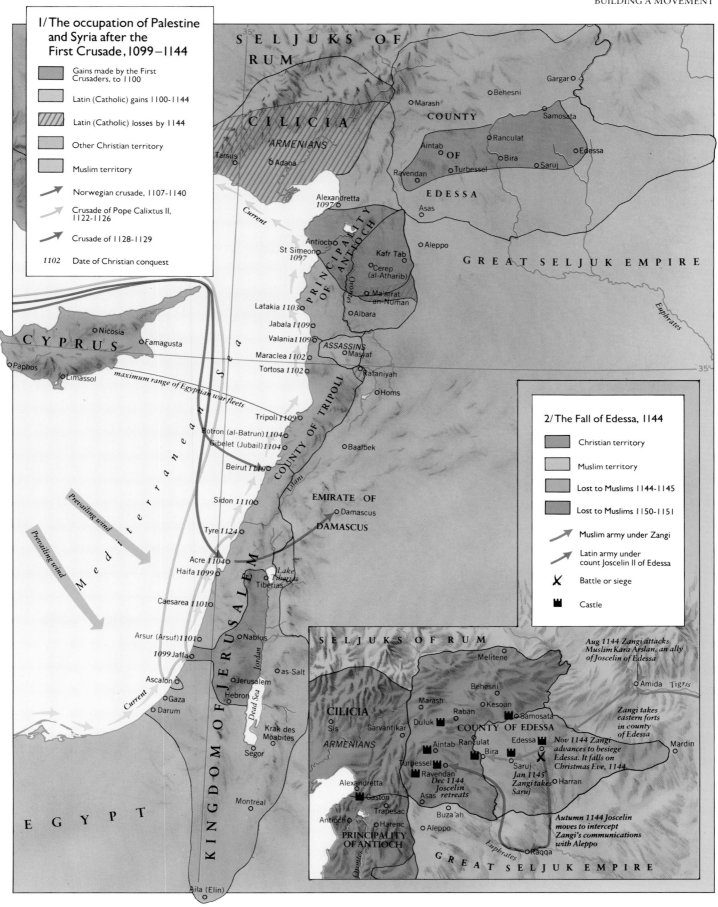

1/ The occupation of Palestine and Syria after the First Crusade, 1099–1144

- Gains made by the First Crusaders, to 1100
- Latin (Catholic) gains 1100–1144
- Latin (Catholic) losses by 1144
- Other Christian territory
- Muslim territory

→ Norwegian crusade, 1107–1140
→ Crusade of Pope Calixtus II, 1122–1126
→ Crusade of 1128–1129

1102 Date of Christian conquest

2/ The Fall of Edessa, 1144

- Christian territory
- Muslim territory
- Lost to Muslims 1144–1145
- Lost to Muslims 1150–1151

→ Muslim army under Zangi
→ Latin army under count Joscelin II of Edessa
✗ Battle or siege
♜ Castle

Aug 1144 Zangi attacks Muslim Kara Arslan, an ally of Joscelin of Edessa

Zangi takes eastern forts in county of Edessa

Nov 1144 Zangi advances to besiege Edessa. It falls on Christmas Eve, 1144

Jan 1145 Zangi takes Saruj

Dec 1144 Joscelin retreats

Autumn 1144 Joscelin moves to intercept Zangi's communications with Aleppo

Rulers and Vassals

The crusader states were run on feudal principles: the rulers devolved great power to the lords in return for their support.

Within the settler states, the crusaders imposed a feudal system very similar to that which existed in Europe. The kingdom of Jerusalem, for example, was fragmented into lordships such as Caesarea. The lords who ruled these areas were the king's tenants-in-chief; and he had little control over their lands. In turn, the lords had complete jurisdiction over their own vassals (rear-vassals). Like lords near the remoter frontiers of Europe, they exercised considerable independence in their relations with their Muslim neighbours.

The king also had his own lordship, the royal domain, which he ruled directly. Its administrative structure served as a model for the other lordships in the kingdom. The relationship of vassal to lord was central to the system; both parties were bound by mutual obligations and, since disputes often arose, courts were essential. Only Catholics could play a full part in feudal courts, so the vassals

– who held the political power – were mostly westerners, except for a few native converts.

A parallel system operated in the three other crusader states, the counties of Tripoli and Edessa, and the principality of Antioch. The settlers adapted much of the existing Muslim administration, especially the system of revenue-gathering, to suit their own preconceptions. Revenue offices such as the *Chaine* and the *Fonde* were also given a judicial function. For their Muslim and Jewish subjects, the crusaders introduced a distinction between 'spiritual' cases, which remained in the hands of the *qadis* and rabbis, and 'secular' ones,

which went to the new Court of the Syrians. The native villages continued to be run by a council of elders.

The feudal system suited settler society and, because military service was among a vassal's obligations, provided manpower for the armies. But there were never enough knights: no more, perhaps, than 2,000 in the whole Latin East. The power of the lords was balanced by the fact that the royal domain provided the king with greater wealth than any of his vassals had; with it, he could pay the mercenaries who were essential to the defence of the kingdom.

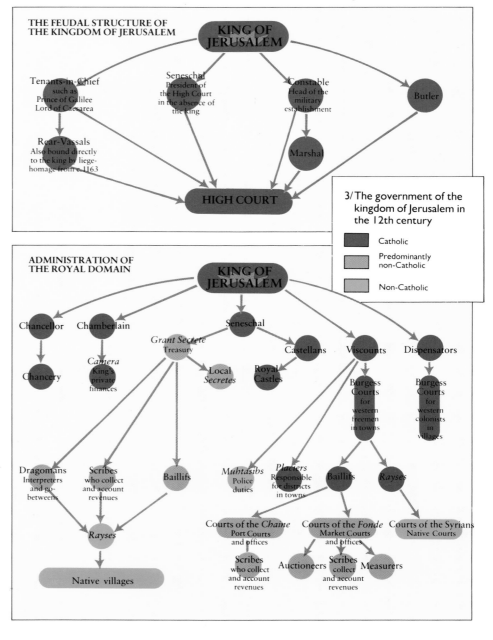

The original ivory cover of a Latin psalter, written and illuminated in Jerusalem, 1131-1143, probably for Queen Melisende. The cover illustrates the life of David, with all its implications for monarchy. David was considered the prototype of true kingship. Members of the dynasty ruling Jerusalem were proud that as descendants of Charlemagne they were sitting on the throne of David.

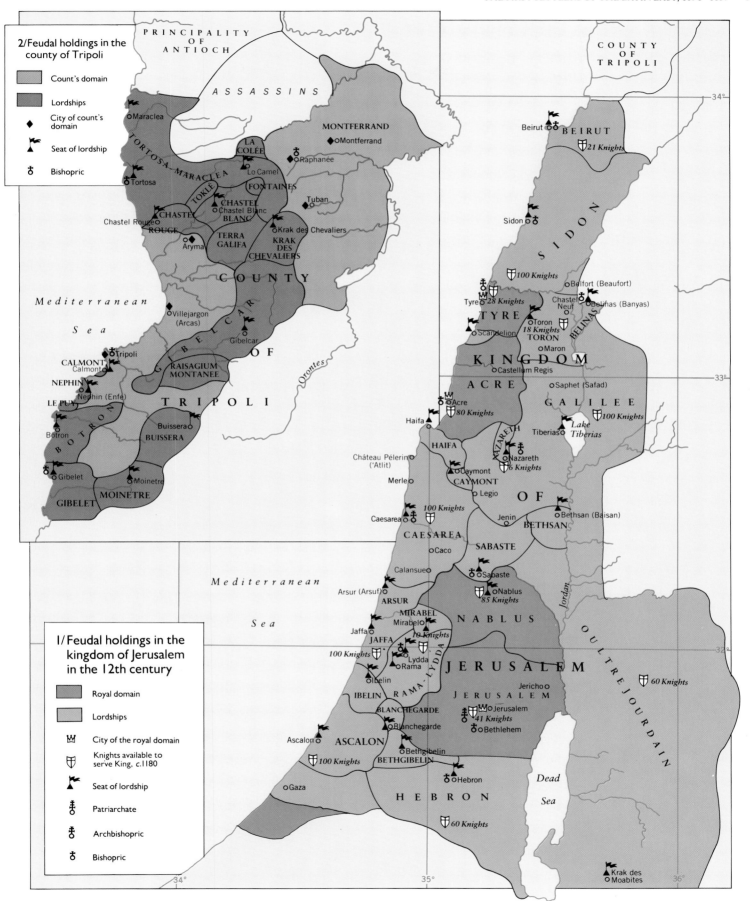

2/Feudal holdings in the county of Tripoli

- Count's domain
- Lordships
- ◆ City of count's domain
- 🏴 Seat of lordship
- ☦ Bishopric

PRINCIPALITY OF ANTIOCH

COUNTY OF TRIPOLI

ASSASSINS

○ Maraclea

MONTFERRAND

◆ Montferrand

TORTOSA-MARACLEA

LA COLÉE

◆ Raphanée

🏴 ○ Tortosa

○ Lo Camel

TOKLÉ

FONTAINES

CHASTEL BLANC

◆ Tuban

CHASTEL ROUGE

○ Chastel Blanc

○ Chastel Rouge

🏴 Krak des Chevaliers

TERRA GALIFA

KRAK DES CHEVALIERS

◆ Aryma

Mediterranean Sea

COUNTY

GIBELCAR

○ Villejargon (Arcas)

OF

○ Gibelcar

RAISAGIUM MONTANEE

TRIPOLI

Orontes

CALMONT

☦ ○ Tripoli

◆ Calmont

NEPHIN

LE PUY

○ Nephin (Enfe)

BOTRON

○ Buissera

○ Botron

BUISSERA

☦ ○ Gibelet

○ Moinetre

GIBELET

MOINETRE

1/Feudal holdings in the kingdom of Jerusalem in the 12th century

- Royal domain
- Lordships
- 👑 City of the royal domain
- 🛡 Knights available to serve King, c.1180
- 🏴 Seat of lordship
- ☩ Patriarchate
- ☦ Archbishopric
- ☦ Bishopric

Mediterranean Sea

○ Beirut   🏴 BEIRUT   ☦ *21 Knights*

COUNTY OF TRIPOLI

SIDON

○ Sidon ☦

🛡 *100 Knights*

○ Belfort (Beaufort)

Tyre ○ ☦ 👑 🏴   Chastel Neuf 🛡   ☦ 🏴 ○ Belinas (Banyas)

28 Knights   BELINAS

TYRE   🏴 ○ Scandelion   ○ Toron 🛡 *18 Knights*   TORON

KINGDOM   ○ Maron

ACRE   ○ Castellum Regis   ○ Saphet (Safad)

GALILEE

🏴 ○ Acre ☦ 👑   🛡 *100 Knights*

🛡 *80 Knights*   ○ Tiberias   🏴 *Lake Tiberias*

○ Haifa   HAIFA   NAZARETH   ☦ ○ Nazareth 🏴   OF   🏴 ○ Bethsan (Baisan)

Château Pèlerin ('Atlit)   CAYMONT   *6 Knights*

○ Merle   ○ Caymont 🏴   BETHSAN

○ Legio   ○ Jenin

Caesarea ○ ☦ 🏴   🛡 *100 Knights*   SABASTE

CAESAREA   ☦ 🏴 Sabaste

○ Caco   ○ Nablus

○ Calansue   🛡 *85 Knights*   NABLUS

Arsur (Arsuf) ○ 🏴   MIRABEL

ARSUR   ○ Mirabel 🏴   JERUSALEM

Jaffa ○ 🏴   *10 Knights* 🛡

JAFFA   ○ Jericho   OUTREJOURDAIN

🛡 *100 Knights*   ○ Lydda ☦   🛡 *60 Knights*

RAMA-LYDDA   ○ Rama

🏴 ○ Ibelin   ☩ ○ Jerusalem 👑

IBELIN   ☦ ○ Bethlehem   *41 Knights* 🛡

🏴 BLANCHEGARDE   ○ Blanchegarde

Ascalon ○ 🏴   ☦ ○ Bethgibelin

ASCALON   🏴 BETHGIBELIN

🛡 *100 Knights*   ☦ ○ Hebron

○ Gaza   HEBRON

Dead Sea

🛡 *60 Knights*   🏴 Krak des Moabites ○

Caesarea: A Settler Town

The Latin settlers in the Holy Land took over existing towns and adapted them to their own needs.

Caesarea is a good example of a medium-sized town of the 12th century. Its Roman heyday was long since past, and by the time it was captured by the crusaders in May 1101, its walls enclosed only one tenth of the town's 6th-century area. Under the crusaders, it became the seat of a secular lord and of an archbishop. The new occupants drove out the Muslim population but did little to alter the existing streets, fortifications, water supply, baths, markets, shops and houses. Even the mosques, to begin with at least, were hastily turned into churches. During the course of the 12th century, the Muslim Great Mosque was demolished and replaced with the new Latin cathedral of St Peter.

The town was relatively prosperous, enjoying both local and some long-distance trade, though not on the scale of the northern ports

of Acre, Tyre and Beirut. On the south side of the harbour stood the castle, consisting of a massive tower with a surrounding wall, cut off from the town by a sea-filled moat. To the north was a mole built of re-used Roman columns. The area thus enclosed represented no more than the inner basin of the harbour built by Roman engineers eleven centuries before, and it was said to be so small that it could accommodate only one ship at a time.

The city walls in the 12th century were essentially those built by the Muslims, enclosing only a central rectangle of the gridded Roman street plan. Large rectangular towers projected from them, and protected the gates. Around the walls was a dry ditch. Many of the houses also dated from the Muslim period, and were built in the oriental fashion, looking inwards on to a central court containing a rainwater cistern. Most had an upper storey, which in at least one case extended on arches over a street. Water was supplied from the Crocodile River, 9 miles (15km) to the north,

along one of the Roman aqueducts which still remained in repair. Outside the walls, a cemetery extended to the south; on the north and east, gardens and orchards spread as far as the encroaching dunes permitted.

> **W**e used to be Westerners; now we are Easterners. You may once have been a Roman or a Frenchman; here, and now, you are a Galilean or a Palestinian. For we have forgotten the lands of our birth; to most of us they are now strange, foreign countries. Some people are now in possession of their own houses and servants as if they had inherited them by right; others are married not only to girls from back home, but also to Syrians, Armenians and even Saracens — but of course only to baptized ones.
>
> Fulcher of Chartres describes his fellow settlers in *Historia Hierosolymitana*

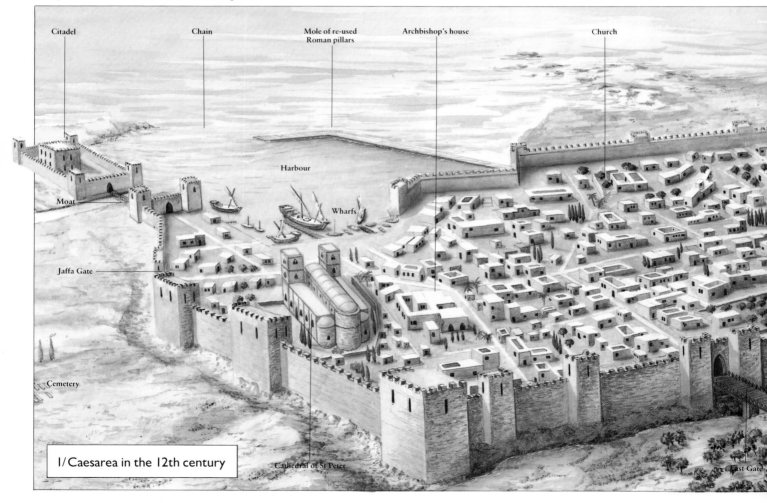

Citadel   Chain   Mole of re-used Roman pillars   Archbishop's house   Church

Harbour

Moat

Wharfs

Jaffa Gate

Cemetery

Cathedral of St Peter

East Gate

1/ Caesarea in the 12th century

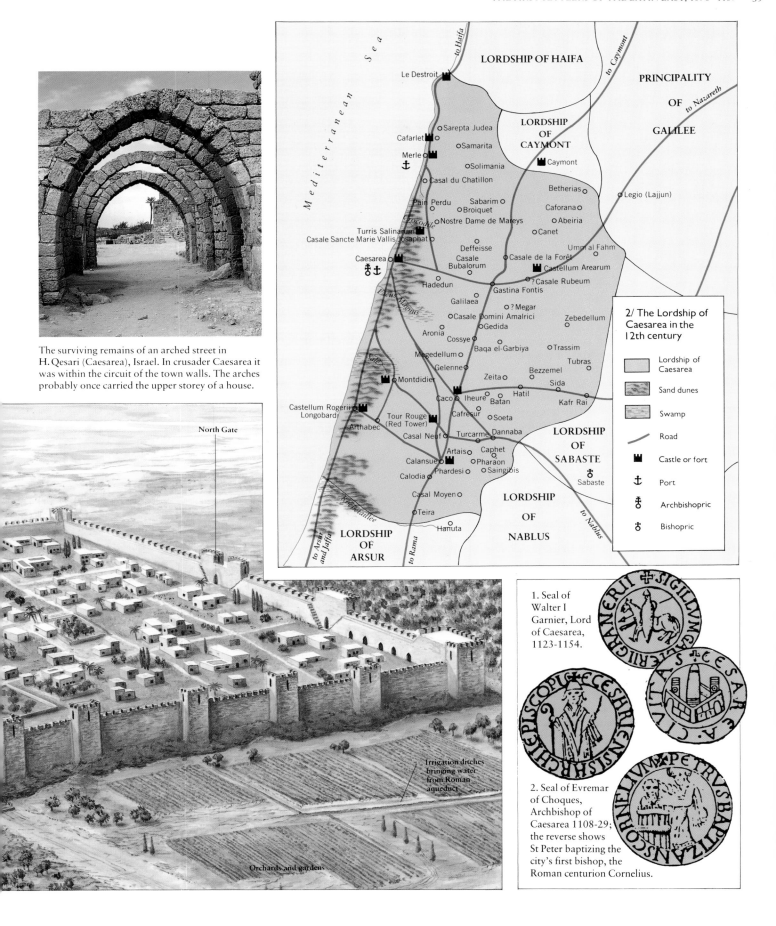

The surviving remains of an arched street in H. Qesari (Caesarea), Israel. In crusader Caesarea it was within the circuit of the town walls. The arches probably once carried the upper storey of a house.

North Gate

Irrigation ditches bringing water from Roman aqueduct

Orchards and gardens

LORDSHIP OF HAIFA

Le Destroit

to Haifa

to Caymont

PRINCIPALITY OF GALILEE

to Nazareth

Mediterranean Sea

Sarepta Judea

LORDSHIP OF CAYMONT

Cafarlet

Samarita

Merle

Solimania

Caymont

Casal du Chatillon

Betherias

Legio (Lajjun)

Pain Perdu

Sabarim

Caforana

Broiquet

Nostre Dame de Mareys

Abeiria

Turris Salinarum

Canet

Casale Sancte Marie Vallis Josaphat

Crocodile

Deffeisse

Ummal Fahm

Caesarea

Casale Bubalorum

Casale de la Forêt

Castellum Arearum

Hadedun

Gastina Fontis

?Casale Rubeum

Lacus Masnus

Galilaea

?Megar

Zebedellum

Casale Domini Amalrici

Aronia

Gedida

Cossye

Baqa el-Garbiya

Trassim

Megedellum

Tubras

Gelenne

Zeita

Bezzemel

Sida

Montdidier

Caco

Iheure

Batan

Hatil

Kafr Rai

Castellum Rogerii Longobardi

Cafresur

Soeta

LORDSHIP OF SABASTE

Arthabec

Tour Rouge (Red Tower)

Turcarme

Dannaba

Casal Neuf

Artais

Caphet

Sabaste

Calansue

Pharaon

Phardesi

Saingibis

Calodia

Casal Moyen

LORDSHIP OF NABLUS

Teira

to Nablus

Hanuta

Valle

Nahr el-taillée

to Arsur and Jaffa

to Rama

LORDSHIP OF ARSUR

2/ The Lordship of Caesarea in the 12th century

Lordship of Caesarea

Sand dunes

Swamp

Road

Castle or fort

Port

Archbishopric

Bishopric

1. Seal of Walter I Garnier, Lord of Caesarea, 1123-1154.

2. Seal of Evremar of Choques, Archbishop of Caesarea 1108-29; the reverse shows St Peter baptizing the city's first bishop, the Roman centurion Cornelius.

Settler Villages

The village of Parva Mahumeria was a pioneering settlement of Christian colonists in the Holy Land.

In the kingdom of Jerusalem, most of the immigrant Frankish population lived in towns or castles; the countryside was populated and worked almost exclusively by native Syrians, both Christians and Muslims. A number of attempts were made, however, to settle westerners on the land. Many of the landowners around Jerusalem promoted this kind of venture, among them the canons of the Holy Sepulchre (▶*page 46*). They were well placed to do so because Godfrey of Bouillon had bequeathed some villages to them on his death in 1100. In 1120, the canons established their first such settlement just north of the city at Magna Mahumeria (al-Bira). The settlers, volunteers from Southern France together with a few Spaniards and Italians, were encouraged by the offer of lands and house plots on very attractive terms. In return, they paid part of their agricultural produce annually to the canons' steward, who lived and worked in the courthouse (*curia*).

By 1155, there were about 450 inhabitants, including three smiths, three carpenters, a mason, a shoemaker and a goldsmith. The population continued to increase, and by 1187 it had reached about 700. The settlers were liable for military service; 65 men from Magna Mahumeria died defending Gaza from Saladin in 1170. A church was also built.

The canons' second venture was Parva Mahumeria (al-Qubaiba). It was built by 1164 on the lands of Bethsurie, on the road between Jerusalem and the coast. Like Magna Mahumeria, it had a church and a courthouse enclosed by vaulted store-rooms. The village houses, set out along a single main street, were of European type, with their living areas built over large vaulted undercrofts, which served as store-rooms or workshops. Of the 29 basements excavated by archaeologists, one was a bakery, one contained a rotary olive-press, and almost half of them contained pressing-floors with stone counter-weights from the pressing machinery, illustrating the importance of wine and olive oil production in the settler villages.

The settlements were short-lived, and were abandoned when Saladin invaded in 1187 (▶ *page 60*). A Jewish traveller passing through Magna Mahumeria in 1210 found the village derelict.

> **N**ow Judaea is for the most part mountainous, and round about the Holy City rises into very lofty ranges... wherever any patches of earth are found among these masses of rock, the land is seen to be fit for the production of every kind of fruit. We have seen the hills and mountains covered with such vineyards and plantations of olive trees and fig trees, and the valleys abounding with corn and garden produce.
>
> German pilgrim Theodoric, c.1170

Olives (above) had been grown around Parva Mahumeria (al-Qubaiba) since ancient times. In the crusader period, production was mostly geared towards local consumption. The oil was extracted in hand presses (right), and used for cooking, lighting and making soap.

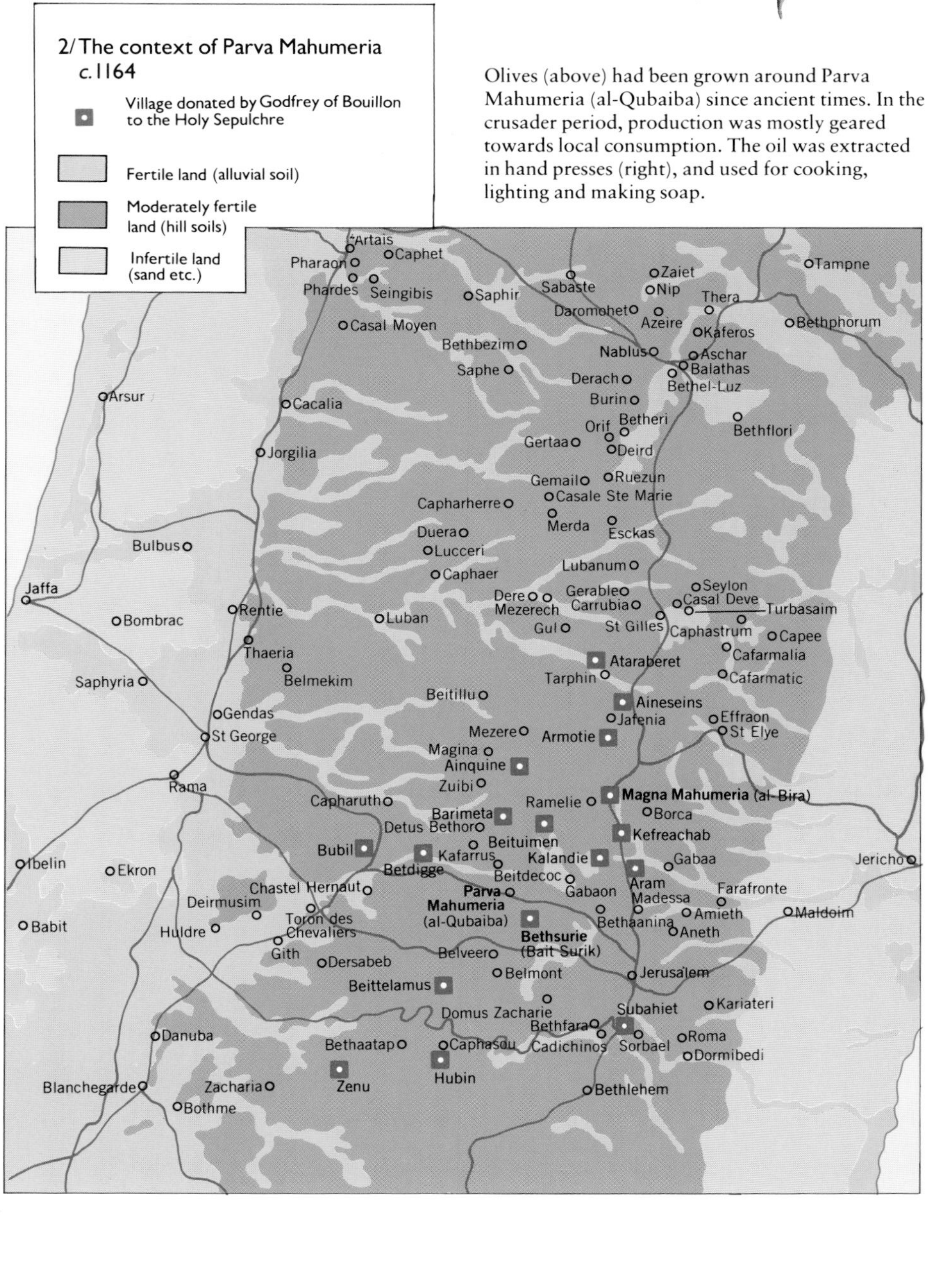

2/ The context of Parva Mahumeria c.1164

- ▣ Village donated by Godfrey of Bouillon to the Holy Sepulchre
- Fertile land (alluvial soil)
- Moderately fertile land (hill soils)
- Infertile land (sand etc.)

[Map showing the region with numerous place names including:]
Pharaon, Caphet, Artais, Phardes, Seingibis, Saphir, Sabaste, Zaiet, Nip, Thera, Tampne, Daromohet, Azeire, Kaferos, Bethphorum, Casal Moyen, Bethbezim, Nablus, Aschar, Saphe, Derach, Balathas, Bethel-Luz, Arsur, Cacalia, Burin, Betheri, Orif, Bethflori, Gertaa, Deird, Jorgilia, Gemail, Ruezun, Capharherre, Casale Ste Marie, Merda, Esckas, Duera, Lucceri, Lubanum, Bulbus, Caphaer, Dere, Gerableo, Seylon, Jaffa, Rentie, Luban, Mezerech, Carrubia, Casal Deve, Turbasaim, Bombrac, Thaeria, Gul, St Gilles, Caphastrum, Capee, Belmekim, Ataraberet, Cafarmalia, Saphyria, Beitillu, Tarphin, Aineseins, Cafarmatic, Gendas, Mezere, Armotie, Jafenia, Effraon, St George, Magina, St Elye, Rama, Ainquine, Zuibi, Caparutho, Barimeta, Ramelie, Magna Mahumeria (al-Bira), Detus Bethoro, Borca, Bubil, Kafarrus, Kalandie, Kefreachab, Betdigge, Beitcdecoc, Gabaa, Jericho, Ibelin, Ekron, Chastel Hernaut, Beituimen, Aram, Farafronte, Deirmusim, Kalandie, Gabaon, Madessa, Maldoim, Babit, Huldre, Toron des Chevaliers, Parva Mahumeria (al-Qubaiba), Bethaanina, Amieth, Aneth, Gith, Dersabeb, Belveero, Bethsurie (Bait Surik), Beittelamus, Belmont, Jerusalem, Kariateri, Domus Zacharie, Subahiet, Danuba, Bethaatap, Caphasdu, Cadichinos, Bethfara, Sorbael, Roma, Dormibedi, Blanchegarde, Zacharia, Zenu, Hubin, Bethlehem, Bothme

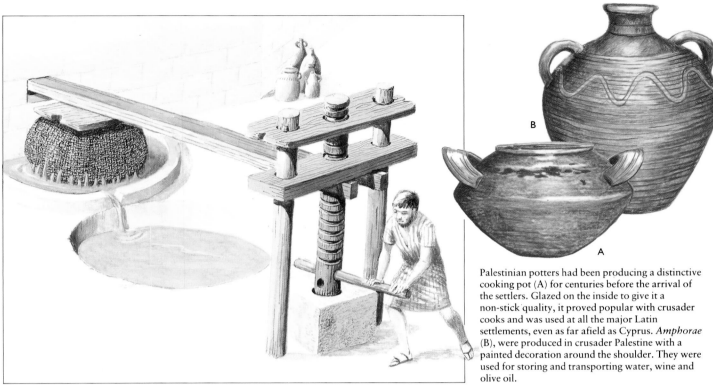

Palestinian potters had been producing a distinctive cooking pot (A) for centuries before the arrival of the settlers. Glazed on the inside to give it a non-stick quality, it proved popular with crusader cooks and was used at all the major Latin settlements, even as far afield as Cyprus. *Amphorae* (B), were produced in crusader Palestine with a painted decoration around the shoulder. They were used for storing and transporting water, wine and olive oil.

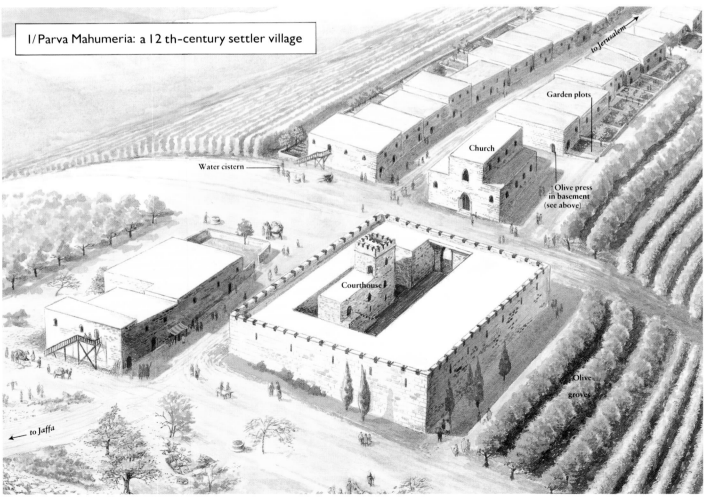

1/Parva Mahumeria: a 12th-century settler village

The Holy Land

The Holy Land had an immense emotional appeal to the Catholic settlers. Every nook and cranny of the landscape could be associated with Christ, the disciples, the saints and the patriarchs and prophets of the Old Testament.

Pilgrimage to the Holy Places of Christendom played an important part in the development of crusading ideology, and few of those who took the cross to go and fight in Palestine would have left for home without first visiting them. The picture they formed of the spiritual geography of the Holy Land was influenced by a variety of sources: literary, oral and even cartographic. Writers of the 12th century added new information, based on personal experience or conversations with monks or churchmen living in the Holy Land. But they often drew as much on what they had read as on what they had actually seen and heard. The flowers that the Englishman Saewulf saw on Mount Tabor in 1102 or 1103, for instance, seem to have been inspired by the words of the Venerable Bede (702-703).

Some well-known Biblical features appear in different places depending on which source of information the writer was using or on how easy a particular place was to reach. Emmaus, for example, was traditionally located by the Greek church at 'Amwas, on the edge of the coastal plain; but during the 12th century the Latins relocated it at Abu Ghosh, closer to Jerusalem. After the loss of Jerusalem, when Christian pilgrims were restricted to using a different road further north, the traditional location was shifted once more, so that today Christ's Resurrection appearance to Cleopas is recalled by Western pilgrims at al-Qubaiba, a village which did not exist before the 12th century (▶page 40).

Many of the more important Holy Places had churches built over them in late Roman and Byzantine times, but most of these had been destroyed before the 12th century. When the crusaders took over, an enormous task of rebuilding was required. Almost all of the principal shrines were placed in the care of monastic houses or cathedral chapters, who concerned themselves with the pilgrims' material as well as spiritual needs. The Templars and Hospitallers (▶page 52) provided a military escort for parties of pilgrims.

An early 12th-century pilgrim, from a contemporary wall painting in the church of St Nicolas in Tavant, France. He carries a palm frond– the sign of a Jerusalem pilgrim – in his left hand. In Jerusalem, palm fronds could be purchased in the Street of Palms, by the church of St Mary Latina.

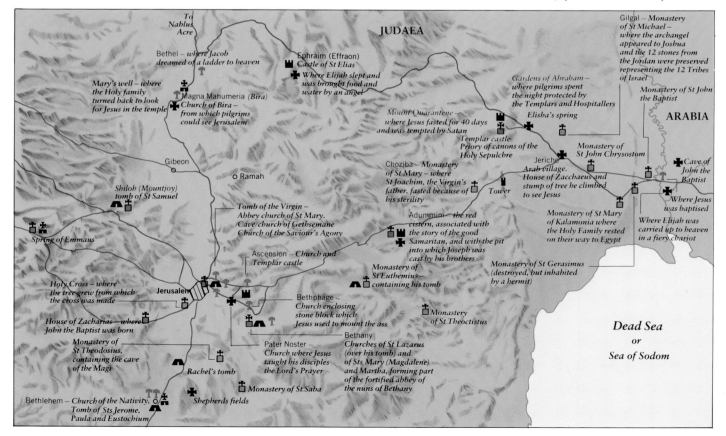

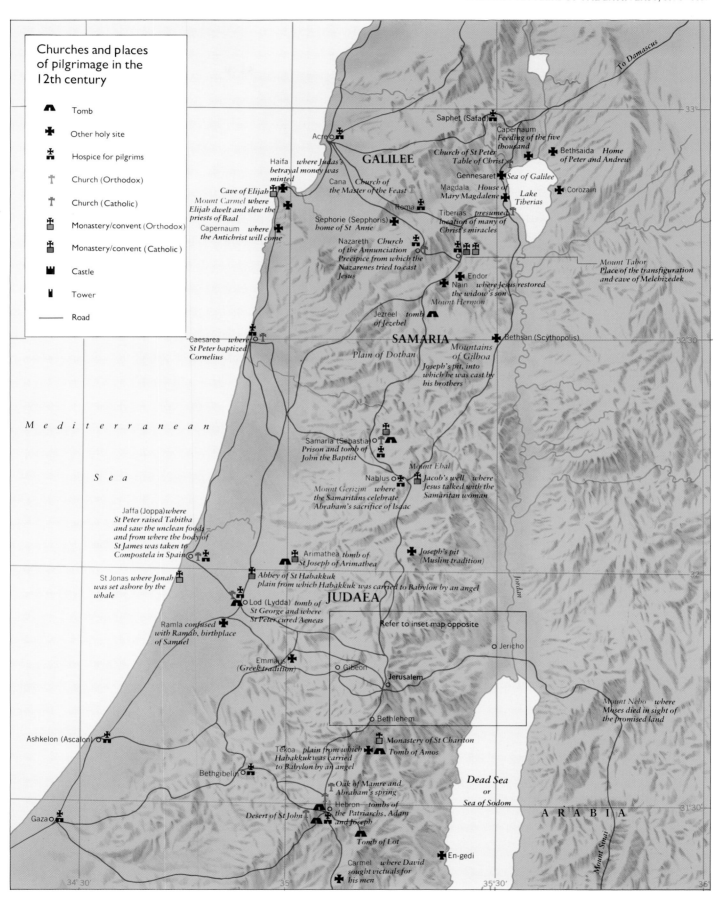

Churches and places of pilgrimage in the 12th century

- ⛰ Tomb
- ✚ Other holy site
- ⛨ Hospice for pilgrims
- ✝ Church (Orthodox)
- ✝ Church (Catholic)
- ▥ Monastery/convent (Orthodox)
- ⛨ Monastery/convent (Catholic)
- ⛫ Castle
- ⛉ Tower
- —— Road

To Damascus

Acre

GALILEE

Saphet (Safad)

Capernaum *Feeding of the five thousand*

Church of St Peter Table of Christ

Bethsaida *Home of Peter and Andrew*

Gennesaret *Sea of Galilee*

Corozain

Magdala *House of Mary Magdalene*

Lake Tiberias

Haifa *where Judas's betrayal money was minted*

Cana *Church of the Master of the Feast*

Roma

Cave of Elijah

Mount Carmel *where Elijah dwelt and slew the priests of Baal*

Capernaum *where the Antichrist will come*

Sephorie (Sepphoris) *home of St Anne*

Tiberias *presumed location of many of Christ's miracles*

Nazareth *Church of the Annunciation Precipice from which the Nazarenes tried to cast Jesus*

Nain *where Jesus restored the widow's son*

Mount Hermon

Mount Tabor *Place of the transfiguration and cave of Melchizedek*

Jezreel *tomb of Jezebel*

Caesarea *where St Peter baptized Cornelius*

SAMARIA

Plain of Dothan

Bethsan (Scythopolis)

Mountains of Gilboa

Joseph's pit, into which he was cast by his brothers

M e d i t e r r a n e a n

S e a

Samaria (Sebastia) *Prison and tomb of John the Baptist*

Mount Ebal

Nablus

Jacob's well *where Jesus talked with the Samaritan woman*

Mount Gerizim *where the Samaritans celebrate Abraham's sacrifice of Isaac*

Jaffa (Joppa) *where St Peter raised Tabitha and saw the unclean foods and from where the body of St James was taken to Compostela in Spain*

Arimathea *tomb of St Joseph of Arimathea*

Joseph's pit *(Muslim tradition)*

St Jonas *where Jonah was set ashore by the whale*

Abbey of St Habakkuk *plain from which Habakkuk was carried to Babylon by an angel*

Jordan

Lod (Lydda) *tomb of St George and where St Peter cured Aeneas*

JUDAEA

Ramla *confused with Ramah, birthplace of Samuel*

Refer to inset map opposite

Jericho

Emmaus *(Greek tradition)*

Gibeon

Jerusalem

Mount Nebo *where Moses died in sight of the promised land*

Bethlehem

Ashkelon (Ascalon)

Monastery of St Chariton

Tekoa *plain from which Habakkuk was carried to Babylon by an angel*

Tomb of Amos

Bethgibelin

Dead Sea or *Sea of Sodom*

Oak of Mamre and Abraham's spring

Hebron *tombs of the Patriarchs, Adam and Joseph*

Desert of St John

Gaza

A R A B I A

Tomb of Lot

Mount Sinai

Carmel *where David sought victuals for his men*

En-gedi

The Holy City

Jerusalem – the Holy City – was now the capital of a Christian kingdom, and soon found itself filled with pilgrims from all quarters of Christendom.

For the first time in 450 years, the city in which Christ had suffered on the cross was in Christian hands. After the terrible siege (▶ *page 30*), the corpses were cleared and the rebuilding began. Jerusalem became the capital of a secular kingdom. A royal palace was built beside the al-Aqsa mosque, in what was believed to be the precinct of the ancient Temple of the Lord. Later the site was granted to the Templars and a new palace built near the Tower of David, a location equally rich in kingly associations.

The city had very little economic importance and was at first greatly underpopulated, but it was the holiest in Christendom, the centre of the world to Christian cartographers. Bells – banned under Muslim rule – were restored to the churches, a Latin patriarch and clergy were installed, and the stream of pilgrims who had visited the city before the First Crusade turned into a flood.

The most important holy places in Jerusalem were those associated with Christ's Passion and Resurrection. The Passion story began with Jesus's entry into Jerusalem through the Golden Gate, continued with his teaching in the Temple precincts, his arrest in Gethsemane, his imprisonment, trial and condemnation in and around the Roman Governor's palace or Praetorium, his carrying of the cross from there to Calvary, and ended with his crucifixion and burial, and his post-Resurrection appearance to the apostles in the Upper Room on Mount Sion. Pilgrims could follow Christ's route – the Way of the Cross – from the Praetorium to Calvary, which, together with his Tomb, was enclosed within the Church of the Holy Sepulchre (▶ *page 46*).

In the early 12th century, pilgrims would normally have entered the city through David's Gate, next to the Citadel (or Tower of David) on the east, and would have proceeded directly to the Church of the Holy Sepulchre, to pray at the Tomb of Christ. During the course of this century, however, other smaller sites and shrines developed. To cater for the influx of Western visitors arriving by sea at the ports of Acre and Jaffa, hostels, such as the one attached to the church of St Mary Latina, developed. The Hospitallers (▶ *page 52*) built a vast hospital with 2,000 beds for sick and

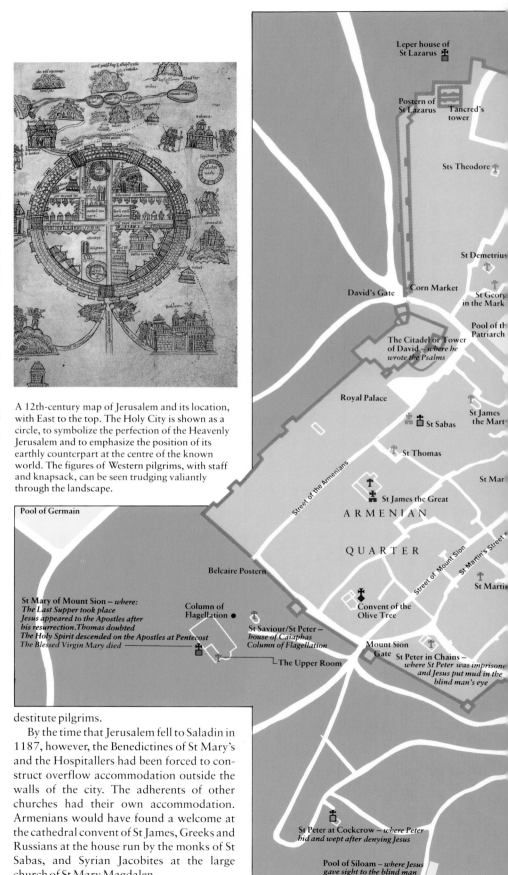

A 12th-century map of Jerusalem and its location, with East to the top. The Holy City is shown as a circle, to symbolize the perfection of the Heavenly Jerusalem and to emphasize the position of its earthly counterpart at the centre of the known world. The figures of Western pilgrims, with staff and knapsack, can be seen trudging valiantly through the landscape.

Pool of Germain

St Mary of Mount Sion – *where:*
The Last Supper took place
Jesus appeared to the Apostles after
his resurrection.Thomas doubted
The Holy Spirit descended on the Apostles at Pentecost
The Blessed Virgin Mary died

Belcaire Postern

Column of Flagellation ●

St Saviour/St Peter – *house of Caiaphas Column of Flagellation*

└The Upper Room

Leper house of St Lazarus

Postern of St Lazarus   Tancred's tower

Sts Theodore

St Demetrius

David's Gate   Corn Market

St George in the Mark

Pool of th Patriarch

The Citadel or Tower of David – *where he wrote the Psalms*

Royal Palace

St James the Mart

St Sabas

St Thomas

St Mar

Street of the Armenians

St James the Great

ARMENIAN

QUARTER

Street of Mount Sion

St Martin's Street

St Martin

Convent of the Olive Tree

Mount Sion Gate   St Peter in Chains – *where St Peter was imprisone and Jesus put mud in the blind man's eye*

St Peter at Cockcrow – *where Peter hid and wept after denying Jesus*

Pool of Siloam – *where Jesus gave sight to the blind man*

destitute pilgrims.

By the time that Jerusalem fell to Saladin in 1187, however, the Benedictines of St Mary's and the Hospitallers had been forced to construct overflow accommodation outside the walls of the city. The adherents of other churches had their own accommodation. Armenians would have found a welcome at the cathedral convent of St James, Greeks and Russians at the house run by the monks of St Sabas, and Syrian Jacobites at the large church of St Mary Magdalen.

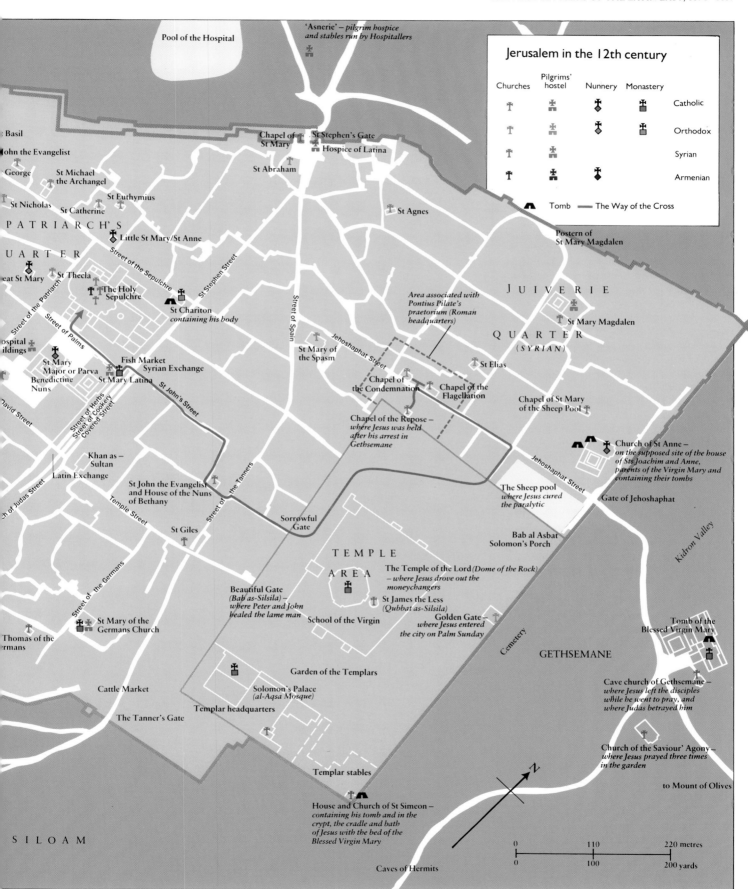

Jerusalem in the 12th century

Churches	Pilgrims' hostel	Nunnery	Monastery	
✝	⛪	✝	⛪	Catholic
✝	⛪	✝	⛪	Orthodox
✝	⛪			Syrian
✝	⛪	✝		Armenian

Tomb ▬ The Way of the Cross

Pool of the Hospital

'Asnerie' – *pilgrim hospice and stables run by Hospitallers*

St Basil

John the Evangelist

George   St Michael the Archangel

St Nicholas   St Euthymius

St Catherine

PATRIARCH'S QUARTER

Little St Mary/St Anne

Great St Mary   St Thecla

Street of the Sepulchre

The Holy Sepulchre

St Chariton *containing his body*

Hospital Buildings

St Mary Major or Parva Benedictine Nuns

Fish Market   Syrian Exchange

St Mary Latina

David Street

Street of the Patriarch

Street of Palms

St John's Street

Street of Herbs
Street of Cookery
Covered Street

Khan as – Sultan

Latin Exchange

Church of Judas Street

St John the Evangelist and House of the Nuns of Bethany

Temple Street

St Giles

Street of the Tanners

Sorrowful Gate

Chapel of St Mary

St Stephen's Gate

Hospice of Latina

St Abraham

St Stephen Street

Street of Spain

St Agnes

St Mary of the Spasm

Jehoshaphat Street

Area associated with Pontius Pilate's praetorium (Roman headquarters)

Chapel of the Condemnation

Chapel of the Flagellation

Chapel of the Repose – *where Jesus was held after his arrest in Gethsemane*

St Elias

Chapel of St Mary of the Sheep Pool

JUIVERIE QUARTER (SYRIAN)

Postern of St Mary Magdalen

St Mary Magdalen

Church of St Anne – *on the supposed site of the house of Sts Joachim and Anne, parents of the Virgin Mary and containing their tombs*

The Sheep pool *where Jesus cured the paralytic*

Jehoshaphat Street

Gate of Jehoshaphat

Kidron Valley

Bab al Asbat Solomon's Porch

TEMPLE AREA

The Temple of the Lord *(Dome of the Rock) – where Jesus drove out the moneychangers*

St James the Less *(Qubbat as-Silsila)*

Beautiful Gate *(Bab as-Silsila) – where Peter and John healed the lame man*

School of the Virgin

Golden Gate – *where Jesus entered the city on Palm Sunday*

Cemetery

GETHSEMANE

Tomb of the Blessed Virgin Mary

Cave church of Gethsemane – *where Jesus left the disciples while he went to pray, and where Judas betrayed him*

Church of the Saviour' Agony – *where Jesus prayed three times in the garden*

to Mount of Olives

Garden of the Templars

Solomon's Palace *(al-Aqsa Mosque)*

Templar headquarters

Cattle Market

The Tanner's Gate

St Mary of the Germans Church

Thomas of the Germans

Street of the Germans

Templar stables

House and Church of St Simeon – *containing his tomb and in the crypt, the cradle and bath of Jesus with the bed of the Blessed Virgin Mary*

SILOAM

Caves of Hermits

N

0	110	220 metres
0	100	200 yards

The Holy Sepulchre

The Church of the Holy Sepulchre in Jerusalem was the emotional centre of the Christian world, built directly over the rock of Calvary and the tomb of Christ.

The church of the Holy Sepulchre visited by Western pilgrims in the 12th century was a composite building of various periods. After the Roman emperor Constantine began to favour Christianity in 313, the tomb of Christ, which for two centuries had lain beneath the pagan temples of Jerusalem's Roman forum, was uncovered once more. The tomb itself was isolated from the surrounding rock and enclosed within a rotunda below a large timber dome. To the east, a large congregational church was built; this was separated from the rotunda by a colonnaded court, enclosing the rock of Calvary at its south-eastern corner and the other sites associated with the Passion.

Although Jerusalem fell to the Muslims in 638, Christian worship was allowed to continue under the care of the Greek Orthodox church until 1009, when the mad caliph al-Hakim utterly destroyed Constantine's church. Between 1042 and 1048, the rotunda and courtyard were rebuilt by the Byzantine emperor Constantine IX Monomachus. The tomb of Christ, which had been levelled to the ground on al-Hakim's orders, was replaced by a masonry replica; around it the rotunda was reconstructed as a circular church, with a gallery and an eastern apse containing the main altar.

After Jerusalem was captured by the crusaders in 1099, a Catholic community of 20 canons was established in the Holy Sepulchre. It soon became obvious that the rebuilt Byzantine church was too small to accommodate the large numbers of pilgrims who began to flock to the city. Over the next 50 years the complex was fashioned into one great Romanesque church; and the belltower, the dome over the crossing and the canons' cloister were completed later in the century.

The new crusader choir – consecrated on 15 July 1149 – was built over the site of the former open court between the rotunda and Constantine's church. The pilgrim approaching it from the market street on the south would have passed beneath an arched colonnade into the *parvis* or courtyard, before the south front of the church. To the left of the *parvis* was a line of three chapels: the chapel of St John below the belltower next to the

church, the domed chapel of the Holy Trinity containing the baptistery, and the chapel of St James, the first bishop of Jerusalem. To the right of the doors was the chapel of St Mary the Egyptian below a richly decorated stair which led up to the domed chapel of the Franks, forming a kind of vestibule to the chapel enclosing the rock of Calvary.

Just inside the double door to the church, around Golgotha or the chapel of Adam below Calvary, lay the tombs of the Latin kings of Jerusalem. The centre of the world was marked in the pavement of the new choir, directly below the dome of the crossing, and near it was the place where Christ's body had been anointed for burial. To the west of this stood the Sepulchre itself, and to the east the high altar, with a mosaic representing Christ's triumph over death in the semi-dome of the apse above it.

On the north side of the church lay the chapel of St Mary, two chapels containing relics of the Holy Cross, and the Prison of Christ. Within the apsidal ambulatory on the east were three chapels (one with an altar to St Longinus), which commemorated the crowning with thorns, the division of Christ's garments, and his flagellation. To the east of this, outside the church and below the canons' cloister, lay the chapel of St Helena, the mother of Constantine, and the rock-cut cistern in which she was said to have found the relic of the Cross.

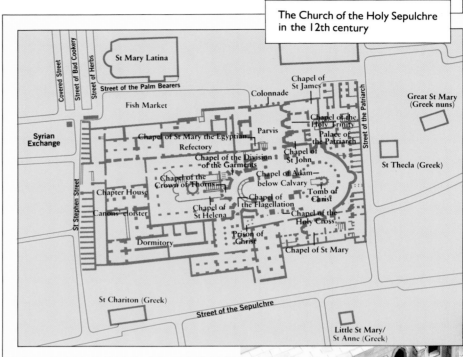

The Church of the Holy Sepulchre in the 12th century

St Mary Latina

Covered Street

Street of Bad Cookery

Street of Herbs

Street of the Palm Bearers

Fish Market

Syrian Exchange

St Stephen Street

Colonnade

Chapel of St James

Chapel of the Holy Trinity

Palace of the Patriarch

Street of the Patriarch

Great St Mary (Greek nuns)

St Thecla (Greek)

Parvis

Chapel of St Mary the Egyptian

Refectory

Chapel of the Division of the Garments

Chapel of St John

Chapel of the Crown of Thorns

Chapter House

Chapel of Adam— below Calvary

Tomb of Christ

Chapel of the Flagellation

Canons' cloister

Chapel of St Helena

Chapel of the Holy Cross

Dormitory

Prison of Christ

Chapel of St Mary

St Chariton (Greek)

Street of the Sepulchre

Little St Mary/ St Anne (Greek)

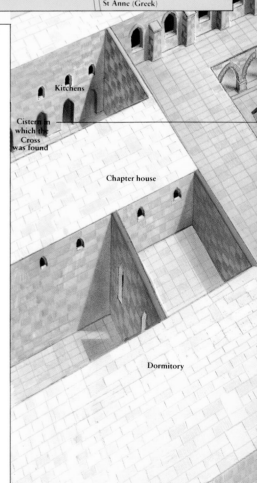

Kitchens

Cistern in which the Cross was found

Chapter house

Dormitory

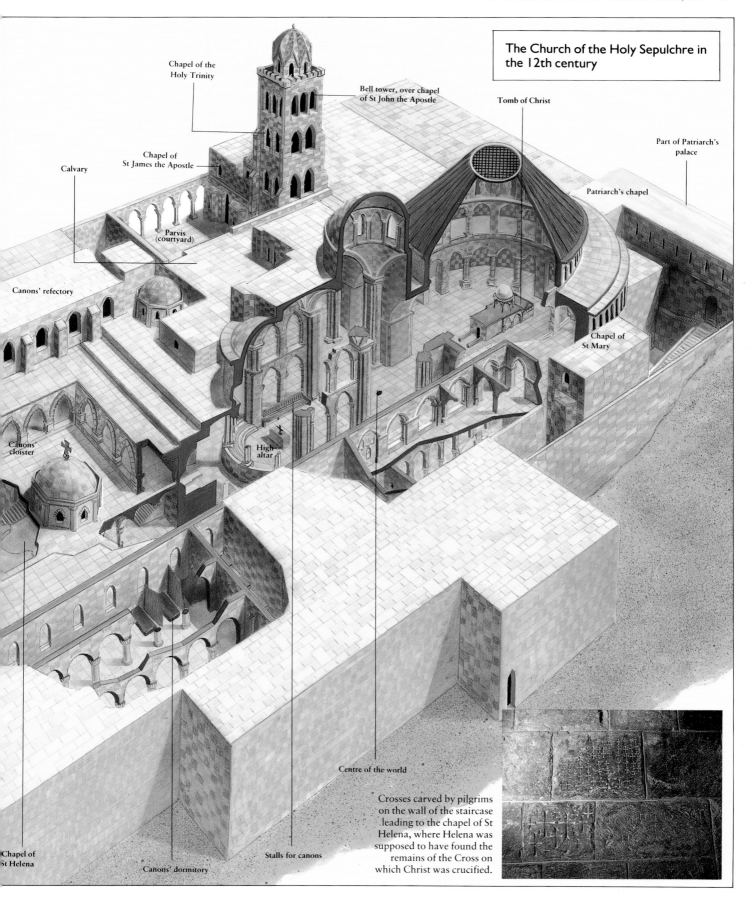

The Church of the Holy Sepulchre in the 12th century

Chapel of the Holy Trinity

Bell tower, over chapel of St John the Apostle

Tomb of Christ

Part of Patriarch's palace

Chapel of St James the Apostle

Patriarch's chapel

Calvary

Parvis (courtyard)

Canons' refectory

Chapel of St Mary

Canons' cloister

High altar

Centre of the world

Chapel of St Helena

Canons' dormitory

Stalls for canons

Crosses carved by pilgrims on the wall of the staircase leading to the chapel of St Helena, where Helena was supposed to have found the remains of the Cross on which Christ was crucified.

The Second Crusade

**The Second Crusade was an
operation on an unprecedented scale:
a war on three fronts in Spain, the
Baltic and the Near East.**

The Second Crusade was inspired by the
plight of the Holy Land. Its course and
conduct revealed how the crusade could be
applied consistently to various theatres of
Christian warfare and, in the preaching of
Bernard of Clairvaux, to the inner spiritual
needs of individual Christians.

On Christmas Eve 1144, the Muslim ruler
of Aleppo and Mosul, Imad al-Din Zangi captured Edessa, which had been in Latin
Christian hands since 1098 (▶ *page 34*). In
December the following year, Pope Eugenius
III called for a new crusade. His letter,
Quantum praedecessores, listed for the first
time the spiritual and material privileges to be
offered to crusaders. The immediate reaction
was muted. In France, Louis VII's declared intention to journey to the Holy Land met with
hostility. It was not until Eugenius reissued his
letter on 1 March 1146 that concerted recruitment began.

Eugenius III's chief contribution was to
appoint Bernard, abbot of Clairvaux, as the
main crusade preacher. He was the leading
spiritual figure of the time, and was sub-
sequently canonized. On Easter Day 1146,
Louis VII and his nobles took the cross at
Vézelay. The crowds were so large that
Bernard had to preach in the fields that
stretched down the hill from the church. To
meet the enthusiastic response Bernard tore
up his own clothes to make enough crosses.

After this dramatic success, Bernard of
Clairvaux travelled through Burgundy and
Flanders. He then turned aside to the
Rhineland to combat the anti-semitic rabble-
rousing of an unauthorized preacher, Radulf.
Where he could not go in person, he sent let-
ters instead. After a tour of the Upper Rhine
and Switzerland, Bernard persuaded King
Conrad III of Germany to take the cross at
Speyer in December 1146.

Bernard appealed directly to individual
hopes of salvation. He was no stranger to
knights' spiritual and martial aspirations,
having written *In Praise of the New
Knighthood* (1128-1137), which welcomed
the ideal of the Templars as knights dedicated
to serving God (▶*page 52*). Now he offered
the 'mighty men of valour' a bargain: in return for taking the cross, they would gain full
remission of sins by fighting in a cause that

> his age is like no other that has gone
> before ... blessed are those who are
> alive in this year pleasing to the Lord, this
> year of remission, this year of veritable
> jubilee. I tell you, the Lord has not done this
> for any other generation before, nor has he
> lavished on our fathers a gift of grace so
> copious. Look at the skill he is using to save
> you. Consider the depth of his love and be
> astonished, sinners. He creates a need – he
> either creates it or pretends to have it – while
> he comes from heaven to help you in your
> necessity. This is a plan not made by man, but
> proceeding from the heart of divine love.
>
> **St Bernard calls for crusaders, 1147**

was spiritually meritorious. For Bernard, the
crusade was not only a military operation but
also an opportunity for personal and collective redemption.

The crusade soon developed in unforeseen
directions. By the spring of 1147, the pope
had authorized King Alfonso VII of Castile to
equate his campaign against the Moors in
Spain with the crusade (▶ *page 72*). With the
help of the Aragonese and a Genoese fleet,
Alfonso captured the port of Almeria. In
October Bernard of Clairvaux gave permission to leaders in Saxony to regard their attack on the pagan Wends as part of the wider
crusading enterprise. In the event, the Danish
and Saxon attack on Dobin in July 1147 and
the larger Saxon offensive against Demmin
and Stettin in August both ended in truces.

The two main forces bound for the East
were the French under Louis VII and the
Germans under Conrad III. They shadowed
one another across central Europe, reaching
Constantinople in the autumn. Many crusaders sailed directly to the Holy Land, including groups of French and Italians under
the counts of Auvergne and Savoy and the
marquis of Montferrat, as well as Provençals
under Alphonso Jordan, count of Toulouse.
A combined fleet of Flemish, Rhinelanders,
Frisians, Normans and English helped the
king of Portugal capture Lisbon from the
Moors in October 1147. The fleet resumed its
journey to the east the following February,
capturing Faro *en route*. Some broke away
from the main fleet to join the count of
Barcelona and the Genoese in the siege of
Tortosa (July-December 1148). With large
armies on Byzantine territory and sea-borne
contingents in the Mediterranean, the crusaders were poised to attempt their original
objective: the recapture of the city of Edessa.

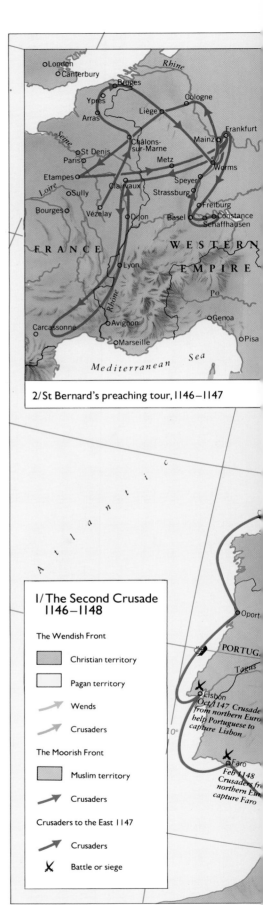

2/St Bernard's preaching tour, 1146–1147

**1/ The Second Crusade
1146–1148**

The Wendish Front

▢ Christian territory

▢ Pagan territory

→ Wends

→ Crusaders

The Moorish Front

▢ Muslim territory

→ Crusaders

Crusaders to the East 1147

→ Crusaders

✕ Battle or siege

Oct 1147 Crusade
from northern Europe
help Portuguese to
capture Lisbon

Feb 1148
Crusaders from
northern Europe
capture Faro

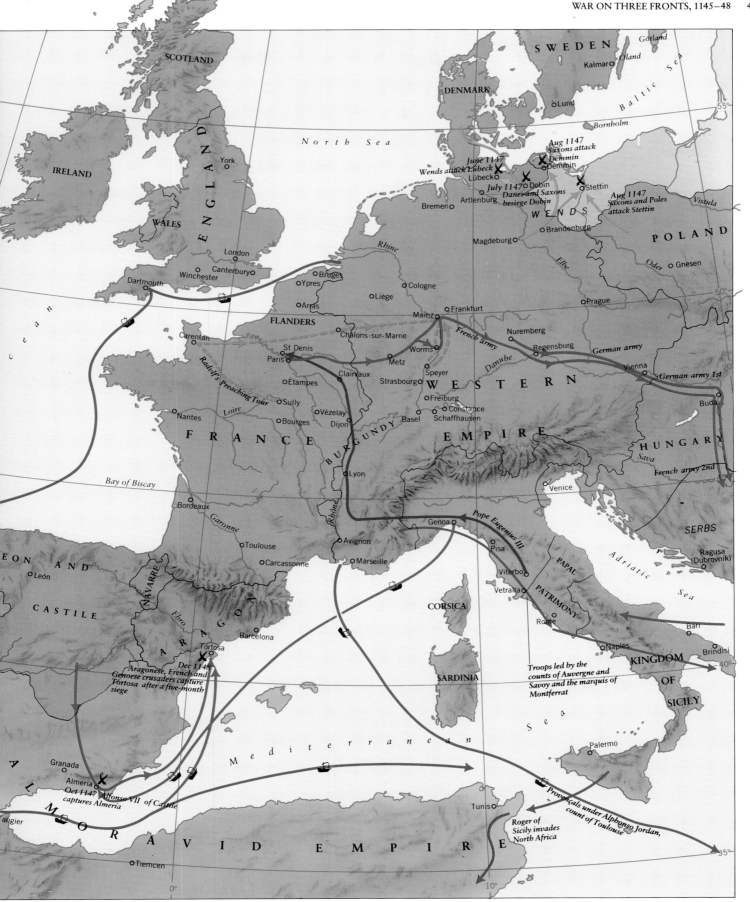

SCOTLAND

IRELAND

ENGLAND

WALES

York

London
Canterbury
Winchester

Dartmouth

North Sea

SWEDEN

Götland

Kalmar   *Oland*

DENMARK

Lund

Bornholm

Aug 1147
Saxons attack
Demmin
June 1147   Demmin
Wends attack Lübeck
Lübeck
July 1147   Dobin
Artlenburg   Danes and Saxons
besiege Dobin

Bremen

Magdeburg

Brandenburg

WENDS

Stettin

Aug 1147
Saxons and Poles
attack Stettin

Vistula

POLAND

Oder   Gnesen

Prague

Bruges
Ypres
Arras
FLANDERS
Carentan
St Denis
Paris
Étampes
Sully
Vézelay
Bourges   Dijon

Liège   Cologne

Rhine

Frankfurt

Mainz
Chálons-sur-Marne   French army
Worms   Nuremberg
Metz   Regensburg   German army
Speyer   Danube
Strasbourg   Vienna   German army 1st
Freiburg   WESTERN
Constance   Buda
Schaffhausen
Basel   EMPIRE

Radulf's Preaching Tour

Nantes

Loire

FRANCE

BURGUNDY

Lyon

HUNGARY

Sava

French army 2nd

SERBS

Bay of Biscay

Bordeaux

Garonne

Toulouse

Carcassonne

Rhône

Avignon

Marseille

Genoa

Pisa

Pope Eugenius III

Venice

PAPAL
PATRIMONY

Viterbo
Vetralla
Rome

Adriatic

Sea

Ragusa
(Dubrovnik)

Bari

Naples

Brindisi

EON AND

León

CASTILE

NAVARRE

ARAGON

Ebro

Tortosa

Barcelona

Dec 1148
Aragonese, French and
Genoese crusaders capture
Tortosa after a five-month
siege

CORSICA

SARDINIA

Troops led by the
counts of Auvergne and
Savoy and the marquis of
Montferrat

KINGDOM

OF

SICILY

Palermo

Mediterranean   *Sea*

Granada

Almeria

Oct 1147 Alfonso VII of Castile
captures Almeria

AL   M   O   R   A   V   I   D   E   M   P   I   R   E

angier

Tiemcen

Tunis

Provençals under Alphonso
Jordan, count of Toulouse

Roger of
Sicily invades
North Africa

The Second Crusade in the East

In the Near East, the Second Crusade proved a fiasco; a long march across hostile terrain, followed by a demoralizing withdrawal.

While the Second Crusade broadened to encompass the conflicts in Spain and the Baltic, its original objective – the recapture of the city of Edessa – was not forgotten.

The French and German armies (▶ *page 48*) crossed the Bosporus into Asia Minor, where the main German force divided. Conrad III's half-brother, Bishop Otto of Freising, led the non-combatant pilgrims towards the Holy Land. Conrad himself led his army into battle with the Turks near Dorylaeum in October, but was heavily defeated. He then fell ill and returned to Constantinople. The remnants of his army joined the French, who were making their way along the coast road to Adalia.

Louis's army found themselves harassed by the Turks, hampered by the winter weather and resentful at the Byzantine authorities' reluctance to provide adequate supplies. The beleaguered force narrowly escaped destruction at Mount Cadmus. The crusaders were rallied by the Templars, who imposed strict discipline, and they reached Adalia in January 1148. A Byzantine fleet was supposed to take them to Syria, but when it turned out to be much smaller than he had hoped for, Louis was forced to abandon most of his army. These crusaders tried to reach Tarsus overland, but most died on the way.

On his arrival in Syria, Louis abandoned his original plan of recapturing Edessa and decided instead to fulfil his vow in Jerusalem. By the end of spring 1148, the main crusader groups had assembled in Palestine, and Conrad, now recovered, had rejoined the party.

At a council in Acre on 24 June, the crusaders and the nobles of the kingdom of Jerusalem, led by King Baldwin III, agreed to attack Damascus together. The assault was launched in late July. The crusaders captured the orchards to the south-west of the city, but when they encountered heavy resistance, transferred to the east where the defences seemed less formidable. This was a disastrous mistake; the terrain there was an open and waterless plain, and they were forced to make an ignominious withdrawal. The mutual recriminations that ensued soured relations between the west and the crusader states for an entire generation.

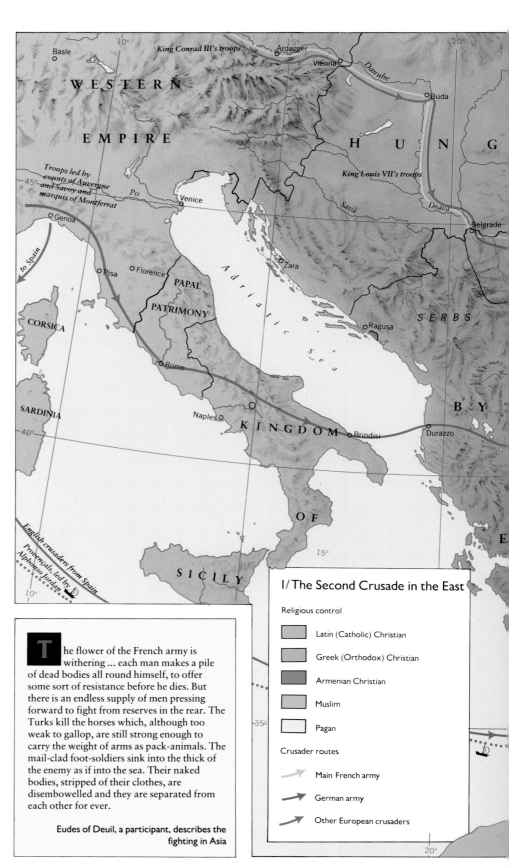

I/ The Second Crusade in the East

Religious control

- Latin (Catholic) Christian
- Greek (Orthodox) Christian
- Armenian Christian
- Muslim
- Pagan

Crusader routes

- Main French army
- German army
- Other European crusaders

The flower of the French army is withering ... each man makes a pile of dead bodies all round himself, to offer some sort of resistance before he dies. But there is an endless supply of men pressing forward to fight from reserves in the rear. The Turks kill the horses which, although too weak to gallop, are still strong enough to carry the weight of arms as pack-animals. The mail-clad foot-soldiers sink into the thick of the enemy as if into the sea. Their naked bodies, stripped of their clothes, are disembowelled and they are separated from each other for ever.

Eudes of Deuil, a participant, describes the fighting in Asia

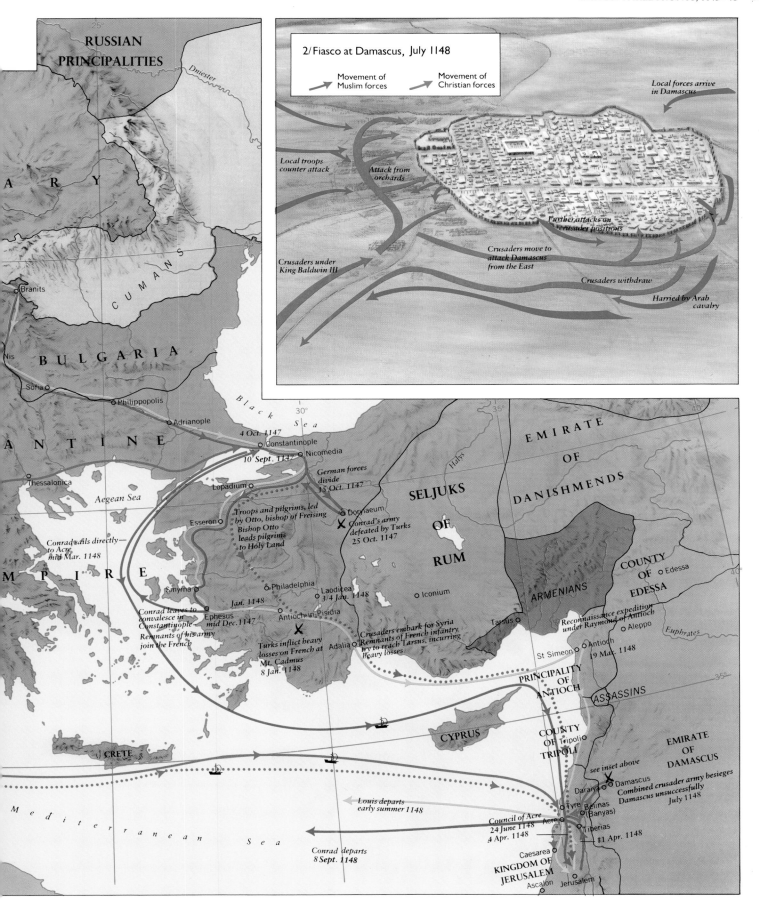

RUSSIAN
PRINCIPALITIES

Dniester

25°

ARY

Branits

C U M A N S

Nis

B U L G A R I A

Sofia

Philippopolis

Adrianople

Black Sea

30°

4 Oct. 1147

Constantinople *Nicomedia*

10 Sept. 1147

ANTINE

Thessalonica

Aegean Sea

Lopadium

German forces
divide
15 Oct. 1147

SELJUKS

Dorylaeum

OF

Conrad's army
defeated by Turks
25 Oct. 1147

Esseron

Troops and pilgrims, led
by Otto, bishop of Freising
Bishop Otto
leads pilgrims
to Holy Land

RUM

Conrad sails directly
to Acre
mid Mar. 1148

M P I R E

Smyrna

Philadelphia

Laodicea
3/4 Jan. 1148

Iconium

Jan. 1148

Conrad leaves to
convalesce in
Constantinople
Remnants of his army
join the French

Antioch in Pisidia
mid Dec. 1147

Ephesus

Turks inflict heavy
losses on French at
Mt. Cadmus
8 Jan. 1148

Crusaders embark for Syria
Remnants of French infantry
try to reach Tarsus, incurring
heavy losses

Adalia

Tarsus

EMIRATE

OF

DANISHMENDS

Halys

35°

ARMENIANS

COUNTY
OF   *Edessa*
EDESSA

40°

Reconnaissance expedition
under Raymond of Antioch

Aleppo

St Simeon *Antioch*
19 Mar. 1148

Euphrates

PRINCIPALITY
OF
ANTIOCH

ASSASSINS

35°

CYPRUS

COUNTY
OF TRIPOLI

TRIPOLI

CRETE

EMIRATE
OF
DAMASCUS

see inset above

Daraiya *Damascus*

Combined crusader army besieges
Damascus unsuccessfully
July 1148

M e d i t e r r a n e a n   S e a

Louis departs
early summer 1148

Council of Acre
24 June 1148
4 Apr. 1148

Tyre *Belinas
(Banyas)*

Acre

Tiberias

11 Apr. 1148

Conrad departs
8 Sept. 1148

Caesarea

KINGDOM OF
JERUSALEM

Ascalon *Jerusalem*

Inset map:

2/ Fiasco at Damascus, July 1148

→ Movement of
Muslim forces

→ Movement of
Christian forces

Local forces arrive
in Damascus

Local troops
counter attack

Attack from
orchards

Further attacks on
crusader positions

Crusaders move to
attack Damascus
from the East

Crusaders under
King Baldwin III

Crusaders withdraw

Harried by Arab
cavalry

Templars and Hospitallers

In the wake of the First Crusade, a new kind of monastic organization had emerged: the Military Orders. These fighting friars soon assumed a crucial role in the defence of the crusader settlements in the East.

Around 1119, a French knight called Hugh of Payns formed a small brotherhood to defend the pilgrim roads to Jerusalem. His initiative won the support of King Baldwin II of Jerusalem, and of Bernard, abbot of Clairvaux. The brothers were given a part of the Temple enclosure as their headquarters (▶ *page 44*), and soon the Knights Templar, as they were now known, were fighting in the armies of the crusader states. The Hospital of St John of Jerusalem had been founded as a charitable institution for the care of the sick in the 11th century. The Hospitallers, or Knights of St John as they came to be known, began to assume military responsibilities in the 1130s.

It has been argued that the Military Orders imitated the Muslim *ribat*, a frontier fortress where Muslims gave temporary service while living devoutly; but there are significant differences between the two institutions. The Military Orders sprang from the Christian background of the time, when the religious and moral obligations of knighthood were being stressed and when fighting the enemies of Christianity was coming to be regarded as a suitable task for men leading a religious life.

Both the Templars and Hospitallers had their headquarters in Jerusalem. They rapidly acquired extensive properties in the West and established convents there which could act as recruiting centres (▶ *page 90*); as a result, rulers and nobles in the crusader states, lacking manpower and resources, gave or sold strongholds to the Orders, which were entrusted with the defence of large stretches of frontier territory. The earliest example is probably the march assigned to the Templars in the Amanus region in northern Antioch, while the Hospitallers were later assigned extensive territories – some actually in Muslim hands – in northern Tripoli and southern Antioch. The brethren also provided field service, although their numbers were not very great: in 1187 the Temple's central convent was said to have been almost annihilated after losing 60 brothers at Cresson and 230 at Hattin. The Orders also used auxiliary troops, including native *turcopoles*.

Their wealth and the importance of the work they did meant that the Masters had become significant political figures in the kingdom of Jerusalem by 1187. Yet, although wider military activities predominated, the Orders did not abandon their obligations to pilgrims. In the Holy Land the Hospitallers are known to have maintained a hospital at Aqua Bella as well as at Jerusalem, and both orders had forts along pilgrim routes, especially those linking Jaffa, Jerusalem and the Jordan (▶*page 42*).

Templar seal, *c.*1202. There are various interpretations of the two knights on one galloping horse, but they probably symbolize the idea of brotherhood among the Templars. The legend reads: SIGIL' MILITVM CRISTI (seal of the knights of Christ).

Seal of the Hospitaller master Cast of Murols, *c.*1170-1172. It shows a man lying before a tabernacle. A 13th century source says that this is the body of a dead man, thus symbolizing the end awaiting all rather than the Hospital's work for the sick. The legend reads: HOSPITALIS IHERVSALEM.

Go forward in safety, knights, and with undaunted souls drive off the enemies of the cross of Christ, certain that neither death nor life can separate you from the love of God which is in Christ Jesus, repeating to yourselves in every peril, *Whether we live or whether we die we are the Lord's.* How glorious are the victors who return from battle! How blessed are the martyrs who die in battle! Rejoice, courageous athlete, if you live and conquer in the Lord, but exult and glory the more if you die and are joined to the Lord. Life indeed is fruitful and victory glorious, but... death is better than either of these things. For if those are *blessed who die in the Lord*, how much more blessed are those who die for the Lord?

St Bernard of Clairvaux, on the Templars, in *De laude novae militiae*

The Hospitaller castle of Belvoir, a few miles south of Lake Tiberias (Sea of Galilee), is the first dateable true concentric castle, built shortly after 1168. The innermost fortifications served not only as a redoubt but as a monastic enclosure for the brothers. The ambitious building programme nearly bankrupted the order and led to its master having a nervous breakdown.

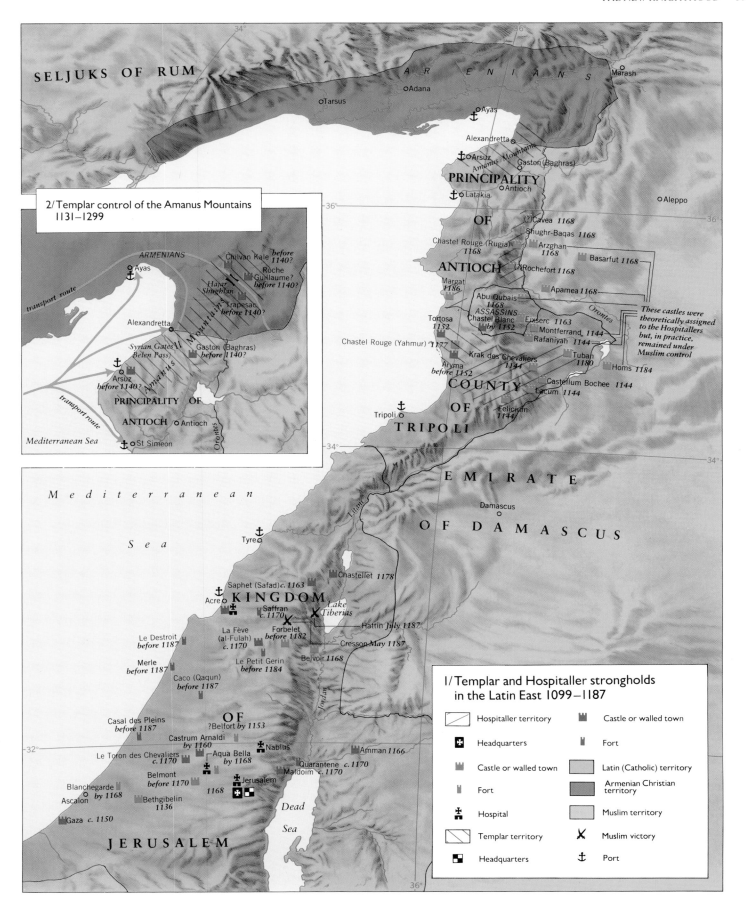

SELJUKS OF RUM

ARMENIANS

Marash

Adana

Tarsus

Ayas

Alexandretta

Arsuz
Gaston (Baghras)
Amanus Mountains

PRINCIPALITY

Antioch

Latakia

Aleppo

OF

(?)Cavea 1168
Shughr-Baqas 1168
Chastel Rouge (Rugia) 1168
Arzghan 1168
Basarfut 1168
Rochefort 1168

ANTIOCH

Margat 1186
Apamea 1168

Abu Qubais 1168
ASSASSINS
Chastel Blanc by 1152
Eixserc 1163
Montferrand 1144
Rafaniyah 1144

Tortosa 1152

These castles were
theoretically assigned
to the Hospitallers
but, in practice,
remained under
Muslim control

Chastel Rouge (Yahmur) 1177

Krak des Chevaliers 1144
Tuban 1180
Homs 1184

Aryma before 1152

COUNTY

Castellum Bochee 1144
Lacum 1144

Tripoli

OF

Felicium 1144

TRIPOLI

EMIRATE

Orontes

Damascus

OF DAMASCUS

2/ Templar control of the Amanus Mountains 1131–1299

ARMENIANS

Ayas

transport route

Chilvan Kale   before 1140?
Roche Guillaume?   before 1140?
Hajar Shughlan
Trapesac   before 1140?

Alexandretta

Syrian Gates
(Belen Pass)
Gaston (Baghras)
before 1140?

Arsuz
before 1140?

transport route

PRINCIPALITY   OF

Antioch

ANTIOCH

Mediterranean Sea

St Simeon

Orontes

Mediterranean

Sea

Tyre

Litani

Chastellet 1178

Saphet (Safad) c. 1163

Acre

KINGDOM

Saffran c. 1170
Lake Tiberias

La Fève (al-Fulah) c. 1170

Le Destroit before 1187

Forbelet before 1182

Hattin July 1187

Cresson May 1187

Merle before 1187

Le Petit Gerin before 1184

Belvoir 1168

Caco (Qaqun) before 1187

Jordan

Casal des Pleins before 1187

?Belfort by 1153

OF

Castrum Arnaldi by 1160

Nablus

Amman 1166

Le Toron des Chevaliers c. 1170

Aqua Bella by 1168

Quarantene c. 1170

Belmont before 1170

Maldoim c. 1170

Blanchegarde by 1168

Jerusalem 1168

Ascalon

Bethgibelin 1136

Dead

Gaza c. 1150

Sea

JERUSALEM

1/ Templar and Hospitaller strongholds in the Latin East 1099–1187

▨	Hospitaller territory	♜	Castle or walled town
✠	Headquarters	▮	Fort
♜	Castle or walled town		Latin (Catholic) territory
▮	Fort		Armenian Christian territory
✚	Hospital		Muslim territory
▨	Templar territory	✗	Muslim victory
▦	Headquarters	⚓	Port

The Military Orders in Spain

Spain was an important field of crusading activity, and with the Templars and Hospitallers busy in the East, new Orders were created to defend Christendom's western frontier.

The Christian rulers in Spain endowed the Hospitallers (from 1108) and Templars (by 1128) more generously than others elsewhere; they gave them estates in the north and castles in central Spain, hoping that they would defend the invasion routes against Muslim armies. But the international Military Orders were reluctant to divert resources from the defence of the Holy Land, and fought only sporadically in Spain. The Spaniards therefore decided to create their own Military Orders in imitation of the Templars. These were usually set up around the nucleus of an existing crusading confraternity such as that of Calatrava (1158), or Cáceres, which became the Order of Santiago (1170).

These orders spread rapidly throughout Christian Spain, where they defended the frontier castles and invasion routes until 1212 and provided the backbone of the armies which were to reconquer the south between 1212 and 1248 (▶ *page 72*). They also played a crucial part in resettling central and southern Spain, and defending it against counter-attacks after 1248, in ransoming Christians from Muslim captivity, in assisting pilgrims, and in other charitable work. They financed all these activities largely from their numerous estates in central and northern Spain.

Other Military Orders were founded between 1158 and 1175, but by 1225 most of them had been absorbed by the four giants, Calatrava, Santiago, the Hospital and the Temple. The Order of Évora (*c.*1166) was affiliated to Calatrava, became its Portuguese branch, moved its headquarters to Avis, and re-named itself 'of Avis'; the Order of San Julián del Pereiro (*c.*1175) was affiliated to Calatrava, became its Leonese branch, and re-named itself after its successive new headquarters, Trujillo (1188) and Alcántara (1218); the Order of Montegaudio (*c.*1173) after several changes of headquarters and name, was divided between Calatrava and the Temple by 1221.

But the size and strength of the Military Orders came to be seen as a challenge to the power of the monarchs, and after 1288 the Orders were fragmented under royal pressure. The pattern of amalgamation was thus replaced by one of disintegration, a process accelerated by the fall of the Templars in 1307 (▶ *page 124*). The Portuguese commanderies of the Temple and Santiago and the Valencian commanderies of the Temple were turned into the independent Orders of Cristo, São Tiago and Montesa; thus by 1320 there were as many as eight Military Orders in Spain and Portugal.

> **K**ing Alfonso VIII of Castile, on the Order of Santiago,
> **E**stablished the Order's headquarters in Uclés, and their duty is the sword of defence
> The pursuer of Arabs lives there, and its inhabitant is the defender of the faith
> The voice of those praising God is heard there, and the joy of desire grows high there;
> The sword reddens with the blood of Arabs, and faith burns bright with the love of their mind
> He [Alfonso] filled the Tagus's banks with settlers, and the woods of Ocaña with defenders;
> He offered that land to the Highest, and dedicated it to the Order of St. James.
> He joined to it the cliffs of Oreja, and the castle of Mora,
> So that he might devote that land to holiness, and share in their religious life.
>
> Archbishop of Toledo, Rodrigo Jiménez de Rada in *De Rebus Hispaniae*

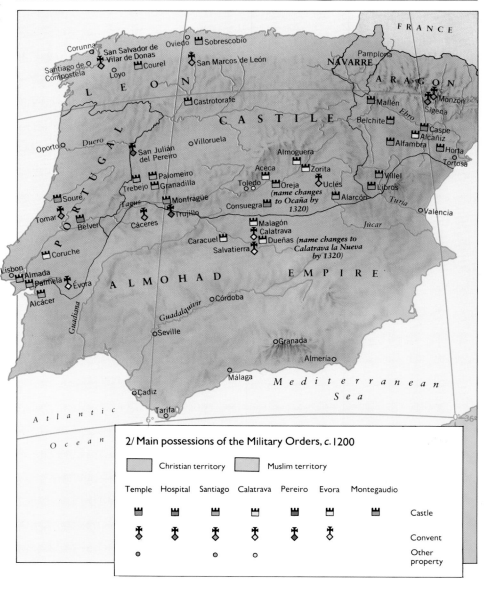

2/ Main possessions of the Military Orders, c. 1200

Christian territory   Muslim territory

	Temple	Hospital	Santiago	Calatrava	Pereiro	Evora	Montegaudio	
Castle	♜	♜	♜	♜	♜	♜	♜	Castle
Convent	⚜	⚜	⚜	⚜	⚜	⚜		Convent
Other	●		●	●				Other property

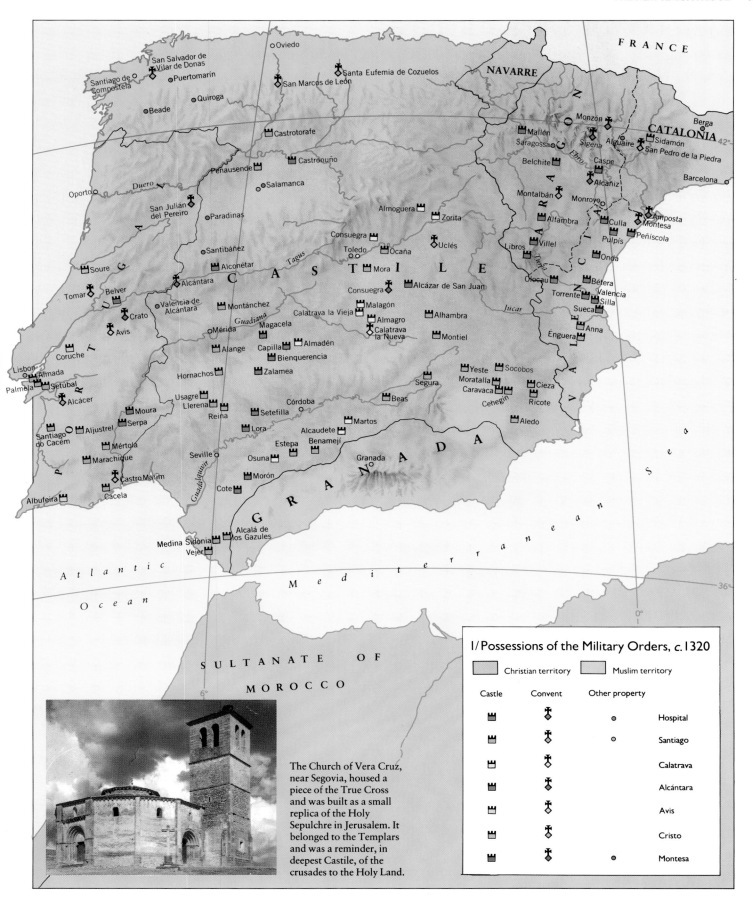

FRANCE

NAVARRE

CATALONIA

Berga

Oviedo

San Salvador de
Vilar de Donas
Santiago de
Compostela
Puertomarín
Santa Eufemia de Cozuelos
San Marcos de León

Beade
Quiroga

Monzón

Mallén
Saragossa
Sigena
Alguaire
Sidamón
San Pedro de la Piedra

Beade
Castrotorafe

Belchite
Caspe

Peñausende
Castronuño
Montalbán
Monroyo
Alcañiz

Oporto
Salamanca
Almoguera
Zorita
Alfambra
Culla
Montesa
Amposta

Duero

San Julián
del Pereiro
Consuegra
Uclés
Libros
Villel
Pulpís
Peñíscola

Paradinas
Toledo
Ocaña
Tortosa

Santibáñez
Mora
Olocau
Bétera

Soure
Alconétar
Alcázar de San Juan
Torrente
Valencia
Silla

Tomar
Belver
Alcántara
Consuegra
Sueca

Crato
Valencia de
Alcántara
Montánchez
Malagón
Alhambra
Énguera
Anna

Avis
Mérida
Magacela
Calatrava la Vieja
Almagro
Calatrava
la Nueva
Montiel

Coruche
Alange
Capilla
Almadén
Bienquerencia

Lisbon
Almada
Hornachos
Zalamea
Yeste
Socobos
Moratalla
Cieza

Setúbal
Palmela
Segura
Caravaca
Ricote

Alcácer
Usagre
Llerena
Setefilla
Beas
Cehegín
Aledo

Moura
Serpa
Reina
Lora
Córdoba

Santiago
do Cacem
Aljustrel
Mértola
Estepa
Benamejí
Alcaudete
Martos

Marachique
Osuna
Morón
Granada

GRANADA

Castro Marim
Cote

Albufeira
Cacela
Alcalá de
los Gazules

Medina Sidonia
Vejer

Atlantic
Ocean

Mediterranean Sea

SULTANATE OF

MOROCCO

The Church of Vera Cruz,
near Segovia, housed a
piece of the True Cross
and was built as a small
replica of the Holy
Sepulchre in Jerusalem. It
belonged to the Templars
and was a reminder, in
deepest Castile, of the
crusades to the Holy Land.

1/Possessions of the Military Orders, *c.*1320

Christian territory   Muslim territory

Castle	Convent	Other property	
		Hospital	Hospital
		Santiago	Santiago
			Calatrava
			Alcántara
			Avis
			Cristo
		Montesa	Montesa

Defence of the Latin East

After the failure of the Second Crusade in the East, the crusaders were mostly on the defensive. Their castles became essential for their survival.

In the north, the Muslim advance continued, and by 1170 the Christians had lost all the territory to the east of the River Orontes. In the south, the crusaders seized the initiative for a while, taking Ascalon in 1153 and launching ambitious campaigns to capture Egypt in the 1160s. But despite laying siege to Alexandria, Damietta and three times to Bilbais, they were unable to prevent the country being united with Muslim Syria in 1169 (▶*page 58*).

The crusaders had begun to build castles almost as soon as they arrived in the East. As in the West, the principal function of a castle was to serve as the residence, and administrative and economic power base of a lord, his family and retainers. But now that the crusaders were on the defensive, they also assumed great military importance.

When the first systematic attempts to map the crusader castles were made in the late 19th and early 20th centuries, it was noticed that many castles appeared to be positioned in lines, defending – or so it seemed – potential invasion routes, such as river valleys or bridge crossings; and that one castle was often visible from the next, so that warnings of enemy movements could be passed by signal or beacon.

More recent researches show such views to be largely erroneous, and to reflect more the military thinking of the years leading up to the Great War than that of the pre-gunpowder and pre-telegraphic age. Medieval castles could rarely block invasion routes, and the evidence for signalling between them is slight. In any case, there could never have been a grand defensive scheme, conceived at any one particular moment, for the hundreds of castles and towers which appear as dots on the archaeologist's map were constructed by different people, at different times, over a span of almost two centuries.

The military importance of a castle depended less on the strength of its walls than on the ability of its garrison to take the field and, with the assistance of garrisons from neighbouring castles, defeat or frighten off an aggressor. The defensive strategy of the kingdom of Jerusalem was likewise based not upon walls of masonry but upon the field army, led by the king or his constable.

Few lords could match the vast resources of the Military Orders, however, and as the century proceeded and the situation became more threatening, it was they who were entrusted with the defence of the most vulnerable areas, where they built some of the largest and most elaborate of all crusading castles, including Krak des Chevaliers (▶*page 106*).

When the crusaders built the castle of Saone (below), their task was made easier by the fact that the site had already been fortified by the Byzantines in the preceding century. In order to cut the massive ditch (above) which defends the eastern side of the castle, some 70,000 cubic metres of solid rock would have to have been removed. There is evidence that the ditch was deepened, possibly in the 12th century, but most of the work had already been done. As at Edessa and Nephin, the Byzantine engineers and their Latin successors left a tall, slender pinnacle of rock to support a timber bridge leading to the original main gate into the castle.

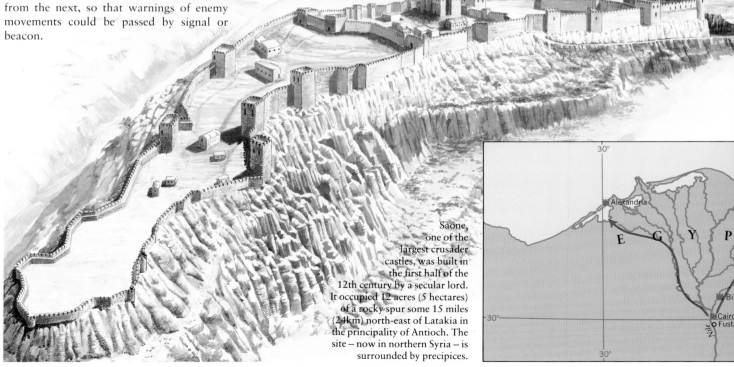

Saone, one of the largest crusader castles, was built in the first half of the 12th century by a secular lord. It occupied 12 acres (5 hectares) of a rocky spur some 15 miles (24km) north-east of Latakia in the principality of Antioch. The site – now in northern Syria – is surrounded by precipices.

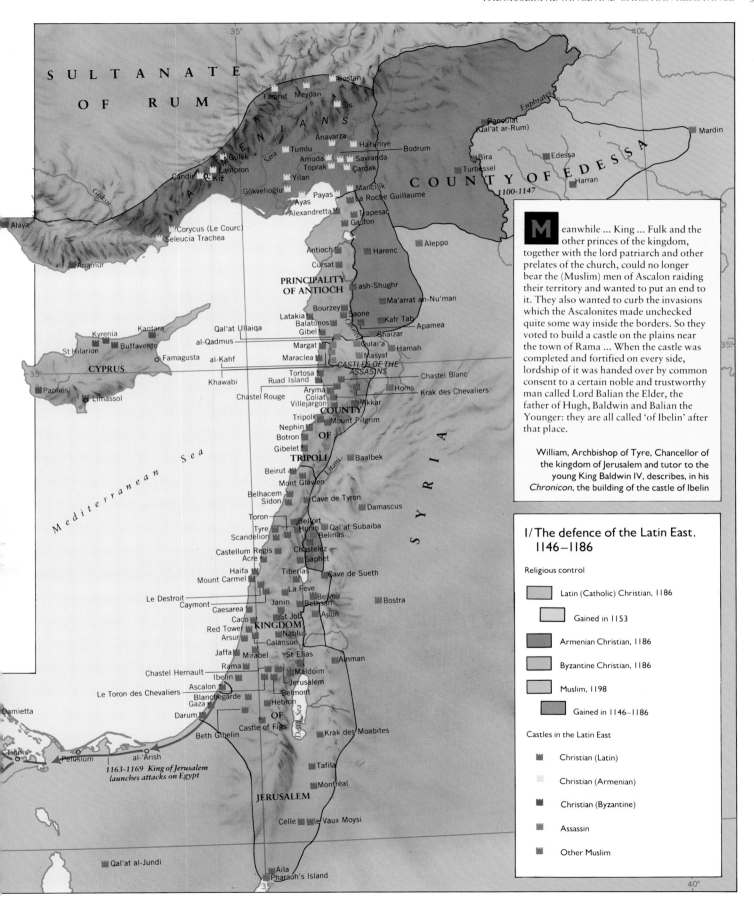

SULTANATE
OF RUM

Bostan
Tamrut Meydan
Sis
A R M E N I A N S
Anavarza
Tumlu   Haruniye — Bodrum
Gülek   Amuda   Savranda
Candir Kiz Lampron Toprak Çardak
Yilan
Gökvelioğlu   Payas
Mancilik
Ayas   La Roche Guillaume
Alexandretta   Trapesac
Corycus (Le Courc)   Gaston
Seleucia Trachea

COUNTY OF EDESSA
1100–1147

Raooulat
(Qal'at ar-Rum)
Bira
Turbessel
Edessa
Mardin
Harran

Aleppo

Antioch   Harenc
Cursat
PRINCIPALITY   ash-Shughr
OF ANTIOCH
Bourzey   Ma'arrat an-Nu'man
Latakia   Saone   Kafr Tab
Balatonos   Apamea
Gibel   Shaizar
Qal'at Ullaiqa   Qulai'a
al-Qadmus   Margat   Masyaf   Hamah
Maraclea   CASTLES OF THE
al-Kahf   ASSASSINS   Chastel Blanc
Tortosa   Homs
Khawabi   Ruad Island   Krak des Chevaliers
Chastel Rouge   Aryma
Coliat   Akkar
Villejargon
COUNTY
Tripoli   Mount Pilgrim
Nephin   OF
Botron
Gibelet   TRIPOLI
Beirut   Baalbek

Kyrenia   Kantara
St Hilarion Buffavento
CYPRUS
Famagusta
Paphos
Limassol

Mont Glavien
Belhacem
Sidon   Cave de Tyron
Toron   Damascus
Belfort
Tyre   Hunin
Scandelion   Belinas   Qal'at Subaiba
Castellum Regis   Chastelez
Acre   Saphet
Haifa   Tiberias
Mount Carmel
Le Destroit   La Feve   Cave de Sueth
Caymont   Belvoir
Caesarea   Janin Bethsan   Bostra
Caco   St Job
Red Tower   Nablus Ajlun
Arsur   Calansue
Jaffa Mirabel   St Elias Amman
Rama   Maldoim
Chastel Hernault Ibelin   Jerusalem
Ascalon   Belmont
Le Toron des Chevaliers   Belmont
Gaza Blanchegarde
Darum   Hebron
OF
Castle of Figs
Beth Gibelin   Krak des Moabites
Damietta
Tinnis
Pelusium   al-'Arish
1163–1169 King of Jerusalem
launches attacks on Egypt   Tafila
JERUSALEM   Montréal

Celle le Vaux Moysi

Qal'at al-Jundi

Aila
Pharaoh's Island

Mediterranean Sea

Euphrates
Sara
Göksu
Orontes
Litani

S Y R I A

Dead Sea

35°
40°
35°
35°
40°

1/ The defence of the Latin East, 1146–1186

Religious control

	Latin (Catholic) Christian, 1186
	Gained in 1153
	Armenian Christian, 1186
	Byzantine Christian, 1186
	Muslim, 1198
	Gained in 1146–1186

Castles in the Latin East

	Christian (Latin)
	Christian (Armenian)
	Christian (Byzantine)
	Assassin
	Other Muslim

Islam Reunified

The Muslim world had been transformed by the arrival of the crusaders. In the course of the 12th century, a series of strong leaders forged a united empire from the Islamic states of the Near East.

After the Seljuks had radically altered the political configuration of the Near East in the 11th century (▶ *page 26*), the conquests of the governors they installed in northern Iraq ironically restored the old division between Egypt and Syria. The Great Seljuk empire was by now long past its peak; the only branch that was capable of offering any effective resistance to the crusaders was that of Mosul, officially ruled by a young prince of the Seljuk dynasty but effectively governed by his *atabeg*, or regent. Imad al-Din Zangi, appointed *atabeg* of Mosul in 1127, occupied Aleppo the following year, embarking on a campaign of expansion that led to his capture of Edessa from the crusaders in 1144 (▶ *page 34*).

Zangi was assassinated in 1146. His son Nur al-Din took Damascus in 1154, and was acclaimed 'king' by the caliph in Baghdad. His next objective was to take Egypt. Its long isolation under the Fatimid dynasty, who were Shi'i Muslims, made it vulnerable to the crusaders, who had made several attempts to invade the country (▶ *page 56*). Nur al-Din gained control of Egypt and in 1169 one of his generals, Saladin was appointed to administer it. Two years later the Fatimids were deposed and orthodox Sunni Islam reinstated.

Nur al-Din died in 1174. Saladin, a Kurd from northern Iraq, was by no means his undisputed successor, but he used his Egyptian power base to wrest control of Syria from his Zangid rivals. By the time he was poised to crush the crusader states, Saladin had acquired Damascus (1174), Aleppo (1183), Mayyafariqin (1185) and the nominal overlordship of Mosul itself.

The Christian position in the East had already been weakened by the crushing defeat inflicted on the Byzantines by the Seljuks of Rum at Myriokephalon; now the crusader states were encircled by a united Muslim power. Saladin pressed home this advantage (▶ *page 60*) and by the time of his death in 1193 had taken most of Palestine. His brother conquered the Yemen, while one of his mamluks invaded North Africa. The dynasty of Saladin's family, the Ayyubids, would dominate the Near East for the next half century (▶ *page 108*).

THE *JIHAD*

The *jihad*, or 'holy war', is a striving after perfection in the self, the community and the world. It is a collective obligation to make war upon non-Muslims until they submit to Muslim rule as converts or as *dhimmi*s, protected persons of a recognized faith such as Judaism or Christianity.

In principle, the Commander of the Faithful or his representatives are required to make an annual expedition into enemy territory. Virtually the only duty specifically laid upon the monarch, it was more honoured in the breach than in the observance. Between the Dar al-Islam (Land of Islam) and the target of *jihad*, the Dar al-Harb (Land of War) there existed a fundamental state of enmity, suspended by the legal fictions of safe conduct and truce. When the *jihad* was resumed, it was almost always for some good political reason.

The *jihad* was invoked by Nur al-Din to justify both his war against the crusaders and his struggles against Muslim rivals.

A manuscript koran of 1167 (below), given in the same year by Muslim leader Nur al-Din to the Hanafi *madrasa* (religious college) in Damascus. Nur al-Din actively promoted Sunni Islam through the official *madrasas*, thus ensuring his reputation as defender of the faith and providing a generation of secretaries willing to support the dynasty.

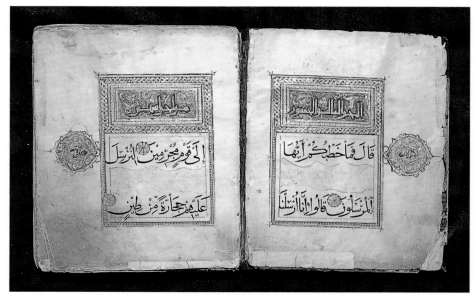

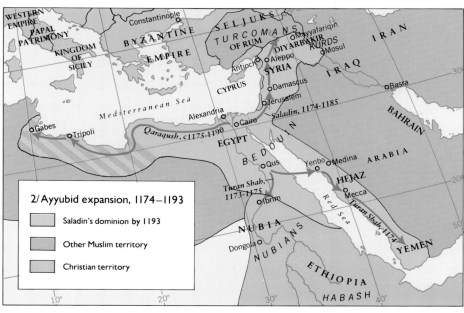

2/ Ayyubid expansion, 1174–1193

- Saladin's dominion by 1193
- Other Muslim territory
- Christian territory

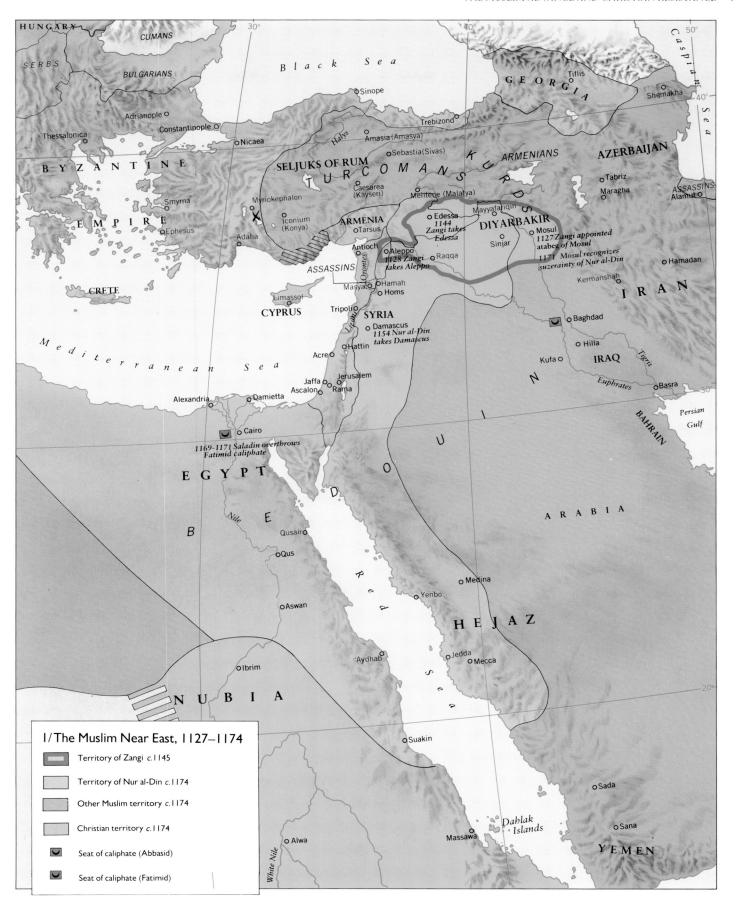

HUNGARY

CUMANS

Black Sea

SERBS

BULGARIANS

Sinope

GEORGIA

Tiflis

Shemakha

Adrianople

Trebizond

Thessalonica

Constantinople

Amasia (Amasya)

KURDS

ARMENIANS

AZERBAIJAN

BYZANTINE

Nicaea

Halys

Sebastia (Sivas)

SELJUKS OF RUM

TURCOMANS

Tabriz

Maragha

ASSASSINS
Alamut

Caesarea
(Kayseri)

Meliteue (Malatya)

Smyrna

Myriokephalon

Edessa
*1144
Zangi takes
Edessa*

Mayyafariqin

DIYARBAKIR

EMPIRE

Iconium
(Konya)

ARMENIA

Tarsus

Mosul

*1127 Zangi appointed
atabeg of Mosul*

Hamadan

Ephesus

Adalia

Antioch

Aleppo
*1128 Zangi
takes Aleppo*

Raqqa

Sinjar

*1171 Mosul recognizes
suzerainty of Nur al-Din*

ASSASSINS

Kermanshah

IRAN

CRETE

Limassol

Masyat

Hamah

Homs

Oronтes

Litani

Baghdad

CYPRUS

Tripoli

SYRIA

Damascus
*1154 Nur al-Din
takes Damascus*

Hilla

Mediterranean Sea

Acre

Hattin

Kufa

IRAQ

Tigris

Jaffa

Jerusalem

Ascalon

Rama

Basra

Alexandria

Damietta

B
E
D
O
U
I
N

Persian
Gulf

BAHRAIN

Cairo
*1169-1171 Saladin overthrows
Fatimid caliphate*

EGYPT

Nile

Euphrates

B

Qusair

ARABIA

Qus

Red
Sea

Aswan

Medina

Yenbo

HEJAZ

Ibrim

NUBIA

Jedda
Mecca

Aydhab

Sada

Suakin

Hamadan

Dahlak
Islands

Sana

White Nile

Alwa

Massawa

YEMEN

I/The Muslim Near East, 1127–1174

Territory of Zangi *c.*1145

Territory of Nur al-Din *c.*1174

Other Muslim territory *c.*1174

Christian territory *c.*1174

Seat of caliphate (Abbasid)

Seat of caliphate (Fatimid)

Saladin's Conquests

The charismatic Muslim leader Saladin wiped out the Christian army at Hattin and, in little more than a year, drove the crusaders out of Palestine and Syria.

Saladin crossed the River Jordan on 30 June 1187 with an army of about 30,000, including 12,000 regular cavalry. The Christian army was commanded by Guy of Lusignan, the king of Jerusalem. Although it was the largest ever raised in the kingdom, it still only came to about 20,000 men, of whom 1,200 were knights. It assembled at Sephorie, a secure position with a good supply of water. To lure the Christian army away from their camp and into hostile terrain, Saladin sent a section of his army to attack Tiberias. The Muslims swiftly overran the town and began a siege of its castle.

After a heated debate, the Christian leaders decided to advance to the relief of Tiberias. Harassed by Muslim archers and skirmishers, Guy's army made slow progress, and soon began to suffer from thirst and heat exhaustion. On the evening of 3 July, as they camped near Meskenah, the Christians decided to strike north in search of water. On the following day, the line of march became dangerously extended, and Guy's army was boxed in by the Muslims on the heights known as Qarn Hattin (the Horns of Hattin). Only a small body of knights under Raymond of Tripoli managed to escape by charging through Taqi al-Din's line to the north-east. Guy and the rest of his following surrendered to Saladin. The army of the kingdom of Jerusalem had been destroyed.

Saladin's troops fanned out through Galilee and Samaria, easily taking such lightly defended places as Nazareth. Saladin himself advanced towards the coast to capture Acre and several other harbour castles to the north. Deprived of their garrisons to swell the ill-fated army of King Guy, they were easy prey. He reconnoitred the defences of Tyre, but decided that they would be too difficult to storm; and without a fleet he was unable to starve the town into surrender. Instead, he moved south to take the port of Ascalon, which the crusaders had used to launch naval raids against Egypt (▶page 34).

Then he besieged Jerusalem. After negotiations, the city surrendered on 2 October. Although it was of negligible strategic importance, its capture was a devastating blow to Christian morale. But it was a propaganda victory that Saladin was unable to exploit to the full, finding it increasingly difficult to keep a large army in the field. As he marched north, he took many of the more vulnerable castles, but avoided the big cities of Tripoli and Antioch.

A second round of campaigning in 1188 brought more gains. Saladin inspected the defences of Tyre once again, but the place seemed more impregnable than ever. In hindsight, his failure to capture Tyre can be seen as a major strategic error which would put all his conquests in jeopardy; in the years to come, the Third Crusade (▶page 62) would reap the benefits. However, in the two years which followed Hattin, Saladin had taken over 50 crusader castles, and the Christians had lost nearly all the kingdom of Jerusalem.

> **T**hen the Muslims returned to the attack against the Franks and they went back up the hill. When I saw them retreating with the Muslims in pursuit, I cried out in joy: 'We have beaten them'. My father turned to me and said: 'Be silent. We shall not defeat them until that (red) tent (of the king) falls'. As he spoke, the tent fell.
>
> A description of the Battle of Hattin by Saladin's son al-Afdal 'Ali

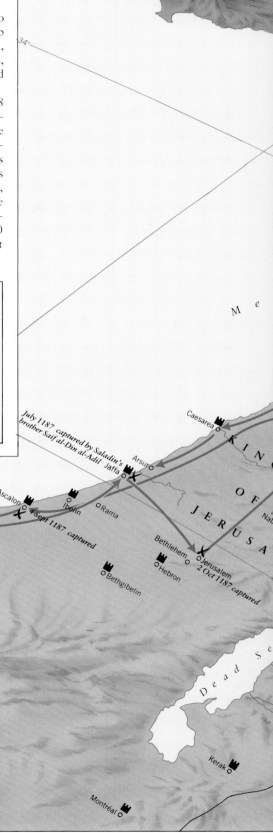

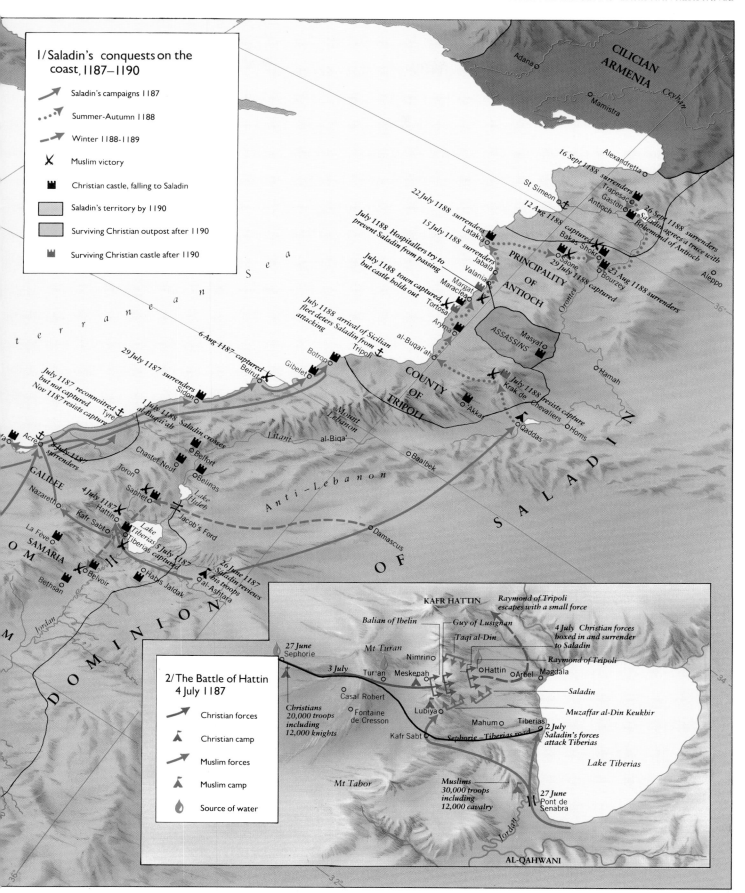

1/Saladin's conquests on the coast, 1187–1190

- Saladin's campaigns 1187
- Summer-Autumn 1188
- Winter 1188-1189
- ✗ Muslim victory
- ♜ Christian castle, falling to Saladin
- Saladin's territory by 1190
- Surviving Christian outpost after 1190
- ♜ Surviving Christian castle after 1190

CILICIAN ARMENIA

Adana

Mamistra

Ceyhan

Alexandretta

16 Sept 1188 surrenders

Trapesac

26 Sept 1188 surrenders

Gaston

Antioch

St Simeon

12 Aug 1188 captured

Bakas Shokr

Saladin agrees a truce with Bohemond of Antioch

22 July 1188 surrenders

15 July 1188 surrenders

Latakia

Ozone

29 July 1188 captured

23 Aug 1188 surrenders

Bourzey

Jabala

PRINCIPALITY

Valania

Aleppo

36°

July 1188 Hospitallers try to prevent Saladin from passing

Margat

OF

July 1188 town captured but castle holds out

Maraclea

Tortosa

ANTIOCH

Orontes

July 1188 arrival of Sicilian fleet deters Saladin from attacking

Anyma

al-Buqai'ah

ASSASSINS

Masyaf

Hamah

6 Aug 1187 captured

Botrop

Tripoli

COUNTY

July 1188 resists capture

Krak de Chevaliers

29 July 1187 surrenders

Gibelet

OF

Homs

Beirut

Akkar

Qaddas

July 1187 reconnoitred but not captured

Nov 1187 resists capture

Tyre

Sidon

1 July 1188 al-Buqai'ah Saladin crosses

TRIPOLI

Mount Lebanon

al-Biqa'

Acre

2 July 1187 surrenders

Chastel Neuf

Belfort

Litani

Baalbek

GALILEE

Toron

Belinas

Anti-Lebanon

DOMINION   OF   SALADIN

Nazareth

Sapheto

4 July 1187 Hattin

Kafr Sabt

Lake Huleh

La Fève

Jacob's Ford

Damascus

SAMARIA

Tiberias 5 July 1187 Tiberias captured

Belvoir

Habis Jaldak

26 June 1187 Saladin reviews his troops

al-Ashtara

Bethsan

Jordan

34°

36°

32°

2/The Battle of Hattin 4 July 1187

- → Christian forces
- ⛺ Christian camp
- → Muslim forces
- ⛺ Muslim camp
- 🜄 Source of water

KAFR HATTIN

Raymond of Tripoli escapes with a small force

Balian of Ibelin

Guy of Lusignan

Taqi al-Din

4 July Christian forces boxed in and surrender to Saladin

27 June Sephorie

Mt Turan

Nimrino

Hattin

Raymond of Tripoli

Arbel

Magdala

3 July

Tur'an

Meskepah

Saladin

Casal Robert

Lubiya

Muzaffar al-Din Keukbir

Christians 20,000 troops including 12,000 knights

Fontaine de Cresson

Mahum

Tiberias

Kafr Sabt

Sephorie–Tiberias road

2 July Saladin's forces attack Tiberias

Mt Tabor

Muslims 30,000 troops including 12,000 cavalry

Lake Tiberias

27 June Pont de Senabra

Jordan

AL-QAHWANI

The Third Crusade

Saladin's onslaught was countered by the Third Crusade, which succeeded in recapturing most of the coastal plain of Palestine.

News of the crushing defeat of the Christian army at Hattin and the loss of Jerusalem on 2 October 1187 (▶ *page 60*) provoked a massive reaction in the West. Pope Urban III died of shock at the news, but his successor Gregory VIII issued a new call to arms, *Audita tremendi*, on 29 October. In November, Richard of Poitou (later Richard I of England) became the first ruler north of the Alps to take the cross, followed by Henry II of England, Philip II of France and the veteran emperor Frederick Barbarossa in the following spring. At that time a fleet sent by William II of Sicily helped relieve the remaining Christian outposts of Antioch, Tripoli and Tyre.

Although internecine feuding and the death of Henry II delayed the departure of the kings of England and France until 1190, fleets from northern Europe, Flanders and England left in May 1189, capturing Silves from the Moors *en route* (▶ *page 72*). A Pisan fleet reached Palestinian waters by the summer of 1189 and in May 1189 the emperor set out from Regensburg at the head of a massive army.

The situation in Syria, however, remained desperate. The remaining settlers were divided in allegiance between the king of Jerusalem, Guy of Lusignan, who had lost at Hattin, and Conrad of Montferrat, whose arrival at Tyre in 1187 had saved the city from Saladin. With a tiny force, Guy began to besiege Acre in August 1188 and it was to Acre that the armies and fleets of the west directed themselves. These included forces from Cologne (1189) and those of Henry of Champagne and Louis of Thuringia (1190) and Leopold of Austria (1191). After a successful march across central Europe and Asia Minor, the great German crusade army fell apart when Frederick Barbarossa accidentally drowned in the river Göksu on 10 June 1190. The meagre remnants of his force reached Acre in October.

In July 1190, the English and French kings set out together from Vézelay. Richard sent an advance guard under Baldwin, archbishop of Canterbury, direct to Acre. The kings spent a winter of political and personal acrimony in Sicily. Philip sailed directly to Acre in March 1191, while Richard turned to wrest Cyprus from its Byzantine ruler Isaac Comnenus before landing at Acre on 8 June. He was to remain in Palestine for 16 months.

1/ Crusade contingents, 1188–1192

- Latin (Catholic) Christian territory
- Greek (Orthodox) Christian territory
- Armenian Christian territory
- Muslim territory
- ✡ Persecution of Jews

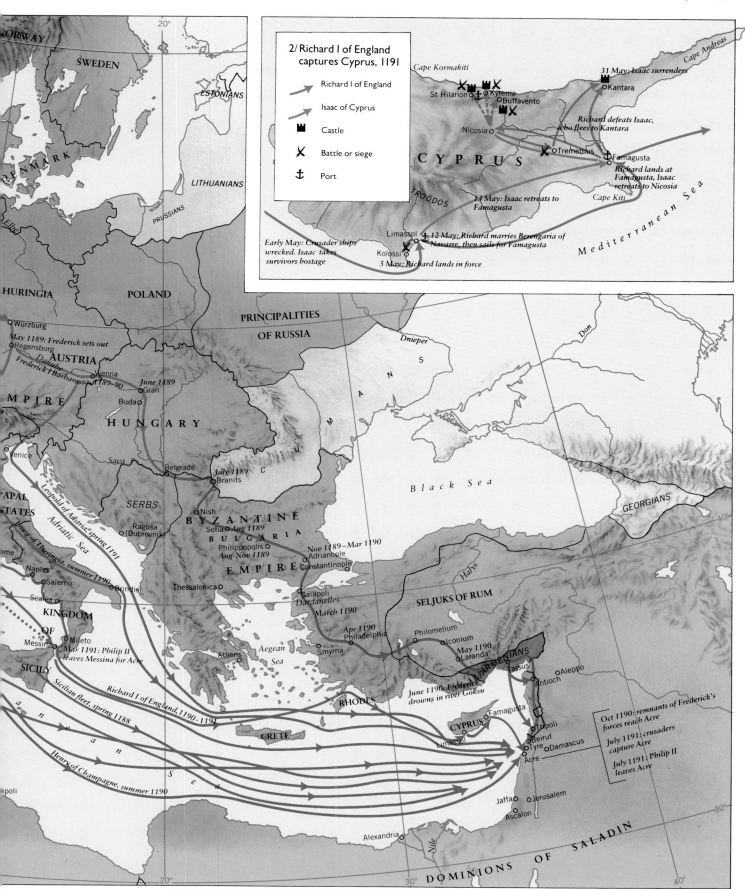

2/ Richard I of England captures Cyprus, 1191

→ Richard I of England

→ Isaac of Cyprus

♜ Castle

✗ Battle or siege

⚓ Port

Cape Kormakiti

Cape Andreas

31 May: Isaac surrenders

St Hilarion ⚓ Kyrenia ♜ ✗
Buffavento ✗
♜ Kantara

Richard defeats Isaac, who flees to Kantara

Nicosia ○

C Y P R U S

✗ ○ Tremethus

⚓ Famagusta
Richard lands at Famagusta, Isaac retreats to Nicosia

TROODOS

Cape Kiti

13 May: Isaac retreats to Famagusta

Mediterranean Sea

Limassol ○

⚓ 12 May: Richard marries Berengaria of Navarre, then sails for Famagusta

Early May: Crusader ships wrecked. Isaac takes survivors hostage

Kolossi ○

5 May: Richard lands in force

NORWAY

SWEDEN

ESTONIANS

DENMARK

LITHUANIANS

PRUSSIANS

Elbe

THURINGIA

POLAND

PRINCIPALITIES

OF RUSSIA

Dnieper

○ Würzburg

May 1189: Frederick sets out

○ Regensburg

Danube

AUSTRIA

Frederick I Barbarossa 1189–90

○ Vienna

June 1189

○ Gran

Budao

HUNGARY

Don

EMPIRE

Sava

Venice ○

Belgrade ○

July 1189

○ Branits

C

Black Sea

GEORGIANS

PAPAL

STATES

Adriatic Sea

Leopold of Austria, spring 1191

SERBS

Ragusa ○
(Dubrovnik)

Nish ○

BYZANTINE

Sofia ○ Aug 1189

BULGARIA

○ Naples

Landgrave of Thuringia, summer 1190

○ Salerno

Philippopolis ○
Aug-Nov 1189

Nov 1189–Mar 1190

Adrianople ○

40°

Scalea ○

Thessalonica ○

EMPIRE

Constantinople ○

Halys

KINGDOM

Gallipoli
Dardanelles

March 1190

SELJUKS OF RUM

OF

Messina ○

○ Mileto

Mar 1191: Philip II leaves Messina for Acre

SICILY

Sicilian fleet, spring 1188

Richard I of England, 1190–1191

Athens ○

Aegean
Sea

Apr 1190
Philadelphia ○

Smyrna ○

Philomelium ○

Iconium ○

May 1190
○ Laranda

ARMENIANS

○ Tarsus

○ Aleppo

Antioch ○

RHODES

June 1190: Frederick drowns in river Göksu

Oct 1190: remnants of Frederick's forces reach Acre

Henry of Champagne, summer 1190

CRETE

CYPRUS

Famagusta ○

Limassol ○

○ Tripoli

Beirut ○

July 1191: crusaders capture Acre

July 1191: Philip II leaves Acre

Tyre ○ ○ Damascus

Acre ○

poli

S   e   a

Jaffa ○ ○ Jerusalem

Ascalon ○

30°

Alexandria ○

Nile

D O M I N I O N S   O F   S A L A D I N

20°   30°   40°

The Recovery of the Coast

Between them, the Third and the German Crusades recovered most of the coastal ports, ensuring a life-line to the West for the settlers.

Once Acre had fallen to the crusaders in July 1191, Philip II of France left for the West. Three weeks later, on 22 August, Richard set off southwards. Nothing demonstrated so well his generalship than the march and battle that followed. For the whole of the march the Christian army was under almost constant attack from Saladin's forces. Richard organized his horsemen in divisions, with the main standard in their midst. An outer line of defence, was provided by half the infantry with the other half marching with the baggage between the knights and the sea-shore. A fleet shadowed the army and kept it supplied. After passing through the Forest of Arsur the army rested for two days on the banks of the river Rochetaillée (al-Faliq). It then emerged on to a plain north of Arsur. Saladin redoubled his efforts and on 7 September the Christians found themselves under heavy attack from light horsemen, whose arrows killed many of their horses. Richard prepared an enveloping assault, but the impatience of some knights in the rear meant that only a frontal charge was launched. After a shaky counter-attack, the Muslims were driven from the field by a final Christian charge.

Richard reached his first objective, Jaffa, on 10 September and he spent the next year in southern Palestine, twice – in December 1191 and June 1192 – advancing to within a few miles of Jerusalem. During this period he began to rebuild Ascalon to secure the southern approaches to a restored kingdom of Jerusalem. After he had spectacularly thwarted Saladin's attempt to recapture Jaffa (August 1192), a treaty was arranged (2 September) according to which the defences of Ascalon were to be demolished, the Christians were to retain control of the coast between Acre and Jaffa and the crusaders were to be allowed to visit the Holy Sepulchre in Jerusalem. Richard sailed for home on 9 October 1192.

Within three years another crusade was being organized, this time by Frederick Barbarossa's son, the emperor Henry VI. Although Henry died before departure, a substantial German army reached Palestine in September 1197 and occupied Sidon and Beirut before disintegrating when the news of the emperor's death reached it.

In these 13th-century tiles from Chertsey Abbey, Surrey, Richard I of England (on left) charges at a Muslim cavalryman who was probably intended to represent Saladin.

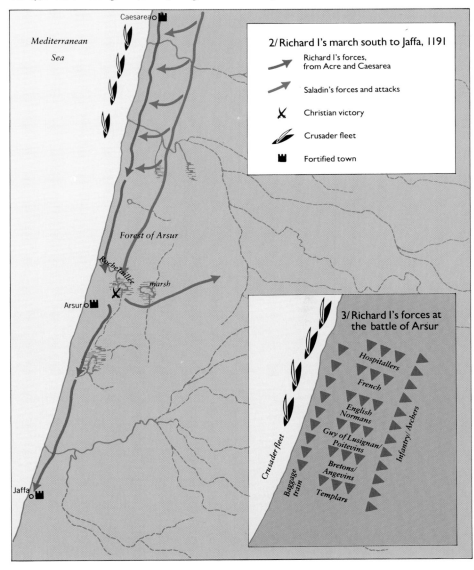

2/ Richard I's march south to Jaffa, 1191

→ Richard I's forces, from Acre and Caesarea

→ Saladin's forces and attacks

✗ Christian victory

Crusader fleet

Fortified town

3/ Richard I's forces at the battle of Arsur

Hospitallers
French
English Normans
Guy of Lusignan/ Poitevins
Bretons/ Angevins
Templars
Infantry/ Archers
Baggage train
Crusader fleet

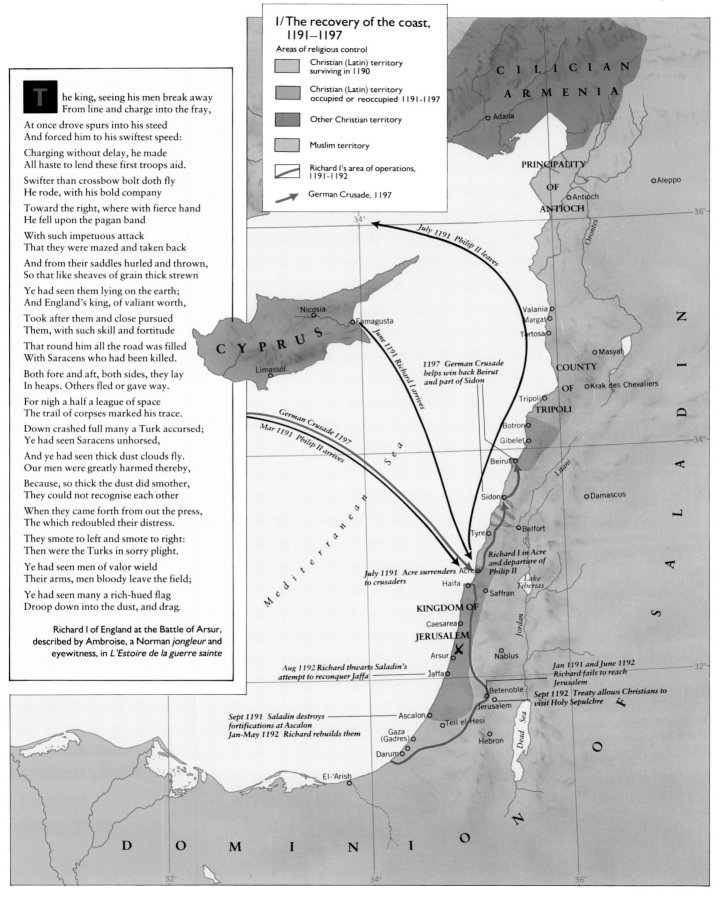

T he king, seeing his men break away
From line and charge into the fray,

At once drove spurs into his steed
And forced him to his swiftest speed:

Charging without delay, he made
All haste to lend these first troops aid.

Swifter than crossbow bolt doth fly
He rode, with his bold company

Toward the right, where with fierce hand
He fell upon the pagan band

With such impetuous attack
That they were mazed and taken back

And from their saddles hurled and thrown,
So that like sheaves of grain thick strewn

Ye had seen them lying on the earth;
And England's king, of valiant worth,

Took after them and close pursued
Them, with such skill and fortitude

That round him all the road was filled
With Saracens who had been killed.

Both fore and aft, both sides, they lay
In heaps. Others fled or gave way.

For nigh a half a league of space
The trail of corpses marked his trace.

Down crashed full many a Turk accursed;
Ye had seen Saracens unhorsed,

And ye had seen thick dust clouds fly.
Our men were greatly harmed thereby,

Because, so thick the dust did smother,
They could not recognise each other

When they came forth from out the press,
The which redoubled their distress.

They smote to left and smote to right:
Then were the Turks in sorry plight.

Ye had seen men of valor wield
Their arms, men bloody leave the field;

Ye had seen many a rich-hued flag
Droop down into the dust, and drag.

Richard I of England at the Battle of Arsur,
described by Ambroise, a Norman *jongleur* and
eyewitness, in *L'Estoire de la guerre sainte*

I/The recovery of the coast, 1191–1197

Areas of religious control

Christian (Latin) territory surviving in 1190

Christian (Latin) territory occupied or reoccupied 1191-1197

Other Christian territory

Muslim territory

Richard I's area of operations, 1191-1192

German Crusade, 1197

CILICIAN ARMENIA

Adana

Aleppo

PRINCIPALITY OF ANTIOCH

Antioch

Orontes

July 1191 Philip II leaves

Nicosia

Famagusta

Valania

Margat

Tortosa

June 1191 Richard I arrives

CYPRUS

Masyaf

Limassol

1197 German Crusade helps win back Beirut and part of Sidon

COUNTY OF TRIPOLI

Krak des Chevaliers

Tripoli

German Crusade 1197

Botron

Gibelet

Mar 1191 Philip II arrives

Beirut

Litani

Mediterranean Sea

Damascus

Sidon

S A L A D I N

Tyre

Belfort

Richard I in Acre and departure of Philip II

July 1191 Acre surrenders to crusaders

Acre

Lake Tiberias

Haifa

Saffran

KINGDOM OF

Caesarea

JERUSALEM

Jordan

Jan 1191 and June 1192 Richard fails to reach Jerusalem

Arsur

Nablus

Sept 1192 Treaty allows Christians to visit Holy Sepulchre

Aug 1192 Richard thwarts Saladin's attempt to reconquer Jaffa

Jaffa

Betenoble

Jerusalem

Sept 1191 Saladin destroys fortifications at Ascalon
Jan-May 1192 Richard rebuilds them

Ascalon

Tell el-Hesi

Dead Sea

O F

Gaza (Gadres)

Hebron

Darum

El-'Arish

D O M I N I O N

O F

Part 2
THE DEFENCE OF CHRISTENDOM

The German crusaders were still in the East when Pope Innocent III (1198-1216) began his reign. Innocent was a vigorous and quick-witted man, highly-educated in theology and law. He had a high view of his position as pope, but he sometimes made hasty judgements, which he was over-inclined to trust. He was well-known for speaking his mind and his put-downs could be crushing. One would have thought that Duke Leopold VI of Austria, who spent huge amounts of energy and money on crusading – he went on the Third and Fifth Crusades to the East, as well as crusading in Spain and Languedoc, and taking the cross on two further occasions – deserved nothing but thanks and praise for his support. But Innocent put him firmly in his place:

> 'There is much more merit in the gibbet of Christ's cross than in the little sign of your cross . . . For you accept a soft and gentle cross; he suffered one that was bitter and hard. You bear it superficially on your clothing; he endured his in the reality of his flesh. You sew yours on with linen and silken threads; he was fastened to his with hard, iron nails.'

In spite of the harshness of his tongue, Innocent was a deeply, even emotionally, religious man, with an obsessive commitment to crusading. He preached crusades to the East three times; proclaimed a crusade in Sicily against an agent of the imperial government called Markward of Anweiler; and authorized the Livonian crusade in the Baltic region, the crusade against the Cathar heretics in south-western France and a crusade in Spain. Crusading was being waged somewhere in every year of his pontificate; and he himself was busy preaching the cross in the weeks leading up

to his death. For the first time we are presented with the movement in full panoply: crusades against Muslims, other non-Christians, heretics and the Church's Christian enemies.

Pope Innocent III, who preached more crusades than any other pope, portrayed granting a charter to the Priory of Subiaco.

Innocent was the kind of man who would want to control this wide spectrum of enterprises. He established elaborate procedures, with an array of appointments, for the preaching of the cross. He instituted a general taxation of the clergy to provide cash to subsidize crusaders, judging, in this case correctly, that it was the expense of crusading that put many people off. He even attempted to close down two crusades (against the Cathars and in Spain) in favour of another to the East. By summoning a great general council, he tried to deal with the problems of the crusade and the reform of the Church. Contemporaries were convinced that these were related, since success in crusading would only proceed from a healthy Christendom. Europe was showered with papal letters, and Innocent's legates and preachers received detailed instructions and answers to queries. The pope's training as a lawyer was also at least partly responsible for the much clearer and often definitive formulations of crusade privileges which appeared at this time.

It hardly needs saying that Innocent's crusading policy was far too ambitious. He completely lost control of the Fourth Crusade as it careered off towards Constantinople. His elaborate scheme for the preaching of the cross was too systematic and was abandoned by his successors. His taxation of the Church for the crusades, though setting an important precedent, could be too easily avoided. The first tax had been instituted in 1199; by 1208 it had still not been raised in parts of Italy and some English assessments were collected only in

1217. Fighting went on in Languedoc in defiance of his desire to phase out the crusade against the Cathars; in fact by undermining that crusade at a crucial time he probably prolonged the misery in south-western France by a decade. His general council instituted major reforms which the bishops would not then enforce. That is a catalogue of failure; and it looks as though Innocent was in danger of over-extending the West's resources. But it is also clear that he was riding on the crest of a wave of enthusiasm for crusading, which manifested itself in such strange forms as the Children's Crusade of 1212.

It was, in fact, in the 13th century that crusading really came into its own as an established institution. The tempo set in Innocent's pontificate continued almost unabated and it is impossible even to estimate how many thousands of nobles, knights, merchants, artisans and peasants took the cross. Everywhere there were public processions, preaching and special prayers in the Mass, taxation, alms-giving – there were boxes in the churches – the encouragement of benefactions in wills and the practice of vow redemptions by which those who were not suited to fighting made crusade vows which they could then redeem for money payments. It would, therefore, have been hard for anyone in Catholic Europe to have escaped being touched in some way or other by the movement. The appeal of crusading was now being reinforced by the reading and recital of history, myth, epic poetry and popular songs. It was, in fact, a genuinely popular devotion.

Although the techniques and technology of warfare had developed, the essentials of crusading had not changed much. Even with papal and royal subsidies it was still immensely expensive and it was a dangerous and uncomfortable penitential exercise. After putting his affairs in order, a man would leave home humbly dressed as a pilgrim and would visit local shrines before setting off on his journey, often involving a sea crossing which many crusaders found terrifying.

In the 13th century the response to crusade appeals was commonly to be found in local networks of lordship and patronage, whereas in the first era of crusading it had been families which had responded collectively. But families were still

The Dispensation of Vows

Crusade vows were solemn and legally binding. It was not easy to avoid censure should a man have second thoughts and try to dodge the consequences of his commitment. When a man was suitable – that is to say he was a knight or a professional soldier – *dispensation*, absolution from the fulfilment of the vow, was extremely hard to obtain; indeed Pope Innocent III, who laid the ground rules, maintained the Roman law concept that the vow was hereditable and should be performed by a son if not fulfilled by his father. But there were some abatements, although they could only be granted by the pope or his agents. They were:

✠ *Deferment*: the right to a delay.

✠ *Commutation*: the performance of another penitential act in place of that vowed, which was sometimes used strategically by the 13th-century popes, who might wish vows to crusade in one theatre of war to be transferred to another.

✠ *Substitution*: the sending of another in the crusader's place.

✠ *Redemption*: dispensation in return for a money payment, theoretically equalling the sum that would have been spent on crusade. Under Innocent III this began to be used as a way of helping to finance crusades. The obviously unsuitable, including the elderly and women, were encouraged to take the cross and then seek redemption, which provided funds. The practice led to abuses, scandal and sporadic criticism throughout the century.

important for the traditions they embodied. Both the Englishman William Peverel, who went East in 1240 with King Henry III's brother, Earl Richard of Cornwall, and King Louis IX of France, who took the cross in 1244, must have been influenced by family commitments which dated back to the First Crusade. They were typical of many. Family tradition also fuelled another element, the chivalric theatre which was to become so prominent in the 14th century. Robert of Clari witnessed the spectacular departure of the Fourth Crusade from Venice in 1202:

'There were at least one hundred pairs of silver and brass trumpets, which all sounded the signal to move off, and so many drums and tabors and other instruments that it was marvellous to see. When the ships were out at sea and had spread their sails and the banners and ensigns were flying high on the ships' castles, it seemed as if the sea itself shook with fear and that it was afire.'

Forty-seven years later John of Joinville saw the arrival in Egypt of the count of Jaffa:

'His galley was painted within and without with escutcheons bearing his coat-of-arms . . . He had a good 300 oarsmen in his galley; each oarsman had a shield with the count's arms on

it and a pennon with the coat-of-arms worked in gold . . . It seemed as if the galley flew . . . and what with the noise of the flapping pennons, the drums and the Saracen horns on board the ship, it seemed as though a thunderbolt was falling from heaven.'

Changes were taking place, of course, and it is worth while comparing Innocent III with an equally enthusiastic successor, Pope Gregory X, who came to the papal throne in 1271, 55 years after Innocent's death. Gregory was in the East as a crusader when he was elected pope and the cardinals certainly hoped that he would do everything he could to save the Holy Land. He threw himself energetically into the task, summoning conferences and another general council, with the aim, like Innocent, of reforming Christendom and promoting a new crusade, although he planned to lead this one himself. He called for written advice from the clergy, issued the most comprehensive crusade constitution since Innocent's pontificate, heroically tried to reconcile the Greek and Latin churches, imposed a new general tax and divided Christendom into collectorates, with the aim of building up a huge financial reserve. He planned to crown a new western emperor on 2 February 1277; two months later he and the emperor would lead a great army to the East, possibly following the path of the First Crusade and re-conquering Asia Minor on the way. But on 10 January 1276, a year before this crusade should have been mustering, he died and his ambitious scheme died with him. Whereas the last crusade planned by Innocent was put in motion by his successor, Gregory's evaporated and the vast sums of money he had collected for it were dissipated in Italy.

It used to be fashionable to explain this fiasco as evidence that crusading was in decline. The volume of criticism, it was maintained, was rising, fuelled by the diversion of the movement into perverse schemes which benefited only individuals and the papacy. The taxation of the Church was arousing bitter resentment, but above all Christians were now demoralized by nearly two centuries of failure. Almost every one of these points can be challenged. The volume of criticism was not rising, but remained static and fairly low-level. And most of it was not fundamental criticism of crusading itself, but was either special pleading by interest groups or expressions of an integral element in crusade ideology, because failure in God's own enterprise was unthinkable except in terms of the inadequacy of the instruments of the divine plan, the crusaders themselves, who had to be portrayed as unworthy if a reverse was to be explained convincingly. It is true that taxation was unpopular – when has it not been? But the campaigns in alternative theatres of war were rarely regarded as perversions of some original ideal. How could they have been when one of the alternatives, crusading in Spain, had been authorized by the originator of the movement, Pope Urban II himself? The authoritative justifications for the use of force against heretics or Christian enemies of the Church were in fact older than the crusading movement. As the extent of the continuing enthusiasm for crusading in the 14th and 15th centuries has become apparent to modern historians, it has become impossible to maintain that late 13th-century Christians were demoralized. On the contrary, as the events after the crusaders' defeat at Hattin in 1187 had shown – they were to be repeated after the loss of the last toe-holds in Palestine in 1291 – crusading thrived on disaster: stories of catastrophe and atrocities actually fuelled enthusiasm.

So how is one to account for the failure of Gregory's plans and also for the fact that it was to prove impossible ever again to mount a really large international crusade of the old type? In the first place, the costs of warfare and the rise of nation states were combining to make old-fashioned crusades impracticable: around 1190 it had been hard enough to bring about the alliances necessary to the Third Crusade, and so preoccupied with the rift between emperor and pope had been the rest of Europe in the late 1240s that Louis IX's first crusade was in the end hardly more than a French affair. Secondly, it was arguable that in the 1270s large-scale crusades were not what was needed. The Christians in the East required a permanent increase in their garrisons, not the spasmodic arrival of large bodies of troops, which, after thoroughly upsetting the

A crusader in an act of prayer. From a 13th-century English psalter.

Heresy

Heresy was, and is, 'false' Christian doctrine, which diverged from the teaching of the Church. A heretic was a baptized Christian who willingly persisted in holding and propagating his or her beliefs against the Church's instructions. The essential feature of the heretic was this refusal to be bound by the Church's teaching, and a distinction could be, and was, made between Catholics who had lapsed into heresy and whose decisions were presumed to be deliberate, and their children, who had been brought up innocently in heresy and had not chosen to deny the Church's function.

The Church maintained that Christ had given it the custody of those truths which God revealed to mankind about himself. A heretic, by refusing to abide by the Church's instructions, was denying that God-given function and was, moreover, rejecting Christ's intentions for mankind. This is why heresy was seen as an active, not a passive, threat and was described as a rebellion; it was viewed as a boil or a cancer within the body of the Church, and medical metaphors of 'lancing' or 'cutting out' were often used.

Since the 4th century, force had been employed against heretics and its use justified. There was very little argument about that – in fact it was easier to justify force against renegade Christians than it was against Muslims – but the Church had traditionally looked to the secular authorities to take the necessary steps. Real problems arose when secular rulers were too weak to impose effective sanctions – the background to the launching of crusades against heretics – or when, as in the 16th century, some rulers themselves came to adhere to heresy.

Muslims, would depart, leaving the original defenders to their fate. At the same time as he had been planning his grandiose crusade, Pope Gregory had been nurturing a scheme whereby Charles of Anjou (Louis IX's younger brother who had conquered southern Italy and Sicily in a crusade, had established suzerainty over Latin Greece and was in the process of buying the crown of Jerusalem from a claimant) would establish an eastern Mediterranean empire, in which the Christian Holy Land would be integrated and its defence assured. This turned out to be no less of a chimera than the papal-imperial crusade. The fact was that the phenomenal success in 1099 and the conviction that crusades were divinely inspired had led to the belief that it was possible to mount a successful expedition to the East. This was surely an illusion, since such a crusade needed more in terms of resources, logistics and planning than the West could ever provide. It was in the more limited crusades on the other frontiers of Christendom that the movement found success.

Success in Spain and Portugal

The holy war in Spain was strengthened by crusading ideas. By the late 13th century only Granada remained in Muslim hands.

After 1140 there were profound changes in the political structure of both Muslim and Christian Spain. The Almoravids were overthrown and replaced by the heretical Almohad sect from north-west Africa (▶*page 32*); and the great Leonese kingdom split into three, Portugal, Castile and León. Each of these kingdoms tried to expand south along the great Roman highways such as the Camino de la Plata from León to Seville, bringing them into conflict with the Almohads.

Although the Reconquest was now equated with crusading (▶ *page 48*), the Spanish Christians received comparatively little help from abroad. But crusading ideas and methods were spreading, and Military Orders were set up to defend the borders (▶*page 54*).

Alfonso VIII of Castile captured Cuenca in 1177 and pushed south-west to Plasencia and Trujillo. Though routed by the caliph at Alarcos in 1195, he avenged this defeat at Las Navas de Tolosa (1212), where he led the

This Almohad banner, captured by Alfonso VIII at the battle of Las Navas de Tolosa, bears the inscription (from the top): 'I take refuge in God from Satan the stoned. In the name of God, the Merciful, the Compassionate, God bless him and give him peace'.

united armies of Castile, Navarre and Aragon, with a few crusaders, to the decisive victory of the whole Reconquest.

After 1224 the Almohad empire disintegrated in a war of succession complicated by religious and racial hatreds. With papal help, the Christians were able to conquer almost all of southern Spain. Alfonso IX of León took Cáceres in 1229 and Badajoz in 1230. His son, Fernando III, had been king of Castile since 1217, and when he inherited León in 1230 the combined forces of the two kingdoms were able to conquer all the Guadalquivir valley. His son Alfonso X suppressed the emirates of Murcia and Niebla, leaving only Granada under Muslim rule. He expelled all the Muslims from Castilian Andalucia, replacing them with thousands of Christian settlers.

In Portugal, the Palmela peninsula and Alcacer had been captured by 1217 by the Military Orders and Rhenish crusaders. King Sancho II conquered as far as the Algarve by 1248, turning most of the area over to the Military Orders for cattle ranching.

James I – 'the Conqueror' – of Aragon, meanwhile, had taken the Balearic Islands (1229-1235) and the city and kingdom of Valencia. He expelled the Muslims from the cities and reduced them to near-serfdom in the countryside under a new landowning aristocracy from Aragon and Catalonia.

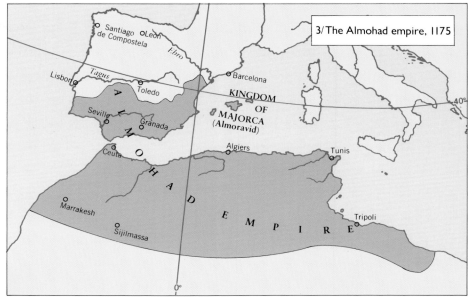

3/ The Almohad empire, 1175

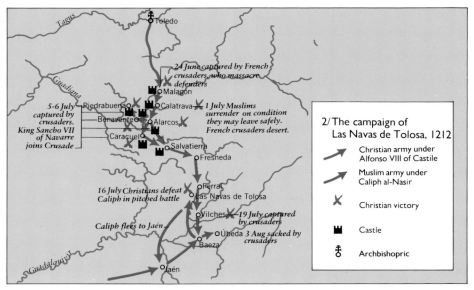

2/ The campaign of Las Navas de Tolosa, 1212

24 June captured by French crusaders, who massacre defenders

5-6 July captured by crusaders. King Sancho VII of Navarre joins Crusade

1 July Muslims surrender on condition they may leave safely. French crusaders desert.

16 July Christians defeat Caliph in pitched battle

Caliph flees to Jaén

19 July captured by crusaders

Úbeda 3 Aug sacked by crusaders

→ Christian army under Alfonso VIII of Castile

→ Muslim army under Caliph al-Nasir

✗ Christian victory

🏰 Castle

☦ Archbishopric

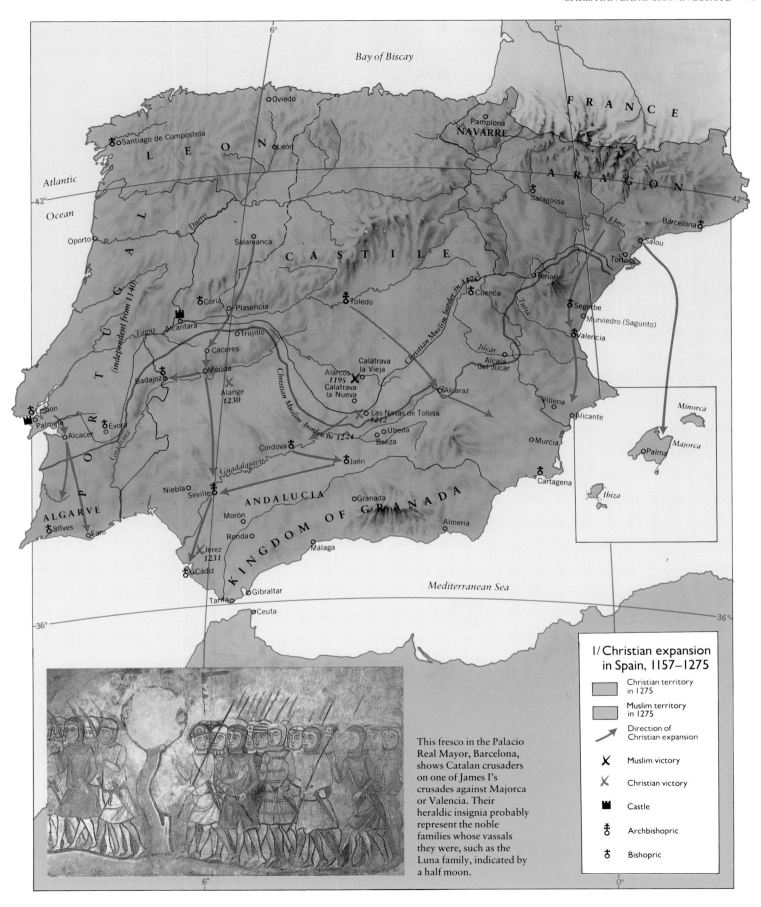

Bay of Biscay

Atlantic

Ocean

42°

FRANCE

Oviedo

Santiago de Compostela

León

Pamplona
NAVARRE

Saragossa

Barcelona

Oporto

Salamanca

Duero

ARAGON

Ebro

Salou

Tortosa

LEON

CASTILE

Teruel

Coria
Plasencia
Alcántara
Tagus

Trujillo

Cáceres

Toledo

Cuenca

Christian Muslim border in 1270

Segorbe
Murviedro (Sagunto)

Júcar

Turia

Mérida

Badajoz
Alange
1230

Calatrava
la Vieja
Alarcos
1195
Calatrava
la Nueva

Alcalá
del Júcar

Valencia

(independent from 1140)

Christian Muslim border in 1224

Las Navas de Tolosa
1212

Alcaraz

Villena

PORTUGAL

Lisbon
Palmela
Alcácer
Évora

Guadiana

Cordova

Guadalquivir

Jaén

Úbeda
Baeza

Alicante

Murcia

Cartagena

Niebla
Seville

ANDALUCÍA

Granada

Morón

KINGDOM OF GRANADA

Almería

ALGARVE

Silves
Faro

Ronda

Jerez
1231

Málaga

Cádiz

Gibraltar

Tarifa

Ceuta

Mediterranean Sea

36°

Minorca

Majorca

Palma

Ibiza

1/Christian expansion in Spain, 1157–1275

Christian territory in 1275

Muslim territory in 1275

Direction of Christian expansion

Muslim victory

Christian victory

Castle

Archbishopric

Bishopric

This fresco in the Palacio Real Mayor, Barcelona, shows Catalan crusaders on one of James I's crusades against Majorca or Valencia. Their heraldic insignia probably represent the noble families whose vassals they were, such as the Luna family, indicated by a half moon.

The Baltic Crusades

On the northern fringes of Europe, extensive pagan regions still existed in the 13th century. Their eradication was one of the goals of crusading.

The conquest by crusaders and the settlement of the eastern Baltic lands really began in the 1190s when Popes Celestine III and Innocent III supported efforts to preserve and extend a missionary church established among the Livs on the lower reaches of the River Dvina. By 1230 Bishop Albert of Riga, with the assistance of a small military order, the Sword Brothers, had conquered Livonia (approximately modern Latvia). Meanwhile the Danes, who had been attacking the Pomeranian coast from Lübeck to Danzig, Finland, Ösel and Prussia, took northern Estonia in 1220. To the north the Swedes were soon to launch a series of campaigns against Finland where they clashed with the Russians.

Between Livonia and Christian Germany, however, there remained a wide belt of pagan territory. Another missionary bishop attempted to convert the pagan Prussians, again with the assistance of a small Military Order, the Knights of Dobrzyń. They failed, and Duke Conrad of Masovia, whose territories were being menaced by the Prussians, called in the Teutonic Knights. This Military Order had grown from modest origins in the late 12th century into a powerful trans-European organization. Although its headquarters were still in Palestine (▶ *page 106*), it had become involved in Europe when the king of Hungary had given the order a section of his frontier in Transylvania. The Knights, however, had been expelled for trying to establish a 'state within a state'.

The Teutonic Knights were invited to Prussia. They rapidly absorbed the Order of Dobrzyń and began carving out a state for themselves, without regard to the legitimate rights of the host, Duke Conrad, or the existing missionary church. In 1226 their master received from the emperor Frederick II the status of imperial prince for all future conquests in Prussia. In 1234 Pope Gregory IX took the Knights' territory under his protection as a papal fief. The Teutonic Knights absorbed the Sword Brothers in Livonia after the latter were defeated by the pagan Lithuanians in 1236. Fears about the Order's ability to resist the Mongols, who were pressing on the east European frontiers in the early 1240s (▶ *page 112*), probably led to the extraordinary privilege, granted in 1245, by

which they could grant plenary crusade indulgences to Germans who assisted them against the Prussians without any specific papal authorization. But by 1250 the Teutonic Knights had established an independent state and could wage a perpetual crusade to support it.

Assisted by merchants from Lübeck and Bremen and by parties of visiting crusaders, they had embarked on the conquest of the indigenous pagan tribes. There were setbacks. After Prussian revolts in 1242 and 1260, the second set off by their defeat by the Lithuanians at Durben, the Order had to fight long wars of recovery. A drive towards Pskov was halted and the Knights were crushed by Prince Alexander Nevsky of Novgorod in the Battle on Lake Peipus (5 April 1242). And they always had to face the might and resilience of successive Lithuanian rulers.

In Prussia itself the Teutonic Knights advanced inexorably, employing a combination of armed force with the preservation of the rights and social status of those who accepted Christianity. They also secured their hold by granting generous terms to the settlers they lured from northern and east central Germany. Broadly speaking, German settlements were relatively dense in West Prussia, declining to a thin upper class the further settlement moved eastwards. Following the loss of Acre in 1291 and a temporary period in Venice, the Order relocated its headquarters to Marienburg in 1309 (▶ *page 128*), thus tacitly acknowledging its true power base and changing realities.

Albert, bishop of Livonia addressed the pope and all the bishops about the difficulties, hostilities and other concerns facing the Church in Livonia... The bishop said: 'We know, holy father, that you constantly watch over the holy land of Jerusalem, which is the land of the Son of God, as the apple of your holiness's eye. In the same way you ought not to cease looking after Livonia, which is the land of the Mother of God...For the Son loves his Mother and just as he does not want his own land to be lost, so he is particularly anxious that the land of his Mother should not be imperilled.' The pope replied: 'We will always make it our concern to favour with the same fatherly love and attention the land of the Mother, just as we do the land of the Son.'

Exchange between the Bishop of Livonia and Pope Innocent III at the Fourth Lateran Council in 1215. From Henry of Livonia, *Chronicon*.

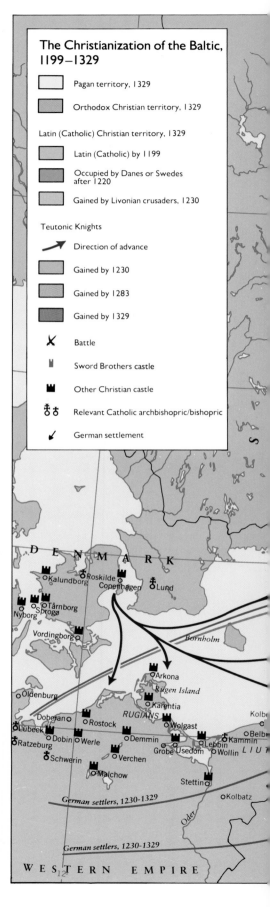

The Christianization of the Baltic, 1199–1329

- Pagan territory, 1329
- Orthodox Christian territory, 1329

Latin (Catholic) Christian territory, 1329
- Latin (Catholic) by 1199
- Occupied by Danes or Swedes after 1220
- Gained by Livonian crusaders, 1230

Teutonic Knights
- Direction of advance
- Gained by 1230
- Gained by 1283
- Gained by 1329
- Battle
- Sword Brothers castle
- Other Christian castle
- Relevant Catholic archbishopric/bishopric
- German settlement

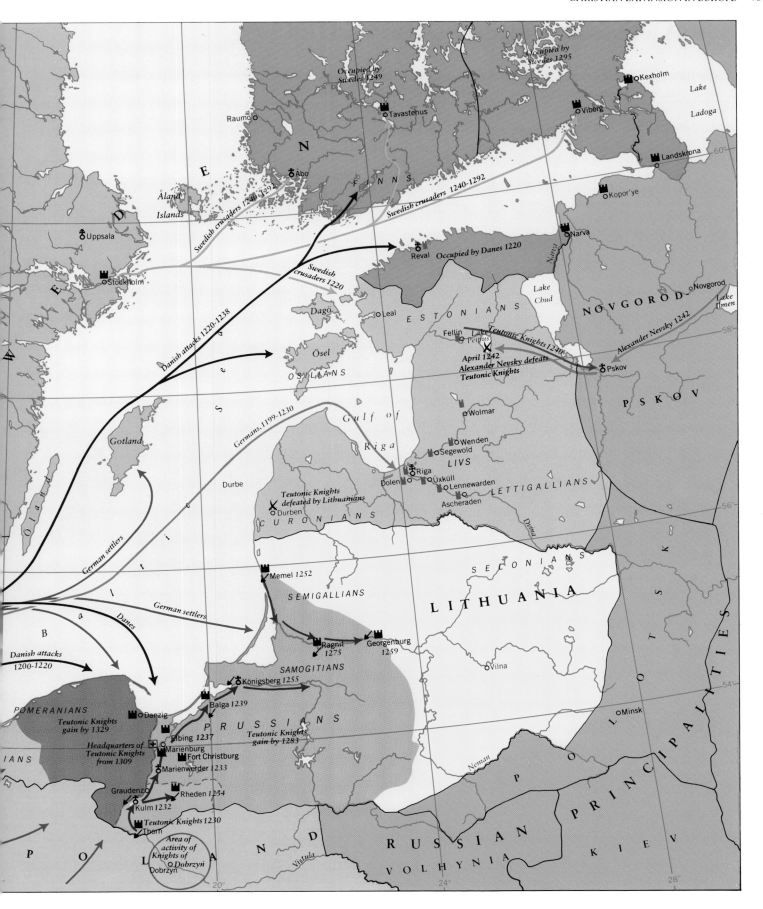

Occupied by
Swedes 1295

○Kexholm

ᛒViborg

Lake
Ladoga

Raumo○

Occupied by
Swedes 1249

○Tavastehus

ᛒ Landskrona

E   N

F I N N S

Swedish crusaders 1240–1292

60°

ᛒ○Kopor'ye

Åbo ♂○

Swedish crusaders 1240–1292

Narva
ᛒ○Narva

♂ᛰUppsala

D

Åland
Islands

Swedish
crusaders 1220

♂Reval   Occupied by Danes 1220

Nova

L A K E

NOVGOROD   ○Novgorod

Lake
Ilmen

E

ᛒ○Stockholm

Dagö

Leal○

E S T O N I A N S

Lake
Chud

58°

Alexander Nevsky 1242

Fellin○   Lake
        Peipus

Teutonic Knights 1240

Danish attacks 1220–1238

Ösel

○Pskov

April 1242
Alexander Nevsky defeats
Teutonic Knights

P S K O V

O S I L I A N S

e

Germans, 1199–1230

Gulf of

Wolmar○

W

S

Riga

○Wenden
ᛒSegewold

L I V S

Gotland

Durbe○

Dolen○♂○Riga
     ○Üxküll
     ᛒLennewarden
Ascheraden○

L E T T I G A L L I A N S

56°

Teutonic Knights
defeated by Lithuanians
✂Durben

Düna

l

C U R O N I A N S

t

German settlers

S E L O N I A N S

i

ᛒMemel 1252

LITHUANIA

c

German settlers

S E M I G A L L I A N S

a

Danes

B

l

ᛒRagnit   ᛒGeorgenburg
  1275   1259

S A M O G I T I A N S

○Vilna

T S K

54°

Danish attacks
1200–1220

ᛰ○Königsberg 1255

P   O   L

○Minsk

POMERANIANS
Teutonic Knights
gain by 1329

ᛒ○Danzig

ᛒ
Balga 1239

P R U S S I A N S

Teutonic Knights
gain by 1283

R U S S I A N   P R I N C I P A L I T I E S

ᛒ
Elbing 1237

ᛰ Marienburg
ᛒFort Christburg

Headquarters of
Teutonic Knights
from 1309

I A N S

♂Marienwerder 1233

Graudenz○

ᛒRheden 1234

○♂Kulm 1232

Neman

ᛒThorn
Teutonic Knights 1230

P   O   L   A   N   D

Area of
activity of
Knights of
○Dobrzyń
Dobrzyń

Vistula

V O L H Y N I A

R U S S I A N

K I E V

20°   24°   28°

The Crusades Against the Cathars

In the war against the heretical Cathar sect, crusading was used to control religious belief within Christian Europe.

The beliefs of the Cathars were so radical that they were hardly Christian at all: they held that there were two Gods, the God of the spiritual world and a God who had created the material world in which the soul was imprisoned. To free their souls, the Cathars tried to give up everything of this world. They did not eat meat, milk or eggs, abstained from sexual relations, denied the Trinity and renounced the Church.

By 1200 the heresy had become so widespread in the remote, mountainous regions of south-west France that the papacy was seriously alarmed. Many Cathars were from noble families, and many senior churchmen in the area had Cathar relatives. In January 1208, a papal legate was murdered by a vassal of Count Raymond VI of Toulouse. Pope Innocent III proclaimed a crusade against the heretics, and in the spring of 1209 a large force gathered at Lyon. Raymond quickly came to terms with the Church, so the crusaders had to content themselves with invading the lands of his vassal Raymond Roger of Trencavel, viscount of Béziers and Carcassonne. In July, Béziers was sacked and 15,000 of its townspeople, Cathar and Catholic alike, were massacred. Carcassonne surrendered in August.

A northern baron, Simon of Montfort, was given control of the Trencavel lands. Over the next two years he took most of the castles and villages in the area that still resisted. In 1211, Count Raymond VI's refusal to help eradicate the Cathars gave Simon of Montfort the pretext to invade the county. He tried to encircle the city of Toulouse itself, but at the end of each campaigning season many crusaders went home, leaving the castles they had taken to defect back to Raymond.

Then, in the summer of 1213, King Peter II of Aragon intervened. Although Peter was an orthodox Catholic, he felt that his interests in the region were threatened by Simon of Montfort's growing power. Simon and his crusaders met the combined forces of Aragon and Toulouse at Muret in September 1213, defeating them utterly and killing Peter himself. Raymond was forced to flee, leaving Simon to pursue his brutal suppression of the Cathars into Quercy.

Raymond and his son – the future Raymond VII – returned from exile in 1216. Simon tried to take Toulouse from them, but in June 1218 he was killed by a stone thrown from the city walls. An expedition in 1219 by Prince Louis, heir to the throne of France, could not prevent the count from recovering his territories. It was only in 1226 that Louis, now king, was able to overcome the region. He left his lieutenant Humbert of Beaujeu to ravage the Toulousain, forcing Count Raymond VII to sue for peace in 1229. Then began the slow erosion of Catharism by the Inquisition, the settlement of outsiders and the dispossession of heretical lords.

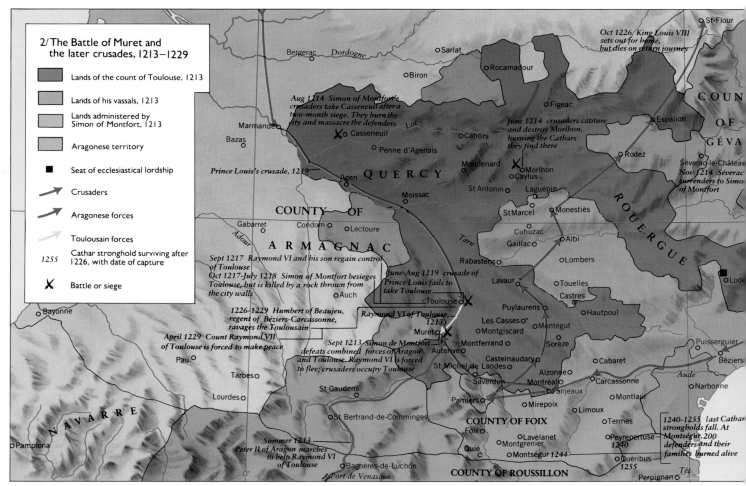

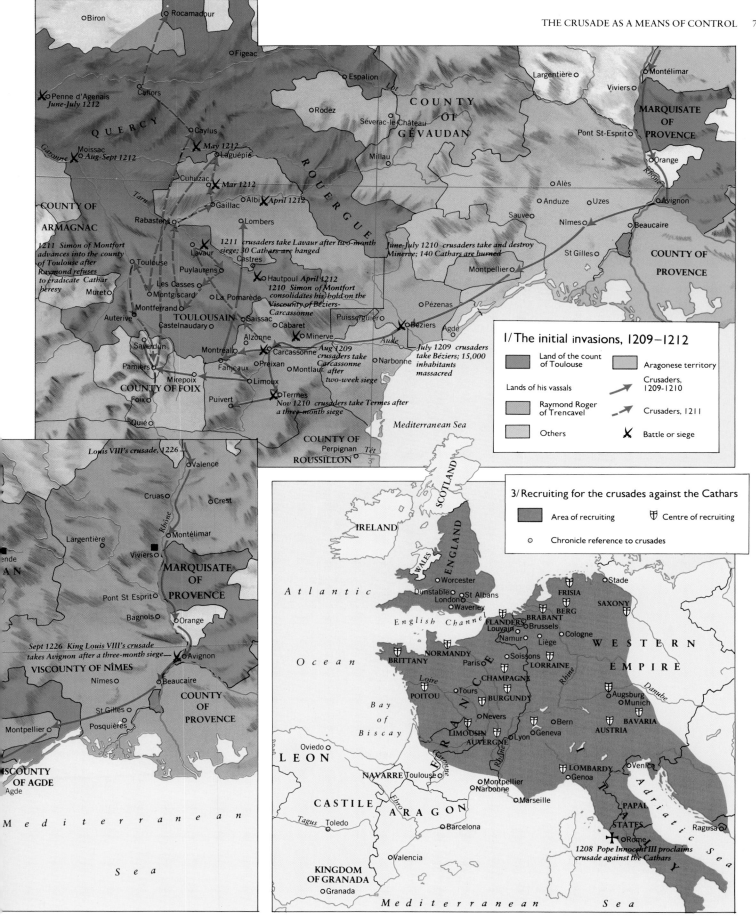

1/ The initial invasions, 1209–1212

- Land of the count of Toulouse
- Aragonese territory
- Lands of his vassals
- Crusaders, 1209–1210
- Raymond Roger of Trencavel
- Crusaders, 1211
- Others
- Battle or siege

1211 Simon of Montfort advances into the county of Toulouse after Raymond refuses to eradicate Cathar heresy

1211 crusaders take Lavaur after two-month siege; 30 Cathars are hanged

June-July 1210 crusaders take and destroy Minerve; 140 Cathars are burned

1210 Simon of Montfort consolidates his hold on the Viscounty of Béziers-Carcassonne

Aug 1209 crusaders take Carcassonne after a two-week siege

July 1209 crusaders take Béziers; 15,000 inhabitants massacred

Nov 1210 crusaders take Termes after a three-month siege

Louis VIII's crusade, 1226

Sept 1226 King Louis VIII's crusade takes Avignon after a three-month siege

3/ Recruiting for the crusades against the Cathars

- Area of recruiting
- Centre of recruiting
- Chronicle reference to crusades

1208 Pope Innocent III proclaims crusade against the Cathars

Crusades in Italy

Heretics were not the only internal enemies of Christendom against whom crusading was aimed; in the 13th and 14th centuries it was also directed against the political opponents of the popes, especially in Italy.

The popes had become the secular rulers of a band of territory across the middle of the Italian peninsula. To the north lay a chequer-board of autonomous cities in Lombardy and Tuscany; to the south the dominant Italian power, the kingdom of Sicily, which then included southern Italy as well as the island itself. The kingdom was ruled directly by the western emperor, Frederick II. Antagonism between him and the papacy reached such a level that, at the time he recovered Jerusalem from the Muslims in 1229 (▶ *page 98*), he was actually an excommunicate.

The whole of Italy was torn between supporters of the papacy, who became known as Guelfs, and the followers of the emperor, the Ghibellines. Between 1198 and 1268 the papacy preached a long series of crusades against its enemies in Italy; after 1239 these were aimed at ousting Frederick, his sons Conrad and Manfred and his grandson Conradin, from Sicily. The most ambitious and successful of these ventures was the invasion of the kingdom in 1265-1266 by Charles of Anjou, a younger brother of Louis IX of France (▶ *page 96*). Charles's victories over Manfred at Benevento in 1266 and Conradin at Tagliacozzo in 1268 established the supremacy of the French Angevin dynasty in Italy.

But in 1282, the island of Sicily rebelled, and adopted members of the Aragonese royal house as its rulers. For the Aragonese, this was an important step in a dynamic process of Mediterranean expansion which had already included the conquest of the Balearic islands (▶ *page 72*) and the establishment of a protectorate over Muslim towns in North Africa, and would later give them control of Sardinia and the duchy of Athens (▶ *page 138*).

Between 1283 and 1302 the papacy launched a number of crusades to restore Angevin rule in Sicily, but the sea power of Aragon was too great and in 1302 the treaty of Caltabellotta ratified the separation of the island from the mainland provinces of the kingdom.

Rome now seemed too insecure a base for the papacy, and in 1305 the new pope

Clement V took up residence in Poitiers, before moving to Avignon in 1309. From its exile, the papacy waged a constant struggle to reassert its political power in Italy. Papal legates such as Cardinal Gil Albornoz rallied the Guelf powers – principally Florence and the mainland remnant of the kingdom of Sicily – in a number of crusades against the Ghibellines. The most aggressive of the Ghibelline lords were the Visconti family in Milan and its dependent cities, and crusades were waged against them in the 1320s and 1360s. Working from an expanded territorial base and using the latest military techniques, the Ghibellines frustrated every attempt by the papacy to pacify northern and central Italy and facilitate its return to Rome.

E piscopal authority and power is counted for little, ecclesiastical censure is despised, souls perish, bodies are slaughtered, cities are burnt, castles are destroyed, travellers are robbed, Saracens and schismatics are set over orthodox Christians, heretics are defended to such an extent that in several places we dare not take action.

Pope Urban IV justifies
the crusade against Manfred in 1264

A 14th-century man-at-arms, carved in stone by an Italian sculptor. Drawn by wages and booty as well as the spiritual attraction of the crusading indulgence, such heavily-armed professional fighters were regularly employed by both the papacy and its opponents.

3/ Aragonese expansion, 1229–1324

Catalan-Aragonese Federation, 1229

Catalan-Aragonese gains, 1229-1324

● Muslim town under Catalan protectorate

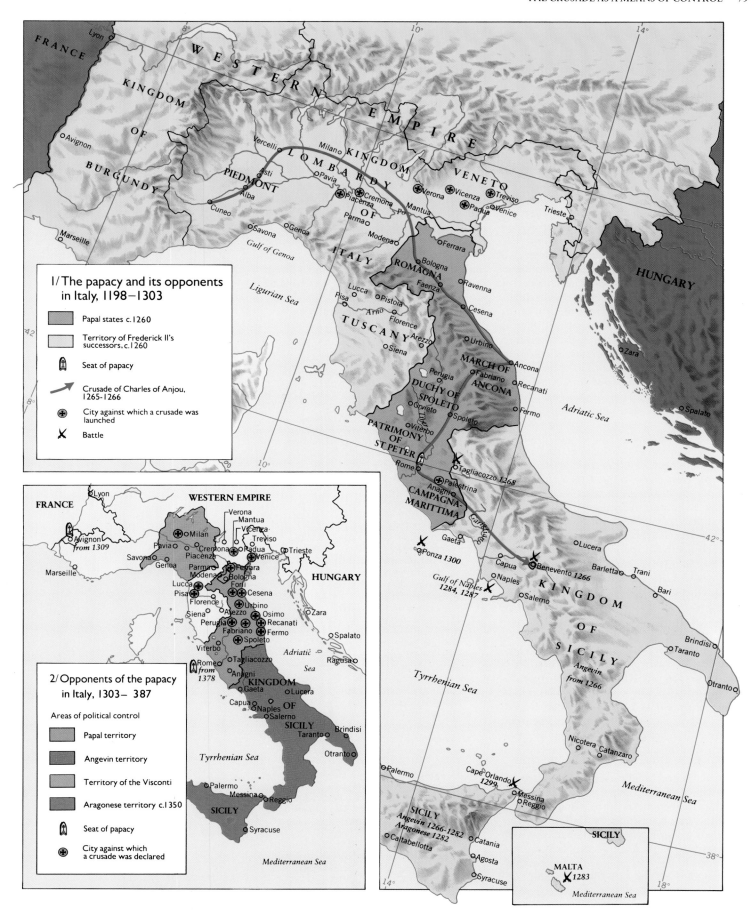

1/ The papacy and its opponents in Italy, 1198–1303

Papal states c.1260

Territory of Frederick II's successors, c.1260

Seat of papacy

Crusade of Charles of Anjou, 1265–1266

City against which a crusade was launched

Battle

2/ Opponents of the papacy in Italy, 1303– 387

Areas of political control

Papal territory

Angevin territory

Territory of the Visconti

Aragonese territory c.1350

Seat of papacy

City against which a crusade was declared

Critics of Crusading

Crusading attracted criticism from the start; but it was mostly directed at abuses of the movement, seldom at the movement itself.

Aspects of the crusading movement attracted criticism almost from the time of Urban II's sermon at Clermont in 1095. The critics themselves were scattered throughout Europe and included both monastic chroniclers and troubadours. They complained that expeditions were encumbered with too many non-combatants; that priests and monks neglected their spiritual and pastoral duties in order to take the cross; and about the presence of female camp-followers. The repeated setbacks suffered by God's army came to be explained as a divine judgement upon human sinfulness, as manifested in the crusaders' greed, pride and immorality. Gerhoh of Reichersberg argued that during the Second Crusade the inhabitants of Jerusalem did not wish for peace with the Muslims, but 'almost solely the acceptance of money, whether from the offerings of pilgrims or from the redemption of the besieged.'

Contemporaries also complained about non-fulfilment of vows and in particular about rulers who delayed their departure; about the harshness of taxes levied by the church and state to finance the crusades; and that the system of vow redemption, intended for those genuinely unable to go on crusade, was being abused for financial gain.

In the 13th century, critics such as the Aragonese chronicler Ramón Muntaner argued that the crusade itself was being abused, and that the campaigns against heretics (▶page 76) schismatic Greeks (▶page 84) and Christian lay powers (▶page 78) were being waged at the expense of the beleaguered kingdom of Jerusalem. Some historians have argued that such criticism reflected public opinion and disillusionment with the crusading movement as a whole, but apart from a few vociferous individuals, critics came from areas which had good reason to oppose papal policy, such as Languedoc and the imperial heartland of Germany. Some critics, such as Freidank and Walther von der Vogelweide, had links with the imperial court. The same critics and arguments can be found in relation to the crusades against the Cathars and the campaigns against Frederick II in Italy, as well as the later papal-Angevin campaigns against Frederick II's heirs, Conrad, Manfred and Conradin, and against Sicily and Aragon.

After events such as the defeat and capture of Louis IX at Mansurah (▶page 96) it was inevitable that some would question whether it was God's will to continue, but others exhorted the faithful to resume the struggle. Criticism of the concept of crusading itself was rare. The only identifiable pacifist groups were the heretic Cathars and Waldensians. There were isolated critics of the idea of crusading, such as Ralph Niger and Joachim of Fiore. The latter's idea that the crusaders would never be victorious by force of arms was taken up by his followers the Joachites, but they were not very numerous and their ideas about the crusades do not seem to have had wide appeal. The crusading movement was still attracting support long after Acre fell to the Mamluks in 1291.

T here are some of these critics who say that it is not in accordance with the Christian religion to shed blood in this way, even that of wicked infidels. For Christ did not act thus...

There are others who say that although one ought not to spare Saracen blood one must, however, be sparing of Christian blood and deaths...Is it wisdom to put at risk in this way so many and such great men of ours?...

There are others who say that when our men go overseas to fight the Saracens the conditions of war are much worse for our side, for we are very few in comparison to their great numbers. We are, moreover, on alien territory...And so it looks as though we are putting God to the test...

There are others who say that, although we have a duty to defend ourselves against the Saracens when they attack us, it does not seem that we ought to attack their lands or their persons when they leave us in peace...

There are others who say that, if we ought to rid the world of Saracens, why do we not do the same to the Jews?...

Other people are asking, what is the point of this attack on the Saracens? For they are not roused to conversion by it but rather are stirred up against the Christian faith....

Others say that it does not appear to be God's will that Christians should proceed against the Saracens in this way, because of the misfortunes which God has allowed and is still allowing to happen to the Christians engaged in this business.

How could the Lord have allowed Saladin to retake the land won with so much Christian blood, the emperor Frederick to perish in shallow water and King Louis to be captured in Egypt...if this kind of proceeding had been pleasing to him?

Humbert of Romans in a report for the Second Council of Lyon, 1274

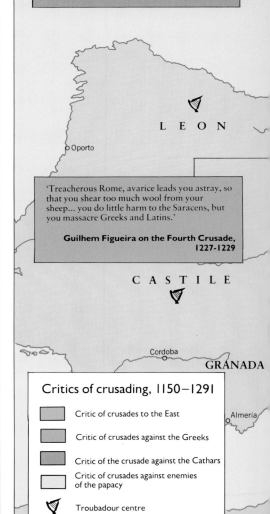

'The Greeks persist in their error because the truth is not preached to them in their own language, and the Saracens too... Nor is war effective against them, since... those who survive, together with their children, are more and more embittered against the Christian faith.'

Roger Bacon, *Opus maius*, 1260

'God is not pleased with a forced service. Whoever seeks to spread the faith through violence, in that way transgresses the discipline of the faith.'

Ralph Niger, *De re militari*, 1187-1188

'An unjust war, in which greed was the spur to action rather than the extermination of the perverse heretics.'

Roger Wendover on the crusade against the Cathars, in *Flores historiarum* c.1226

'Treacherous Rome, avarice leads you astray, so that you shear too much wool from your sheep... you do little harm to the Saracens, but you massacre Greeks and Latins.'

Guilhem Figueira on the Fourth Crusade, 1227-1229

O Oporto

L E O N

C A S T I L E

Cordoba

GRANADA

Almeria

Critics of crusading, 1150–1291

Critic of crusades to the East

Critic of crusades against the Greeks

Critic of the crusade against the Cathars

Critic of crusades against enemies of the papacy

Troubadour centre

Location of other critic

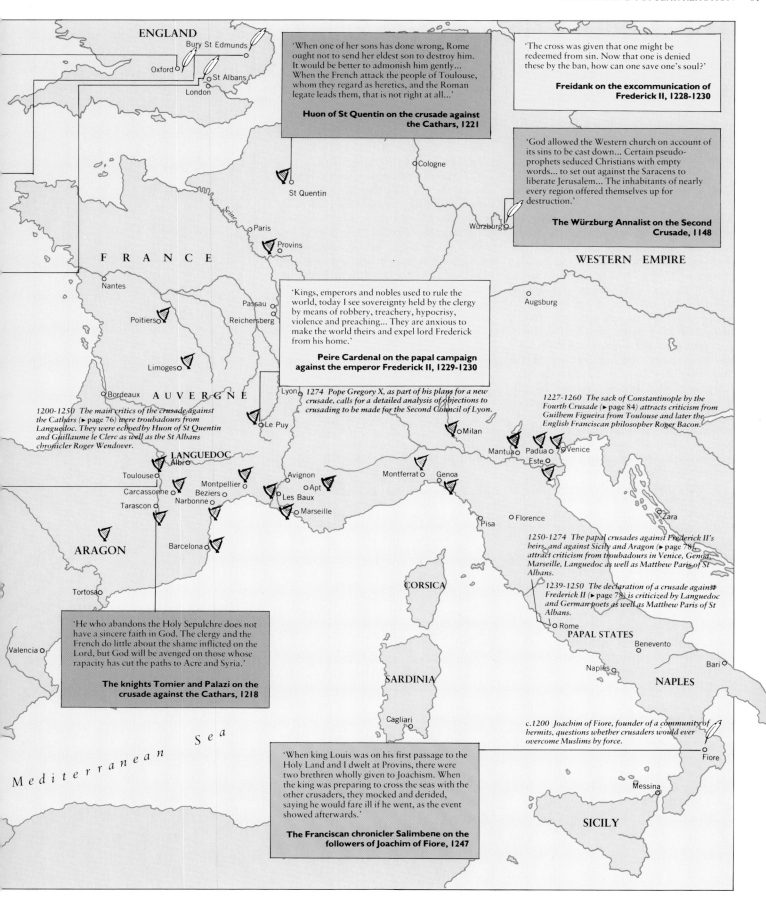

ENGLAND
Bury St Edmunds
Oxford
St Albans
London

'When one of her sons has done wrong, Rome ought not to send her eldest son to destroy him. It would be better to admonish him gently... When the French attack the people of Toulouse, whom they regard as heretics, and the Roman legate leads them, that is not right at all...'

Huon of St Quentin on the crusade against the Cathars, 1221

'The cross was given that one might be redeemed from sin. Now that one is denied these by the ban, how can one save one's soul?'

Freidank on the excommunication of Frederick II, 1228-1230

Cologne

St Quentin

'God allowed the Western church on account of its sins to be cast down... Certain pseudo-prophets seduced Christians with empty words... to set out against the Saracens to liberate Jerusalem... The inhabitants of nearly every region offered themselves up for destruction.'

The Würzburg Annalist on the Second Crusade, 1148

Würzburg

WESTERN EMPIRE

F R A N C E

Seine

Paris
Provins

Nantes

Passau
Reichersberg

Augsburg

Poitiers

'Kings, emperors and nobles used to rule the world, today I see sovereignty held by the clergy by means of robbery, treachery, hypocrisy, violence and preaching... They are anxious to make the world theirs and expel lord Frederick from his home.'

Peire Cardenal on the papal campaign against the emperor Frederick II, 1229-1230

Limoges

Bordeaux A U V E R G N E

Lyon *1274 Pope Gregory X, as part of his plans for a new crusade, calls for a detailed analysis of objections to crusading to be made for the Second Council of Lyon.*

1227-1260 The sack of Constantinople by the Fourth Crusade (▶ page 84) attracts criticism from Guilhem Figueira from Toulouse and later the English Franciscan philosopher Roger Bacon.

1200-1250 The main critics of the crusade against the Cathars (▶ page 76) were troubadours from Languedoc. They were echoed by Huon of St Quentin and Guillaume le Clerc as well as the St Albans chronicler Roger Wendover.

Le Puy

Milan

Mantua Padua Venice
Este

LANGUEDOC
Albi
Toulouse
Carcassonne Montpellier
Beziers
Narbonne
Tarascon

Avignon
Apt
Les Baux
Marseille

Montferrat Genoa

Pisa Florence

Zara

ARAGON Barcelona

CORSICA

1250-1274 The papal crusades against Frederick II's heirs, and against Sicily and Aragon (▶ page 78), attract criticism from troubadours in Venice, Genoa, Marseille, Languedoc as well as Matthew Paris of St Albans.

Tortosa

1239-1250 The declaration of a crusade against Frederick II (▶ page 78) is criticized by Languedoc and German poets as well as Matthew Paris of St Albans.

Rome PAPAL STATES

Benevento

Valencia

'He who abandons the Holy Sepulchre does not have a sincere faith in God. The clergy and the French do little about the shame inflicted on the Lord, but God will be avenged on those whose rapacity has cut the paths to Acre and Syria.'

The knights Tomier and Palazi on the crusade against the Cathars, 1218

SARDINIA

Naples Bari

NAPLES

Cagliari

c.1200 Joachim of Fiore, founder of a community of hermits, questions whether crusaders would ever overcome Muslims by force.

Fiore

M e d i t e r r a n e a n   S e a

'When king Louis was on his first passage to the Holy Land and I dwelt at Provins, there were two brethren wholly given to Joachism. When the king was preparing to cross the seas with the other crusaders, they mocked and derided, saying he would fare ill if he went, as the event showed afterwards.'

The Franciscan chronicler Salimbene on the followers of Joachim of Fiore, 1247

Messina

SICILY

The Popular Crusades

Criticism of crusading helped to fuel the outbreak of spontaneous, popular crusades: if the rich and powerful could not liberate Jerusalem, maybe the poor and humble could.

The 13th and early 14th centuries saw a number of movements of crusading enthusiasm which drew their support largely from the young and rootless among the rural labouring poor: the Children's crusade of 1212, the Shepherd's crusade of 1251, the Popular crusade of 1309 and the Shepherds' crusade of 1320. Except for the French version of the Children's crusade (for which there is no solid evidence of crusading intention), they all originated in a broad band of territory stretching from Normandy to the Rhineland; the borderlands between France and the Western Empire were particularly sensitive to this type of popular piety. None of the crusades lasted for more than a few months, usually beginning around Easter and expiring by late summer. None reached the East, and many of those taking part did not even reach the Mediterranean ports. Attacks on Jews were often associated with them.

Reliable evidence of their chronology and intentions is difficult to piece together, because most clerical commentators were either hostile or uncomprehending, and the participants left no witness of their own. But their very existence offers a glimpse of an underclass otherwise largely ignored in contemporary sources, which could be fired by charismatic popular preaching.

All of these outbreaks appear to have been influenced by contemporary crusading propaganda, although not in the ways that the papacy and the secular rulers had hoped for. The Children's Crusade, for example, was set off by the ferment aroused by popular preach-ing for the crusade against the Cathars (▶ *page 76*); the Shepherds' Crusade of 1251 by the news of the disasters that had overtaken Louis IX of France in Egypt (▶ *page 96*); and the Popular Crusade of 1309 and the Shepherds' Crusade of 1320 by the renewal of preaching to recover the Holy Land.

The Master of Hungary, the demagogue who led the 1251 Shepherds' Crusade, carried a letter he claimed had been given to him by the Blessed Virgin Mary, and which spelled out a recurrent theme of the popular crusades: that the failure of the crusades to retake Jerusalem proved that it was not the proud and rich – the members of the military classes – who were destined to liberate the Holy City, but the innocent and humble.

> **T**here was a 60-year-old Hungarian... This imposter, who could speak French, German and Latin, wandered about everywhere preaching without papal authority or the licence of any prelate, falsely claiming that he had received an order from Blessed Mary, the mother of the Lord, to summon shepherds and herdsmen... He said that heaven had granted them in their humility and simplicity the privilege of recovering the Holy Land ... for the pride in arms of the French (nobility) had not pleased God... He summoned all sorts of shepherds and they gradually began to follow him, leaving their flocks, herds and studs without asking their lords or relatives and without bothering about what they would eat... Their numbers greatly multiplied to such an extent that, mustering 100,000 or more, they made themselves military standards and a lamb bearing a flag was drawn on the banner of their master: the lamb as a sign of humility and innocence; the flag with the cross as a sign of victory.
>
> **Matthew Paris describes the first Shepherds' Crusade in *Historia Maiora*, 1251**

English peasants in the early 14th century, fulfilling what was seen as their proper function, working the land. The popular crusades were viewed by contemporary chroniclers as a distortion of the social order.

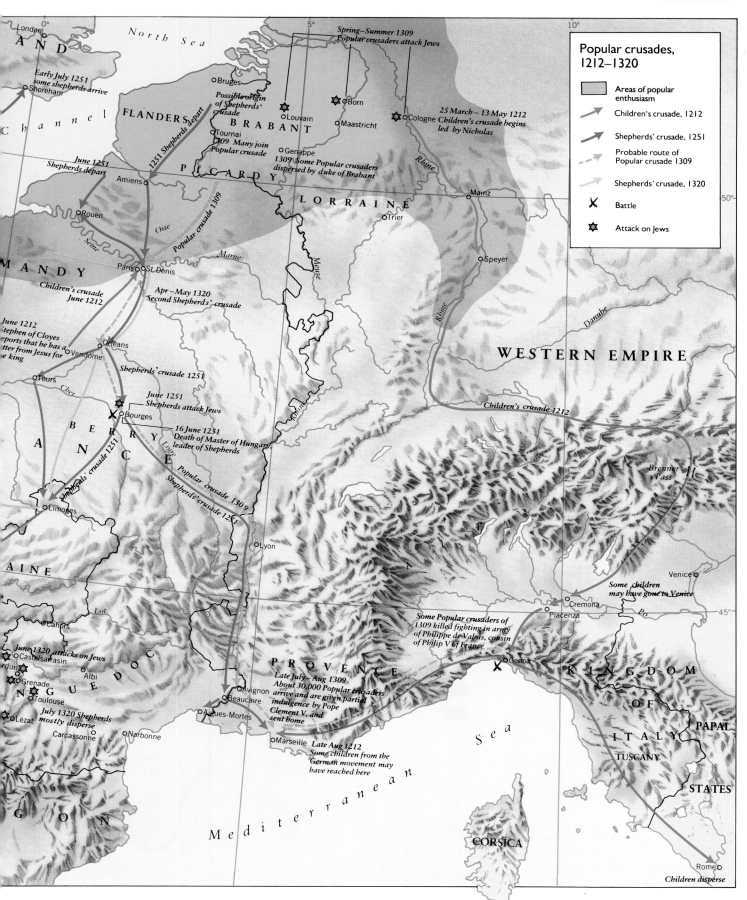

London

North Sea

A N D

Early July 1251
some shepherds arrive
Shoreham

C h a n n e l

FLANDERS

Bruges

BRABANT

Possible origin
of Shepherds'
crusade

1251 Shepherds depart

Tournai
1309 Many join
Popular crusade

Louvain

Born

Maastricht

Genappe

P I C A R D Y

June 1251
Shepherds depart

Amiens

June 1251
Shepherds depart

Spring–Summer 1309
Popular crusaders attack Jews

Cologne   25 March – 13 May 1212
Children's crusade begins
led by Nicholas

Rhine

L O R R A I N E

1309 Some Popular crusaders
dispersed by duke of Brabant

Mainz

Trier

Speyer

M A N D Y

Rouen

Oise

Seine

Marne

Meuse

Popular crusade 1309

Paris   St Denis

Children's crusade
June 1212

Apr – May 1320
Second Shepherds' crusade

Rhine

WESTERN EMPIRE

Danube

June 1212
Stephen of Cloyes
reports that he has a
letter from Jesus for
the king

Vendôme

Orleans

Tours

Cher

F R A N C E

Shepherds' crusade 1251

June 1251
Shepherds attack Jews

Bourges

16 June 1251
Death of Master of Hungary,
leader of Shepherds

B E R R Y

Loire

Popular crusade 1309

Shepherds' crusade 1251

Limoges

A I N E

Lot

Cahors

G U E D O C

June 1320 attacks on Jews
Castelsarrasin

Albi

N G U E

Grenade

Toulouse

Lézat   July 1320 Shepherds
mostly disperse

Carcassonne

Narbonne

G O N

Lyon

Rhône

A L P S

Brenner
Pass

Children's crusade 1212

Venice

Some children
may have gone to Venice

Cremona

Piacenza

Po

Some Popular crusaders of
1309 killed fighting in army
of Philippe de Valois, cousin
of Philip V of France

P R O V E N C E

Late July – Aug 1309
About 30,000 Popular crusaders
arrive and are given partial
indulgence by Pope
Clement V, and
sent home

Avignon

Beaucaire

Aigues-Mortes

Marseille   Late Aug 1212
Some children from the
German movement may
have reached here

Genoa

K I N G D O M

O F

I T A L Y

TUSCANY

PAPAL

STATES

M e d i t e r r a n e a n   S e a

CORSICA

Rome

Children disperse

The Fourth Crusade

The controversial Fourth Crusade turned away from Egypt and ended in the destruction of the Christian Byzantine empire.

In August 1198, Pope Innocent III declared a new crusade. The initial response was disappointing, but some inspired local preaching, and Innocent's unprecedented decision to tax the church to subsidize the crusaders, helped to create the nucleus of a force around the counts of Champagne, Blois and Flanders, and several important lords of the Ile de France. The destination of the crusade was to be Egypt, the centre of Muslim power in the Near East (▶*page 58*). Venice agreed to provide the transport, and in April 1201 contracted to ship 4,500 knights, 9,000 squires and 20,000 foot soldiers to Egypt for the sum of 85,000 marks. When only a third of the force had reached Venice by October 1202, the crusade leaders were unable to raise this sum. In lieu of payment, they agreed to help the Venetians recover Zara, lost to Hungary in 1186. Despite Innocent III's instructions that no Christian city be attacked, they took Zara the following month.

The Byzantine empire, meanwhile, was in the throes of a dynastic crisis. The emperor Isaac Angelus had been deposed and blinded by his brother Alexius III. Isaac's son (Alexius IV) fled to the west for aid, and now made a startling proposition to the crusaders. If they restored him and his father to power, he would pay them 200,000 marks, reunite the Orthodox Church with Rome, and contribute a large force for operations in the Holy Land. The Venetians and most of the crusade leaders agreed, but to many crusaders it was quite unacceptable, and they left the main force and sailed direct to the Holy Land.

On 24 June the main army disembarked at Chalcedon, opposite Constantinople. They crossed the Bosporus from Scutari, stormed Galata on 6 July, and then marched alongside the Golden Horn. The Venetians, meanwhile, prepared to attack the city from the sea. On 17 July, following a general assault, Alexius III fled and Isaac was released.

The young Alexius IV, crowned co-emperor with his father, tried to meet his obligations to his allies, who remained camped just outside the city walls. The clergy and people of Constantinople, however, resented the terms of the agreement and the presence of the crusaders, and anti-western feelings exploded in riots and street fighting. In January 1204,

Alexius IV and his father were deposed and murdered. The new emperor Alexius V was overtly anti-western. The crusaders, isolated and increasingly threatened, decided to take Constantinople for themselves. In March, the crusaders and the Venetians signed a treaty which dismembered the Byzantine empire and divided the spoils. By 15 April, after three days of terrible pillaging, the city was theirs. Count Baldwin of Flanders was crowned the first Latin emperor of Constantinople in the cathedral of St Sophia, and most of southern Greece was conquered during the following winter.

> **W**hen the victors were eagerly looting the conquered city, Abbot Martin made for a church which was held in great veneration... He found there an old man... The abbot shouted fiercely at him: 'Come now, you perfidious old man, show me where you keep the more potent relics you have or rest assured that you will be punished at once with the penalty of death'... Then the old man opened an iron chest... When the abbot saw it he swiftly and avidly plunged in both hands and he and the chaplain, briskly tucking up their habits, filled the folds with holy sacrilege... As he hurried to the ships, he was seen by those who knew him. They asked him joyfully whether he had carried anything off. He answered with a smiling face, as usual, and merry words, 'We have done well'. To which they replied, 'Thanks be to God'.
>
> Gunther of Pairis describes the sack of Constantinople

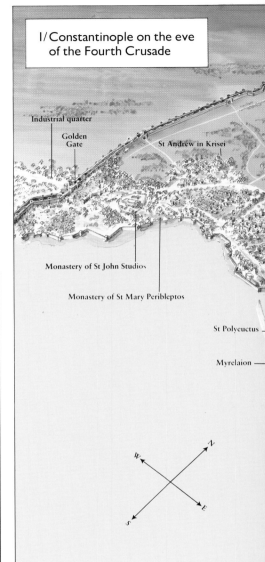

1/ Constantinople on the eve of the Fourth Crusade

Industrial quarter
Golden Gate
St Andrew in Krisei
Monastery of St John Studios
Monastery of St Mary Peribleptos
St Polyeuctus
Myrelaion

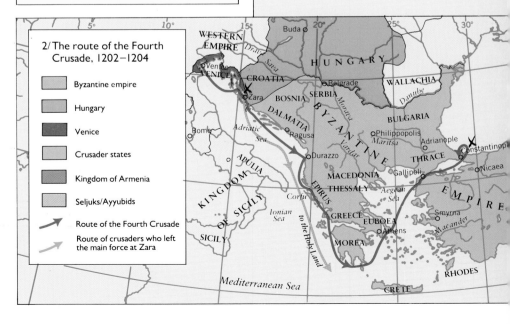

2/ The route of the Fourth Crusade, 1202–1204

- Byzantine empire
- Hungary
- Venice
- Crusader states
- Kingdom of Armenia
- Seljuks/Ayyubids
- ⟶ Route of the Fourth Crusade
- ⟶ Route of crusaders who left the main force at Zara

WESTERN EMPIRE
Buda
HUNGARY
Drau
Sava
VENICE
CROATIA
Belgrade
WALLACHIA
Zara
BOSNIA
SERBIA
Danube
DALMATIA
BYZANTINE
BULGARIA
Rome
Adriatic Sea
Ragusa
Morava
Philippopolis
Maritsa
Adrianople
Constantinople
Durazzo
THRACE
Nicaea
APULIA
MACEDONIA
Gallipoli
KINGDOM
EPIRUS
THESSALY
Aegean Sea
EMPIRE
Corfu
Smyrna
Ionian Sea
GREECE
EUBOEA
Maeander
OF SICILY
Athens
SICILY
MOREA
RHODES
Mediterranean Sea
CRETE
to the Holy Land

Land walls of Theodosius

Crusader camp 1203-1204

17 July 1203 Crusaders attack by land

Christ in Chora

Blachernae Palace

Cistern of Aetius

Cistern of St Mokius

Cistern of Aspar

Crusaders 8 and 12 April 1204

Land walls of Constantine

17 July 1203 Venetians

Monastery of Constantine Lips

Forum of Arcadius

Church of Christ Euergetes

Monastery of Christ Pantepoptes

attack by sea

Forum Bovis

Church of the Holy Apostles

Monastery of Christ Pantokrator

Aqueduct of Valens

GALATA

Golden Horn

Harbour of Eleutherion

GENOESE QUARTER

July 1203

Galata Tower

Forum of Theodosius

Mosque

Chain

New Harbour

6 July 1203 Crusaders take Galata and break chain across Golden Horn

Forum of Constantine

Bosporus

VENETIAN QUARTER

AMALFITAN QUARTER

St Mary of the Coppersmiths

Hippodrome

PISAN QUARTER

Sts Sergius and Bacchus

GENOESE QUARTER

Great Palace

Bucoleon Palace and imperial landing stage

Lighthouse

Sea walls

Nea Ekklesia (New Church)

Augusteum

Cathedral of St Sophia

St Irene

Acropolis

Orphanage of St Paul

St George in Mangana

Sea of Marmara

35°

45°

Black Sea

Sinope

Halys

40°

SELJUKS OF RUM

Adana

Aleppo

Antioch

Oronte

35°

CYPRUS

Latin Greece

The Fourth Crusade led to the establishment of new crusader states in Greece; but their existence was always insecure.

Once Constantinople had fallen to the crusaders (▶ *page 84*), much of the Byzantine empire was partitioned into new crusader states. The territories around Constantinople itself, on both the European and Asiatic sides of the Bosporus, were controlled by the Latin emperors of the houses of Flanders and Courtenay. Around the northern Aegean as far as Athens, there was a new, Latin 'kingdom' of Thessalonica. And in the Morea, Geoffrey of Villehardouin established what was to be the most permanent of the crusader states in Greece, the principality of Achaea.

The Villehardouin family, who were technically vassals of the Latin emperor at Constantinople, maintained a brilliant chivalric court at Andravida. Their predominantly agrarian crusader state was run on feudal lines that closely paralleled those of the kingdom of Jerusalem (▶ *page 36*). The prince had his own domain, which was administered through the feudal assizes, or law code. His chief vassals in the Morea were the high barons (including the archbishop of Patras), ensconced in their powerful and often spectacular castles. The Military Orders – the Templars, Hospitallers and Teutonic Knights – held lands as well. Latin settlement was concentrated around the coasts and on the larger islands. The settlers confined themselves to the towns and the castles, and scarcely occupied the countryside. In some of these Latin centres, archbishoprics, bishoprics and abbeys were established. But the Latin bishops were often absentee, and the bulk of the population remained loyal to the Greek Orthodox church.

The prince of Achaea was also the overlord of other Latin rulers beyond the Morea itself, including the lords of Thebes and Athens, the dukes of Archipelago and the Orsini family of Cephalonia. But Latin rule in Greece was never secure. From the start, it was compromised by concessions made to the Venetians in return for their support during the Fourth Crusade. The Venetians controlled a large part of Constantinople itself; they held the strategic naval bases of Modon and Coron; and in Crete, which they occupied from 1212, they set up a colonial regime with Italian settlers. Elsewhere they avoided the administrative and defensive costs of direct rule: Naxos and the surrounding islands were held by the Venetian Sanudo family - the dukes of Archipelago - as a fief of the princes of Achaea. Venice also exercised an overlordship in Negroponte.

Another check on the power of the crusader states came from the surviving outposts of Byzantine rule in Nicaea and Epirus. The despotate of Epirus conquered the Latin kingdom of Thessalonica in 1224. The Bulgarians, who were allied to the crusaders, took it in 1230, but by 1246 Thessalonica had been swallowed up by the empire of Nicaea. This was now the emergent power in the region; by 1235 it had taken all the Latin territories on the Asiatic side of the Bosporus. In 1259, the Nicaean emperor Michael Palaeologus defeated William of Villehardouin at the battle of Pelagonia. William and many of his lords were taken prisoner, and in 1261 he was forced to surrender the strongholds of Monemvasia, Maina and Mistra to Michael as part of his ransom. That same year, Michael recaptured Constantinople and re-established the Byzantine empire.

The principality of Achaea survived, but on William's death in 1275 it passed to his son-in-law Philip of Anjou. He was the son of Charles I of Naples, and from then on the principality was governed from Italy.

> ld Sir Nicholas de St-Omer, because he was a great and noble man and had a lot of money...came and took the princess of Morea as his wedded wife... With his great wealth and dominions which he held, he constructed the castle of St-Omer which was in Thebes and he built this castle to be an extremely strong one; he made dwellings within it fit for a basileus [emperor]. Indeed, he built it and constructed it and inside he covered its walls with murals depicting how the Franks conquered Syria.
>
> *The Chronicle of the Morea*

Clermont Castle, illustrated below, is situated 37 miles (60km) south-west of Patras. It was built in *c*.1205, immediately after the Latin conquest, by Prince Geoffrey I of Villehardouin. The castle overlooked the sea near the administrative capital at Glarentsa and the court of the Villehardouins at Andravida. A hexagonal inner keep, with great vaulted halls, provided extensive living accommodation. The large outer courtyard provided a first line of defence.

3/ The crusader castle at Clermont

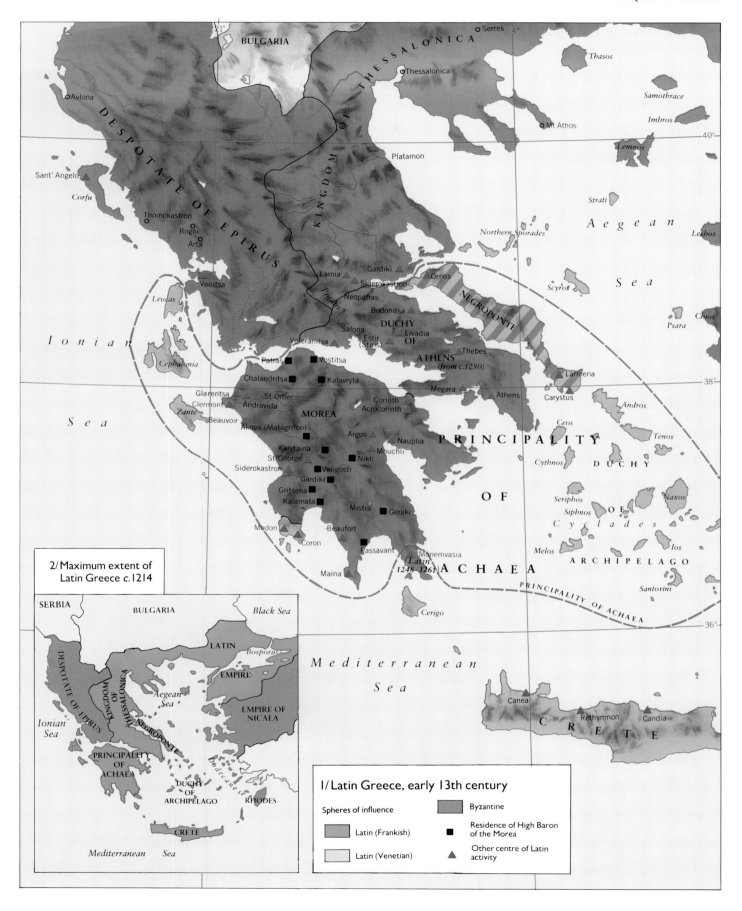

2/ Maximum extent of Latin Greece *c.*1214

SERBIA

BULGARIA

Black Sea

DESPOTATE OF EPIRUS

KINGDOM OF THESSALONICA

Bosporus

LATIN EMPIRE

Aegean Sea

EMPIRE OF NICAEA

Ionian Sea

NEGROPONTE

PRINCIPALITY OF ACHAEA

Dodecanese

DUCHY OF ARCHIPELAGO

RHODES

CRETE

Mediterranean   Sea

1/ Latin Greece, early 13th century

Spheres of influence

Latin (Frankish)

Latin (Venetian)

Byzantine

■ Residence of High Baron of the Morea

▲ Other centre of Latin activity

BULGARIA

○ Serres

○ Thessalonica

KINGDOM OF THESSALONICA

○ Avlona

Thasos

Samothrace

Imbros

DESPOTATE OF EPIRUS

Sant' Angelo ▲

Corfu

Thomokastron ○

Rogoi ○

Arta ○

● Mt Athos

Platamon

40°

Lemnos

Strati

A e g e a n

Lesbos

Vonitsa

Leucas

Lamia

Gardiki ▲

Siderokastron

Neopatras

Oreos

NEGROPONTE

Scyros

Northern Sporades

Chios

Psara

S e a

I o n i a n

Cephalonia

Bodonitsa ▲

Salona

Veteranitsa ▲

Estir (Stiris) ▲

DUCHY OF ATHENS *(from c.1280)*

Livadia

Thebes

Patras ■

Vostitsa ■

Chalandritsa ■

Kalavryta ■

Larmena ▲

38°

S e a

Glarentsa ▲

Zante

Clermont

St Omer ▲

Andravida

MOREA

Megara

Athens

Carystus

Andros

Beauvoir

Akova (Matagrifon) ■

Corinth ▲

Acrocorinth

Ceos

Tenos

St George ▲

Karytaina ■

Argos ▲

Nauplia

Mbuchli

PRINCIPALITY

Cythnos

DUCHY

Siderokastron ▲

Nikli ■

Veligosti ■

Gardiki ■

Gritsena ■

Kalamata ■

Mistra

Geraki ■

OF

Seriphos

Siphnos

OF

Naxos

Modon ▲

Coron

Beaufort

Passavant ■

Maina

Monemvasia *(Latin 1248–1261)*

ACHAEA

Melos

Ios

C y c l a d e s

ARCHIPELAGO

Santorini

PRINCIPALITY OF ACHAEA

36°

Cerigo

M e d i t e r r a n e a n

S e a

Canea ▲

C R E T E

Rethymnon ▲

Candia ▲

Mobilization in England and Wales

England has a wealth of church and state records to show how crusades were mobilized and what impact they had on society at home.

English crusaders were prominent in the Third Crusade under Richard I (▶*page 62*); in the crusade of 1227 led by the bishops of Winchester and Exeter; and in Richard, earl of Cornwall's crusade of 1240 (▶*page 98*). A contingent under William Longsword joined St Louis in Egypt in 1250, and many crusaders followed the future Edward I to the Holy Land in 1270-1272 (▶*page 96*). Throughout the period, the resources of the English crown were mobilized in the cause of crusading; among the many who took the cross were the kings Richard I, John, Henry III and Edward I.

The northern recruitment for the 1270 expedition shows that contingents were formed out of the existing social bonds of lordship, vassalage, tenure, kinship and neighbourhood. When such bonds were absent, as happened with the fleets of 1147, 1189, 1190 and 1217, association was sworn. To bind men to a leader who was not necessarily their lord for lengthy service abroad, written contracts were developed by the time of Richard of Cornwall's crusade of 1240.

England supplied money as well as men. Richard I raised huge sums through a special crusade tax, the Saladin Tithe; wealthy individuals put their fortunes at the service of crusading; and vow redemption, legacies, gifts and church tithes all swelled the coffers. Funds were also raised by carefully organized preaching, such as the tour of Wales conducted by Baldwin, archbishop of Canterbury in 1188, and the campaign of Archbishop Romeyn, who instructed 35 Franciscan and Dominican friars to preach the cross simultaneously, at specified locations in the diocese of York, on 14 September 1291.

By the end of the 13th century the crusade had become an established feature of English religious life, with regular appeals for money, special services, processions and prayers built into the liturgy, frequent grants of indulgences and taxation and the near permanent presence in many parish churches of collection chests for the crusades. Crusading also affected English politics; during the civil wars of 1215-1217 and 1264-1265, both sides sought to depict their causes as crusades.

There was a more sinister side to the English experience. Wives and widows of crusaders were assaulted and even killed in attempts to appropriate their husband's property. Moneylenders, especially the monasteries, accumulated estates at the expense of crusaders who had sold or mortgaged land to raise money for the journey. And in Lent 1190, anti-Jewish massacres spread north from London to Stamford and King's Lynn, culminating in the hideous butchery of the Jewish community in York, ushering in a century of persecution.

The chapel of the Holy Sepulchre, Winchester Cathedral, which was redecorated *c*.1220-1230, with scenes depicting incidents of Christ's life on earth. The Holy Sepulchre in Jerusalem (▶*page 46*) is depicted in the Entombment of Christ. The frescoes were perhaps painted on the order of Bishop Peter des Roches of Winchester (1204-1238) who crusaded with Frederick II, 1227-1231 (▶*page 98*).

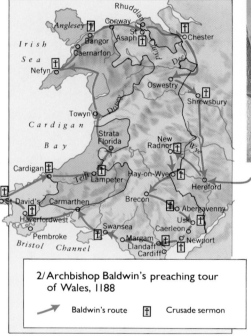

2/ Archbishop Baldwin's preaching tour of Wales, 1188

→ Baldwin's route   ✝ Crusade sermon

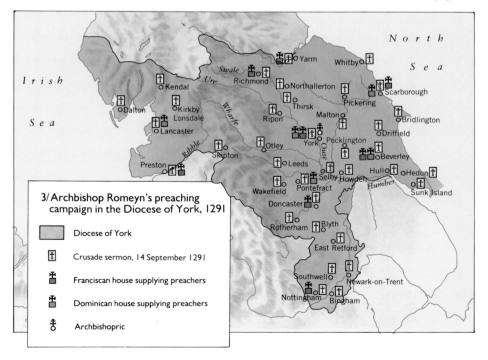

3/ Archbishop Romeyn's preaching campaign in the Diocese of York, 1291

▢ Diocese of York

✝ Crusade sermon, 14 September 1291

✠ Franciscan house supplying preachers

✠ Dominican house supplying preachers

✟ Archbishopric

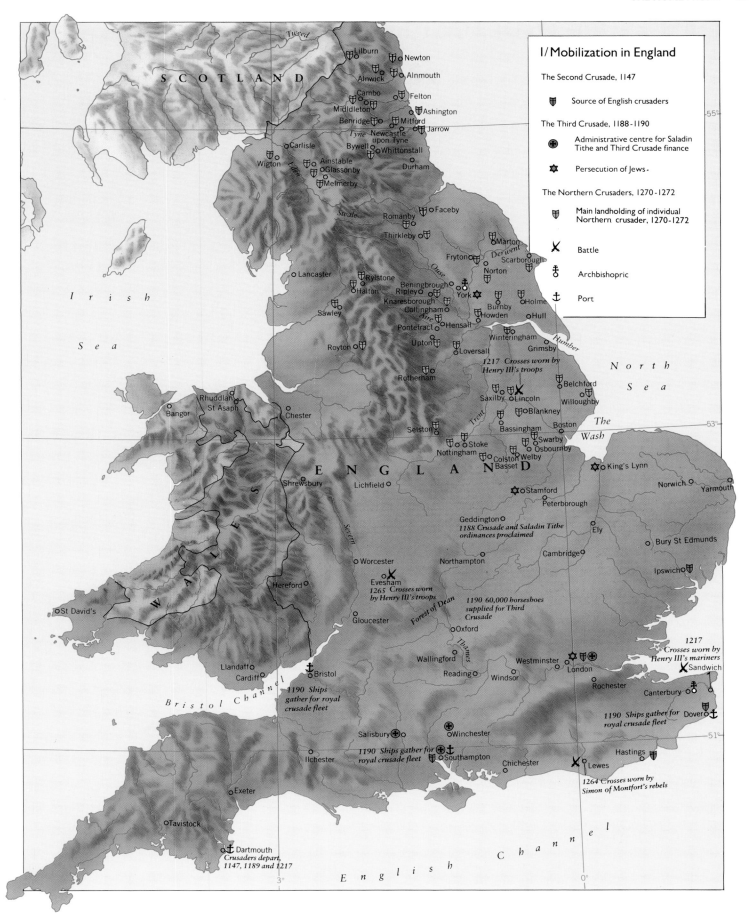

SCOTLAND

Tweed

Lilburn
Newton
Alnwick
Alnmouth
Cambo
Felton
Middleton
Ashington
Benridge
Mitford
Tyne
Jarrow
Whittonstall
Newcastle
upon Tyne
Carlisle
Bywell
Wigton
Eden
Ainstable
Glassonby
Durham
Melmerby

Swale
Romanby
Faceby
Thirkleby

Marton
Fryton
Derwent
Lancaster
Scarborough
Ouse
Norton
Rylstone
Beningbrough
Halton
York
Holme
Knaresborough
Burnby
Sawley
Collingham
Howden
Hull
Aire
Hensall
Pontefract
Royton
Upton
Winteringham
Humber
Loversall
Grimsby
1217 Crosses worn by
Henry III's troops
Rotherham
Belchford
Saxilby Lincoln
Willoughby

I r i s h

S e a

N o r t h

S e a

Rhuddlan
St Asaph
Blankney
Bangor
Chester
Trent
Bassingham
Boston
Selston
Swarby The
Stoke
Osbournby Wash
Nottingham
Colston Welby
Basset
E N G L A N D
King's Lynn
Shrewsbury
Lichfield
Norwich
Yarmouth
Stamford
Peterborough
Geddington
Ely
Bury St Edmunds
1188 Crusade and Saladin Tithe
ordinances proclaimed
Cambridge
Ipswich
W A L E S
Worcester
Northampton
Severn
Evesham
1265 Crosses worn
by Henry III's troops
Hereford
Forest of Dean
1190 60,000 horseshoes
supplied for Third
Crusade
St David's
Gloucester
Oxford
Thames
1217
Crosses worn by
Henry III's mariners
Wallingford
Westminster
Llandaff
Reading
London
Sandwich
Cardiff
Windsor
Bristol
Rochester
1190 Ships gather
for royal crusade fleet
Canterbury
1190 Ships gather for
royal crusade fleet
Dover
Salisbury
Winchester
Ilchester
Hastings
1190 Ships gather for
royal crusade fleet
Southampton
Chichester
Lewes
1264 Crosses worn by
Simon of Montfort's rebels
Exeter

B r i s t o l   C h a n n e l

Tavistock
Dartmouth
Crusaders depart,
1147, 1189 and 1217

E n g l i s h   C h a n n e l

1/Mobilization in England

The Second Crusade, 1147

Source of English crusaders

The Third Crusade, 1188-1190

Administrative centre for Saladin
Tithe and Third Crusade finance

Persecution of Jews.

The Northern Crusaders, 1270-1272

Main landholding of individual
Northern crusader, 1270-1272

Battle

Archbishopric

Port

The Resources of the Military Orders

The Military Orders had extensive holdings in Western Europe; these provided the money, supplies and manpower essential to their role in the Holy Land.

As the Military Orders assumed an important role in the defence of the Latin East (▶ *page 52*), they acquired property throughout Western Europe. The income it provided financed the Orders' operations in the East. From their headquarters in the kingdom of Jerusalem, the Grand Masters of the Templars, the Hospitallers and the Teutonic Knights each presided over a three-tier organizational structure. At the top was the headquarters itself, where the Grand Master was assisted by groups of officials, some of whom had their counterparts in secular courts: the leading military official, for example, was the marshal (▶ *page 36*). The majority of the remaining brothers were western knights. The majority of Templars and Hospitallers sent to the East came from France, where these Orders had the most property; Germany was the Teutonic Knights' main source of revenues and manpower.

The next tier down consisted of the European provinces (the Hospital used the term priory), which were governed by provincial masters (or priors). Templar and Hospitaller provinces were normally obliged to send a third of their revenues to the East annually, besides supplying brethren. Payments were often in kind.

Within each province were a considerable number of convents, or religious houses, which formed the bottom tier of the organizational structure. They were primarily administrative centres, usually staffed by a handful of brethren. Most convents were for brothers, but several Military Orders had some houses for sisters. Heads of male convents were usually called commanders or *preceptors*. Assisted by a chamberlain or *claviger*, they were responsible for the administration of the Order's properties in their district and paid a proportion of the income from these to the province or priory of which they were a part. Apart from the Grand Master, who was elected, officials were imposed from above. Chapters were held at each level – conventual chapters met weekly, provincial ones annually – and officials were obliged to seek counsel or consent on certain issues; but chapters often had no seal of their own, and in practice officials enjoyed considerable freedom of

action. Because of distance, Grand Masters could not closely supervise Western provinces, so brothers – called 'masters *deça mar*', 'grand commanders' or 'visitors' – were delegated to represent the Grand Master in the West.

2/ Hospitaller priory of England, 13th century
- ■ Priory headquarters
- ■ House of Hospitaller brethren
- ■ House of Hospitaller sisters

The crypt of the 12th-century church of the Hospitaller priory of England at Clerkenwell, London (right). The priory was the administrative centre of all Hospitaller commanderies in England, Wales and Scotland.

> **I** tem, it is decreed that every prior beyond the sea [in the West] should have a register, which he should keep in his treasury, in which register should be entered all the rents, lands, vines and meadows. Every commander should receive from the prior that part of the register which relates to his commandery.
>
> **Hospitaller statutes decreed by a general chapter held in Palestine in 1242**

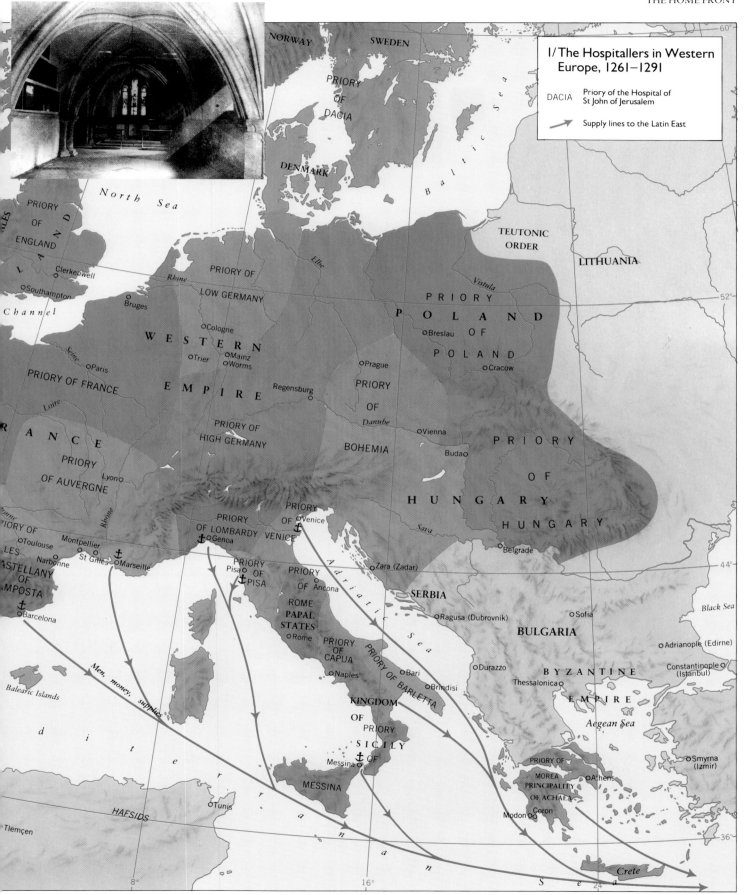

NORWAY

SWEDEN

PRIORY OF DACIA

Baltic Sea

DENMARK

TEUTONIC ORDER

LITHUANIA

North Sea

PRIORY OF ENGLAND

Clerkenwell

Southampton

Rhine

Bruges

PRIORY OF LOW GERMANY

Elbe

Cologne

PRIORY OF POLAND

Breslau

Vistula

Channel

Seine

Paris

WESTERN

Trier

Mainz
Worms

Prague

Cracow

PRIORY OF FRANCE

Loire

Regensburg

EMPIRE

PRIORY OF

PRIORY OF HIGH GERMANY

Danube

BOHEMIA

Vienna

Budao

PRIORY

F R A N C E

PRIORY OF AUVERGNE

Lyon

Rhône

OF

HUNGARY

HUNGARY

PRIORY OF

PRIORY OF LOMBARDY

PRIORY OF VENICE

Venice

Genoa

Sava

Belgrade

Toulouse

Montpellier

St Gilles

Narbonne

Marseille

Pisa

PRIORY OF PISA

PRIORY OF ANCONA

Ancona

Adriatic

Zara (Zadar)

SERBIA

Black Sea

CASTELLANY OF AMPOSTA

Barcelona

ROME
PAPAL
STATES

Rome

PRIORY OF CAPUA

Ragusa (Dubrovnik)

Sofia

BULGARIA

Adrianople (Edirne)

Balearic Islands

Men, money, supplies

Naples

PRIORY OF BARLETTA

Bari

Brindisi

Durazzo

Thessalonica

BYZANTINE

Constantinople (Istanbul)

d

i

t

e

KINGDOM

OF

PRIORY OF

SICILY

OF

Messina

MESSINA

r

r

a

Tunis

HAFSIDS

Tlemçen

n

e

a

n

16°

PRIORY OF

MOREA
PRINCIPALITY
OF ACHAEA

Modon
Coron

EMPIRE

Aegean Sea

Smyrna
(Izmir)

Athens

Sea

Crete

24

60°

52°

44°

36°

8°

Mobilization in France

The crusade led by St Louis in 1248 took years of preparation. But it was probably the best-equipped and best-supplied crusade ever to journey to the East.

After taking vows in December 1244, Louis IX spent nearly four gruelling years preparing a crusade to recover Jerusalem (▶ *page 96*). Recruiting began in early 1245. The efforts of local preachers and prelates, and Louis's own influence, induced many of the great lords of France to take the cross, including Louis's brothers Robert of Artois, Charles of Anjou and Alphonse of Poitiers, and magnates like Counts John of Montfort and Peter of Vendôme. Where such men led, others followed through lordship, kinship and neighbourhood bonds, helping to explain the geographical pattern of recruitment.

The raising of an army was only the beginning. In 1246 Louis contracted for 36 ships of Genoa and Marseille to transport his force. His agents began to purchase all manner of supplies and stores, much of which was sent ahead to Cyprus. Aigues-Mortes, chosen for embarkation, was rapidly converted from a sleepy fishing village into a major royal port and arsenal. These, and other preparations were hugely expensive; further charges were incurred by Louis's commitment to subsidize, through contracts and loans, perhaps half of the crusaders who were to accompany him to the East. The cost of the crusade to the French crown was later estimated at 1,537,570 *livres tournois*.

Louis's average annual income was only *c*.250,000 *l.t.* To meet costs, he sharply reduced expenditure, took measures to exploit the royal domain more intensively, and resorted to various expedients to raise cash, but he also decided to look elsewhere. Despite grumblings, the French church paid a tenth of ecclesiastical revenues for five years: some 950,000 *l.t.* were raised as a result, covering two thirds of Louis's expenses. The towns of the royal domain, including those in Normandy and Languedoc, however large or small, were squeezed, some making two, even three, grants to the king. Municipal grants perhaps totalled *c*.274,000 *l.t.* From 1245 to 1248, Louis toured the royal domain, a journey that was at least in part connected with the need to raise funds for his crusade. Remarkably, he remained solvent for four of his five years in the East, a measure of his foresight and determination.

T o have perfect joy in paradise
I must leave the land I love so much,
Where she lives whom I thank every day.
Her body is noble and spirited, her face
fresh and lovely...
And my true heart surrenders all to her.
But my body must take its leave of her;
I am departing for the place where God
suffered death
To ransom us on a Friday...
No more than a child can endure hunger –
And no one can chastise him for crying
because of it –
Do I believe that I can stay away
From you, whom I am used to kiss and to
embrace,
Nor have I in me such power of abstinence.
A hundred times a night I shall recall your
beauty:
It gave me such pleasure to hold your body!
When I no longer have it I shall die of
desire...
Beautiful Isabel, I commend you to God's
will.
I cannot stay with you any longer;
Into the land of the paynim, to a race of
unbelievers
I must go for the love of God.
I am going there with the good intention of
saving my soul;
But remember well, beautiful and noble
love,
That if anyone ever died for loving loyally
I do not think I will survive even as far as
the seaport.

Por joie avoir perfite en paradis – Anon.
A typical crusader song

2/ The currency of medieval France

Several different currencies, based on different weight standards, circulated side by side in medieval France. The reason for this lay in the feudal origins of the coinage; a number of princes, dukes and bishops exercised the right to mint coins.

The regal coinage only gradually came to dominate these rivals. It was struck by the king not in his capacity as ruler of France, but as the count of Tours, Paris or Sens. The pound of Paris (*livre parisis*) was worth more than the pound of Tours (*livre tournois*).

The pound was purely an accounting unit; the highest value coin struck by St Louis at the beginning of his reign was the silver *denier*, of which there were 240 to the pound. The *denier parisis* (1) was therefore a larger coin than the *denier tournois* (2), which could be identified by its symbolic representation of the castle of Tours.

In 1266, St Louis introduced two higher value denominations, the *gros tournois* (3), worth 12 *deniers tournois*, and the gold *écu*.

A contemporary illumination of Louis IX, with his mother Blanche of Castile, queen of France. Blanche played a crucial role as Louis's regent in France during his crusade absence. She was also a domineering mother who exerted great influence upon Louis.

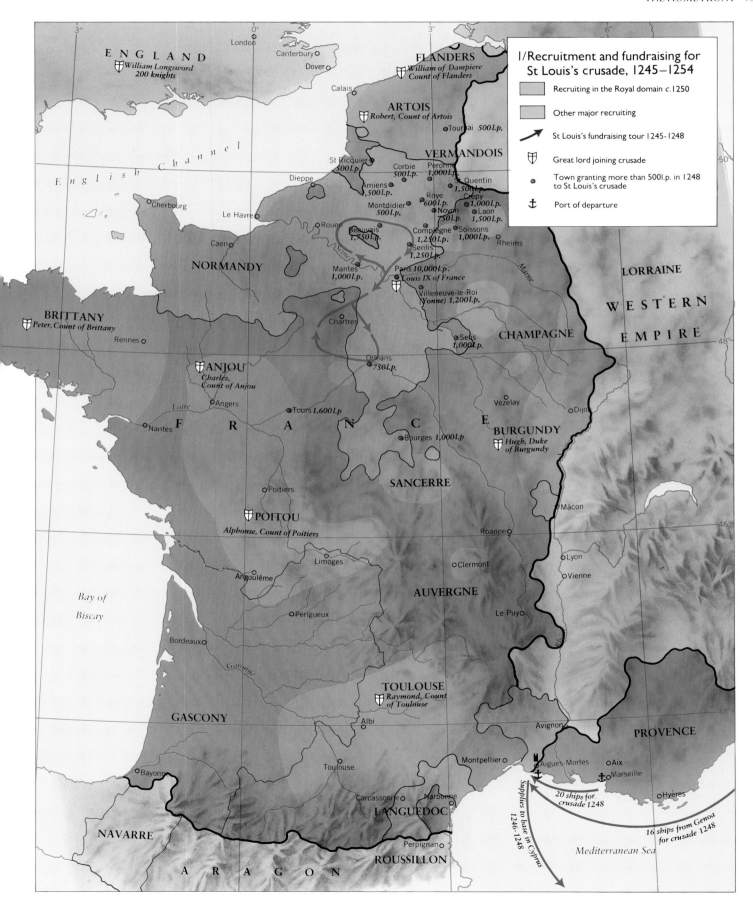

ENGLAND
London
William Longsword
200 knights

Canterbury
Dover
Calais

FLANDERS
William of Dampiere
Count of Flanders

ARTOIS
Robert, Count of Artois

Tournai 500 l.p.

VERMANDOIS

St Ricquier
500 l.p.

Corbie
500 l.p.

Peronne
1,000 l.p.

Quentin

Dieppe

Amiens
1,500 l.p.

Roye
600 l.p.

Crepy
1,500 l.p.

Cherbourg

Montdidier
500 l.p.

Noyon
750 l.p.

1,000 l.p.

Laon
1,500 l.p.

Le Havre

Rouen

Beauvais
1,750 l.p.

Compiegne
1,250 l.p.

Soissons
1,000 l.p.

Caen

Senlis
1,250 l.p.

Rheims

NORMANDY

Mantes
1,000 l.p.

Paris 10,000 l.p.
Louis IX of France

Villeneuve-le-Roi
(Yonne) 1,200 l.p.

LORRAINE

WESTERN

Chartres

BRITTANY
Peter, Count of Brittany

Rennes

ANJOU
Charles,
Count of Anjou

Orleans
750 l.p.

Sens
1,000 l.p.

CHAMPAGNE

EMPIRE

Angers

Tours 1,600 l.p.

Vézelay

Dijon

Nantes

F   R   A   N   C   E

Bourges 1,000 l.p.

BURGUNDY
Hugh, Duke
of Burgundy

Poitiers

SANCERRE

Mâcon

POITOU
Alphonse, Count of Poitiers

Roanne

Lyon

Limoges

Clermont

Vienne

Angoulême

AUVERGNE

Bay of
Biscay

Périgueux

Le Puy

Bordeaux

GASCONY

TOULOUSE
Raymond, Count
of Toulouse

Albi

Avignon

PROVENCE

Toulouse

Montpellier

Aigues-Mortes

Aix
Marseille

Bayonne

Carcassonne

Narbonne

LANGUEDOC

Hyères

NAVARRE

Supplies to base in Cyprus
1246-1248

20 ships for
crusade 1248

16 ships from Genoa
for crusade 1248

Perpignan

ROUSSILLON

Mediterranean Sea

A   R   A   G   O   N

English Channel

Loire

Seine

Marne

Garonne

**1/Recruitment and fundraising for
St Louis's crusade, 1245–1254**

Recruiting in the Royal domain c.1250

Other major recruiting

St Louis's fundraising tour 1245-1248

Great lord joining crusade

Town granting more than 500 l.p. in 1248
to St Louis's crusade

Port of departure

The Fifth Crusade

It was European commitment that made possible the most ambitious crusades of the 13th century. Their aim was to ensure the survival of the crusader states by conquering Egypt itself.

In the second decade of the 13th century, crusade enthusiasm was running high, but Jerusalem itself was still in Muslim hands. It was the great ambition of Pope Innocent III to recapture the Holy City; in April 1213 he called for a new crusade to the East, but he died in July 1216 before he could see his plans come to fruition.

Duke Leopold VI of Austria was the first ruler to depart, joined soon afterwards at Acre by King Andrew of Hungary, King Hugh I of Cyprus and by contingents from throughout the Western Empire. The crusaders spent the winter of 1217-1218 in Palestine, fighting small-scale operations against the Muslims. Some contingents were only signed up for a limited period, and the Christian forces were weakened when King Andrew left for home in January. But when reinforcements, including large fleets from northern Europe, arrived in the spring, the crusaders devised a bolder plan: the invasion of Egypt. In May 1218, they established a bridgehead on an island west of Damietta; in August, they captured a defensive tower in the Nile. Despite Egyptian counter-attacks, they succeeded in dredging an abandoned canal, allowing supplies and reinforcements to be brought in closer, and in November 1219 they finally took Damietta.

The Egyptian sultan al-Kamil offered to surrender the entire territory of the kingdom of Jerusalem (except for Transjordan) if the crusaders would evacuate Egypt. But the Christians were paralysed by a leadership conflict between John of Brienne (the king of Jerusalem) and the papal legate Pelagius of Albano. John wanted to accept the sultan's terms, but Pelagius refused. For 20 months Pelagius waited for the western emperor Frederick II, who never came (▶ *page 98*). Only an advance force under Duke Louis I of Bavaria had arrived when the general march south began in July 1221. Ignoring King John's advice, the crusaders halted opposite Mansurah, which had been heavily fortified while the crusaders delayed. The Egyptians blocked the supply lines from Damietta and broke the dykes to flood the surrounding land. The crusaders were doomed, and on 30 August they agreed to leave Egypt.

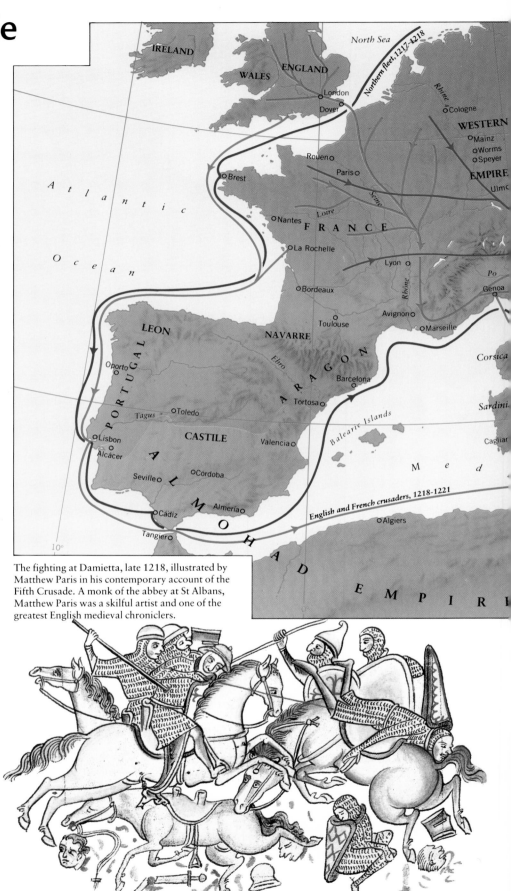

The fighting at Damietta, late 1218, illustrated by Matthew Paris in his contemporary account of the Fifth Crusade. A monk of the abbey at St Albans, Matthew Paris was a skilful artist and one of the greatest English medieval chroniclers.

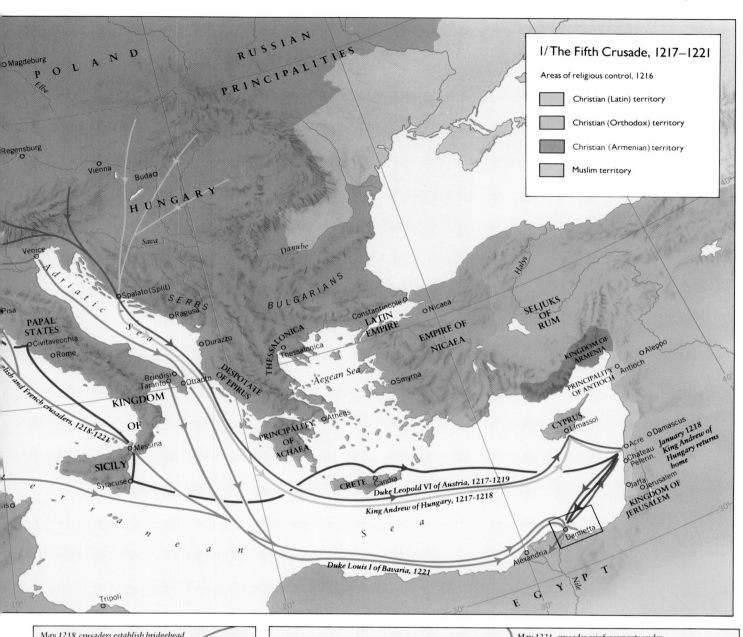

I/ The Fifth Crusade, 1217–1221

Areas of religious control, 1216

- Christian (Latin) territory
- Christian (Orthodox) territory
- Christian (Armenian) territory
- Muslim territory

POLAND

RUSSIAN

PRINCIPALITIES

Magdeburg

Elbe

Regensburg

Vienna

Buda

HUNGARY

Sava

Danube

Venice

Spalato (Split)

SERBS

Pisa

PAPAL STATES

Civitavecchia

Rome

Ragusa

Durazzo

BULGARIANS

Constantinople

LATIN EMPIRE

Nicaea

EMPIRE OF NICAEA

SELJUKS OF RUM

Halys

KINGDOM OF ARMENIA

Aleppo

English and French crusaders, 1218-1221

Brindisi

Taranto

Otranto

KINGDOM OF SICILY

Messina

Syracuse

DESPOTATE OF EPIRUS

THESSALONICA

Thessalonica

Aegean Sea

Smyrna

PRINCIPALITY OF ANTIOCH

Antioch

PRINCIPALITY OF ACHAEA

Athens

CYPRUS

Limassol

Acre

Chateau Pelerin

Damascus

January 1218 King Andrew of Hungary returns home

CRETE

Candia

Duke Leopold VI of Austria, 1217-1219

King Andrew of Hungary, 1217-1218

Jaffa

Jerusalem

KINGDOM OF JERUSALEM

Tripoli

Duke Louis I of Bavaria, 1221

Alexandria

Damietta

Nile

EGYPT

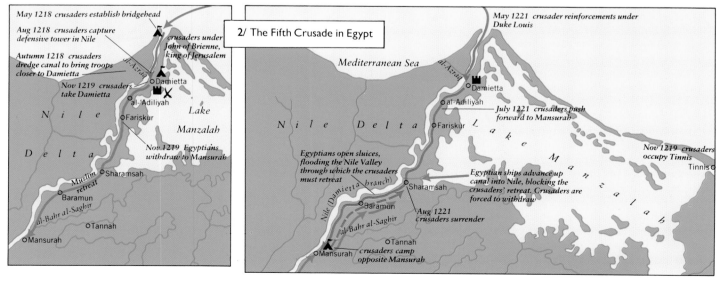

2/ The Fifth Crusade in Egypt

May 1218 crusaders establish bridgehead

Aug 1218 crusaders capture defensive tower in Nile

Autumn 1218 crusaders dredge canal to bring troops closer to Damietta

Nov 1219 crusaders take Damietta

crusaders under John of Brienne, king of Jerusalem

al-Azraq

Damietta

al-'Adiliyah

Fariskur

Nile Delta

Lake Manzalah

Nov 1219 Egyptians withdraw to Mansurah

Muslim retreat

Sharamsah

Baramun

al-Bahr al-Saghir

Tannah

Mansurah

May 1221 crusader reinforcements under Duke Louis

Mediterranean Sea

al-Azraq

Damietta

al-'Adiliyah

July 1221 crusaders push forward to Mansurah

Fariskur

Nile Delta

Lake Manzalah

Nov 1219 crusaders occupy Tinnis

Tinnis

Egyptians open sluices, flooding the Nile Valley through which the crusaders must retreat

Nile (Damietta branch)

Baramun

al-Bahr al-Saghir

Shatamsah

Egyptian ships advance up canal into Nile, blocking the crusaders' retreat. Crusaders are forced to withdraw

Aug 1221 crusaders surrender

Tannah

Mansurah

crusaders camp opposite Mansurah

The Crusades of St Louis

The two crusades of St Louis were disasters: on the first, his army was surrounded and he was made prisoner; the second ended when disease ravaged his knights and caused his own death at Tunis.

Despite the impressive French mobilization for St Louis's first crusade (▶ *page 92*), political rivalries in Western Europe minimized international support. As a result, his army of some 15,000 men, including about 2,500 knights, was recruited mainly from the French crown lands, Flanders, Champagne, Burgundy, Brittany and Poitou. This force was bolstered by small contingents from Lorraine, Italy and Scotland, and around 200 English knights.

Louis sailed from Aigues-Mortes on 25 August 1248 and landed at Limassol, Cyprus on 17 September. Here, the army gradually mustered, departing for Egypt the following May. On 6 June the crusaders took Damietta with minimal losses; this, however, was to prove their only real success. Following further reinforcement from France in October, they began their march towards Cairo on 20 November, down the Damietta branch of the Nile. While the crusaders were advancing, the Sultan al-Salih Ayyub (▶ *page 108*) died, and Egyptian morale collapsed.

The crusaders halted on the north bank of the al-Bahr al-Saghir, opposite Mansurah where the bulk of the Egyptian forces were positioned, but were unable to cross the waterway. Eventually a local revealed the existence of an unguarded ford downstream, and on 8 February 1250 the vanguard renewed the advance. After crossing the ford, however, Count Robert of Artois, Louis's brother, disobeyed instructions to wait and rashly led the vanguard to destruction in the narrow streets of Mansurah.

It was the turning-point: Egyptian morale recovered with the arrival at Mansurah of the new sultan, Turan Shah, and Louis's army had lost too many men to advance any further. Exposed, increasingly outnumbered, and ravaged by disease, they retreated halfway to Damietta. On 6 April, near Sharamsah, Louis was surrounded and forced to surrender. On payment of a huge ransom on 6 May, he sailed not for France but Acre, a measure of his remarkable commitment. Louis remained in the East for four years, effectively taking over the government, negotiating truces and massively fortifying Acre, Jaffa, Caesarea

Louis IX of France, on 5 June 1249, rides towards Damietta, which is defended by Muslim archers. The crusade fleet is in the background. From an illuminated manuscript painted in Acre shortly after 1277. This school of illuminators was probably founded by Louis himself during his stay in Palestine, 1250-1254.

and Sidon. On 24 April 1254 he finally left Acre, landing at Hyères in July.

Louis took the cross again on 24 March 1267. Once more he found that support beyond France was limited, consisting mainly of 300 English knights under Prince Edward of England, joined by a Frisian fleet in the Mediterranean and some Scots. Even his subjects' response was lukewarm this time; only around 10,000 men took part. Louis sailed from Aigues-Mortes on 2 July 1270 for the rendezvous at Cagliari, Sardinia, where he announced that Tunis was the target; news had reached him that the Emir Muhammad I of Tunis wanted to be baptized.

No sooner had the fleet landed outside Tunis on 18 July, than many of the crusaders were struck down by disease. On 25 August, Louis himself died. Louis's brother Charles of Anjou was now in effective command, and once he had secured a treaty beneficial to himself from Muhammad, the crusaders sailed for Sicily in November. The army rapidly disintegrated. Philip III, Louis's heir, bore his father's remains back to France. Of the other leaders, only Prince Edward proceeded to Acre, where he landed in May 1271. His brother Edmund joined him with reinforcements, but even then their forces were too limited to achieve much. After surviving an assassination attempt, Edward sailed home in September 1272.

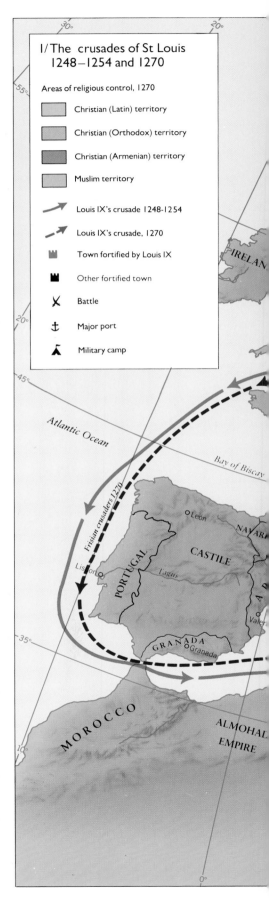

1/ The crusades of St Louis 1248–1254 and 1270

Areas of religious control, 1270

- Christian (Latin) territory
- Christian (Orthodox) territory
- Christian (Armenian) territory
- Muslim territory

→ Louis IX's crusade 1248-1254

↗ Louis IX's crusade, 1270

♜ Town fortified by Louis IX

♜ Other fortified town

✗ Battle

☩ Major port

⚐ Military camp

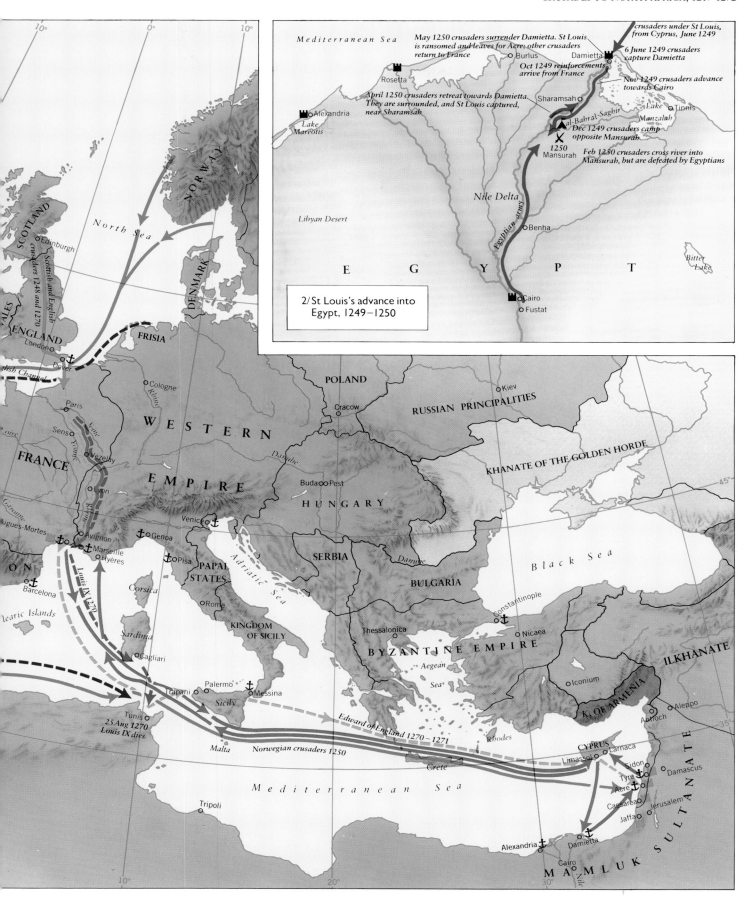

2/St Louis's advance into Egypt, 1249–1250

May 1250 crusaders surrender Damietta. St Louis is ransomed and leaves for Acre; other crusaders return to France

Oct 1249 reinforcements arrive from France

crusaders under St Louis, from Cyprus, June 1249

6 June 1249 crusaders capture Damietta

Nov 1249 crusaders advance towards Cairo

April 1250 crusaders retreat towards Damietta. They are surrounded, and St Louis captured, near Sharamsah

Dec 1249 crusaders camp opposite Mansurah

Feb 1250 crusaders cross river into Mansurah, but are defeated by Egyptians

Mediterranean Sea

Burlus

Rosetta

Damietta

Alexandria

Lake Mareotis

Sharamsah

al-Bahr-al-Saghir

Manzalah

Lake Tinnis

1250 Mansurah

Libyan Desert

Nile Delta

Benha

Bitter Lake

E G Y P T

Cairo

Fustat

SCOTLAND

Edinburgh

Scottish and English crusaders 1248 and 1270

North Sea

NORWAY

DENMARK

FRISIA

ENGLAND

London

Dover

English Channel

Cologne

Rhine

Paris

Sens

Vezelay

Yonne

WESTERN EMPIRE

POLAND

Cracow

Kiev

RUSSIAN PRINCIPALITIES

Danube

FRANCE

Lyon

Budapest

HUNGARY

KHANATE OF THE GOLDEN HORDE

Garonne

Aigues-Mortes

Avignon

Marseille

Hyères

Louis IX 1270

Genoa

Pisa

Venice

PAPAL STATES

Adriatic Sea

Danube

SERBIA

BULGARIA

Black Sea

Barcelona

Corsica

Rome

Balearic Islands

Sardinia

Cagliari

KINGDOM OF SICILY

Thessalonica

Constantinople

BYZANTINE EMPIRE

Nicaea

Aegean Sea

ILKHANATE

Iconium

K. OF ARMENIA

Aleppo

Trapani

Palermo

Messina

Sicily

Tunis

25 Aug 1270 Louis IX dies

Edward of England 1270–1271

Rhodes

Antioch

CYPRUS

Larnaca

Limassol

Malta

Norwegian crusaders 1250

Crete

Tyre

Sidon

Damascus

Acre

Caesarea

Jaffa

Jerusalem

Mediterranean Sea

Tripoli

Alexandria

Damietta

Cairo

Nile

MAMLUK SULTANATE

The Crusader States Revived

From the Third Crusade on, the Christians had held most of the Near Eastern coast; during the first half of the 13th century, they extended their control inland.

When Queen Yolande of Jerusalem died in 1228, her husband, the western emperor Frederick II, became regent on behalf of their son Conrad. Frederick, who had not fulfilled his pledge to join the Fifth Crusade in 1217, assembled a new crusade in 1227, but fell ill and was unable to depart. Excommunicated by the pope for delaying again, he finally set out in 1228, and the following year negotiated a treaty with the Egyptians which restored parts of Palestine, including the city of Jerusalem, to Christian control. These gains were extended by a crusade of 1239-1241, led by Count Thibald of Champagne and Earl Richard of Cornwall. Despite Thibald's defeat by the Egyptians at Gaza, the ensuing negotiations left the kingdom of Jerusalem controlling more territory than at any time since 1187.

The commercial importance of the ports of Acre (▶ *page 102*) and Tyre brought prosperity to the Europeans, who now lived almost entirely in the towns. The settlements in Palestine and Syria were no longer as isolated as they had been before 1187; crusader states now existed in Cyprus (▶ *page 62*) and Greece (▶ *page 86*), and relations developed with Cilician Armenia, which had now submitted to the papacy and was heavily influenced by western culture.

The close relations between the Christian settlements were fraught with tensions. The royal family of Armenia and the princes of Antioch were related by marriage. Each wanted their own candidate to inherit the principality of Antioch and, at the beginning of the 13th century, the Armenians launched a series of invasions in support of their candidate. In 1216 they briefly captured Antioch itself.

In the following decade, civil war broke out in Cyprus. Frederick II, the island's overlord, had entrusted its government to five Cypriot knights known as *baillis*. His chief antagonist, John of Beirut, invaded Cyprus in 1229. The struggle continued until John's victory in 1233, and spilled over onto the mainland.

The Christian states were well integrated in the Near East, engaging in trade and diplomacy with their Muslim neighbours. But an attempt to intervene in Muslim politics by allying with the prince of Damascus against the sultan in Egypt led to the loss of Jerusalem and the destruction of the Christian army by the Egyptians at La Forbie in 1244. And after 1250, a new, more aggressive Muslim power – the Mamluks – took control in Egypt (▶ *page 108*).

June 1232
John pursues imperial forces
and defeats them at Agridi

April 1233
John's forces take Kyrenia and
regain control of Cyprus

Kyrenia
St Hilarion
Agridi   Buffavento
Nicosia

July 1229 John defeats ba
1229-1230
John captures northern
castles and controls Cypru

Paphos

C Y P

Limassol

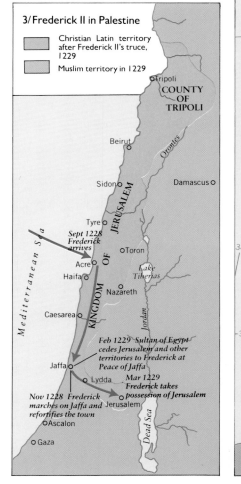

3/Frederick II in Palestine

- Christian Latin territory after Frederick II's truce, 1229
- Muslim territory in 1229

Tripoli
COUNTY OF TRIPOLI

Beirut

Sidon

Damascus

Tyre

Sept 1228
Frederick
arrives

Toron

Acre

Lake
Tiberias

Haifa

Nazareth

Caesarea

Feb 1229 Sultan of Egypt
cedes Jerusalem and other
territories to Frederick at
Peace of Jaffa

Jaffa

Lydda

Mar 1229
Frederick takes
possession of Jerusalem

Nov 1228 Frederick
marches on Jaffa and
refortifies the town

Jerusalem

Ascalon

Gaza

Dead Sea

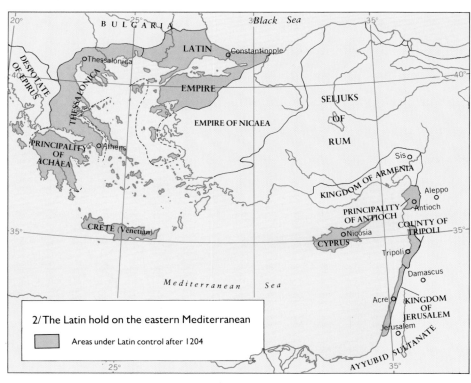

2/The Latin hold on the eastern Mediterranean

Areas under Latin control after 1204

BULGARIA

Black Sea

LATIN   Constantinople

Thessalonica

DESPOTATE OF EPIRUS

THESSALONICA

EMPIRE

EMPIRE OF NICAEA

SELJUKS
OF
RUM

PRINCIPALITY
OF
ACHAEA

Athens

Sis

KINGDOM OF ARMENIA

Aleppo

PRINCIPALITY
OF ANTIOCH

Antioch

CRETE (Venetian)

Nicosia

COUNTY OF
TRIPOLI

CYPRUS

Tripoli

Mediterranean   Sea

Damascus

Acre   KINGDOM
OF
JERUSALEM

Jerusalem

AYYUBID SULTANATE

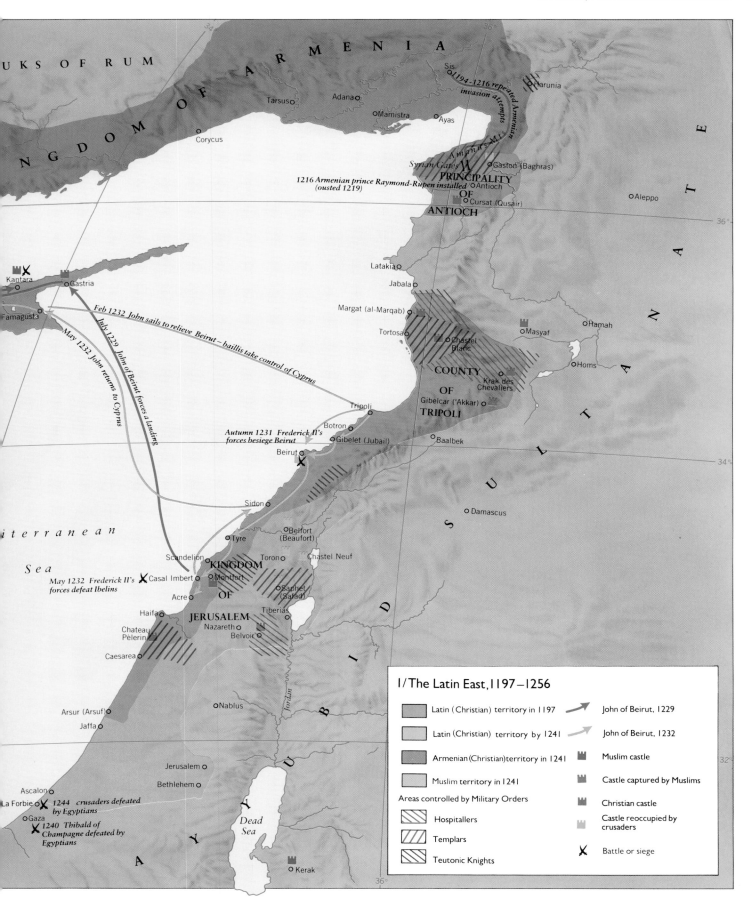

UKS OF RUM

NGDOM OF ARMENIA

Corycus

Tarsuso

Adana○

○Mamistra

Ayas○

Sis○ *1194-1216 repeated Armenian*
invasion attempts

○Harunia

Amanus Mts

Syrian Gates

Gaston (Baghras)○

1216 Armenian prince Raymond-Rupen installed   ○Antioch
(ousted 1219)

○Cursat (Qusair)

PRINCIPALITY OF ANTIOCH

○Aleppo

Latakia○

Jabala○

Margat (al-Marqab)○

Tortosa○

○Masyaf

○Hamah

Chastel Blanc

○Homs

COUNTY OF TRIPOLI

Krak des Chevaliers

Gibelcar ('Akkar)○

Feb 1232 John sails to relieve Beirut – baillis take control of Cyprus

July 1229 John of Beirut forces a landing

May 1232 John returns to Cyprus

Kantara✘

○Gastria

Famagusta○

Tripoli○

Botron○

Gibelet (Jubail)○

○Baalbek

Autumn 1231 Frederick II's
forces besiege Beirut

Beirut○✘

Sidon○

Belfort (Beaufort)○

○Damascus

iterranean

Sea

Scandelion○

Tyre○

Toron○

Chastel Neuf○

May 1232 Frederick II's
forces defeat Ibelins ✘ Casal Imbert

KINGDOM

Acre○

OF

Montfort□

Safhet (Safad)○

Tiberias○

Haifa○

JERUSALEM

Nazareth○

Belvoir○

Chateau Pèlerin○

Caesarea○

SULTANATE

Arsur (Arsuf)○

○Nablus

Jaffa○

AYUBID

Jordan

Jerusalem○

Bethlehem○

Ascalon○

La Forbie○✘ *1244 crusaders defeated*
by Egyptians

Gaza○✘

✘ *1240 Thibald of*
Champagne defeated by
Egyptians

Dead Sea

○Kerak

1/The Latin East, 1197–1256

Latin (Christian) territory in 1197   → John of Beirut, 1229

Latin (Christian) territory by 1241   → John of Beirut, 1232

Armenian (Christian) territory in 1241   ⬛ Muslim castle

Muslim territory in 1241   ⬛ Castle captured by Muslims

Areas controlled by Military Orders

▨ Hospitallers   ⬛ Christian castle

▨ Templars   ⬛ Castle reoccupied by crusaders

▨ Teutonic Knights   ✘ Battle or siege

The Carrying Trade

The crusader states depended on western merchant shipping for their revenues and communication with Europe. By 1150, these merchant fleets had turned the Mediterranean into a Christian-dominated sea.

The appearance of the Italians off the Syrian coast during the First Crusade (▶ *page 30*) had been a dramatic moment in a lengthy struggle against Islam that Pisa, Genoa and Venice had been conducting for a century and a half. In 1087 Pisan and Genoese forces, with papal approval, had gone to attack Mahdia in Tunisia, a focal point in the trade in African gold dust. After the First Crusade, Pisa attempted to conquer the Balearic Islands (1113-1115). The war for the recovery of Jerusalem, therefore, fitted in well with the Italians' military and economic expansion.

The Latin rulers in the Near East needed Italian help to conquer the maritime towns of Palestine. A grant to Genoa (1104) and a treaty with Venice (1123) provided examples of the powerful incentives offered to the Italians: a third of the conquered towns and some freedom from commercial taxes. The rulers often had second thoughts about such generosity, although the increased trade brought them other revenues. By 1200 the Italians were mainly concentrated in Acre and Tyre; they acted as intermediaries between western Europe and Islam, exporting armaments (to the horror of the Church), textiles and foodstuffs, and receiving medicaments, silks, pepper, cotton and sugar.

Acre and Tyre were the command centres for a network that extended to the fabled sources of spices in the Far East. However, from Alexandria in the south and Damascus in the east, the Christian merchants were excluded from direct participation in trade. By 1200 Muslim merchants known as the Karimis controlled the passage of spices from India to their native Egypt. But the rise of the Mongol empire (▶ *page 112*) created an alternative route for eastern luxury goods by way of the Black Sea and central Asia which flourished in the late 13th and 14th centuries.

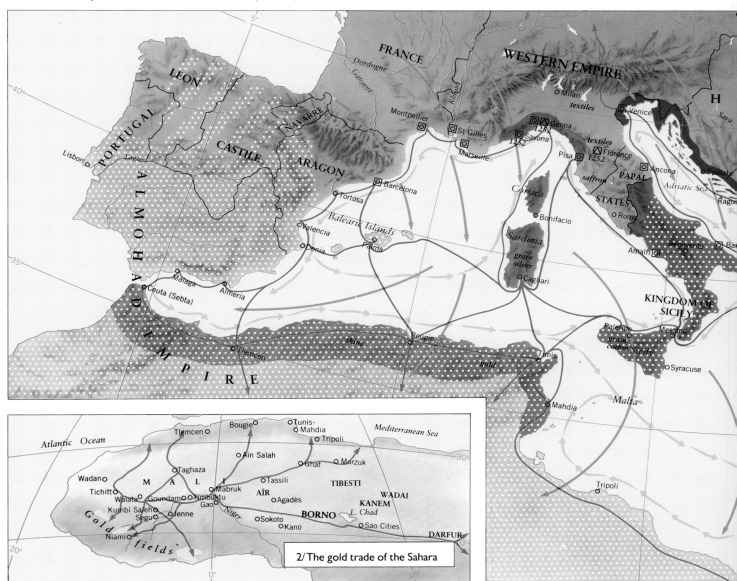

2/ The gold trade of the Sahara

Until the mid-13th century, the states of Western Europe relied upon silver for their coinage; gold was struck only in the Muslim world and the Byzantine empire. It was the Italian mercantile cities, at the forefront of Mediterranean trade, who led the way. The gold *fiorino* or florin took its name from Florence, where it was first produced in 1252 (1). Genoa followed the same year (2), and in 1284, under the doge Giovanni Dandolo, the Venetians introduced their gold ducat (3).

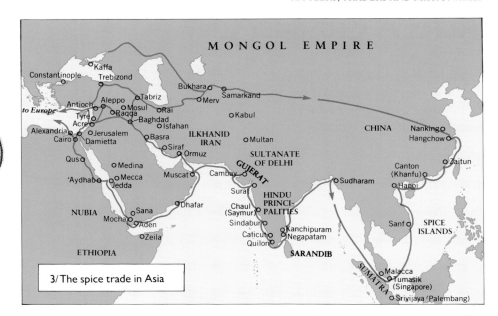

3/ The spice trade in Asia

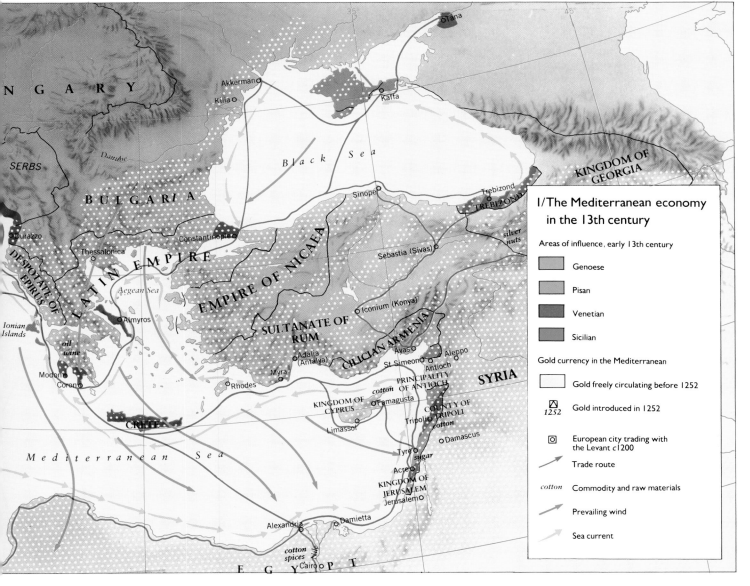

1/ The Mediterranean economy in the 13th century

Areas of influence, early 13th century

Genoese

Pisan

Venetian

Sicilian

Gold currency in the Mediterranean

Gold freely circulating before 1252

1252   Gold introduced in 1252

European city trading with the Levant c1200

Trade route

cotton   Commodity and raw materials

Prevailing wind

Sea current

Acre: A Crusader City

The bustling, cosmopolitan port of Acre was the largest city in the kingdom of Jerusalem. In the 13th century, it was also its capital.

Acre is situated on a low sandstone promontary at the northern end of a sandy bay. The city had developed in ancient times, and by the Islamic period was an important military shipyard and trading port. The original layout of the crusader city was dictated by the line of the old Muslim defences. In the first decade of the 13th century, however, the suburb of Montmusard was also enclosed and a second, outer wall was added to protect both parts of the city.

The harbour was far from ideal, but better than any further south. Large ships had to anchor outside; small boats then ferried goods and passengers to the wharfs. Merchandise was then taken to the Court of the Chain, which combined the functions of customs house, bonded warehouse and market. The main commercial street led – as it still does today – from the Chain quarter northeast to the main gates in the city walls. On either side of it, the merchants of Italy and Provence had their autonomous quarters. The rivalry between the Venetians and Genoese was so intense that open warfare erupted between them in 1256.

Royal authority was exercised by the king in person, or by his constable. The cathedral of the Holy Cross was the seat of the bishop of Acre; but after the loss of Jerusalem in 1187 (▶page 60) the patriarch of Jerusalem established himself in an adjacent quarter and in 1262 took over the see completely. Other cathedral chapters and religious houses from parts of the kingdom lost to the Muslims also settled in Acre in the 13th century, so that there were more than 60 church buildings in the city. Several Military Orders had their headquarters in Acre (▶page 106).

Despite the numbers of churches and churchmen and women in 13th-century Acre, the aspect of the city most forcefully evoked by writers such as Bishop James of Vitry (1216) and the Dominican Friar Burchard of Mount Sion (c.1283) is the level of vice and moral depravity. Its population were gathered from every part of Europe, and included a large criminal element as a result of the practice in western European courts of commuting sentences to settlement in the Holy Land, which became a kind of penal colony as a result.

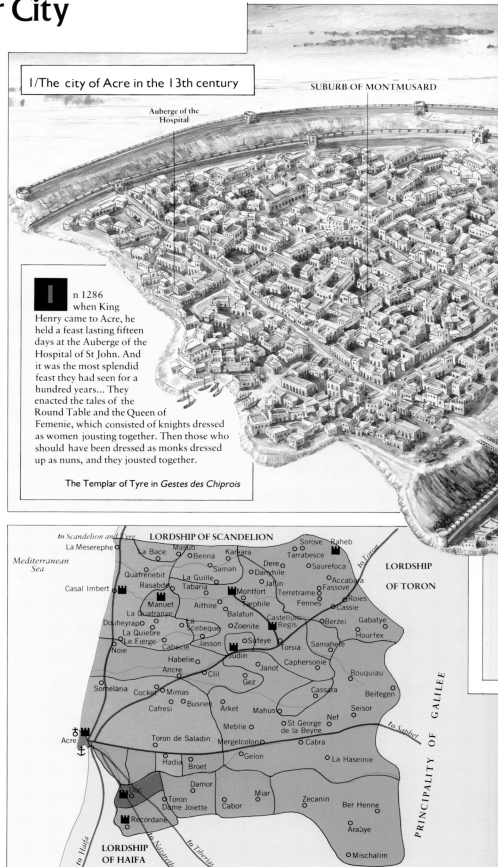

1/The city of Acre in the 13th century

SUBURB OF MONTMUSARD

Auberge of the Hospital

In 1286 when King Henry came to Acre, he held a feast lasting fifteen days at the Auberge of the Hospital of St John. And it was the most splendid feast they had seen for a hundred years... They enacted the tales of the Round Table and the Queen of Femenie, which consisted of knights dressed as women jousting together. Then those who should have been dressed as monks dressed up as nuns, and they jousted together.

The Templar of Tyre in *Gestes des Chiprois*

to Scandelion and Tyre — **LORDSHIP OF SCANDELION**

La Meserephe · La Bace · Masub · Benna · Karkara · Sorove · Raheb · Tarrabesce

Mediterranean Sea

Quafrenebit · La Guille · Samah · Dere · Danyhile · Saurefoca · **LORDSHIP OF TORON**

Casal Imbert · Rasabde · Tabaria · Jallin · Terretrame · Accabara · Fassove

Manuet · Aithire · Montfort · Tarphile · Fennes · Roies · Cassie

La Quatranye · Balatun · Castellum · Berzei · Gabatye

Douheyrapo · La Scebeque · Zoenite · Regis · Hourfex

La Quiebre · Jasson · Sufeye · Torsia · Samahere

Le Fierge · Cabecie · Judin · Caphersonie · Bouquiau

Noie · Habelie · Janot · Beitegen

Ancre · Clil · Gez · Cassara · Seisor

Somelaria · Cocker · Mimas · Busnen · Arket · Mahus · Nef

Cafresi · Meblie · St George de la Beyne · Cabra

Acre · Toron de Saladin · Mergelcolon

Hadia · Broet · Gelon · La Haseinie

Damor · Miar · Zecanin · Ber Henne

Doc · Toron Dame Joiette · Cabor · Arabye

Recordane · Mischalim

LORDSHIP OF HAIFA · *to Haifa* · *to Nazareth* · *to Tiberias* · *to Saphet*

PRINCIPALITY OF GALILEE

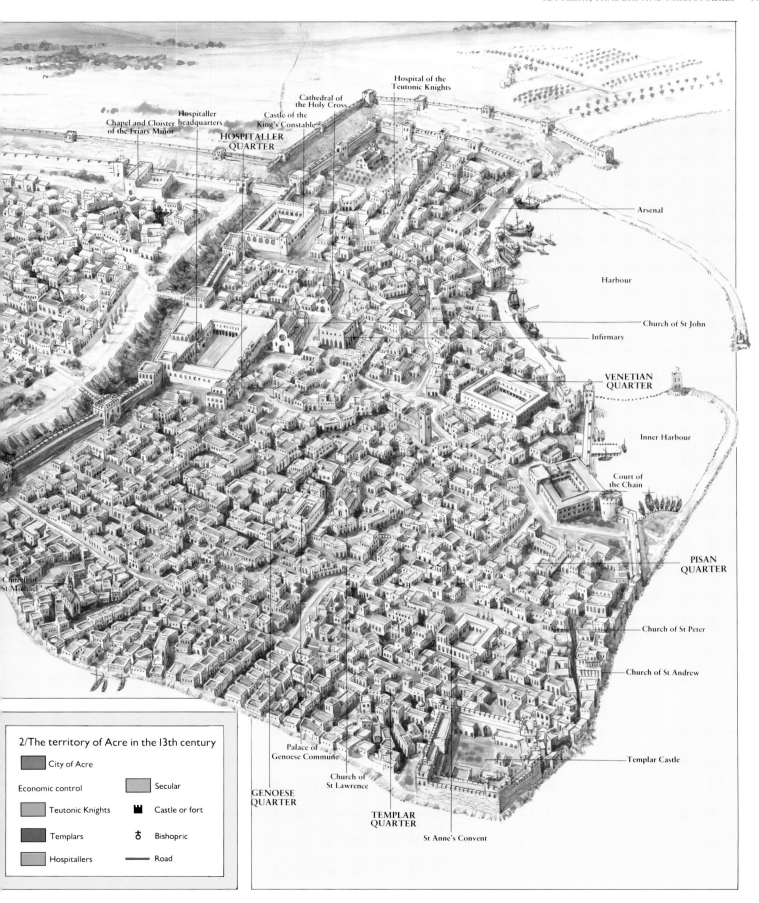

Hospital of the
Teutonic Knights

Cathedral of
the Holy Cross

Hospitaller
Chapel and Cloister headquarters
of the Friars Minor

Hospitaller
Castle of the
King's Constable

HOSPITALLER
QUARTER

Arsenal

Harbour

Church of St John

Infirmary

VENETIAN
QUARTER

Inner Harbour

Court of
the Chain

Church of
St Michael

PISAN
QUARTER

Church of St Peter

Church of St Andrew

Palace of
Genoese Commune

Templar Castle

Church of
St Lawrence

GENOESE
QUARTER

TEMPLAR
QUARTER

St Anne's Convent

2/The territory of Acre in the 13th century

- City of Acre

Economic control

- Teutonic Knights
- Templars
- Hospitallers
- Secular
- Castle or fort
- Bishopric
- Road

The Catholic Mission in the East

A Catholic church hierarchy was established in the crusader states, and soon after the development of missions in the 13th century, it was extended to the Far East.

After the First Crusade (▶*page 30*) the conquerors installed western clerics as patriarchs of Jerusalem and Antioch and created a network of Latin archbishoprics and bishoprics in the area. The Eastern Christians became theoretically subject to their control, but this was rarely more than nominal.

The Latins were never more than a small minority of the population and there were few Latin parishes. However, they established a number of monastic foundations, especially in the holy places (▶*page 42*). All the major western religious communities came to be represented. In the 13th century these were joined by the mendicant orders including the Carmelites, an order which originated in the Latin East. When the crusaders began to lose control of the area to the Muslims, some of these Latin bishoprics survived as titular sees, especially if they had endowments in the territories that remained in Christian hands, or in the West.

The popes also gave bishoprics to the Christian missionaries they were sending to the East. From the first half of the 13th century members of the Franciscan and Dominican orders undertook diplomatic and spiritual missions to Asia, especially to those lands ruled by the Mongols (▶*page 112*). Some missionaries established a more permanent presence in towns on the Black Sea, in Greater Armenia and western Iran, for the benefit of European merchants and oriental Christians. Later missionaries moved further east, into India and China.

In 1307 the Franciscan John of Montecorvino was consecrated as archbishop in Tartary, and established his see at Khanbalik (Beijing). His province initially included all the Mongol realms, but a few years later a second province was set up, staffed by Dominicans and based on Sultaniyeh in Iran. Following this success, large numbers of missionary bishoprics were founded but they frequently proved ephemeral. The Catholic missions were often defeated by plague, by political upheavals and by the fact that many rulers of central Asia were being won over to Islam. By the end of the 14th century missionary activity was largely restricted to the Black Sea region and Caucasia.

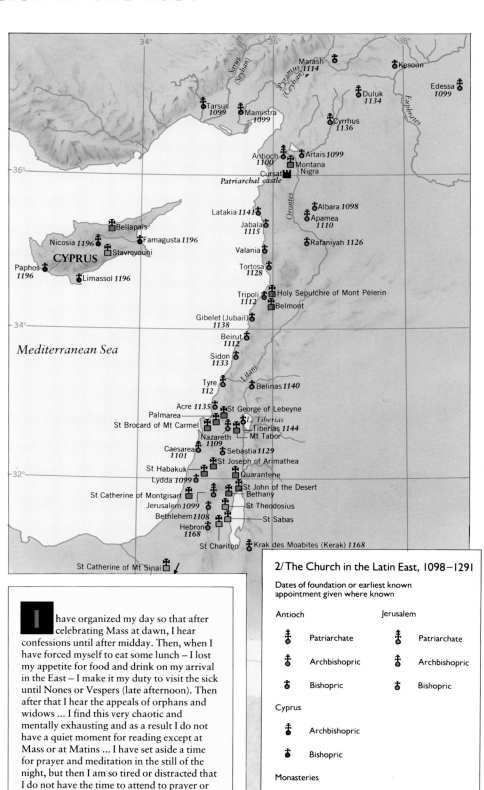

I have organized my day so that after celebrating Mass at dawn, I hear confessions until after midday. Then, when I have forced myself to eat some lunch – I lost my appetite for food and drink on my arrival in the East – I make it my duty to visit the sick until Nones or Vespers (late afternoon). Then after that I hear the appeals of orphans and widows ... I find this very chaotic and mentally exhausting and as a result I do not have a quiet moment for reading except at Mass or at Matins ... I have set aside a time for prayer and meditation in the still of the night, but then I am so tired or distracted that I do not have the time to attend to prayer or to considering my own weaknesses.

James of Vitry describing his day as newly-arrived bishop of Acre in 1216

2/ The Church in the Latin East, 1098–1291

Dates of foundation or earliest known appointment given where known

Antioch	Jerusalem
Patriarchate	Patriarchate
Archbishopric	Archbishopric
Bishopric	Bishopric

Cyprus

Archbishopric

Bishopric

Monasteries

Latin (Catholic) Christian

Greek (Orthodox) Christian

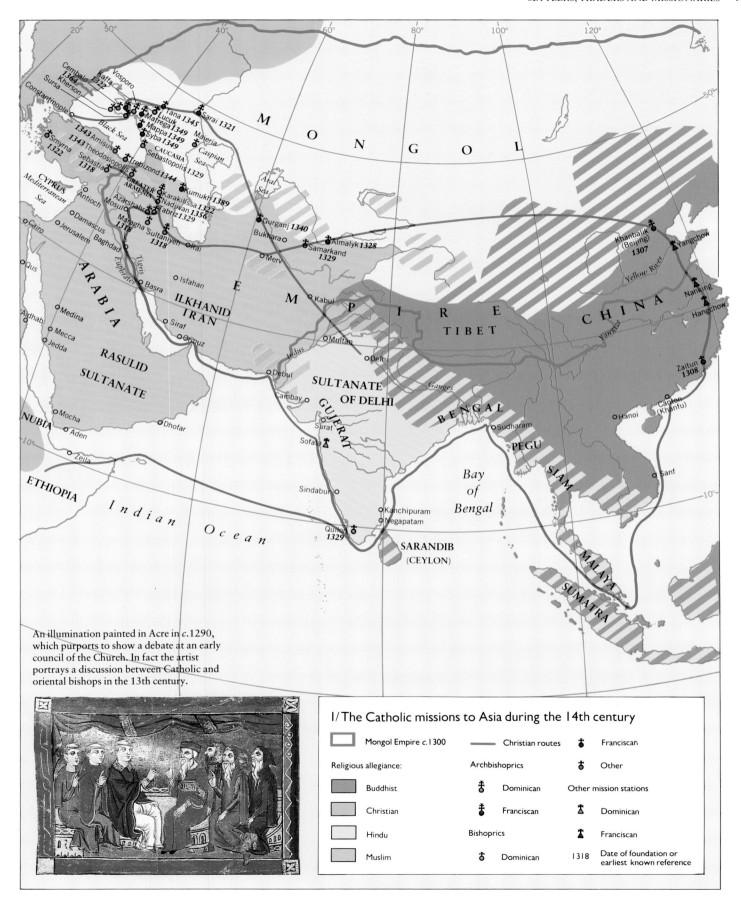

An illumination painted in Acre in c.1290,
which purports to show a debate at an early
council of the Church. In fact the artist
portrays a discussion between Catholic and
oriental bishops in the 13th century.

1/ The Catholic missions to Asia during the 14th century

Mongol Empire c.1300

Religious allegiance:

Buddhist

Christian

Hindu

Muslim

Christian routes

Archbishoprics

☦ Dominican

☦ Franciscan

Bishoprics

☦ Dominican

☦ Franciscan

☦ Other

Other mission stations

⚱ Dominican

⚱ Franciscan

1318 Date of foundation or
      earliest known reference

Guardians of the Latin East

During the 13th century the Military Orders reasserted their control in the Holy Land, reoccupying old castles and building new ones.

Most of the Military Orders' castles in Syria had been lost in the aftermath of the battle of Hattin in 1187; the only important strongholds retained by the Hospitallers were Krak des Chevaliers and Margat. But once the crusaders regained control of the coast (▶ *page 64*) the Orders' holdings increased again. Some castles were recovered as Christian frontiers advanced; others, such as Château Pèlerin, were newly constructed to meet the needs of changed boundaries; and many were given or sold to the Orders, often by lords no longer capable of defending them.

In the early 13th century the Orders' main responsibilities lay in the north, but in the middle of the century a growing number of strongholds in the kingdom of Jerusalem passed under their control. Most were assigned to the Templars or Hospitallers, but the Teutonic Order, which had assumed military functions in 1198, also took on defensive responsibilities, particularly in the hinterland of Acre (▶ *page 102*). But no strongholds appear to have been entrusted to the minor orders of St Thomas of Acre and St Lazarus.

Besides assuming a predominant role in the garrisoning of castles – the Templar castle of Saphet had a complement of 80 brothers and 350 auxiliary troops, together with 820 labourers and 400 slaves – the Military Orders provided a considerable proportion of the forces which the crusader states put into the field, even though the total manpower in the East of the leading Orders was little more than 300 brothers. Their importance allowed them not only to exercise a powerful influence in military and political counsels, especially in the frequent absence of a king, but also to undertake independent action: in the north, for example, they pursued aggressive policies which allowed them to exact tribute from places such as Homs and Hamah, as well as from the Assassins. Yet their independent stance in political as well as in military matters provoked criticism, which increased when they showed themselves incapable of stemming the Mamluk advance (▶*page 114*). From the 1260s onwards they were losing numerous strongholds, in many cases after only short sieges; and in 1291 the orders abandoned the Holy Land, although they still retained some holdings in Armenia.

The Hospitaller castle of Krak des Chevaliers, situated on the high point of Hisn al-Akrad, 25 miles (40km) west of Homs, Syria. The outer wall was added about the beginning of the 13th century, when the inner defences were also strengthened. Despite its impressive fortifications, the stronghold surrendered to the Mamluks in 1271 after a siege of little more than a month.

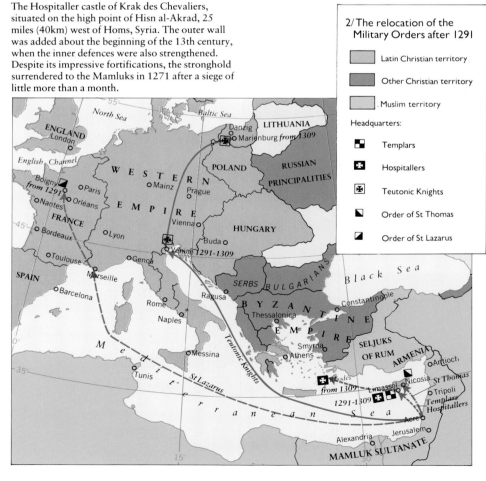

2/ The relocation of the Military Orders after 1291

Latin Christian territory

Other Christian territory

Muslim territory

Headquarters:

■ Templars

✦ Hospitallers

✦ Teutonic Knights

◣ Order of St Thomas

◪ Order of St Lazarus

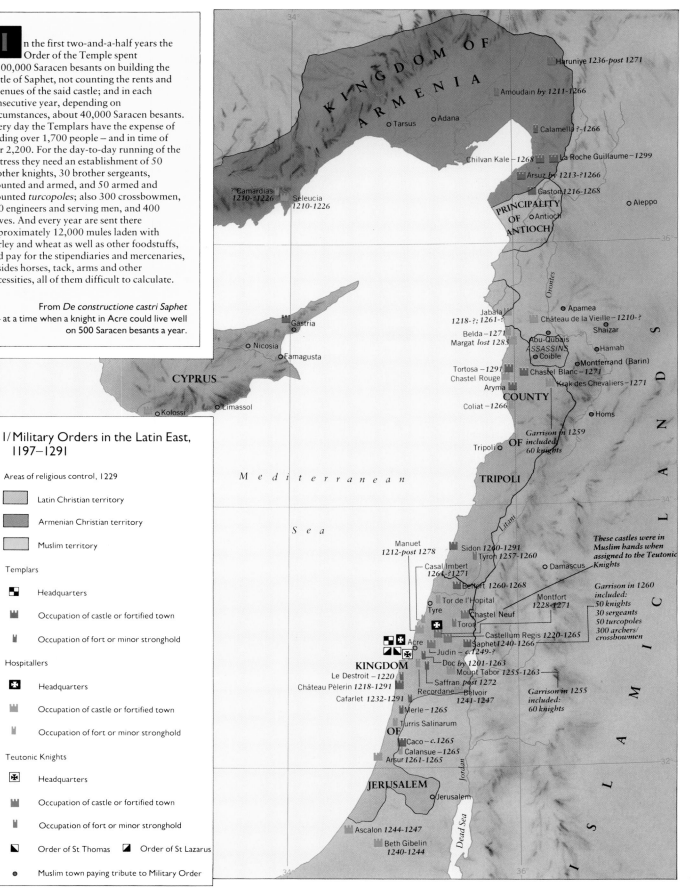

In the first two-and-a-half years the Order of the Temple spent 1,100,000 Saracen besants on building the castle of Saphet, not counting the rents and revenues of the said castle; and in each consecutive year, depending on circumstances, about 40,000 Saracen besants. Every day the Templars have the expense of feeding over 1,700 people – and in time of war 2,200. For the day-to-day running of the fortress they need an establishment of 50 brother knights, 30 brother sergeants, mounted and armed, and 50 armed and mounted *turcopoles*; also 300 crossbowmen, 820 engineers and serving men, and 400 slaves. And every year are sent there approximately 12,000 mules laden with barley and wheat as well as other foodstuffs, and pay for the stipendiaries and mercenaries, besides horses, tack, arms and other necessities, all of them difficult to calculate.

From *De constructione castri Saphet* – at a time when a knight in Acre could live well on 500 Saracen besants a year.

I/Military Orders in the Latin East, 1197–1291

Areas of religious control, 1229

Latin Christian territory

Armenian Christian territory

Muslim territory

Templars

Headquarters

Occupation of castle or fortified town

Occupation of fort or minor stronghold

Hospitallers

Headquarters

Occupation of castle or fortified town

Occupation of fort or minor stronghold

Teutonic Knights

Headquarters

Occupation of castle or fortified town

Occupation of fort or minor stronghold

Order of St Thomas   Order of St Lazarus

Muslim town paying tribute to Military Order

KINGDOM OF ARMENIA

Haruniye *1236–post 1271*

Amoudain *by 1211–1266*

Tarsus

Adana

Calamella *?–1266*

Chilvan Kale *–1268*   La Roche Guillaume *–1299*

Arsuz *by 1213–?1266*

?Camardias *1210–1226*

Seleucia *1210–1226*

Gaston *1216–1268*

PRINCIPALITY OF ANTIOCH

Antioch

Aleppo

Orontes

Apamea

Jabala *1218–?; 1261–?*

Château de la Vieille *–1210–?*

Shaizar

Belda *–1271*

Margat *lost 1285*

Abu-Qubais

ASSASSINS

Coible

Hamah

Tortosa *–1291*

Chastel Rouge

Aryma

Montferrand (Barin)

Chastel Blanc *–1271*

Krak des Chevaliers *–1271*

COUNTY

Coliat *–1266*

Homs

Garrison in 1259 included 60 knights

Tripoli

OF

TRIPOLI

Mediterranean

CYPRUS

Gastria

Nicosia

Famagusta

Kolossi

Limassol

Sea

Litani

Manuet *1212–post 1278*

Sidon *1260–1291*

Tyron *1257–1260*

Casal Imbert *1261–?1271*

Damascus

Beaufort *1260–1268*

Montfort *1228–1271*

These castles were in Muslim hands when assigned to the Teutonic Knights

Tor de l'Hopital

Tyre

Chastel Neuf

Garrison in 1260 included: 50 knights 30 sergeants 50 turcopoles 300 archers/ crossbowmen

Toron

Castellum Regis *1220–1265*

Saphet *1240–1266*

Acre

Judin – *c.1249–?*

Doc *by 1201–1263*

KINGDOM

Mount Tabor *1255–1263*

Le Destroit *–1220*

Saffran *post 1272*

Garrison in 1255 included: 60 knights

Château Pèlerin *1218–1291*

Recordane

Belvoir *1241–1247*

Cafarlet *1232–1291*

Merle *–1265*

Turris Salinarum

OF

Caco – *c.1265*

Calansue *–1265*

Arsur *1261–1265*

Jordan

JERUSALEM

Jerusalem

Ascalon *1244–1247*

Beth Gibelin *1240–1244*

Dead Sea

ISLAMIC

LANDS

The Ayyubid Empire and its Fall

Saladin had left his family a vast empire stretching from Egypt to Asia Minor. Yet within 60 years it was taken from them by their soldier-slaves, the Mamluks.

Saladin's successors acquired the bulk of Diyarbakir in 1232, completing an empire that stretched from Aswan in southern Egypt to the highlands of Anatolia. At the head of the dynasty was the sultan at Cairo. The sultans were not absolute monarchs, but presided over a family conglomerate of princes reigning from capitals such as Damascus, Aleppo and Mayyafariqin. This pattern of government, inherited from the Seljuks, had all the advantages and disadvantages of decentralization. On the one hand, the Ayyubids' hold on their disparate territories was secured; on the other, it was prey to family quarrels, which were sustained by the bands of mamluks – soldier-slaves from southern Russia – in the service of each prince.

The succession to Saladin as sultan was disputed for seven years until his brother, al-Adil Sayf al-Din (Saphadin) took power in Egypt in 1200. This position was maintained by his son al-Kamil (1218-1238) and al-Kamil's son al-Salih. In this way the Ayyubids remained united and strong enough to defeat the Fifth Crusade (▶page 94), but weak enough to prefer negotiation to war when dealing with the emperor Frederick II (▶page 98).

Under al-Salih (1240-1249), the balance began to change. To suppress opposition to his rule, he recruited a large new mamluk regiment, the Bahri (River) Mamluks, named after their island barracks in the Nile at Cairo. Al-Salih died just after the crusade of St Louis had arrived in Egypt (▶page 96), and in the following year the Bahri Mamluks murdered his son Turan Shah and seized power for themselves.

Syria remained loyal to the Ayyubid dynasty; al-Nasir Yusuf, a great-grandson of Saladin, was proclaimed sultan in Damascus. In December 1250 he tried unsuccessfully to reassert Ayyubid control by invading Egypt. But the victory of the Mamluks was assured in 1260, when the Ayyubids of Syria were almost all overthrown by the invading Mongols (▶page 112). Later that year at 'Ayn Jalut, the Mongols were in turn defeated by the Mamluks, who thus acquired virtually all the old Ayyubid empire. They were to rule it in a very different manner from their predecessors.

The citadel of Aleppo, reconstructed by Saladin's son al-Zahir Ghazi at the beginning of the 13th century. It was part of a vast programme of fortification undertaken by Muslims and Christians alike. Aleppo itself was in Muslim hands throughout the period. It prevented the crusaders from securing their hold on northern Syria, while guarding the route from Damascus to Iraq.

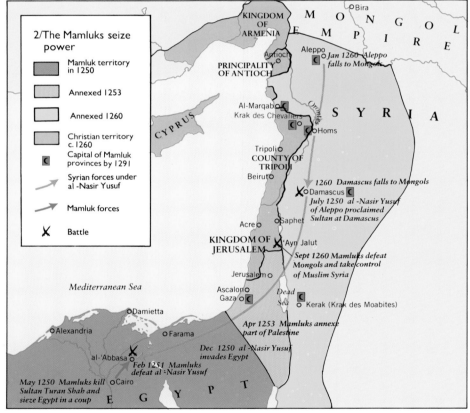

2/The Mamluks seize power

- Mamluk territory in 1250
- Annexed 1253
- Annexed 1260
- Christian territory c.1260
- **C** Capital of Mamluk provinces by 1291
- Syrian forces under al-Nasir Yusuf
- Mamluk forces
- ✗ Battle

KINGDOM OF ARMENIA

PRINCIPALITY OF ANTIOCH

CYPRUS

Al-Marqab **C**
Krak des Chevaliers **C**

Tripoli
COUNTY OF TRIPOLI

Beirut

Acre
Saphet

KINGDOM OF JERUSALEM

Jerusalem

Ascalon
Gaza **C**

Mediterranean Sea

Damietta

Alexandria

al-'Abbasa

Cairo

Farama

E G Y P T

Bira

M O N G O L
E M P I R E

Aleppo **C**
Jan 1260 Aleppo falls to Mongols

Antioch

S Y R I A
Orontes

Homs

1260 Damascus falls to Mongols

✗ Damascus **C**

July 1250 al-Nasir Yusuf of Aleppo proclaimed Sultan at Damascus

✗ 'Ayn Jalut

Sept 1260 Mamluks defeat Mongols and take control of Muslim Syria

Dead Sea
Kerak (Krak des Moabites)

Apr 1253 Mamluks annexe part of Palestine

Dec 1250 al-Nasir Yusuf invades Egypt

Feb 1251 Mamluks defeat al-Nasir Yusuf

May 1250 Mamluks kill Sultan Turan Shah and sieze Egypt in a coup

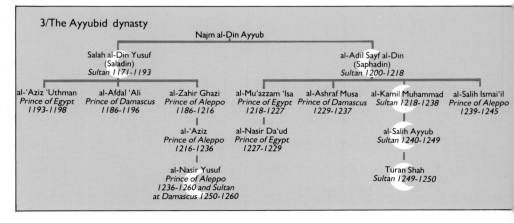

3/The Ayyubid dynasty

Najm al-Din Ayyub

Salah al-Din Yusuf (Saladin)
Sultan 1171-1193

al-Adil Sayf al-Din (Saphadin)
Sultan 1200-1218

al-'Aziz 'Uthman
Prince of Egypt 1193-1198

al-Afdal 'Ali
Prince of Damascus 1186-1196

al-Zahir Ghazi
Prince of Aleppo 1186-1216

al-Mu'azzam 'Isa
Prince of Egypt 1218-1227

al-Ashraf Musa
Prince of Damascus 1229-1237

al-Kamil Muhammad
Sultan 1218-1238

al-Salih Ismai'il
Prince of Aleppo 1239-1245

al-'Aziz
Prince of Aleppo 1216-1236

al-Nasir Da'ud
Prince of Egypt 1227-1229

al-Salih Ayyub
Sultan 1240-1249

al-Nasir Yusuf
Prince of Aleppo 1236-1260 and Sultan at Damascus 1250-1260

Turan Shah
Sultan 1249-1250

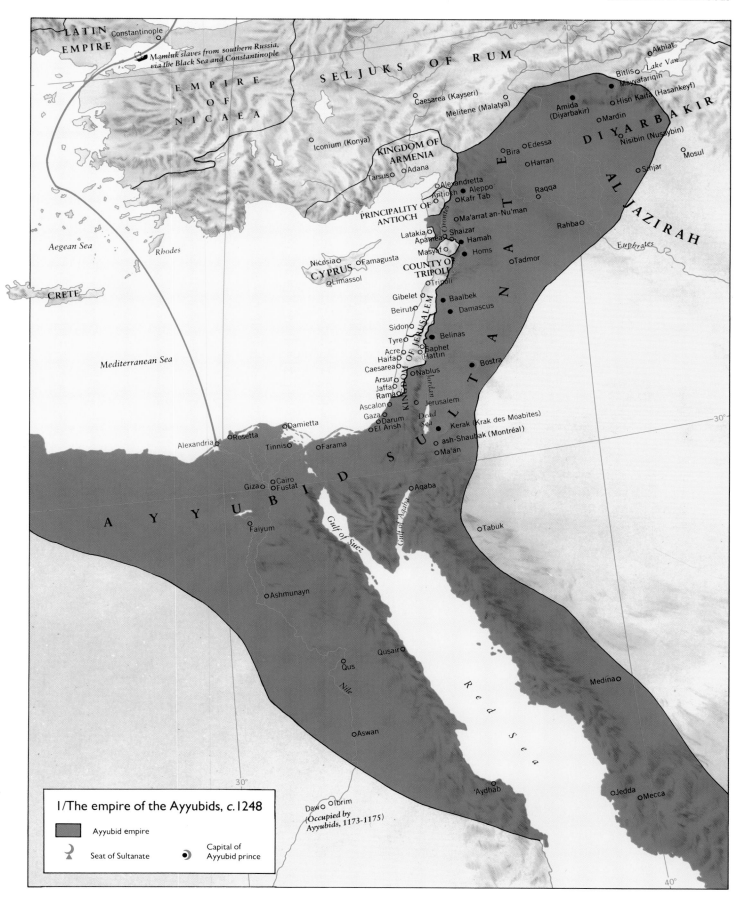

Mamluk slaves from southern Russia,
via the Black Sea and Constantinople

EMPIRE
OF
NICAEA

SELJUKS OF RUM

Akhlat

Bitlis○ ○Lake Van

Mayyafariqin

Caesarea (Kayseri)

Amida
(Diyarbakir)

Hisn Kaifa (Hasankeyf)

Mardin

Iconium (Konya)

KINGDOM OF
ARMENIA

Bira○ ○Edessa

DIYARBAKIR

Nisibin (Nusaybin)

Tarsus○ ○Adana

○Harran

○Mosul

Alexandretta

Antioch ○Aleppo

Raqqa

AL JAZIRAH

PRINCIPALITY OF
ANTIOCH

○Kafr Tab

○Sinjar

Latakia○

○Ma'arrat an-Nu'man

Apamea○ ○Shaizar

Euphrates

Masyaf○

Hamah

Rahba○

Nicosia○

○Homs

Rahba○

CYPRUS ○Famagusta

○Tadmor

○Limassol

COUNTY OF
TRIPOLI

○Tripoli

Gibelet○

○Baalbek

Beirut○

●Damascus

Sidon○

Tyre○

Belinas

Acre○

Saphet
Hattin

Haifa○

Caesarea○

○Nablus

Arsur○

Bostra

Jaffa○

Rama○

Ascalon○

○Jerusalem

Dead
Sea

Gaza○

○Darum

●Kerak (Krak des Moabites)

○El Arish

ash-Shaubak (Montréal)

Aegean Sea

Rhodes

Mediterranean Sea

CRETE

Alexandria○

○Rosetta

○Damietta

Tinnis○

○Farama

○Ma'an

Giza○

○Cairo

○Fustat

○Aqaba

○Tabuk

Faiyum○

AYYUBIDS

Gulf of Suez

Gulf of Aqaba

○Ashmunayn

Qusair○

Qus○

Nile

Red Sea

Medina○

Aswan○

'Aydhab○

○Jedda ○Mecca

Dawo ○Ibrim
(Occupied by
Ayyubids, 1173-1175)

I/The empire of the Ayyubids, c.1248

▨ Ayyubid empire	
☾ Seat of Sultanate	☾● Capital of Ayyubid prince

The Mamluk Chain of Command

Onto the existing civil administration of Egypt and Syria, the Mamluks imposed their own strongly centralized military government.

The Mamluks were a class of soldier-slaves, captured as children from the south Russian steppes. Mostly pagans of Kipchak Turkish origin, they were converted to Islam when they were brought to Egypt to be trained. After they siezed control of the government of Egypt (▶ *page 108*), the flow of slaves continued, providing successive generations of soldiers and administrators. From the mid-14th century, Mamluk slaves mostly came from Christian Circassia in the Caucasus.

Mamluk government owed much to its Fatimid and Ayyubid predecessors: many offices survived from these earlier regimes, although some gained in importance while others declined. But in place of the loose network of Ayyubid principalities, the Mamluks created a rigorously centralized state that posed a far more formidable threat to the Latin settlements. There was very little dele-gation; many officers and officials reported directly to the sultan. Power was exercised through the military, and all the senior Men of the Sword were Mamluks. Directly below the sultan were the Emirs of the Council, who formed what was in effect a military government. The Men of the Sword encroached on areas that had previously been dominated by civilian Men of the Turban (mostly Arab Muslims) and Men of the Pen (mostly Arab Muslims and Christians). The lesser financial departments, or *diwans*, for example, were staffed by Arabs but inspected by Mamluk *shadds*, military officers with financial expertise.

Outside Egypt itself, the provinces – such as Damascus, Aleppo, Kerak and Safad – were governed by Mamluk *naibs*, each of whom reported directly to the sultan in Cairo. As a check against the danger of the *naib* leading a provincial revolt, the citadels of Damascus and Aleppo had their own military governors, known as *walis*. Hamah was technically ruled by an Ayyubid prince who paid tribute to the sultan; in practice, it was treated as Mamluk province.

Three Mamluk officers of the Circassian period. They are wearing the Taqiyya headdress, distinctive of the Mamluk class.

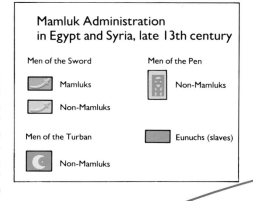

PROVINCIAL GOVERNMENT OF SYRIA

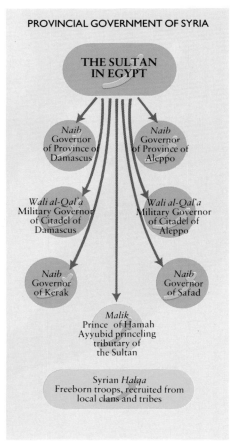

THE SULTAN IN EGYPT

Naib Governor of Province of Damascus

Naib Governor of Province of Aleppo

Wali al-Qal'a Military Governor of Citadel of Damascus

Wali al-Qal'a Military Governor of Citadel of Aleppo

Naib Governor of Kerak

Naib Governor of Safad

Malik Prince of Hamah Ayyubid princeling tributary of the Sultan

Syrian Halqa Freeborn troops, recruited from local clans and tribes

Mamluk Administration in Egypt and Syria, late 13th century

Men of the Sword
- Mamluks
- Non-Mamluks

Men of the Turban
- Non-Mamluks

Men of the Pen
- Non-Mamluks

Eunuchs (slaves)

MEN OF THE PEN

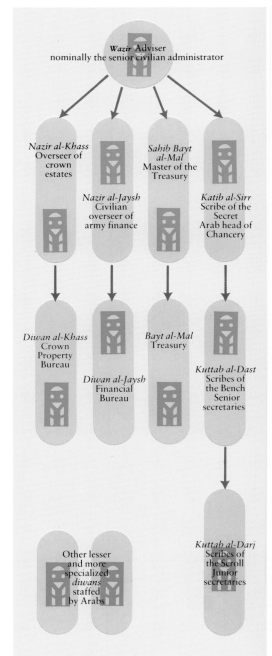

Wazir Adviser nominally the senior civilian administrator

Nazir al-Khass Overseer of crown estates

Nazir al-Jaysh Civilian overseer of army finance

Sahib Bayt al-Mal Master of the Treasury

Katib al-Sirr Scribe of the Secret Arab head of Chancery

Diwan al-Khass Crown Property Bureau

Diwan al-Jaysh Financial Bureau

Bayt al-Mal Treasury

Kuttab al-Dast Scribes of the Bench Senior secretaries

Other lesser and more specialized diwans staffed by Arabs

Kuttab al-Darj Scribes of the Scroll Junior secretaries

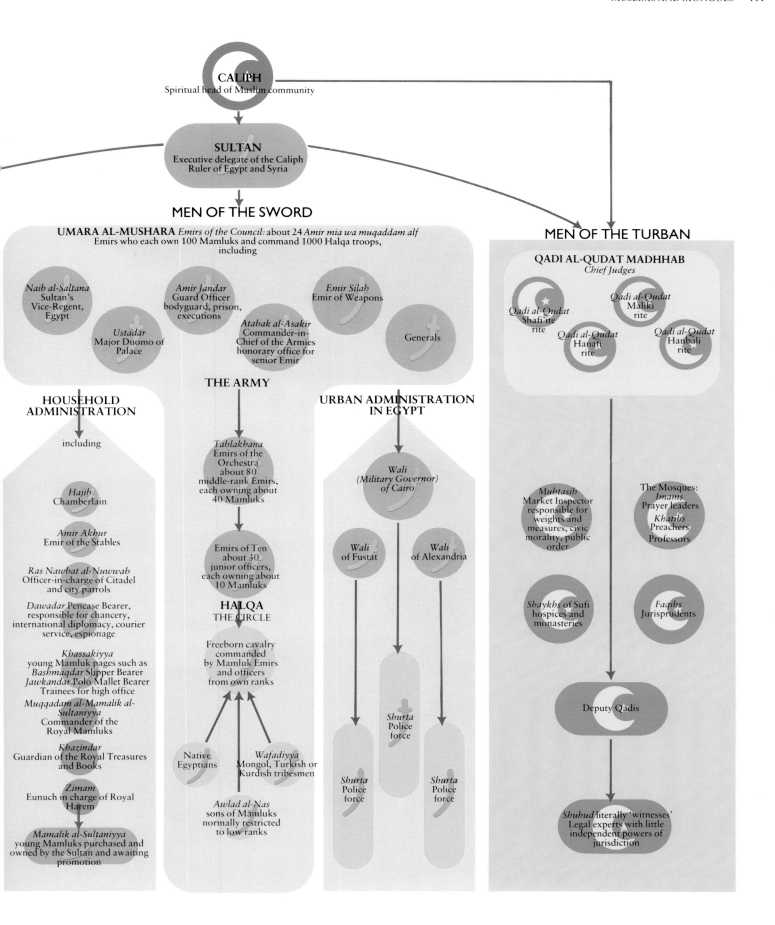

CALIPH
Spiritual head of Muslim community

SULTAN
Executive delegate of the Caliph
Ruler of Egypt and Syria

MEN OF THE SWORD

UMARA AL-MUSHARA *Emirs of the Council:* about 24 *Amir mia wa muqaddam alf*
Emirs who each own 100 Mamluks and command 1000 Halqa troops,
including

Naib al-Saltana
Sultan's
Vice-Regent,
Egypt

Ustadar
Major Duomo of
Palace

Amir Jandar
Guard Officer
bodyguard, prison,
executions

Atabak al-Asakir
Commander-in-
Chief of the Armies
honorary office for
senior Emir

Emir Silah
Emir of Weapons

Generals

MEN OF THE TURBAN

QADI AL-QUDAT MADHHAB
Chief Judges

Qadi al-Qudat
Shafi'ite
rite

Qadi al-Qudat
Maliki
rite

Qadi al-Qudat
Hanafi
rite

Qadi al-Qudat
Hanbali
rite

HOUSEHOLD
ADMINISTRATION

including

Hajib
Chamberlain

Amir Akhur
Emir of the Stables

Ras Nawbat al-Nuwwab
Officer-in-charge of Citadel
and city patrols

Dawadar Pencase Bearer,
responsible for chancery,
international diplomacy, courier
service, espionage

Khassakiyya
young Mamluk pages such as
Bashmaqdar Slipper Bearer
Jawkandar Polo Mallet Bearer
Trainees for high office

*Muqqadam al-Mamalik al-
Sultaniyya*
Commander of the
Royal Mamluks

Khazindar
Guardian of the Royal Treasures
and Books

Zimam
Eunuch in charge of Royal
Harem

Mamalik al-Sultaniyya
young Mamluks purchased and
owned by the Sultan and awaiting
promotion

THE ARMY

Tablakhana
Emirs of the
Orchestra
about 80
middle-rank Emirs,
each owning about
40 Mamluks

Emirs of Ten
about 30
junior officers,
each owning about
10 Mamluks

HALQA
THE CIRCLE

Freeborn cavalry
commanded
by Mamluk Emirs
and officers
from own ranks

Native
Egyptians

Wafadiyya
Mongol, Turkish or
Kurdish tribesmen

Awlad al-Nas
sons of Mamluks
normally restricted
to low ranks

URBAN ADMINISTRATION
IN EGYPT

Wali
(Military Governor)
of Cairo

Wali
of Fustat

Wali
of Alexandria

Shurta
Police
force

Shurta
Police
force

Shurta
Police
force

Muhtasib
Market Inspector
responsible for
weights and
measures, civic
morality, public
order

The Mosques:
Imams
Prayer leaders
Khatibs
Preachers
Professors

Shaykhs of Sufi
hospices and
monasteries

Faqihs
Jurisprudents

Deputy Qadis

Shuhud literally 'witnesses'
Legal experts with little
independent powers of
jurisdiction

Friend or Enemy? The Mongols

The sudden and dramatic rise of the Mongol Empire under Chinggis Khan and his successors posed a common threat to Muslims and Christians alike.

The Mongol empire was founded by Chinggis (Genghis) Khan (?1167-1227). Recognized as supreme ruler of the nomadic Mongol tribes to the north of China in 1206, he set in motion a wave of expansion that continued for half a century after his death. The Mongol army was a highly-trained and manoeuvrable force of cavalry archers, whose tactics owed much to nomadic hunting and herding practices. The army's weakness in siege warfare was remedied by the creation of corps of Chinese (and later Muslim) siege engineers.

When one of Chinggis Khan's grandsons, Batu, invaded Russia and eastern Europe from 1236 to 1242, the Mongols came into direct conflict with Christian Europe. Crusades were preached against them by a number of German bishops, followed by Popes Gregory IX and Innocent V. But little came of them in military terms: Europe was saved more by the withdrawal of the Mongol forces in 1242 than by the efforts of the crusaders.

Hülegü, another of Chinggis's grandsons, exterminated the Assassins of Alamut in 1256 and took Baghdad in 1258. Hülegü then tried to invade Syria, but was defeated by the Mamluks at 'Ayn Jalut in 1260 (▶page 108). This Mongol invasion of Syria posed a dilemma for the crusader states in the East, since the main adversary of the Mongols was their own enemy, the Mamluk sultanate. The crusaders decided that the Mongols were the greater enemy, and adopted a policy of neutrality favourable to the Mamluks.

From 1262 the situation changed. The Mongol empire had now split into four independent – and often antagonistic – khanates under different branches of the Chinggisid family: the Great Khanate in China and Mongolia, the Chaghatai Khanate in Central Asia, the Golden Horde in Russia, and the Ilkhanate in Iran, Iraq and parts of Asia Minor. When the Golden Horde formed an alliance with the Mamluks, the Ilkhans tried to combine forces with the Christians. Very little, however, was achieved in practice: the problems of military co-ordination over such vast distances proved insuperable. In due course the Mongols of the Ilkhanate were themselves converted to Islam, and in 1322 made peace with the Mamluks.

The portrait below is said to be of Hülegü Khan, grandson of Chinggis Khan. Hülegü suppressed the Assassins of north Iran in 1256, and took Baghdad in 1258, killing the last 'Abbasid caliph. His troops were defeated by the Mamluks at 'Ayn Jalut in Palestine in 1260. He died in 1265, having established the Ilkhanate, the Mongol kingdom in Iran and Iraq.

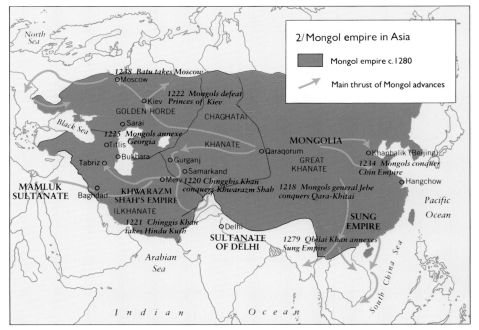

2/ Mongol empire in Asia

Mongol empire c.1280

Main thrust of Mongol advances

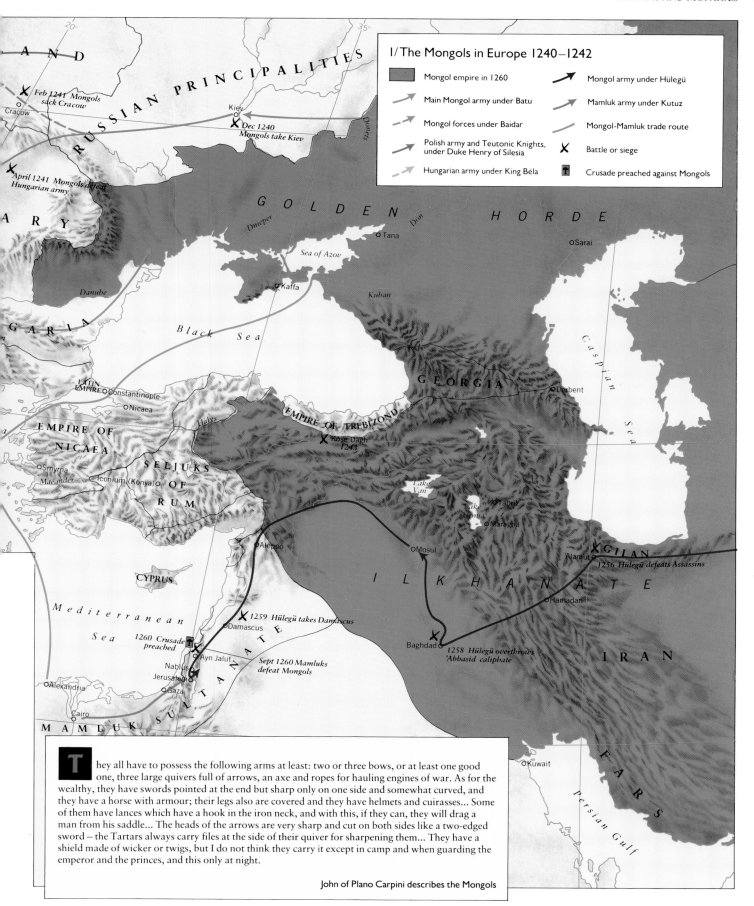

I/The Mongols in Europe 1240–1242

- Mongol empire in 1260
- Main Mongol army under Batu
- Mongol forces under Baidar
- Polish army and Teutonic Knights, under Duke Henry of Silesia
- Hungarian army under King Béla
- Mongol army under Hülegü
- Mamluk army under Kutuz
- Mongol-Mamluk trade route
- Battle or siege
- Crusade preached against Mongols

Feb 1241 Mongols sack Cracow
Cracow
Dec 1240 Mongols take Kiev
Kiev
April 1241 Mongols defeat Hungarian army

RUSSIAN PRINCIPALITIES

Dnieper
Don
Dniester
Danube

GOLDEN HORDE

Tana
Sarai
Sea of Azov
Kaffa
Kuban

Black Sea

Caspian Sea

LATIN EMPIRE Constantinople
Nicaea
EMPIRE OF TREBIZOND
GEORGIA
Derbent

EMPIRE OF NICAEA
Smyrna
Maeander
Iconium (Konya)
Halys
SELJUKS OF RUM

Köse Dagh 1243

Lake Van
Lake Urmia
Tabriz
Maragha

ILKHANATE

Aleppo
Mosul
GILAN
Alamut
1256 Hülegü defeats Assassins

CYPRUS

Mediterranean Sea

1259 Hülegü takes Damascus
Damascus
1260 Crusade preached
Ayn Jalut
Nablus
Jerusalem
Gaza
Alexandria
Cairo

Sept 1260 Mamluks defeat Mongols

MAMLUK SULTANATE

Hamadan

Baghdad
1258 Hülegü overthrows 'Abbasid caliphate

IRAN

FARS

Kuwait

Persian Gulf

They all have to possess the following arms at least: two or three bows, or at least one good one, three large quivers full of arrows, an axe and ropes for hauling engines of war. As for the wealthy, they have swords pointed at the end but sharp only on one side and somewhat curved, and they have a horse with armour; their legs also are covered and they have helmets and cuirasses... Some of them have lances which have a hook in the iron neck, and with this, if they can, they will drag a man from his saddle... The heads of the arrows are very sharp and cut on both sides like a two-edged sword – the Tartars always carry files at the side of their quiver for sharpening them... They have a shield made of wicker or twigs, but I do not think they carry it except in camp and when guarding the emperor and the princes, and this only at night.

John of Plano Carpini describes the Mongols

The Triumph of Islam

In the second half of the 13th century, the Mamluks closed their grip on the crusader settlements until the last outposts were swept away in 1291.

Factional struggles in Cairo and the Muslim cities of Syria gave the western settlers a breathing space in the 1250s. The Mongol invasion of Syria in 1259 (▶ *page 112*) did a great deal of damage to the Muslim hinterland and it seemed likely in the early 1260s that they would return. But their defeat at 'Ayn Jalut in 1260 left the Mamluks in control of most of the former Ayyubid empire (▶*page 108*), and in 1263 the Mamluk sultan Baybars I (1260-1273) was able to turn his attention to the crusader states and launch the first of a series of destructive raids in Galilee. Thereafter, Baybars and his lieutenants directed almost annual attacks against the coast. They were aimed at city suburbs, orchards, crops, and flocks with the intention of damaging the economies of the crusader states. Strongholds were taken methodically: many of those which were on the coast were razed to the ground to prevent their use as bases by any future crusade.

The first important crusader towns to fall to the Mamluks were Caesarea and Arsur in 1265. Babyars's conquest of Saphet in 1266 gave the Mamluks their first important forti-fied base west of the Jordan. From then on the town served as a centre of Mamluk government (▶*page 108*) and a base for operations against the Latins in the south. In 1268 the Mamluks destroyed Antioch, the greatest Latin city in the north.

After 1271, Baybars turned his attentions towards Asia Minor. The succession conflict after his death and another Mongol invasion of Syria in 1280 gave the Latins a second breathing space, although they themselves were now divided over the rival claims to the throne of King Hugh of Cyprus and Charles of Anjou, the king of Sicily. But in 1285, the new Mamluk sultan Kalavun went back onto the offensive against the Hospitallers in the north, who had been ready to ally themselves with the Mongols (▶*page 112*). Fears of a Genoese occupation of Tripoli provoked Kalavun to attack and destroy it in 1289. The settlers appealed for help from the West, and in August 1290, a fleet of 25 Venetian and Aragonese galleys arrived with crusaders from the north of Italy. But it was too little, too late. In March 1291 Kalavun's son and successor, al-Ashraf Khalil, set out from Egypt with a massive army. Joined by contingents from all over the Mamluk sultanate, it arrived at Acre on 5 April. After a grim seven-week siege, the city fell at the end of May. In the months that followed the remaining Latin settlements were easily occupied by the victorious Mamluks.

he Franks did not close most of their gates but left them open and fought in them. The contingent of Hamah was stationed at the head of the right wing, as was their custom, so we were beside the sea, with the sea on our right as we faced Acre. Ships with timber vaulting covered with ox-hides came to us firing arrows and quarrels. There was fighting in front of us from the direction of the city, and on our right from the sea. They brought up a ship carrying a mangonel which fired on us and our tents... This caused us distress until one night there was a violent storm of wind, so that the vessel was tossed on the waves and the mangonel ... smashed to pieces... During the siege, the Franks came out at night, surprised the troops and put the sentries to flight. They got through to the tents and became entangled in the ropes. One of their knights fell into an *amir's* latrine and was killed there... The Franks fell back routed to the town. The troops of Hamah killed a number of them, and when morning came... the lord of Hamah hung a number of heads of Franks on the necks of the horses which the troops had taken from them, and brought them to the sultan... When the Muslims stormed Acre, some of its inhabitants took flight in ships... Then the sultan demanded the surrender of all who were holding out in the towers... and they were beheaded around Acre to the last man. Then at his command the city of Acre was demolished and razed to the ground.

The eyewitness Abu'l Fida describes the fall of Acre to the Mamluks in 1291

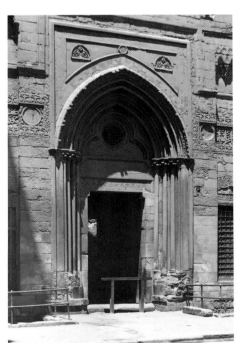

This Gothic marble doorway (left) was taken from the Church of St Andrew in Acre after the capture of the city in 1291. Incorporated into the *madrasa* (religious college) of the Sultan al-Nasir Muhammad ibn Kalavun in Cairo, it served to remind the Mamluks' subjects of the triumph of Islam over the crusaders.

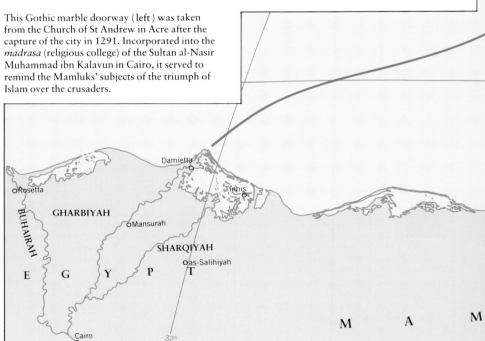

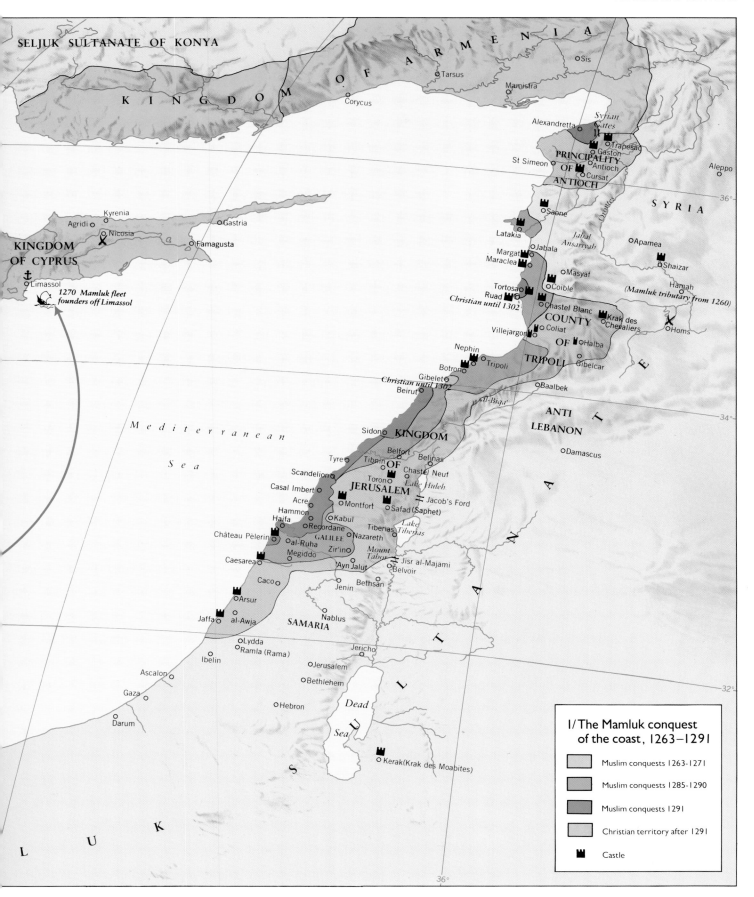

SELJUK SULTANATE OF KONYA

KINGDOM OF ARMENIA

Sis

Tarsus

Corycus

Manistra

Syrian Gates

Alexandretta

Trapesac

Gaston

St Simeon

PRINCIPALITY

Antioch

Aleppo

Cursat

OF

ANTIOCH

SYRIA

Saone

36°

Latakia

Jabala

Jabal Ansariyah

Apamea

Margat

Maraclea

Masyaf

Shaizar

Tortosa

Coible

Hamah

Ruad

Christian until 1302

Chastel Blanc

(Mamluk tributary from 1260)

Krak des Chevaliers

COUNTY

Coliat

Homs

Villejargon

OF

Halba

KINGDOM OF CYPRUS

Kyrenia

Nephin

Gibelcar

Agridi

Nicosia

Gastria

Botron

Tripoli

TRIPOLI

Famagusta

Gibelet

Baalbek

Christian until 1302

Beirut

al-Biqa

Limassol

ANTI

LEBANON

1270 Mamluk fleet founders off Limassol

Sidon

KINGDOM

Damascus

34°

Mediterranean

Tyre

Belfort

Belinas

Sea

Tibnin

OF

Chastel Neuf

Scandelion

Toron

Lake Huleh

Casal Imbert

JERUSALEM

Jacob's Ford

Acre

Montfort

Safad (Saphet)

Hammon

Kabul

Haifa

Recordane

Tiberias

Nazareth

Lake Tiberias

Château Pèlerin

al-Ruha

GALILEE

Zir'ino

Mount Tabor

Jisr al-Majami

Megiddo

Belvoir

Caesarea

'Ayn Jalut

Jenin

Bethsan

Caco

Arsur

Nablus

Jaffa

al-Awja

SAMARIA

Lydda

Ramla (Rama)

Ibelin

Jericho

Ascalon

Jerusalem

32°

Gaza

Bethlehem

Darum

Hebron

Dead Sea

Kerak (Krak des Moabites)

36°

	1/The Mamluk conquest of the coast, 1263–1291
	Muslim conquests 1263–1271
	Muslim conquests 1285–1290
	Muslim conquests 1291
	Christian territory after 1291
	Castle

Part 3
CRUSADING AND THE AGE OF CHIVALRY

The triumph of the Mamluks in Palestine and Syria in 1291 did not end crusading, which continued in several theatres of war. In the 14th century, visiting crusaders from western Europe would return to the Teutonic Knights' headquarters at Marienburg after taking part in one of their regular winter or summer armed sweeps through pagan Lithuanian territory. The vast red-brick castle, which could be seen from many miles away across the plain, consisted of three courts, stretching one after the other along the bank of the River Nogat, an offshoot of the Vistula. After riding through an outer court with its stables, workshops and stores, the visitors would pass under an imposing gateway into the middle court. Ahead of them towered the High Castle, the conventual residence of the Teutonic Knights, who, like the Hospitallers of St John, were professed religious living in a monastic enclosure. The Grand Master's palace, linking the High Castle with the rest of the fortress, stood in the far right corner of the middle court as seen from the entrance arch. To the visitors' left there stretched their lodgings, a range of apartments which were superbly appointed with large rooms and finely traceried windows, ending in a chapel reserved for their use. Immediately opposite the lodgings and taking up almost the whole length of the court to their right, was a magnificent dining hall, kept warm in the fiercely cold winters by an advanced system of underfloor heating. It was in this hall that there took place the feasts which began or ended the *Reisen*, as the campaigns were called, and so delighted contemporaries. Each banquet had a Table of Honour and badges for the most distinguished guests; the Teutonic Knights instituted an 'Order of the Table', in imitation of King Arthur's legendary company of knights.

The Grand Master of the Teutonic Knights, Luther of Brunswick (1331-1334). An able musician, it was during his reign that Marienburg became the scene of German song contests.

The packaged crusading and chivalric theatre arranged by the Teutonic Knights had an immense appeal. Thousands of nobles and knights took the road or the sea voyage to Prussia and had their coats-of-arms depicted in stained glass or hung on the walls of castles and churches at Marienburg or Königsberg. The same practice seems to have been followed in Rhodes, off the coast of Asia Minor, where knights visiting the Hospitallers of St John would hang their shields as mementoes in a 'House of Honour'. A striking variation on this sort of heraldic display can still be seen stretching across the face of the English Tower on the walls of the Hospitaller castle of Bodrum on the mainland of Asia Minor: the arms of King Henry IV and six other members of his family, and a further 19 shields, registering the contributions of leading figures at the English court to the cost of building the tower.

The golden hazy penumbra of chivalric extravagance also swathed the ceremonies surrounding the taking of the cross, nowhere more so than at the Feast of the Pheasant at Lille in 1454, when Duke Philip of Burgundy and his companions made their crusade vows, binding themselves to accomplish high deeds of arms against the Turks with hands held over a live pheasant wearing a collar of gold. This followed a joust and a series of tableaux arranged during the banquet, which had culminated in a weeping girl, representing the Church and drawing attention to her suffering at the hands of the Muslims.

Chivalric theatre looks frivolous to us, but underlying its flamboyance was an international culture and a serious ideology which was in many ways distinct from Christian piety, although it was flecked with Christian ideals. One question is whether chivalry, in its way a kind of layman's response to the Christianity of churchmen, had replaced more conventional piety as a mainspring for crusaders' actions. The way European knights chose the safer, although certainly still expensive, outlet for their crusading impulses provided by the Teutonic Knights' Lithuanian *Reisen* might suggest this, were it not for the fact that so many of them journeyed to the East as well, to fight in even more expensive and much less comfortable ventures. In fact the variety of options available to potential crusaders was as wide as ever. Geoffrey Chaucer's knight in *The Canterbury Tales*, a brilliant and topical invention, had 'reysed' in Prussia, where 'ful ofte tyme he hadde the borde bigonne' – in other words he had had a seat at the Table of Honour – Livonia and Russia, and had crusaded in Spain, North Africa and Asia Minor. Chaucer's knight was only a slight exaggeration of reality. John Boucicaut, the marshal of France, crusaded in Prussia, North Africa, the Balkans and at sea in the eastern Mediterranean. Henry Grosmont, duke of Lancaster, went to Spain, Prussia, Rhodes and Cyprus; and there is evidence in the records of the English Court of Chivalry of individual English gentlemen who had been to Prussia and the Near East or the Balkans. These men had experienced different theatres of war; and alongside them were even more who had chosen one theatre – not only Prussia, but also southern Spain, the eastern Mediterranean, the Balkans or Bohemia – as the sole expression of their commitment. Chivalry provided a decorative gloss and helped to fuel the desire of knights to take part in crusading and of their sons to enter the Military Orders. It enhanced and reinforced the traditional devotional aspects of crusading, but it did not replace them.

Chivalry

Chivalry was a system of thought and behaviour which had its origins in the 11th century, reached maturity in the 14th and was in decline in the 16th century. Some of its ideas, particularly the notion of 'honour', still survive today. In it, aristocratic, martial and Christian elements, each of them a compound of different concepts, were fused to form an original synthesis. Nobility, for instance, was symbolized by the bearing of distinctive coats-of-arms. It comprised descent by blood, recognition by the sovereign, a way and a condition – generally a wealthy condition – of life, and a predisposition to a particular ideal of virtue, expressed in the concept of honour. The profession of arms involved a hereditary capacity to fight on horseback. Christianity provided a system of ethics, also expressed in crusading, which gave chivalry a purpose, and a pre-history in stories such as that of the Holy Grail.

It would be wrong to regard chivalry merely as a knightly expression of Christianity. It had its own internal and distinct coherence, its own literature in the epics of Charlemagne, Arthur and Godfrey of Bouillon, its own symbolism in heraldry and liturgy in the ceremonies of dubbing to knighthood, its own priests and sages in the heralds. Whether or not it was a counter-culture to the Christianity of the Church, an adaptation of Christian ideals made by secular knights to suit themselves, is arguable. But chivalry certainly gave rise to a serious and attractive culture.

Chivalry is normally associated with land-based warfare. It was, of course, the case that knights on chargers were in action in Spain and eastern Europe, sometimes indulging in those rashly futile gestures which were a feature of the 14th century: charging into a marsh at Halmyros or up a hill into a thicket of pointed stakes at Nicopolis. And all the theatres of war were peppered with heavily fortified bases, garrisoned by knights and mercenary troops: the city of Rhodes, which by the early 15th century was one of strongest fortresses in the world, is the best surviving example. But after the loss of the Palestinian mainland in 1291 and the withdrawal of Catholic government to islands – Cyprus, Crete, Naxos, Chios, Lesbos, Rhodes – eastern crusading took to the sea. Sea warfare, with fleets of galleys prowling the Mediterranean between one adamantine outpost and another, was to remain dominant until the 17th century. A lead was taken by the Hospitallers of St John. Within six months of their evacuation from Palestine they were, with the help of the papacy, assembling a war fleet and by 1300 they had ten galleys under the command of an admiral. On Rhodes and later on Malta, their flotilla usually consisted of seven or eight galleys, and it was on these that the young knights of St John were expected to make their *caravans*, the period of active service at sea after which they would be eligible for promotion. The galleys of the Order of St John joined those of other committed powers in the fleets of the leagues which were a feature of crusading from the 14th century onwards: Adramyttium (1334), Smyrna (1344), Lampsacus (1359), Mitylene (1457), Antalya and Smyrna (1472) established a tradition of league victories that lay behind Lepanto (1571). But the expense of maintaining the fortifications and the fleets were immense. This explains why, even after being granted most of the western properties of the suppressed Templars – on paper it was one of the richest religious Orders in Christendom – the Order of St John was forever teetering on the edge of bankruptcy, although this forced it to become one of the most efficient estate managers of the Middle Ages.

Rhodes and Prussia represented a new development in the late medieval period, the creation of Order states. This was a response to the deep crisis for the crusading movement with which the 14th century had opened. The Holy Land had been lost, and western Europe was swept by the conflicting emotions of despair and enthusiasm. Soldiers, kings and armchair strategists circulated memoranda on the recovery of the Holy Land, a goal beyond the resources and logistical abilities of western Europe now that the beach-head in Palestine had been lost. Since disaster was explained in terms of the unworthiness of the men entrusted with carrying out God's intentions, it is not surprising that the Military Orders were under a cloud. Like many other powerful institutions, they had attracted criticism for more than a century. Recurring charges had been that they had deliberately withheld money that should have been spent on crusading and that their rivalry and selfishness had impeded the reconquest of the Holy Land. The criticism was uninformed and unfair, but it had been persistent enough for the union of at least the Templars and the Hospitallers to have been proposed from the 1270s; by 1291 it was being considered by the papacy.

In the end only the Templars succumbed, but throughout the 14th century the popes periodically demanded that the Hospitallers reform themselves; one of them even went as far as to say that he would reform the Order of St John himself if the Hospitallers would not. For a time the Teutonic Knights were also in deep trouble, accused, with some justification, of corruption, brutality, a failure to defend Livonia properly and the hindering of missionary work: a standard complaint was that their cruelty alienated the heathen and made evangelization much more difficult.

It was no coincidence that in 1309, when the Templar crisis was at its height, the Hospitallers and the Teutonic Knights should have moved their headquarters to Rhodes and Prussia respectively establishing the conditions in which their institutions could function, and could be seen to be functioning, purposefully and effectively. These Order states, populated by natives and colonists and

A knight, representing the city of Prato in Italy, wearing the arms of the Angevin kings of Naples. From an address by the people of Prato to King Robert of Naples.

ruled by the Masters of the German Order and the Order of St John, allowed the Teutonic Knights and the Hospitallers to function relatively independently of outside controls. In 1226 the German Grand Master had been given the status of imperial prince by the western emperor, and eight years later the pope had recognized Prussia as a papal fief. The Hospitallers' possession of Rhodes, which they began to occupy in 1306, was much less clearly defined. So Prussia's legal position was stronger than that of Rhodes, which may help to explain why the Hospitallers suffered so much more from papal intervention in the late Middle Ages than did the Teutonic Knights; although it is also true to say that their situation, being more exposed, dangerous and costly, demanded more attention.

On Rhodes, however, the Hospitaller Masters – they were Grand Masters from 1489 – developed an efficient chancery, minted their own coins, sent ambassadors to other Christian courts and from perhaps as early as the 15th century granted honorary knighthoods to laymen associated in a confraternity with the Order. In practice, therefore, they behaved, like the Grand Masters of the German Order, as independent princes. They continued to consider themselves in this light on Malta, which they were given in 1530 after the loss of Rhodes, even though Malta was a fief of the kingdom of Sicily and there was a political crisis in 1753, when King Charles VII of Naples claimed his rights as sovereign. In 1607, 400 years after the Grand Master of the Teutonic Knights had been elevated, the Hospitaller Grand Master was also given the title of imperial prince, which lent him some of the attributes of sovereignty. Manoel Pinto (Grand Master, 1741-1773) completed the process when he unilaterally proclaimed himself a full sovereign by adopting a royal crown.

Crusading survived the crisis of the early 14th century partly, of course, because the predominance of chivalric culture bathed it in a warm romantic glow. But far more important than that was the fact that it could still be perceived to be necessary. Indeed the need for effective crusading had grown because the Ottoman Turks, originating in a little Muslim frontier barony in Asia Minor, were expanding fast. They established a beach-head in Europe by 1348 and from then on, apart from a breathing space of 20 years following a Mongol invasion of Asia Minor in the early 15th century, the Ottoman advance was inexorable. By 1370 the papacy was waking up to the threat, and the following three centuries were punctuated by appeals to westerners to help defend Christianity. The appeals became more pressing than ever as the Ottomans advanced towards the heart of Europe; for a year in 1480-1481 they even occupied Otranto on the heel of Italy. And for his zeal for war against the infidel, Innocent XI, who was pope at the time of the Turkish siege of Vienna in 1683, can be compared with his 13th-century predecessors Innocent III and Gregory X.

But of course the movement was in decline by 1500. It had been a sign of its vitality that it could compete with great inter-state conflicts like the Hundred Years' War, but the transformation of European kingdoms into sovereign nation states and the development of diplomacy, a form of international exchange in which the distinctiveness and autonomy of each state was always stressed, told against the supra-nationalism that has been an intrinsic feature of crusading.

A partial answer to growing national demands had been found in the formation of leagues, which was to become a regular method of crusading in the eastern Mediterranean theatre of war until the late 17th century. The soldiers and sailors taking part could take the cross and enjoy crusade privileges, including the indulgence; and the papacy granted them the proceeds of crusade taxes. It should be stressed that the operations of the leagues were technically not crusades, that is to say wars fought by forces representing Christendom as a whole and engaged in the defence of Christendom seen as a single entity; they were the actions of alliances of individual Christian powers, often coping with a threat particular to themselves, to which were attached the privileges of crusading. But although adaptations of crusade ideology to new political circumstances, they could not halt the gradual decline. One can discern an ebbing of interest among the masses, who were still moved in the early 14th century, but were largely indifferent by 1500, and among those kings, nobles and knights whose homes were distant from the remaining theatres of war in the later 15th century. Nevertheless, there was still hardly a year of the 14th and 15th centuries in which a crusade was not being fought somewhere. And crusading would have a major part to play in the 16th century.

A Crusade that Never Was

Despite the fall of Acre in 1291, many plans were made for the recovery of the Holy Land. One of the most detailed and ambitious was the work of the Venetian nobleman Marino Sanudo.

Throughout the 13th century, there was a constant flow of written advice aimed at the restoration of Christian rule in Palestine. Some of these plans were little more then travellers' tales; others were detailed and sober works on military feasibility of such a project; while others constituted ambitious plans for global political reorganization. Most of these works appeared before 1340, when the loss of the Holy Land was most recent.

The courts of the popes and the kings of France were the main centres of interest in crusading, and attracted most writers. Courtiers and civil servants at the French court, such as Guillaume de Nogaret (*c*.1311), Guillaume Durand the Younger (?1319) and Guy of Vigevano (1335), were directly or indirectly encouraged by the government to produce such plans. Missionaries, clerics and laymen with experience of the East, such as Guillaume d'Adam (*c*.1313) and the Armenian Prince Hayton (1307), gave advice. Military experts, such as the Masters of the Temple and Hospital, Jacques de Molay and Fulques de Villaret, had their say.

The most comprehensive plan came from the Venetian Marino Sanudo Torsello (1270-1343). A relative of the dukes of Archipelago (▶ *page 86*), he devoted much of his life to producing a definitive scheme for Christian political and commercial domination of the eastern Mediterranean. His plan aimed to undermine the power of Mamluk Egypt by a combination of economic embargo, political alliances and concerted military pressure. It suggested that the conquest of Egypt – and hence Palestine – could be achieved by a small, professional sea-borne expeditionary force, followed at an interval by a mass crusade in the traditional manner established by the First and Third Crusades.

Other schemes, such as those of the early 14th-century Catalan mystic Ramon Lull and the French propagandist Pierre Dubois, were more apocalyptic. Some, like those of Dubois and Philippe de Mézières (1327-1405), called for the conquest to be entrusted to a new, united Military Order, and throughout the period the role of the Hospitallers on the island of Rhodes was seen as pivotal.

In addition to a ban on trade with Egypt, alliances with powers further east were suggested, revealing the new horizons opened by the missionaries and merchants of the 13th century (▶*pages 100 and 104*). But a lack of understanding of the Ottoman advance in the second half of the 14th century did little to inject any realism into these crusade plans. As late as 1505 the king of Portugal sent Henry VII of England 'a little book of instruction' on the recovery of Jerusalem; by that time, little more than an impossible dream. But despite their impracticality, these plans are a striking reminder of the tenacious hold that crusading maintained on the minds of western Europeans.

> **T**he required annual expenditure on the said 15,000 foot-soldiers, 300 cavalry and their ship transports, plus food and other necessities... would be 210,000 florins by instalments over three years... That is to say, 60,000 gold florins annually to pay the said cavalry and infantry, and for suitable food and for such expenses as occur. In the same way, we would need 30,000 gold florins over the whole three-year period for ships, timber, iron and such materials as are necessary for the building of living quarters, as well as for sundry military matters and the replacement of such horses as might be destroyed or lost... In this way our expenses would reach the sum total of 210,000 florins.
>
> Marino Sanudo

An illustration of a crusader galley from a contemporary manuscript of Marino Sanudo's *Liber secretorum fidelium crucis* (The Crusaders' Book of Secrets), in which he outlined his plan for the reconquest of the Holy Land.

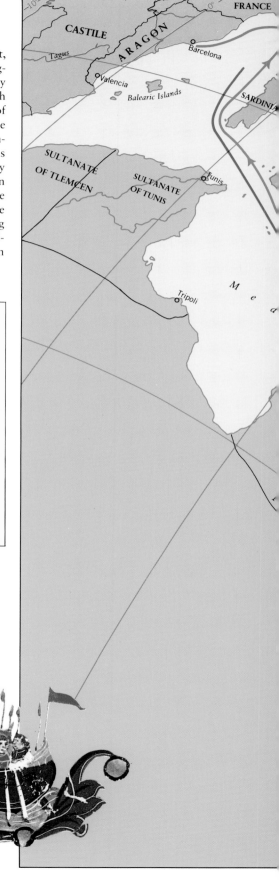

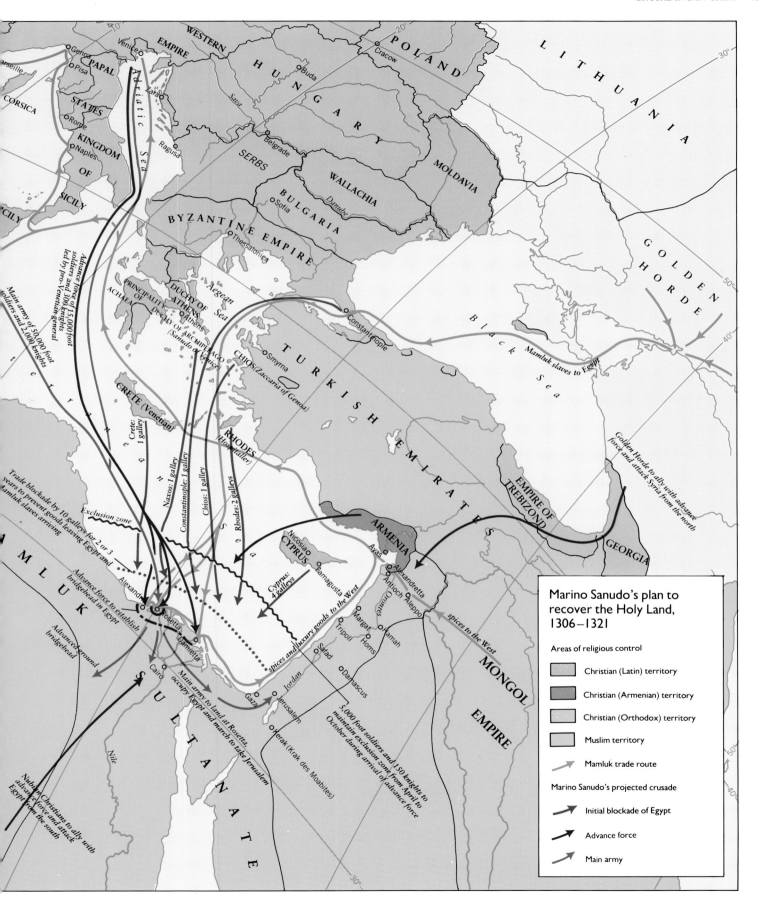

Marino Sanudo's plan to recover the Holy Land, 1306–1321

Areas of religious control

- Christian (Latin) territory
- Christian (Armenian) territory
- Christian (Orthodox) territory
- Muslim territory

→ Mamluk trade route

Marino Sanudo's projected crusade

→ Initial blockade of Egypt

→ Advance force

→ Main army

The Fall of the Templars

The power and prosperity of the Templars made them the object of envy and suspicion. When King Philip IV of France ordered their arrest on charges of heresy, their downfall was rapid.

The recriminations which followed the loss of Acre in 1291 inevitably involved the Order of the Temple, for its chief justification was the war in the Holy Land. Proposals were raised to reform the Order, to amalgamate it with the Hospital of St John, and to bring in fresh leadership from outside, perhaps drawn from the French royal house. The Templars' resistance to these ideas did nothing to enhance their fading reputation, and in October 1307, King Philip IV ordered the sudden arrest of all the Templars in France. The Templars were accused of forcing all entrants to undergo an obscene and heretical initiation ceremony during which they denied Christ and spat on the cross. Harassed and tortured, most of the knights confessed, although many retracted later.

Pope Clement V, who had not been consulted, was highly indignant; the Templars were an exempt Order and their arrest was therefore an affront to his papal authority. In November 1307 he tried to take over the affair by ordering the arrest of the Templars in other lands. At the Council of Vienne in 1312 the pope eventually suppressed the Order and granted its lands to the Hospitallers: in March 1314, the Grand Master Jacques de Molay and the preceptor of Normandy, Geoffroi de Charney, were burned at the stake. Some exceptions were made in the Iberian peninsula, where the papacy allowed Templar possessions to be used to create the new Orders of Montesa in Aragon and Christo in Portugal.

The affair caused widespread scandal; many European rulers, together with a considerable proportion of the literate population, were unconvinced of the Templars' guilt. Philip IV himself seems to have been driven by a powerful and at times morbid religious belief, which he identified almost completely with the imposition of royal overlordship. Moreover, about two-thirds of all Templar houses lay within the reach of the French monarchy. Situated in the prosperous agricultural areas of the north, in key trading regions like Champagne, and along the vital route to the Mediterranean, they represented a rich financial prize.

The arrest and trial of the Templars, 1307–1314

Sept 14 1307 Secret orders sent out by Philip IV of France, to prepare for arrest of the Templars.

Oct 13 1307 Arrest of Templars in France.

Oct 19 1307 Hearings begin in Paris before officials of the Inquisition.

Oct 24 1307 Jacques de Molay, Grand Master of the Temple, confesses to most of the accusations.

Nov 22 1307 Papal bull, *Pastoralis praeeminentiae*, orders the arrest of the Templars throughout Christendom.

Dec 24 1307 Molay revokes his confession in front of the papal representatives.

Feb 1308 Clement V suspends proceedings.

Mar – June 1308 Philip IV campaigns to have trial restarted.

Aug 12 1308 Papal bulls *Faciens misericordiam* and *Regnans in coelis* authorize episcopal inquiries into

individuals and set up papal inquiry into the Order as a whole.

Spring 1309 Beginning of episcopal inquiries.

Nov 22, 1309 First hearings of the papal commission.

Mar 28 1310 Mass meeting of Templars ready to defend the Order.

Apr 7 1310 Defence of the Templars conducted by Pierre de Bologna and Renaud de Provins.

May 12 1310 Burning of 54 Templars in Paris.

June 5 1311 Papal commission ends.

Oct 16 1311 Council of Vienne opens.

Mar 22 1312 Papal bull *Vox in excelso* suppresses Order of the Temple.

May 2 1312 Templar property granted to the Order of the Hospital of St John.

Mar 18 1314 Burning of Jacques de Molay and Geoffroi de Charney.

This late 14th-century miniature shows the execution of Jacques de Molay, Grand Master of the Temple, and Geoffroi de Charney, preceptor of Normandy, on the Ile-des-Javiaux in Paris. Philip IV, king of France, had ordered them to be burnt to death in the evening of March 18, 1314, following their confessions earlier that day.

2/ The new owners of Templar properties in Spain and Portugal, early 14th century

Most Templar properties in area granted to:

▨	Hospitallers
▨	Order of Montesa
☐	Order of Cristo

Other Templar property granted to:

◕	Hospitallers	◕	Order of Alcántara
◕	Order of Cristo	●	King of Castile
◕	Order of Santiago	◕	Council of Seville

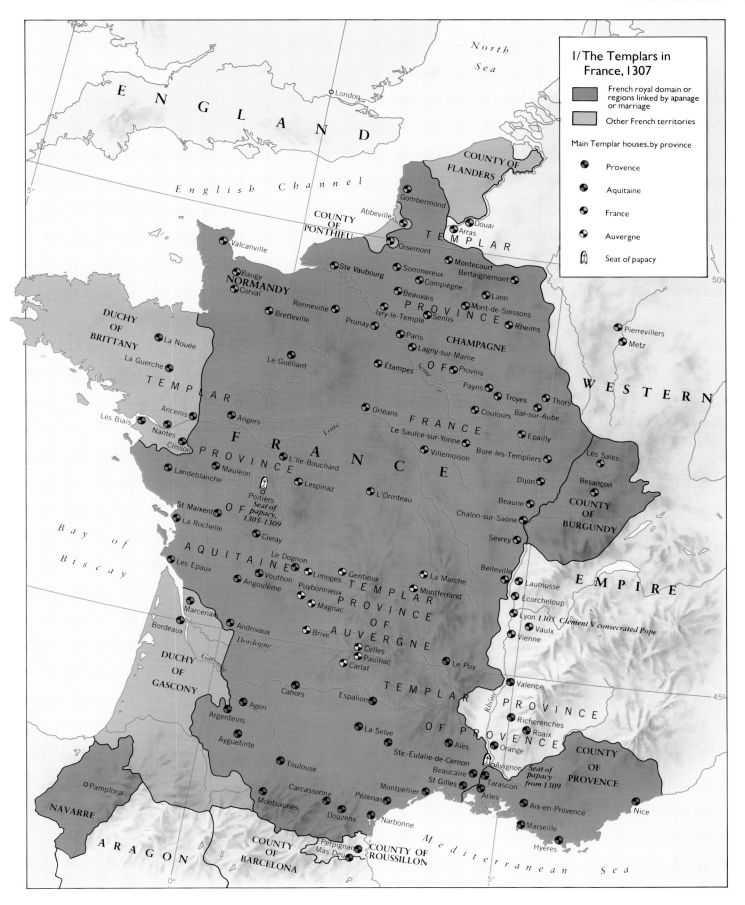

I/The Templars in France, 1307

French royal domain or regions linked by apanage or marriage

Other French territories

Main Templar houses, by province

- Provence
- Aquitaine
- France
- Auvergne
- Seat of papacy

North Sea

ENGLAND

London

English Channel

COUNTY OF FLANDERS

COUNTY OF PONTHIEU

TEMPLAR

Gombermond

Abbeville

Douai

Arras

Oisemont

Valcanville

Ste Vaubourg

Sommereux

Montcourt

Bertaignemont

Baugy

NORMANDY

Compiègne

Corval

Beauvais

Laon

Renneville

Mont-de-Soissons

Bretteville

Prunay

Ivry-le-Temple

Senlis

Rheims

PROVINCE

DUCHY OF BRITTANY

Paris

CHAMPAGNE

Pierrevillers

Metz

La Nouée

Le Guéliant

Lagny-sur-Marne

OF

TEMPLAR

Étampes

Provins

WESTERN

La Guerche

Payns

Troyes

Thors

Ancenis

Angers

Orléans

FRANCE

Coulours

Bar-sur-Aube

Les Biais

Le Saulce-sur-Yonne

Epailly

Nantes

FRANCE

Epailly

Clisson

L'Ille-Bouchard

Villemoison

Bure-les-Templiers

PROVINCE

Les Sales

Mauléon

Dijon

Besançon

Landeblanche

Lespinaz

L'Ormteau

Beaune

St Maixent

Poitiers

OF

Seat of papacy, 1305-1309

Civray

Chalon-sur-Saône

COUNTY OF BURGUNDY

Bay of Biscay

AQUITAINE

Sevrey

Les Epaux

Le Dognon

Limoges

Gentioux

La Marche

Belleville

Vouthon

Puybonnieux

Montferrand

Laumusse

Angoulême

Magnac

TEMPLAR

Ecorcheloup

Marcenais

Brive

PROVINCE

Lyon 1305 *Clement V consecrated Pope*

Bordeaux

Andrivaux

OF

Vaulx

Dordogne

AUVERGNE

Vienne

Celles

EMPIRE

Garonne

Paulhac

Le Puy

DUCHY OF GASCONY

Carlat

Cahors

Espalion

TEMPLAR

Valence

Agen

PROVINCE

Argenteins

Richerenches

Ayguetinte

La Selve

OF

Roaix

Toulouse

Ste-Eulalie-de-Cernon

Alès

Orange

PROVENCE

COUNTY OF PROVENCE

Rhône

Carcassonne

Pézenas

Beaucaire

Avignon

NAVARRE

Montsaunes

Montpellier

St Gilles

Tarascon

Seat of papacy from 1309

Pamplona

Douzens

Arles

Aix-en-Provence

Nice

ARAGON

Perpignan

Narbonne

Marseille

COUNTY OF BARCELONA

Mas Deu

COUNTY OF ROUSSILLON

Mediterranean Sea

Hyères

Spain: The Final Victory

Civil war in Spain delayed the conquest of Muslim Granada; but after the union of Aragon and Castile in 1479, it finally succumbed to the crusading armies of Ferdinand and Isabella.

The last two centuries of the Spanish Reconquest followed a pattern of intermittent advances, between which the Muslims won a series of temporary reprieves. The kingdom of Granada was theoretically a vassal of Castile; but its mountains, its fortresses, its large and determined population and the diplomatic skill of its sultans allowed it to keep its practical independence until 1492.

Morocco was now ruled by the Marinid (or Banu Marin) tribe, who were fanatically orthodox Muslims. In 1275 they launched a holy war against Christian Spain. The sultan of Granada gave them a base on the Straits of Gibraltar from which to raid the lower Guadalquivir valley, and although they failed to capture any cities their raids drew Castile's fire away from Granada. Moroccan volunteers, meanwhile, helped to protect Granada's other borders and even to recover some towns that had fallen to the Christians.

Aragon and Portugal had almost abandoned the Reconquest until, in 1340, Alfonso IV of Portugal helped Alfonso XI of Castile to defeat the Muslims on the river Salado. This led to the capture of Algeciras in 1344 and ended Moroccan intervention in Spain. But

from 1350, civil war in Castile allowed Granada to take and sack Jaén and other cities.

After 1388 the Castilian monarchy rebuilt its strength, captured Antequera in 1410 and defeated the sultan at La Higueruela in 1431; but from then until 1480, both Granada and Castile were absorbed in civil wars, and frontier skirmishing was left to subordinates. All along the frontier, castles controlling the invasion routes into and out of Granada were held by the Military Orders of Calatrava and Santiago (▶*page 54*) and by noble clans like the Guzmáns and Fajardos, who skirmished endlessly with the Muslims, taking and capturing castles, slaves and other booty. As in previous centuries, they were supported by occasional foreign crusaders, and by papal crusading bulls, indulgences and subsidies; but now they also collaborated with Granada to suppress cross-border crime.

In 1479, however, King Ferdinand V and Queen Isabella of Castile inherited Aragon. Their unified kingdom of Spain, inspired by crusading ideas, spelt the end of Muslim Granada. Between 1482 and 1492 the monarchs conquered it, using traditional crusading techniques and the latest artillery, and playing rival sultans off against each other. In 1492 they captured the city of Granada itself, ending 800 years of Muslim rule in Spain.

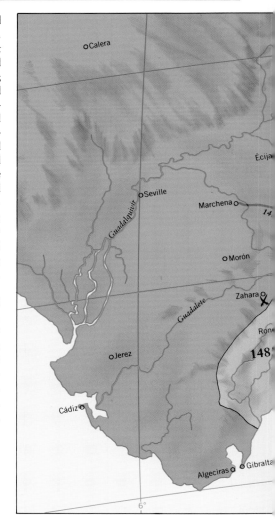

The coat of arms of the united kingdom of Spain, showing the arms of Castile quartered with those of Aragon. The pomegranate at the base of the shield represents the newly-conquered kingdom of Granada.

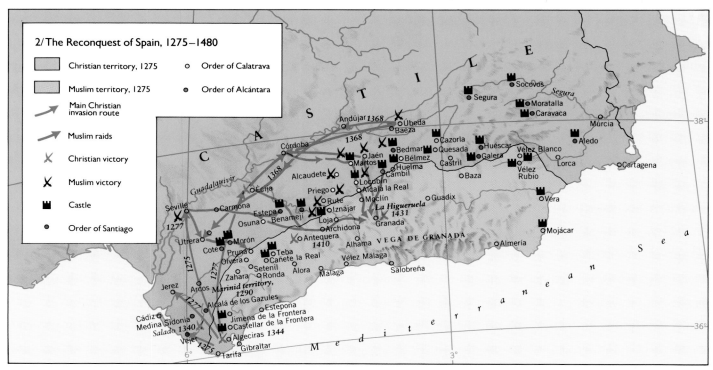

2/ The Reconquest of Spain, 1275–1480

- ▨ Christian territory, 1275
- ▨ Muslim territory, 1275
- → Main Christian invasion route
- → Muslim raids
- ✗ Christian victory
- ✗ Muslim victory
- ♜ Castle
- ● Order of Santiago
- ○ Order of Calatrava
- ● Order of Alcántara

C A S T I L E

Socovos
Segura
Moratalla
Caravaca
Murcia
Aledo
Andújar *1368*
Úbeda
Baeza
Córdoba
1368
Cazorla
Bedmar
Quesada
Huéscar
Vélez Blanco
Jaén
Bélmez
Castril
Galera
Martos
Huelma
Vélez Rubio
1368
Alcaudete
Cambil
Locubín
Baza
Vera
Priego
Alcalá la Real
Rute
Moclín
Guadix
Guadalquivir
Écija
La Higueruela
1431
Seville
Estepa
Iznájar
Granada
Mojácar
1277
Osuna
Benameji
Loja
Almería
Archidona
Carmona
Antequera
1410
Alhama *VEGA DE GRANADA*
Utrera
Cote
Morón
Pruna
Olvera
Cañete la Real
Vélez Málaga
Zahara
Setenil
Álora
Salobreña
Ronda
Málaga
Marinid territory,
Jerez
1290
Arcos
1277
Alcalá de los Gazules
Estepona
Cádiz
Medina Sidonia
Jimena de la Frontera
Salado 1340
Castellar de la Frontera
Vejer
Algeciras *1344*
1275
Tarifa
Gibraltar

M e d i t e r r a n e a n   S e a

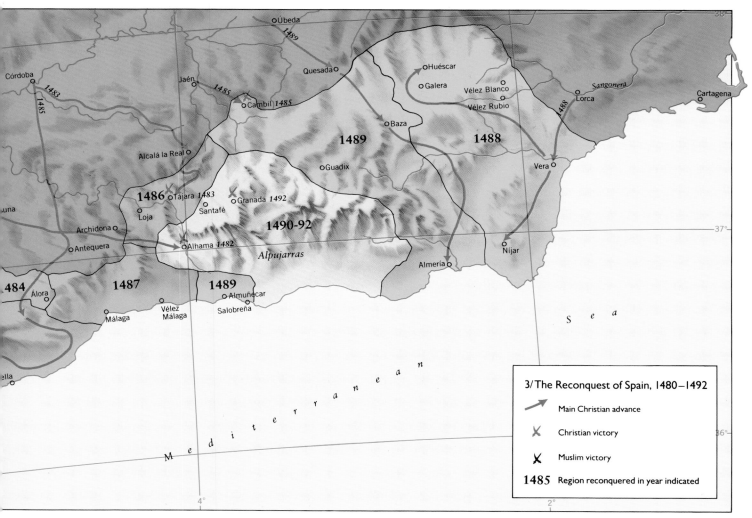

Úbeda
1489
Córdoba
Jaén
Quesada
Huéscar
1483
1485
Galera
Vélez Blanco
1485
Cambil *1485*
Vélez Rubio
Sangonera
Cartagena
Alcalá la Real
Baza
Lorca
1489
1488
Guadix
Vera
Archidona
1486
Tájara *1483*
Granada *1492*
Santafé
Antequera
1490-92
Nijar
Alhama *1482*
Almería
Alpujarras
484
Álora
1487
1489
Almuñécar
Vélez
Málaga
Salobreña
Málaga

S e a

M e d i t e r r a n e a n   S e a

3/ The Reconquest of Spain, 1480–1492

- → Main Christian advance
- ✗ Christian victory
- ✗ Muslim victory
- **1485** Region reconquered in year indicated

The Teutonic Knights

The Teutonic Knights reached their zenith in the late 14th century, as their Prussian Order state gave them a leading role in Baltic trade and a base from which to raid Lithuania.

The loss of the Holy Land in 1291 deprived the Military Orders of their Eastern possessions and led to the question of their principal *raison d'être*: the defence of the Latin East. The Templars were suppressed, and the Hospitallers found a new base on Rhodes. The Teutonic Knights, who already had extensive possessions in Prussia, Pomerelia and Neumark, as well as territories in Livonia (► *page 74*), made Prussia the basis of an Order state. In 1309, the Knights moved their headquarters to Marienburg.

From their Prussian fortresses, the senior officers of the Order governed a complex society: its upper echelons consisted of German urban patricians and a German, Polish and Prussian landed gentry. The peasantry was made up of relatively privileged Germans and underprivileged Prussians, who laboured on the Order's extensive domains. The Knights themselves formed the administrative class, keeping in touch through a sophisticated courier system.

The rich agricultural lands of Prussia and the Knights' involvement in the trading activities of the Hanseatic League made the 14th century a time of considerable prosperity for the Order. Many foreign knights, including King John of Bohemia, Henry of Lancaster and Henry of Derby (later King Henry IV of England), were attracted to Prussia to take part in the Order's sweeping raids – called *Reisen* – into pagan Lithuania.

But the conversion of the Lithuanians to Catholicism and their union with Poland undermined the Order state. In 1410 the Polish-Lithuanian forces crushed the Knights at Tannenberg; the Grand Master, most of the senior knights and 400 of the knight brothers were slain. The large war indemnity imposed on them forced the Knights to adopt grasping fiscal policies and to undermine the rights they had previously granted to entice German settlers to Prussia.

With few pagans left to fight, the Order seemed to have become a rest home for minor German nobility. Opposition crystallized in an association of German urban patricians and landed gentry called the Prussian *Bund*. When King Wladyslaw of Poland renewed the war against the Order in the 1450s, the *Bund* decided it was time to overthrow the Knights. The resulting Thirteen Years War (1454-1466) ended with the loss of the Order's prosperous West Prussian territories to Poland. The Grand Master became a vassal of the Polish king; and Marienburg itself was sold to the Poles by the Order's mercenaries to recoup their unpaid wages.

The castle and palace at Marienburg (left), now Malbork, Poland. From 1309 to 1457 it was the headquarters of the Teutonic Knights and seat of the Grand Master. Vast cliffs of brickwork concealed lavishly-furnished interiors.

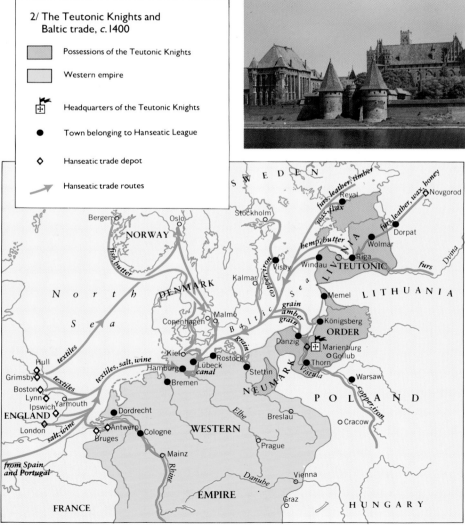

2/ The Teutonic Knights and Baltic trade, *c.*1400

- Possessions of the Teutonic Knights
- Western empire
- ✠ Headquarters of the Teutonic Knights
- ● Town belonging to Hanseatic League
- ◇ Hanseatic trade depot
- → Hanseatic trade routes

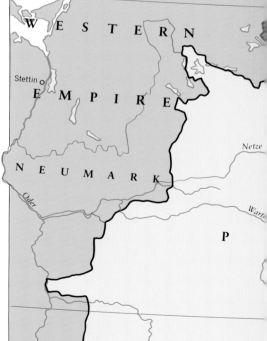

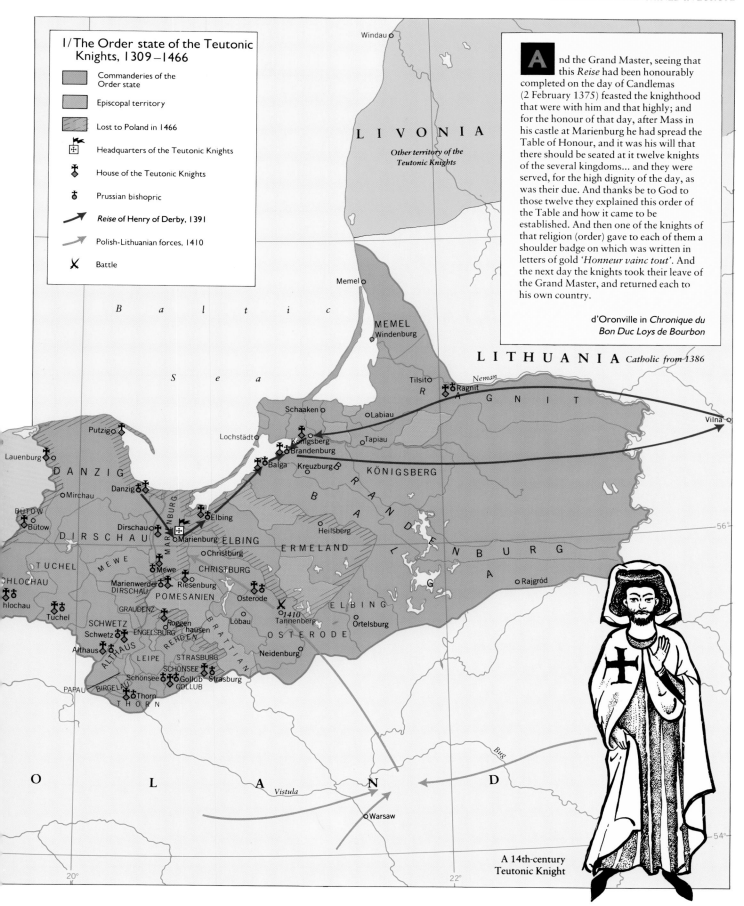

1/The Order state of the Teutonic Knights, 1309–1466

- Commanderies of the Order state
- Episcopal territory
- Lost to Poland in 1466
- Headquarters of the Teutonic Knights
- House of the Teutonic Knights
- Prussian bishopric
- *Reise* of Henry of Derby, 1391
- Polish-Lithuanian forces, 1410
- Battle

And the Grand Master, seeing that this *Reise* had been honourably completed on the day of Candlemas (2 February 1375) feasted the knighthood that were with him and that highly; and for the honour of that day, after Mass in his castle at Marienburg he had spread the Table of Honour, and it was his will that there should be seated at it twelve knights of the several kingdoms... and they were served, for the high dignity of the day, as was their due. And thanks be to God to those twelve they explained this order of the Table and how it came to be established. And then one of the knights of that religion (order) gave to each of them a shoulder badge on which was written in letters of gold '*Honneur vainc tout*'. And the next day the knights took their leave of the Grand Master, and returned each to his own country.

d'Oronville in *Chronique du Bon Duc Loys de Bourbon*

A 14th-century Teutonic Knight

Crusades Against the Hussites

The Czech religious leader Jan Hus was burned in 1415, but his teachings became the focus of a nationalist movement which five crusades proved unable to suppress.

The crusades against the Hussites arose from a combination of religious, nationalist and political developments in Bohemia. During the weak rule of King Wenceslas IV a heretical movement, which derived its name and most of its beliefs from Jan Hus (c.1369-1415), flourished in close association with Czech national feeling. The burning of Hus in 1415 failed to suppress the heretics, whose demands included a reform of the clergy and a review of the church's temporal possessions.

When Wenceslas died in 1419 he was succeeded by his brother, King Sigismund of Hungary. Sigismund was emperor-elect, and he faced resistance to his political authority, joined with growing religious unorthodoxy and anti-German sentiments. He responded by accepting the suggestion of Pope Martin V that he should subdue Bohemia by leading a crusade against the Hussites with the assistance of the German princes. Sigismund reached Prague in 1420 and was crowned in the royalist stronghold Hradčany Castle, but was defeated by the Hussites at Vitkov and Výsehrad, and had to leave Bohemia in the spring of 1421.

This expedition was the first of five great crusades, all of which failed to subjugate the Hussites. The crusaders had allies in the Catholic, German towns of western Bohemia, and they enjoyed the advantage of the deep internal division between the moderate Hussites and the radical Taborites of the south. But they were hindered by poor leadership and lack of discipline. And, as their defeats accumulated their morale slumped. The Hussites, on the other hand, were brilliantly led by Jan Žižka and Prokop the Bald. They made devastating use of innovative tactical devices, especially mobile barriers of war wagons in conjunction with crossbows, cannon and handguns.

The crusades of 1427 and 1431 all but melted away in the face of the Hussite advance, and from 1427 the Hussites skilfully augmented their defence of Bohemia with a series of destructive raids – the 'beautiful rides' – into neighbouring German territory. Unable to bring his subjects to heel, Sigismund reluctantly came to a religious compromise with them in 1436.

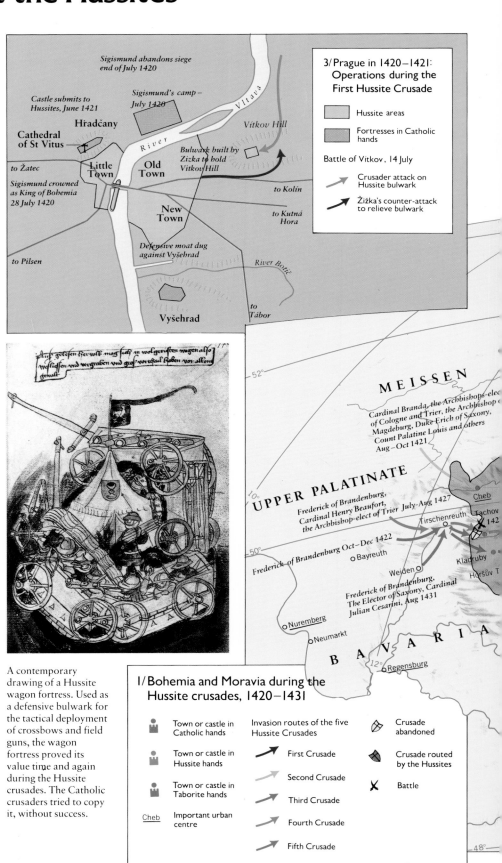

A contemporary drawing of a Hussite wagon fortress. Used as a defensive bulwark for the tactical deployment of crossbows and field guns, the wagon fortress proved its value time and again during the Hussite crusades. The Catholic crusaders tried to copy it, without success.

3/Prague in 1420–1421: Operations during the First Hussite Crusade

1/Bohemia and Moravia during the Hussite crusades, 1420–1431

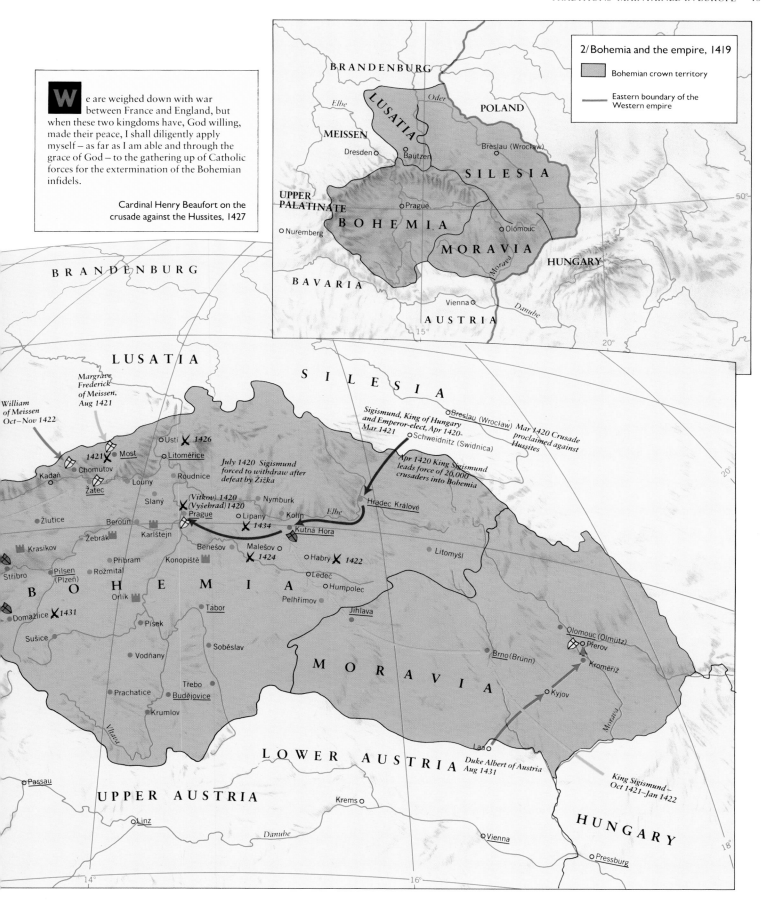

2/Bohemia and the empire, 1419

Bohemian crown territory

Eastern boundary of the Western empire

W e are weighed down with war between France and England, but when these two kingdoms have, God willing, made their peace, I shall diligently apply myself – as far as I am able and through the grace of God – to the gathering up of Catholic forces for the extermination of the Bohemian infidels.

Cardinal Henry Beaufort on the crusade against the Hussites, 1427

BRANDENBURG

LUSATIA

MEISSEN

Dresden

Bautzen

Oder

Elbe

POLAND

Brèslau (Wrocław)

SILESIA

UPPER PALATINATE

Prague

Olómouc

Nuremberg

BOHEMIA

MORAVIA

HUNGARY

BAVARIA

Morava

Vienna

Danube

AUSTRIA

50°

15°

20°

BRANDENBURG

LUSATIA

Margrave Frederick of Meissen, Aug 1421

William of Meissen Oct–Nov 1422

SILESIA

Breslau (Wrocław)

Mar 1420 Crusade proclaimed against Hussites

Usti

1426

Sigismund, King of Hungary and Emperor-elect, Apr 1420-Mar 1421

1421

Most

Litoměřice

Schweidnitz (Swidnica)

Chomutov

Žatec

Roudnice

July 1420 Sigismund forced to withdraw after defeat by Žižka

Apr 1420 King Sigismund leads force of 20,000 crusaders into Bohemia

Kadaň

Louny

Slaný

Nymburk

Žlutice

Beroun

(Vitkov) 1420 (Vyšehrad) 1420 Prague

Lipany

Kolín

Elbe

Hradec Králové

Zebrák

Karlštejn

1434

Kutná Hora

Krasíkov

Příbram

Benešov

Malešov

Habry

1422

Litomyšl

Stříbro

Pilsen (Plzeň)

Rožmital

Konopiště

1424

Ledeč

20°

BOHEMIA

Orlík

Humpolec

Domažlice

1431

Tábor

Pelhřimov

Sušice

Písek

Jihlava

MORAVIA

Olomouc (Olmütz)

Přerov

Vodňany

Soběslav

Kroměříž

Prachatice

Třebo

Brno (Brünn)

Budějovice

Kyjov

Krumlov

Vltava

Morava

LOWER   AUSTRIA

Laa

Duke Albert of Austria Aug 1431

King Sigismund Oct 1421–Jan 1422

Passau

UPPER   AUSTRIA

Krems

Vienna

HUNGARY

Linz

Danube

Pressburg

18°

14°

16°

The Revolution in Shipping

Crusading made the Mediterranean safer for European shipping, which in turn prolonged the survival of the crusader states.

The 12th-century trading boom (▶*page 100*) had created a demand for ocean-going ships with more space for cargo. Once the capture of Majorca by Aragonese-Catalan crusaders (▶*page 72*) had lifted the threat from Muslim fleets, ships developed rapidly. By 1277, the Catalans and Italians were building vessels sturdy enough to sail through the Straits of Gibraltar against the strong incoming current. This enabled them to open up sea routes linking Italy with Flanders, England and Atlantic Morocco.

The traditional galley was a fast, low-slung vessel that combined oar and sail power. Now that it had to cope with the high seas of the Atlantic, it became much larger, with higher gunwales to reduce the danger of swamping. The result of these changes was essentially a new ship: the 'great galley' of the 14th and 15th centuries. The Mediterranean cocha, or cog, was also enlarged, and this sturdy round cargo ship carried grain, oil, wine, and alum from the Black Sea as far as Bruges.

The shipping boom also transformed the instruments of navigation. The compass had been known in the Mediterranean before 1200 but, in an age when most shipping hugged the coastline, its use had been limited. Cartography flourished; by the 1320s, fine sea charts were being created in Venice and Majorca. Commercial manuals, such as those of the Florentine, Pegolotti, gave precise details of tax privileges in foreign ports.

After the fall of Acre in 1291, the crusaders were left with a string of island and coastal settlements. Shipping was their lifeline, and in 1309 the Hospitallers transferred their headquarters to Rhodes (▶*page 136*), where they could command the trade routes of the Aegean and eastern Mediterranean. Many Christian strategists of the day were convinced that a total economic embargo of Egypt would weaken its resistance to a new crusade. The popes threatened to excommunicate merchants who ignored the blockade, and authorized the Hospitallers to intercept vessels and confiscate cargoes. The effectiveness of this blockade was debatable; indeed, ports like Ayas and Famagusta, which could act as intermediaries between Christian and Muslim merchants, prospered, and in 1344 the embargo was lifted.

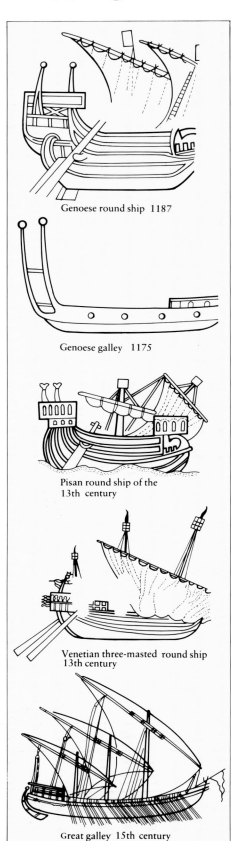

Genoese round ship 1187

Genoese galley 1175

Pisan round ship of the 13th century

Venetian three-masted round ship 13th century

Great galley 15th century

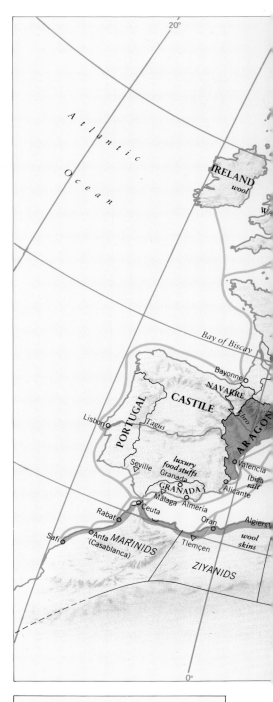

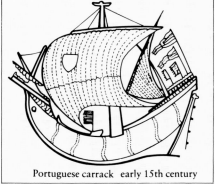

Portuguese carrack early 15th century

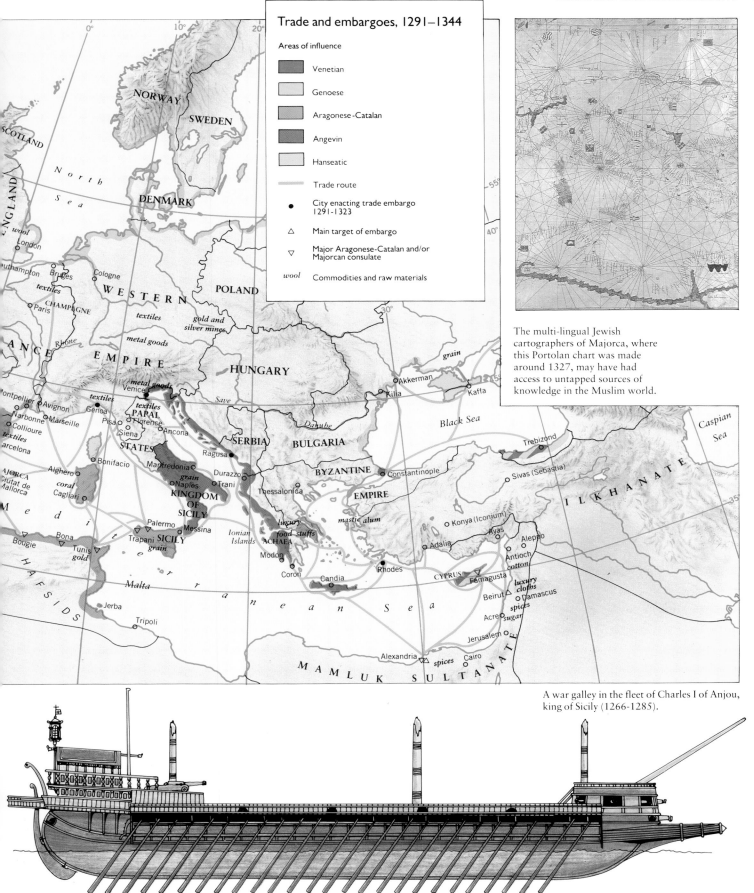

Trade and embargoes, 1291–1344

Areas of influence

Venetian

Genoese

Aragonese-Catalan

Angevin

Hanseatic

—— Trade route

● City enacting trade embargo 1291-1323

△ Main target of embargo

▽ Major Aragonese-Catalan and/or Majorcan consulate

wool Commodities and raw materials

The multi-lingual Jewish cartographers of Majorca, where this Portolan chart was made around 1327, may have had access to untapped sources of knowledge in the Muslim world.

A war galley in the fleet of Charles I of Anjou, king of Sicily (1266-1285).

NORWAY

SWEDEN

SCOTLAND

North Sea

DENMARK

ENGLAND

wool

London

Southampton

Bruges

Cologne

textiles

WESTERN

POLAND

CHAMPAGNE

Paris

textiles

gold and silver mines

Rhone

metal goods

EMPIRE

HUNGARY

30°

Montpellier

Avignon

textiles

Venice

metal goods

textiles

Genoa

PAPAL

Pisa

Florence

textiles

Siena

Ancona

SERBIA

BULGARIA

Save

Danube

grain

Akkerman

Kilia

Kaffa

Black Sea

Caspian Sea

Narbonne

Marseille

Collioure

Barcelona

textiles

STATES

Ragusa

Trebizond

Bonifacio

Manfredonia

grain

Durazzo

Trani

Thessalonica

BYZANTINE

Constantinople

Sivas (Sebastia)

ILKHANATE

MAJORCA

Ciutat de Mallorca

Alghero

coral

Cagliari

Naples

KINGDOM OF SICILY

EMPIRE

mastic alum

Konya (Iconium)

Ayas

Aleppo

Bona

Bougie

Tunis

gold

Palermo

Trapani

Messina

SICILY

grain

luxury food stuffs

Ionian Islands

ACHAEA

Modon

Coron

Candia

Rhodes

Adalia

CYPRUS

Famagusta

Antioch

cotton

luxury cloths

Beirut

Damascus

Acre

spices

sugar

HAFSIDS

Jerba

Malta

Tripoli

Mediterranean Sea

Jerusalem

Alexandria

spices

Cairo

MAMLUK SULTANATE

Cyprus under the Lusignan Kings

Under the kings of the Lusignan dynasty, Cyprus became a vital new force in the Latin East.

After conquering Cyprus in 1191(▶*page 62*), Richard I sold the island to his friend Guy of Lusignan, the former king of Jerusalem. Guy founded a dynasty that was to rule Cyprus until 1489. He brought with him other settlers from Palestine, and imposed a strict feudal system with laws closely modelled on those of the kingdom of Jerusalem, holding the indigenous Greek population in subservience. No member of the aristocracy was ever allowed to hold a castle as part of their feudal inheritance, in case the lords grew too powerful.

Despite the civil war that shook the island from 1229 to 1233 (▶*page 96*), its relative stability and its favourable position soon brought considerable prosperity. The Lusignan capital, Nicosia, became the most splendid in the Latin East. Limassol was originally the main port, but by the end of the 13th century, Famagusta had outstripped it; ideally placed to trade with Cilician Armenia and the ports of northern Syria, it embarked on a period of great prosperity.

The mountains to the north of Nicosia were dominated by three castles which had been built when the island was under Byzantine rule: St Hilarion (which controlled the pass to Kyrenia), Buffavento and Kantara. There were few other fortified points, although the towns Famagusta and Kyrenia were both enclosed by formidable defences.

The Military Orders were richly endowed, especially in the wine-growing south of the island. The Hospitallers had a commandery, or fortress-cum-administrative centre, at Kolossi and the Templars one at Gastria. After the fall of Acre in 1291, both the Templars and Hospitallers chose Cyprus as the location for their new headquarters. When the Templars were suppressed early in the 14th century (▶ *page 124*), their lands were transferred to the Hospitallers, who became extremely wealthy as a result.

The Latin church hierarchy consisted of an archbishop of Nicosia and suffragan bishops of Paphos, Limassol and Famagusta. The Praemonstratensian order had a major abbey at Bellapaïs and the Benedictines took over the Greek Orthodox monastery at Stavrovouni. But the majority of the population remained loyal to the Orthodox rite. Their bishops were subordinated to the Latins, but the Greeks continued to maintain their own monasteries such as Ayios Neophitos near Paphos, and a new Orthodox cathedral was built in the western, gothic style at Famagusta in the 14th century.

The Lusignan kingdom reached its zenith in the mid-14th century under the energetic Peter I (▶*page 142*). But in 1373 the Genoese took Famagusta, ushering in a century of decline. A Mamluk invasion in 1426 forced the Cypriots to recognize the suzerainty of the sultan in Egypt, and finally, in 1489, the Venetians took over the island.

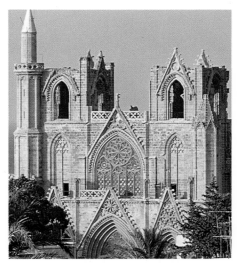

Above: The early 14th-century Catholic Cathedral at Famagusta. The outstanding example of Gothic architecture from the Latin East, since the Ottoman conquest it has been a mosque.

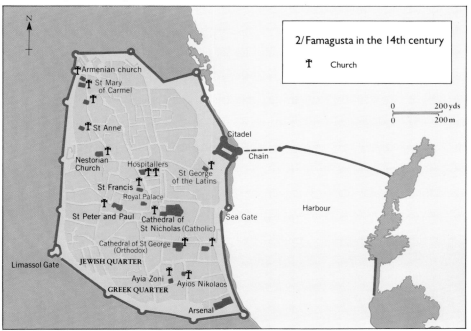

2/ Famagusta in the 14th century

✝ Church

0   200 yds
0   200 m

Armenian church
St Mary of Carmel
St Anne
Nestorian Church
Hospitallers
St George of the Latins
St Francis
Royal Palace
St Peter and Paul
Cathedral of St Nicholas (Catholic)
Cathedral of St George (Orthodox)
JEWISH QUARTER
Ayia Zoni
Ayios Nikolaos
GREEK QUARTER
Limassol Gate
Citadel
Chain
Sea Gate
Harbour
Arsenal

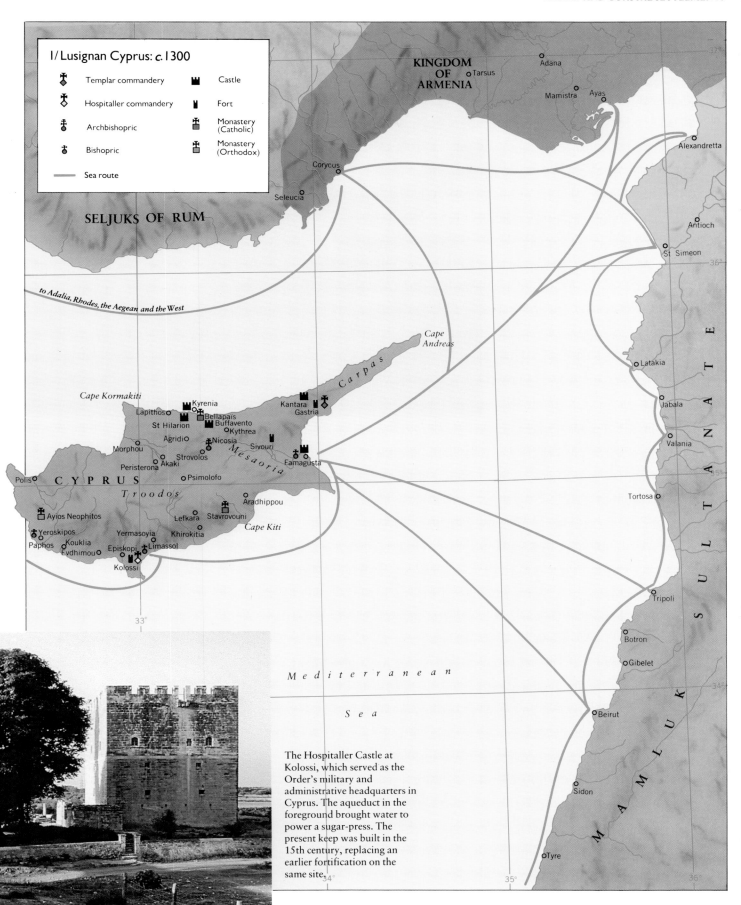

I/Lusignan Cyprus: c. 1300

- ✠ Templar commandery
- ✠ Hospitaller commandery
- ✠ Archbishopric
- ✠ Bishopric
- ⬛ Castle
- ▮ Fort
- ✠ Monastery (Catholic)
- ✠ Monastery (Orthodox)
- ——— Sea route

KINGDOM OF ARMENIA

Adana

Tarsus

Mamistra

Ayas

Corycus

Seleucia

Alexandretta

SELJUKS OF RUM

Antioch

St Simeon

to Adalia, Rhodes, the Aegean and the West

36°

Cape Andreas

Latakia

Carpas

Jabala

Cape Kormakiti

Kyrenia

Lapithos

St Hilarion

Bellapais

Buffavento

Kythrea

Agridio

Nicosia

Sivouri

Morphou

Strovolos

Akaki

Peristerona

Famagusta

Psimolofo

Polis

CYPRUS

Troodos

Kantara

Gastria

Mesaoria

Valania

Tortosa

Aradhippou

Lefkara

Stavrovouni

Ayios Neophitos

Khirokitia

Cape Kiti

Yeroskipos

Kouklia

Yermasoyia

Paphos

Evdhimou

Episkopi

Limassol

Kolossi

33°

Tripoli

Botron

Gibelet

Mediterranean

Sea

Beirut

Sidon

MAMLUK

SULTANATE

Tyre

34°

35°

36°

The Hospitaller Castle at Kolossi, which served as the Order's military and administrative headquarters in Cyprus. The aqueduct in the foreground brought water to power a sugar-press. The present keep was built in the 15th century, replacing an earlier fortification on the same site.

Hospitaller Rhodes

Driven from the Holy Land, the Hospitallers found a new base on the island of Rhodes.

After the fall of Acre in 1291, the Hospitallers retreated to Cyprus, and by 1310 had conquered the Byzantine island of Rhodes. This became their headquarters, where the brethren of each *langue* or tongue resided in their hostels or *auberges* within a walled area of the town, the *collachium*. The city and harbour were fortified, Greek and Latin farmers and merchants settled, a commercial emporium developed and the rural population of the island protected.

The Order's western possessions produced the men and money to sustain several hundred brethren, together with sufficient mercenaries and galleys to defend Rhodes and the dependent islands; the Cypriot commandery with its rich sugar plantations at Kolossi provided further incomes.

The majority of the Hospitallers were French, and the Order was supported by the French popes at Avignon, but after the great plague of 1348 and the papal schism of 1378 it became increasingly difficult to recruit and finance brethren. When a long series of French Masters ended in 1377, the Order's rulers became more international.

The conquest of Rhodes, Cos and the other islands was followed by a succession of naval victories which partly drove the ships of the neighbouring emirate of Menteşe off the seas. The Hospital collaborated in Latin operations which culminated in the capture of Smyrna in 1344 (▶ page 140). This diverted Turkish expansion further north, and in 1354 the Ottomans established themselves in Europe and began to overrun the Balkans. The Hospitallers took part in crusades such as those to Alexandria in 1365 and to Nicopolis in 1396; and they intervened, notably in 1377 and 1397, on mainland Greece. When Smyrna fell to the Mongol leader Timur in 1402 (▶ page 146), it was replaced by a new castle at Bodrum.

The Hospitallers repulsed serious Mamluk attacks on Rhodes in 1440 and again in 1444, and a major Ottoman siege was heroically resisted in 1480. The city walls were immensely strengthened to resist ever more powerful Turkish cannons, but finally a new Ottoman attack led by the Sultan Bayezid proved too powerful; the Hospitallers held out courageously, but help never came, and Rhodes finally surrendered in December 1522.

Fra' Alberto Arringhieri painted by Pinturicchio in 1504. The view of Rhodes in the background was copied from a woodcut illustrating the 1480 siege. It is stylized and back to front.

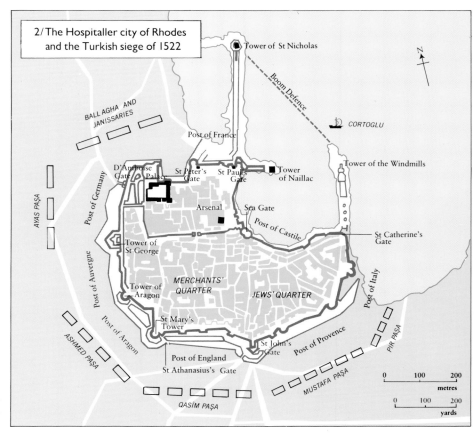

2/ The Hospitaller city of Rhodes and the Turkish siege of 1522

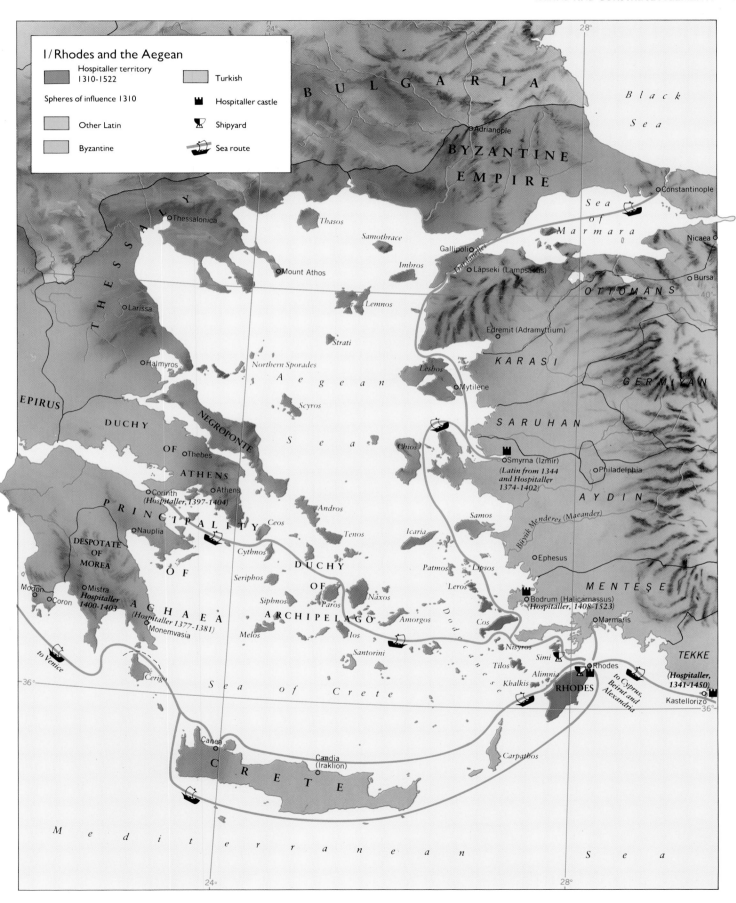

I/Rhodes and the Aegean

Hospitaller territory
1310-1522

Turkish

Spheres of influence 1310

Hospitaller castle

Other Latin

Shipyard

Byzantine

Sea route

BULGARIA

Black Sea

BYZANTINE EMPIRE

Adrianople

Constantinople

Sea of Marmara

Nicaea

Gallipoli

Dardanelles

Lâpseki (Lampsacus)

OTTOMANS

Bursa

Thessalonica

Thasos

Samothrace

Imbros

Lemnos

Mount Athos

Edremit (Adramyttium)

KARASI

Strati

Larissa

Lesbos

Mytilene

SARUHAN

GERMIYAN

Halmyros

Northern Sporades

Scyros

A e g e a n

S e a

Chios

Smyrna (Izmir)
(Latin from 1344
and Hospitaller
1374-1402)

Philadelphia

EPIRUS

THESSALY

DUCHY

OF

NEGROPONTE

Thebes

ATHENS

Andros

Samos

AYDIN

Corinth
(Hospitaller, 1397-1404)

Athens

Tenos

Icaria

Büyük Menderes (Maeander)

Ceos

Nauplia

PRINCIPALITY

Cythnos

Patmos

Lipsos

Ephesus

DESPOTATE
OF
MOREA

Mistra
Hospitaller
1400-1403

OF

Seriphos

DUCHY

Leros

Cos

MENTEŞE

Modon

Coron

ACHAEA

(Hospitaller 1377-1381)

Monemvasia

Siphnos

Paros

Naxos

OF

ARCHIPELAGO

Amorgos

Bodrum (Halicarnassus)
(Hospitaller, 1408-1523)

Marmaris

Melos

Ios

Santorini

Nisyros

Simi

Tilos

TEKKE

to Venice

Cerigo

S e a   o f   C r e t e

Khalkis

Alimnia

Rhodes

RHODES

to Cyprus,
Beirut and
Alexandria

(Hospitaller,
1341-1450)

Kastellorizo

Canea

Candia
(Iraklion)

Carpathos

C R E T E

M e d i t e r r a n e a n   S e a

Dodecanese

The Fragmentation of Latin Greece

To the north-west of Cyprus lay the crusader states of Greece; but a combination of unruly mercenaries, internecine rivalries and the rise of the Ottomans undermined their precarious stability.

At the beginning of the 14th century, the Latin settlements in Greece consisted of the principality of Achaea, the duchy of Athens and, in the Aegean, the duchy of Archipelago and a number of other island lordships (▶ *page 86*). The cohesion of these settlements was shattered in 1311 when the Catalan Company slaughtered Walter of Brienne, duke of Athens, and much of his nobility and knighthood. The Catalans were mercenaries who had been imported by the Byzantine emperor into Asia Minor to fight the Turks; from the Byzantine enclave of Philadelphia they moved to Gallipoli, and by 1309 were in Thessaly.

After their victory at Halmyros, the Catalans set up a state based on Thebes and Athens. They accepted the overlordship of the Aragonese royal family, so that Athens became a part of Aragon's expanding Mediterranean empire. The principality of Achaea, however, was subject to the Angevin rulers of the kingdom of Naples. The arrival of the Catalans thus turned Greece into another arena for the conflict between Aragon and Anjou that was already racking southern Italy (▶ *page 78*).

Athens and Achaea were both torn by internal conflicts between rival claimants. Achaea was menaced by the Byzantines of Mistra and by periodic Ottoman attacks and between 1377 and 1381 it was ruled by the Hospitallers of Rhodes. Navarrese mercenaries then took control; one of them, Peter of St Superan, secured the princely title in 1396. His successor, Centurione Zaccaria, was dispossessed by the Byzantine despot of Mistra in 1432, and the principality of Achaea ceased to exist.

The Navarrese and the Hospitallers also intervened in the duchy of Athens, capturing Thebes in 1379. But Catalan domination of Athens was only ended in 1388 when Nerio Acciaiuoli, the Florentine lord of Corinth, siezed the duchy. His successors ruled Athens until the last remnants of Latin rule in Greece were swept away by the advancing Ottoman empire in 1456 (▶ *page 150*).

The island settlements proved more enduring: the Hospitallers held Rhodes until 1522 (▶ *page 136*); the Genoese occupied Chios – the world centre for the production of mastic – until 1566; while the Venetians retained Crete until 1669 (▶ *page 166*). Ultimately, it was these Italian merchant cities, whose ships provided the means of communication, which reaped the most enduring benefits from the Latin settlements in Greece.

The Latin settlers built many towers throughout Greece. The best-preserved of the 30 that survive is at Markopoulo (below), some 15 miles (25 kilometres) north-east of Athens.

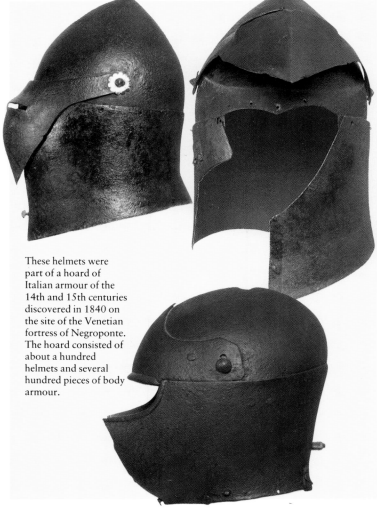

These helmets were part of a hoard of Italian armour of the 14th and 15th centuries discovered in 1840 on the site of the Venetian fortress of Negroponte. The hoard consisted of about a hundred helmets and several hundred pieces of body armour.

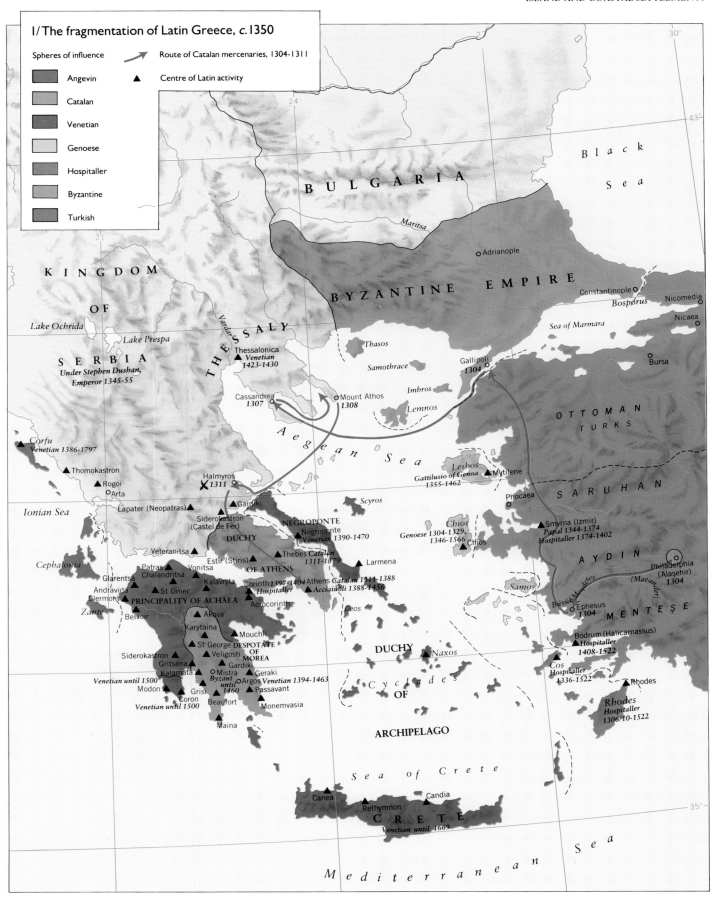

I/ The fragmentation of Latin Greece, *c.*1350

Spheres of influence

Angevin

Catalan

Venetian

Genoese

Hospitaller

Byzantine

Turkish

→ Route of Catalan mercenaries, 1304-1311

▲ Centre of Latin activity

BULGARIA

Black Sea

Maritsa

○ Adrianople

BYZANTINE EMPIRE

Constantinople ○

Bosporus

Nicomedia ○

Nicaea ○

Sea of Marmara

KINGDOM

OF

Lake Ochrida

Lake Prespa

SERBIA

Under Stephen Dushan, Emperor 1345-55

THESSALY

Vardar

▲ Thessalonica *Venetian 1423-1430*

Cassandrea *1307*

Mount Athos ○ *1308*

Thasos

Samothrace

Imbros

Lemnos

Gallipoli ○ *1304*

Bursa ○

OTTOMAN

TURKS

Corfu ▲ *Venetian 1386-1797*

▲ Thomokastron

▲ Rogoi

○ Arta

Ionian Sea

Halmyros ✕ *1311*

▲ Gardiki

Aegean Sea

Scyros

Leshos Gattilusio of Genoa 1355-1462

▲ Mytilene

Phocaea ○

SARUHAN

Cephalonia

Lapater (Neopatras) ▲

Siderokastron *(Castel de Fer)*

DUCHY

Veteranitsa ▲

NEGROPONTE

Negroponte *Venetian 1390-1470*

▲ Estir (Stiris)

Thebes *Catalan 1311-1379* ▲

▲ Larmena

Chios Genoese 1304-1329, 1346-1566

Chios ○

▲ Smyrna (Izmir) *Papal 1344-1374 Hospitaller 1374-1402*

AYDIN

Philadelphia *(Alaşehir) 1304*

Zante

Patras ▲ Vonitsa ▲

Glarentsa ▲ Chalandritsa ▲

Andravida ▲ St Omer ▲ Kalavryta ▲

Clermont ▲

PRINCIPALITY OF ACHAEA

Belvoir ▲

Corinth *1397-1404 Hospitaller* Acrocorinth ▲

Athens *Catalan 1311-1388* ▲ Acciaiuoli *1388-1456*

Ceos

DUCHY

Samos

Büyük Menderes

Ephesus ○ *1304*

MENTEŞE

Bodrum (Halicarnassus) ▲ *Hospitaller 1408-1522*

Akova ▲

Karytaina ▲

Mouchli ▲

St George ▲ Veligosti ▲ Gardiki ▲

DESPOTATE OF MOREA

Naxos ▲

OF

C y c l a d e s

Maeander

Siderokastron ▲

Gritsena ▲

Kalamata ▲ Mistra ○ Geraki ▲

Argos *Venetian 1394-1463* Byzant. *until 1460*

Passavant ▲

Venetian until 1500

Modon ▲ Grisi ▲ Beaufort ▲ Monemvasia ▲

Coron ▲

Venetian until 1500

Maina ▲

Cos Hospitaller 1336-1522

▲ Rhodes

Rhodes Hospitaller 1306/10-1522

OF

ARCHIPELAGO

Sea of Crete

Canea ▲ Rethymnon ▲ Candia ○

C R E T E

Venetian until 1669

M e d i t e r r a n e a n   S e a

Crusading Leagues in the Aegean

The rise of the Turks of Asia Minor gave rise to a new crusading strategy: the formation of crusading leagues.

In the early 14th century, the Latin rulers of Greece and the Aegean islands (▶ *page 86*) began to face a new Muslim threat. The old Seljuk sultanate had collapsed as a result of the Mongol invasions (▶ *page 112*), and in its place, a group of Turkish maritime emirates had formed along the western coast of Asia Minor. The emirates, which were effectively independent of Mongol rule, were governed by men like the redoubtable Umur of Aydin, exponents of vigorous holy war who welcomed the opportunity to lead their warriors in raids by land and especially by sea.

The westerners, especially the Venetians, Hospitallers and Cypriots, tried to co-ordinate a response in the form of naval leagues. Their appeals to the papacy to grant crusading status to these leagues were successful, and the result was a new type of crusading venture: the granting of crusade indulgences, privileges and taxes for the assembly of relatively small flotillas of fighting galleys, provided and financed by a group of powers for a specified length of time.

Although there were many attempts to form crusading leagues, only three reached the stage of action in the 14th century. The first, in 1334, demonstrated by a victory near Adramyttium that the Latins still possessed superiority over the Turks at sea. A second league, formed under the enthusiastic patronage of Pope Clement VI, was more ambitious and successful. In 1344 it captured and held on to Smyrna, the finest of the Turkish ports and the sea outlet of Umur of Aydin. The capture of this superb harbour was one of the greatest achievements of the crusading movement in the 14th century, and generated grandiose hopes in the West. Humbert II, the Dauphin of Viennois, recruited crusaders in a number of north Italian cities with the aim of leading an expeditionary force to Smyrna. But his hopes were frustrated by the hostility of the Genoese – who saw the league as a Venetian enterprise – the unreliability of his Venetian allies, and the absence of a clear plan of operations.

It was not until 1359 that another league was formed. In that year, the pope's legate Peter Thomas won an important victory at Lampsacus and backed Peter I of Cyprus's expansion onto the southern coast of Asia

Minor (▶ *page 142*).

In the second half of the 14th century, the maritime emirates were eclipsed by the rise of the Ottomans, and crusading activity was redirected towards Constantinople and the Balkans (▶ *page 148*). But the naval league remained a characteristic form of anti-Turkish crusade for decades to come, and provided the blueprint for the Holy League that defeated the Ottomans at Lepanto in 1571 (▶ *page 164*).

> **F**or some time now (the Turks) have assembled their strength, including a massive number of armed ships, and have invaded by sea the lands of the Christians in the region of Romania (Latin Greece) and other territories of the faithful adjacent to them. They have launched naval raids against the Christians, their lands and islands with awful ferocity, savaging and depopulating them ... and putting them to flame. What is worse, they take the Christians themselves as booty, subjecting them to horrible and perpetual slavery, selling them like animals and forcing them to renounce their Catholic faith.
>
> **Pope Clement VI decrees crusade preaching against the Turkish maritime emirates, 1343**

The coronation of Pope Clement VI in 1342. During his pontificate, the strategy of crusading leagues was developed, and levies were raised in church provinces to send galleys to the Aegean.

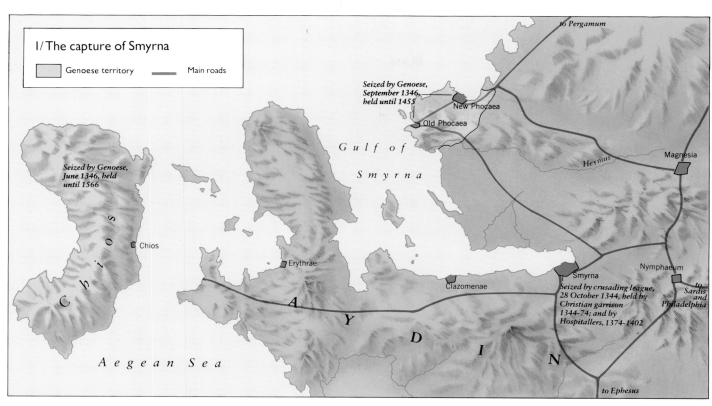

1/ The capture of Smyrna

- Genoese territory
- Main roads

Seized by Genoese, September 1346, held until 1455
New Phocaea
Old Phocaea

to Pergamum

Gulf of Smyrna

Magnesia
Hermus

Seized by Genoese, June 1346, held until 1566

Chios

Chios

Erythrae

Clazomenae

Smyrna
Seized by crusading league, 28 October 1344, held by Christian garrison 1344-74; and by Hospitallers, 1374-1402

Nymphaeum
to Sardis and Philadelphia

A Y D I N

Aegean Sea

to Ephesus

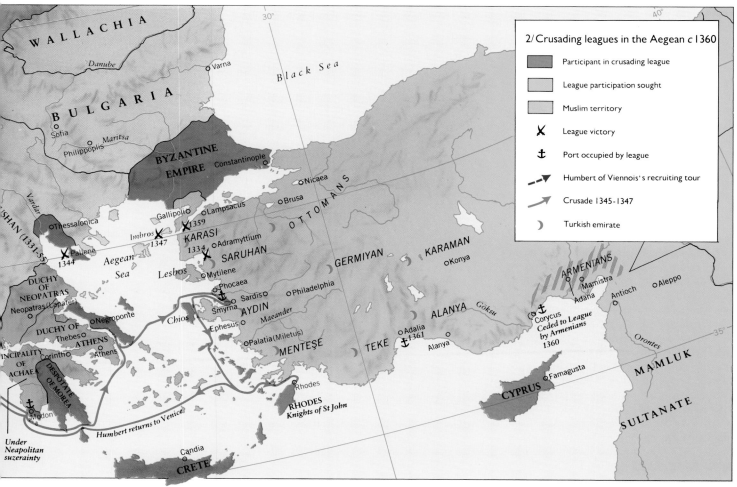

2/ Crusading leagues in the Aegean c 1360

- Participant in crusading league
- League participation sought
- Muslim territory
- ✗ League victory
- ⚓ Port occupied by league
- ◄-- Humbert of Viennois's recruiting tour
- → Crusade 1345-1347
- ☾ Turkish emirate

WALLACHIA

Danube

BULGARIA

Black Sea

Varna

Sofia
Philippoplis   *Maritsa*

BYZANTINE EMPIRE   Constantinople

Nicaea

Brusa
Lampsacus
Gallipoli
OTTOMANS
...SHAN (1331-55)
Thessalonica
Imbros ✗1359
1347
KARASI
1334 ✗ Adramyttium
SARUHAN
Pallene
1344 ✗
Aegean Sea
Lesbos
Mytilene
DUCHY OF NEOPATRAS
Neopatras (Sidari)
Phocaea
Sardis
Philadelphia
GERMIYAN
KARAMAN
Konya
ARMENIANS
Mamistra
Adana
Antioch
Aleppo
Negroponte
Chios
Smyrna
AYDIN
DUCHY OF ATHENS
Thebes
Maeander
Ephesus
Palatia (Miletus)
MENTEŞE
TEKE
ALANYA
Göksu
Corycus
Ceded to League by Armenians 1360
Corinth
Athens
PRINCIPALITY OF ACHAEA
Adalia
⚓1361
Alanya
Orontes
DESPOTATE OF MOREA
Rhodes
RHODES
Knights of St John
CYPRUS
Famagusta
MAMLUK
Modon
Humbert returns to Venice
SULTANATE
Under Neapolitan suzerainty
Candia
CRETE

The Crusade of Peter I of Cyprus

King Peter I of Cyprus briefly revived the dream of liberating Jerusalem; but his most celebrated exploit, the sack of Alexandria, was a short-lived success.

It is sometimes said that Peter was an 'old-fashioned' crusade enthusiast, who dreamed of restoring Christian rule in Jerusalem; more likely he was concerned primarily with the security of Cyprus and the preservation of its share of east-west trade. It was during his reign (1359-1369) that the Lusignan kingdom of Cyprus (▶ *page 134*) reached the zenith of its power and prosperity, and became a centre for anti-Muslim aggression.

At first, Peter concentrated on waging war on the Turkish emirates of southern Asia Minor (▶ *page 140*), whose ships were raiding his kingdom and preying on Christian merchants. In 1360 he was handed control of Corycus by its Armenian inhabitants. The next year he seized the important port of Adalia, and this was followed by a series of smaller raids on towns along the Turkish coast in 1362 and 1363.

Cypriot resources alone were inadequate for any larger undertaking, and in 1362 the king set off to the West to enlist support. The pope gave his enterprise the status of a crusade, and Peter visited France, England, the Low Countries, Germany, Bohemia and Poland in his quest for men and money. In 1365 his recruits sailed from Venice and met up with the Cypriots at Rhodes. In October they captured and sacked the major Egyptian port of Alexandria. But they were unable to retain it and withdrew, laden with plunder, to Cyprus a few days later.

Cyprus was now at war with the Mamluk sultanate of Egypt, and for the next five years negotiations for peace were interspersed with naval raids. A major expedition in January 1367 foundered in bad weather, and Turkish attack on Corycus and a mutiny at Adalia then diverted the king's attention. But there were raids on northern Syria and Cilicia later in 1367 and on Palestine in 1368. Finally, there was a small-scale but extremely wide-ranging expedition in 1369, although Peter himself had already been murdered in a palace *coup* at the beginning of the year. His efforts, in fact had largely run out of steam; and a second visit to the West in 1367 had achieved little. Peace with the Mamluks was agreed in 1370, and Adalia was relinquished to its former Turkish ruler in 1373.

A silver gros of King Peter I (1359-1369). The gros was introduced in the late 13th century and remained current for 200 years. The obverse shows the king with his symbols of regality, while the reverse has the Cross of Jerusalem, and declares him to be king of both Cyprus and Jerusalem.

T he conquest of Alexandria by Peter I, king of Cyprus, was a great and memorable achievement, which would have created a powerful basis for the spread of our religion if only the valour demonstrated in its capture had been matched in its holding.

Petrarch on the taking of Alexandria

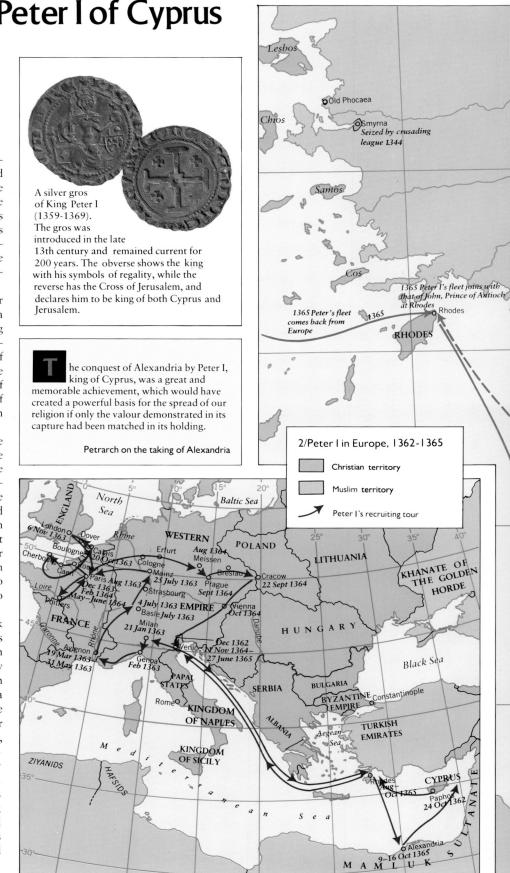

2/Peter I in Europe, 1362-1365

Christian territory

Muslim territory

Peter I's recruiting tour

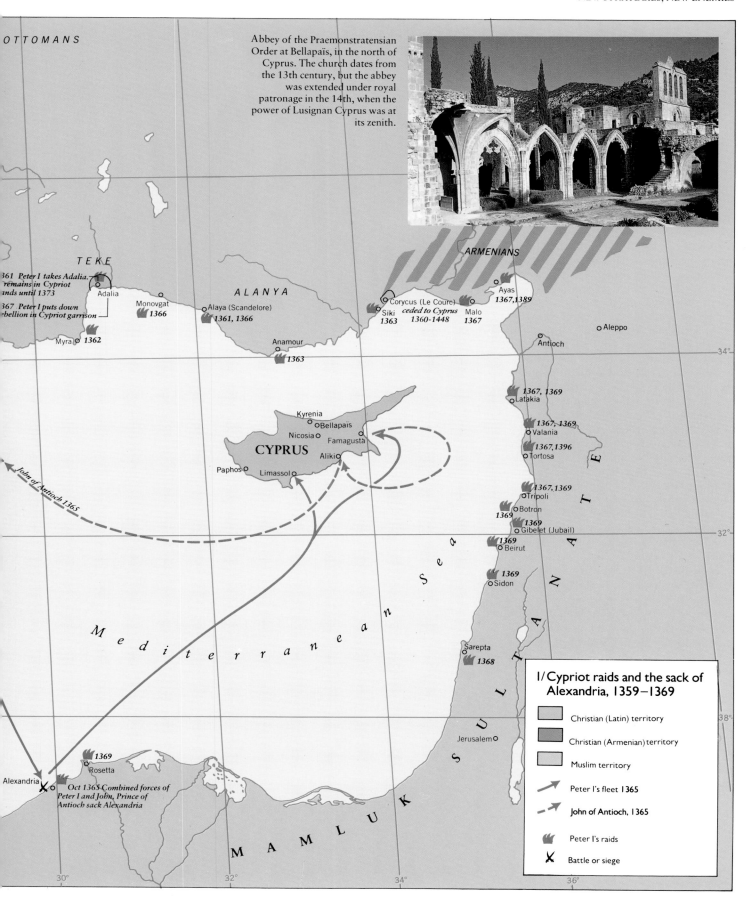

Abbey of the Praemonstratensian Order at Bellapaïs, in the north of Cyprus. The church dates from the 13th century, but the abbey was extended under royal patronage in the 14th, when the power of Lusignan Cyprus was at its zenith.

OTTOMANS

TEKE

861 *Peter I takes Adalia.* *remains in Cypriot* *ands until 1373*

367 *Peter I puts down* *bellion in Cypriot garrison*

Adalia

Monovgat
1366

Myra ○ **1362**

ALANYA

Alaya (Scandelore)
1361, 1366

Anamour
1363

ARMENIANS

Corycus (Le Courc)
Siki   *ceded to Cyprus*
1363   *1360-1448*

Ayas
1367, 1389

Malo
1367

○ Aleppo

Antioch

1367, 1369
Latakia

1367, 1369
○ Valania

1367, 1396
○ Tortosa

Kyrenia
○ Bellapais
Nicosia ○
Famagusta
CYPRUS
Alikio
Paphos ○   Limassol ○

John of Antioch 1365

M e d i t e r r a n e a n   S e a

1367, 1369
○ Tripoli
○ Botron
1369
1369
○ Gibelet (Jubail)

1369
○ Beirut

1369
○ Sidon

S U L T A N A T E

Sarepta
1368

M A M L U K   S U L T A N A T E

Jerusalem ○

1369
Rosetta

Alexandria ✗ ○ *Oct 1365 Combined forces of*
Peter I and John, Prince of
Antioch sack Alexandria

34°

32°

38°

30°   32°   34°   36°

1/Cypriot raids and the sack of Alexandria, 1359–1369

	Christian (Latin) territory
	Christian (Armenian) territory
	Muslim territory

→ Peter I's fleet 1365

⇢ John of Antioch, 1365

♛ Peter I's raids

✗ Battle or siege

Crusades of the Great Schism

In 1378, the Catholic church split, and Europe was torn between the followers of rival popes. Each side was eager to use crusading against the other.

The papacy's long exile in Avignon (▶page 78) caused considerable dissatisfaction. In 1378 a new pope – Urban VI – was elected at Rome. When he showed himself to be unsuitable, a rival – Clement VII – was proclaimed at Avignon. Europe was divided between the followers of one pope or the other, and each pope proclaimed crusades against the supporters of his rival. The two most important of these ventures were fought by the English, who supported Rome. In 1383 the bishop of Norwich, Henry Despenser, led a crusade against the count of Flanders, an ally of France and an adherent of Avignon. The English took several channel towns, but were forced to abandon the siege of Ypres when the French army approached. Three years later, John of Gaunt led a crusading army against Castile, in association with the king of Portugal.

This crusade was no more successful than Henry Despenser's, and generally such attempts to resolve the schism by warfare were eclipsed by the idea that a crusade against the Muslims might be the way to restore Christian unity. In 1390 Count Louis of Bourbon led a crusade against the port of Mahdia in Tunisia. The expedition was suggested by the Genoese, who supplied it with shipping. Most of Louis's army were French, but it included supporters of both Rome and Avignon. Whatever its benefits to Christian morale, the military achievements of the crusade were minimal, and it was abandoned after a nine-week siege. The only beneficiaries were the Genoese, who extracted valuable trading privileges from the emir of Tunis.

Much ambitious and well-intentioned diplomacy at the courts of England, France and Burgundy went into the planning of the great crusade which set out for Nicopolis in 1396 (▶page 148). Although it too was a military failure, it was clearly intended as an expression, and an instrument, of Christian unity, and was proclaimed by both popes.

The schism itself became even more complex when an attempt to resolve it at the Council of Pisa resulted in the election of yet a third rival. It was only in 1417 that the Council of Constance was able to elect a pope – Martin V – who was recognized by all of Western Europe.

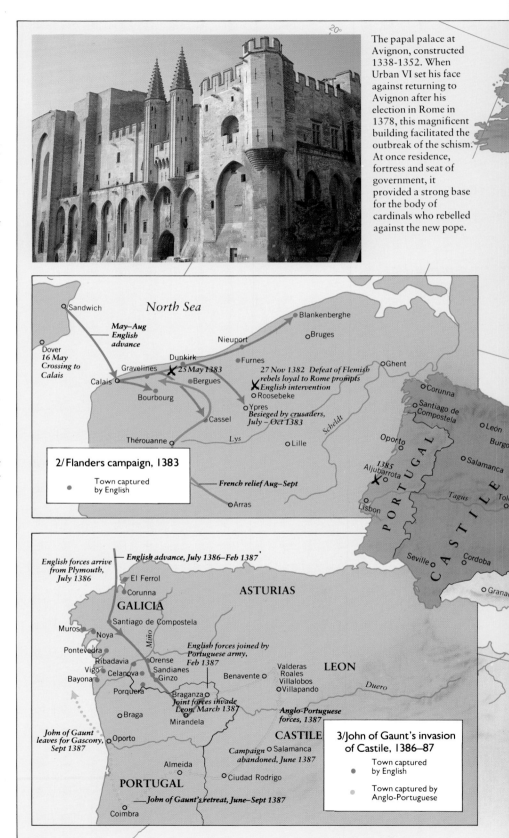

The papal palace at Avignon, constructed 1338-1352. When Urban VI set his face against returning to Avignon after his election in Rome in 1378, this magnificent building facilitated the outbreak of the schism. At once residence, fortress and seat of government, it provided a strong base for the body of cardinals who rebelled against the new pope.

2/Flanders campaign, 1383
● Town captured by English

May–Aug English advance
Sandwich
North Sea
Dover 16 May *Crossing to Calais*
Calais
Gravelines
Bourbourg
Thérouanne
Cassel
Bergues
Dunkirk
✕ 25 May 1383
Nieuport
Furnes
Roosebeke
Ypres *Besieged by crusaders, July – Oct 1383*
Blankenberghe
Bruges
Ghent
27 Nov 1382 Defeat of Flemish rebels loyal to Rome prompts ✕ *English intervention*
Scheldt
Lys
Lille
French relief Aug–Sept
Arras

Corunna
Santiago de Compostela
León
Burgo
Oporto
1385 Aljubarrota ✕
PORTUGAL
Salamanca
Tagus
Lisbon
CASTILE
Tol

3/John of Gaunt's invasion of Castile, 1386–87
● Town captured by English
● Town captured by Anglo-Portuguese

English forces arrive from Plymouth, July 1386
— *English advance, July 1386–Feb 1387*
El Ferrol
Corunna
GALICIA
ASTURIAS
Muros
Santiago de Compostela
Noya
Pontevedra
Miño
Ribadavia
Orense
Vigo
Celanova
Sandianes
Bayona
Ginzo
Porquera
Braganza
Joint forces invade León, March 1387
Braga
Mirandela
John of Gaunt leaves for Gascony, Sept 1387
Oporto
English forces joined by Portuguese army, Feb 1387
Benavente
Valderas
Roales
Villalobos
Villapando
LEON
Duero
Anglo-Portuguese forces, 1387
CASTILE
Campaign abandoned, June 1387
Salamanca
Almeida
Ciudad Rodrigo
PORTUGAL
Seville
Cordoba
Granada
— *John of Gaunt's retreat, June–Sept 1387*
Coimbra

NORWAY

Uppsala
Stockholm

SWEDEN

Visby

SCOTLAND

Edinburgh

DENMARK

North Sea

Copenhagen

Baltic Sea

LIVONIA

Riga

Pskov

Novgorod

ELAND

Dublin

York

WALES

ENGLAND

Lincoln

Oxford

London

Winchester

Plymouth

Canterbury

Calais   Lille

Under
English rule

FLANDERS

Aachen

Cologne

Lübeck

Elbe

Magdeburg

changing local allegiances

Erfurt

Königsberg

Marienburg

PRUSSIA

Gniezno

Kalisz

POLAND

Vilnius

LITHUANIA

(converted to
Catholicism after 1386)

Caen

Rouen

Rheims

Seine

Paris

Chartres

Loire

Orléans

FRANCE

Dijon

Troyes

W E S T E R N

Nuremberg

Regensburg

Straubing

Rhine

Passau

Danube

Prague

Lublin

Cracow

Lvov

Poitiers
1356

Limoges

Under English rule

Bordeaux

Garonne

E M P I R E

Montbéliard

Constance

1417: Church Council ends Schism

Vienna

Buda

HUNGARY

MOLDAVIA

ay of
iscay

Lyon

Rhône

Po

Genoa

Venice

Zagreb

WALLACHIA

Nicopolis
1396

NAVARRE

Toulouse

Avignon

PROVENCE

Marseille

1409: Church Council
attempts to end Schism

Pisa

PAPAL

Zara

Durazzo

SERBIA

OTTOMAN

Adrianople

ARAGON

Saragossa

Barcelona

Tarragona

Peñiscola

Ebro

CORSICA

Plombino

STATES

Rome

1390

Terracina

Capua

Naples

KINGDOM

OF

NAPLES

Ragusa

EMPIRE

Constantinople

Valencia

BALEARIC ISLANDS

SARDINIA

Attacked by crusaders
at instigation of Genoese

Cagliari
1390

M e d i t e r r a

Messina

SICILY

n e a n

Algiers

Bougie

Tunis

S e a

Mahdia
1390

The Rise of the Ottomans

In little over 100 years, the Ottoman state transformed itself from a small Turkish emirate into the most vigorous power in the Islamic world.

The Ottoman state, named after its founder Osman, came into existence around 1300 as one of a number of Turkish emirates in the old Seljuk-Byzantine borderlands (▶page 140). Overshadowed at first by its neighbours, it gradually metamorphosed from a nondescript warband into an aggressive and expansionist Islamic power. By the accession of Mehmet II in 1451, it had occupied most of central and western Asia Minor and from a bridgehead at Gallipoli had annexed Bulgaria, Serbia and much of Albania. Constantinople, stripped of most of its empire, was surrounded.

The rise of this new Islamic power had not gone unnoticed in the west. Scarcely had the Ottomans established their bridgehead in Europe than they became the object of a series of crusading movements such as the crusade of Amadeus of Savoy in 1366 (▶page 148). The conquest of Adrianople around 1369 laid open the road to central Europe. From then on, the curbing of Ottoman power was to become a major objective of crusading.

There are parallels between certain aspects of Ottoman expansion in this period and crusading itself, particularly the concept of holy war (▶page 58). In Muslim dogma this is embodied in the concept of *jihad*, the duty to fight for the faith. The holy war itself, the *ghaza*, is undertaken by *ghazis*, the fighters for the faith. There is a debate about whether the emerging Ottoman empire was actually a *ghazi* state. Like the crusader states in the Near East, the Ottoman conquests in Europe were subject to the political administration of a dominant but – in both religious and ethnic terms – a minority elite. But while the crusades were long-distance operations conducted along extended and vulnerable lines of supply, the Ottoman empire expanded over land, so that despite occasional setbacks such as the invasion of Asia Minor by Timur in 1402, its conquests were far more secure than those of the crusaders.

With the Ottomans there came into existence a dramatic new potential: the possibility of creating a universal state based on religious faith and an imperial vision. To realise this vision, the Ottomans needed an imperial capital. Such a city existed already, poised between Europe and Asia. That Constantinople, not Jerusalem, was the ultimate prize in the 'world's debate' was a truth obscured to the West by emotion and faith. The Ottomans, however, perceived it from their beginnings and in 1453, the sultan Mehmet II was able to profit from this knowledge as the imperial city fell into his hands.

Mehmet II's conquest of Constantinople in 1453 was the culmination of a century and a half of Ottoman expansion. This portrait by Gentile Bellini shows the sultan towards the end of his life.

2/ Timur's invasions, 1400-1402

→ Invasion route

✗ Battle

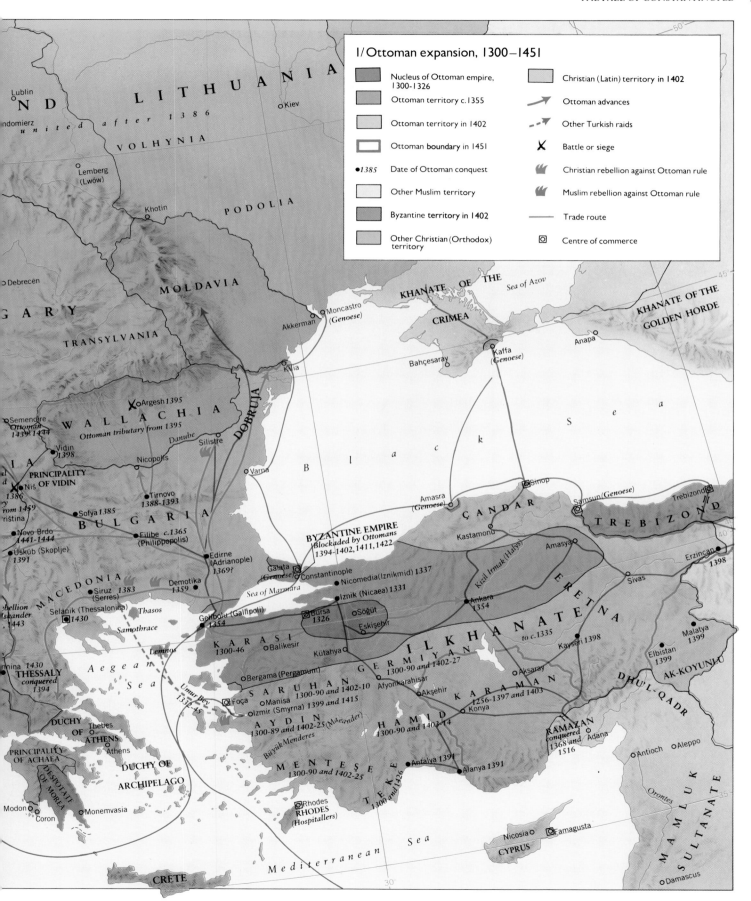

1/Ottoman expansion, 1300–1451

- Nucleus of Ottoman empire, 1300-1326
- Ottoman territory c.1355
- Ottoman territory in 1402
- Ottoman boundary in 1451
- •1385 Date of Ottoman conquest
- Other Muslim territory
- Byzantine territory in 1402
- Other Christian (Orthodox) territory
- Christian (Latin) territory in 1402
- Ottoman advances
- Other Turkish raids
- Battle or siege
- Christian rebellion against Ottoman rule
- Muslim rebellion against Ottoman rule
- Trade route
- Centre of commerce

Lublin

ND   L I T H U A N I A

Kiev

andomierz   *united after 1386*

VOLHYNIA

Debrecen

Lemberg (Lwów)

Khotin

PODOLIA

MOLDAVIA

GARY

TRANSYLVANIA

Moncastro (Genoese)

Akkerman

Kilia

KHANATE OF THE CRIMEA

Sea of Azov

KHANATE OF THE GOLDEN HORDE

Anapa

Bahçesaray

Kaffa (Genoese)

Argesh 1395

WALLACHIA

Ottoman tributary from 1395

S e a

a

Semendre Ottoman 1439, 1444

Vidin 1398

Danube

Silistre

DOBRUJA

B l a c k

Nicopolis

PRINCIPALITY OF VIDIN

Niš 1386

from 1459

riština

Tirnovo 1388-1393

Sofya 1385

BULGARIA

Varna

Amasra (Genoese)

Sinop

Samsun (Genoese)

Trebizond

Novo Brdo 1441-1444

Uskub (Skoplje) 1391

Filibe c.1365 (Philippopolis)

Edirne (Adrianople) 1369?

BYZANTINE EMPIRE *Blockaded by Ottomans 1394-1402, 1411, 1422*

Galata (Genoese)

Constantinople

ÇANDAR

Kastamonu

Kizil Irmak (Halys)

Amasya

T R E B I Z O N D

Erzincan

Sivas

1398

MACEDONIA

Demotika 1359

Siruz 1383 (Serres)

Nicomedia (Iznikmid) 1337

Iznik (Nicaea) 1331

E R E T N A

to c.1335

rebellion skander 1443

Selanik (Thessalonica) 1430

Thasos

Sea of Marmara

Gelibolu (Gallipoli) 1354

Bursa 1326

Söğüt

Ankara 1354

Kayseri 1398

Malatya 1399

AK-KOYUNLU

Samothrace

Lemnos

K A R A S I 1300-46

Balikesir

Eskişehir

I L K H A N A T E

Elbistan 1399

nina 1430

THESSALY *conquered 1394*

A e g e a n

S e a

Umur Bey 1332-45

Bergama (Pergamum)

Kütahya

G E R M I Y A N 1300-90 and 1402-27

Aksaray

D H U ' L - Q A D R

S A R U H A N 1300-90 and 1402-10

Manisa

Afyonkarahisar

Akşehir

K A R A M A N 1256-1397 and 1403

DUCHY OF ATHENS

Thebes

Athens

Foça

Olzmir (Smyrna) 1399 and 1415

A Y D I N 1300-89 and 1402-25

Büyük Menderes (Maeander)

H A M I D 1300-90 and 1403-14

Konya

RAMAZAN *conquered 1368 and 1516*

Adana

Antioch

Aleppo

PRINCIPALITY OF ACHAEA

DUCHY OF ARCHIPELAGO

DESPOTATE OF MOREA

Modon

Coron

Monemvasia

M E N T E Ş E 1300-90 and 1402-25

T E K E 1300 and 1326

Antalya 1391

Alanya 1391

Orontes

M A M L U K   S U L T A N A T E

Rhodes RHODES (Hospitallers)

S e a

Nicosia

Famagusta

CYPRUS

CRETE

M e d i t e r r a n e a n

Damascus

Crusades in Support of Constantinople

Only Constantinople stood between the Ottomans and Balkan domination. Western men, arms and money poured in to defend it.

As the Ottomans advanced into Europe, a series of crusades was organized to free the Christians of the Balkans and to assist the rapidly shrinking Byzantine empire.

The first of these expeditions was led by Amadeus of Savoy, and set out from Venice in 1366. It succeeded in recapturing Gallipoli from the Ottomans; but on arriving at Constantinople, Amadeus discovered that his cousin, the Byzantine emperor John V, had been taken prisoner by the Bulgarians. This forced him to divert his fleet into the Black Sea to rescue the emperor.

In 1394 the Ottomans invaded the Morea and blockaded Constantinople. Both the popes, at Rome and Avignon, proclaimed crusades against the Ottomans. A Hungarian and French army of 10,000 crusaders under King Sigismund of Hungary and John of Nevers, advanced down the Danube, a fleet of Hospitallers, Venetians and Genoese sailed upriver from the Black Sea to meet it. But due to the impetuosity of the French and the desertion of the Wallachians and Transylvanians, the crusaders suffered a crushing defeat at Nicopolis.

In 1399 the famous French captain Marshal Boucicaut led a contingent of troops which succeeded in temporarily lifting the Ottoman blockade of Constantinople and bringing the Byzantine emperor Manuel II to the West to appeal for help. In 1403, Boucicaut went on to lead a series of daring raids on Ottoman and Mamluk ports. But it was not until 1443 that another great expedition was launched against the Turks. In January of that year, Pope Eugenius IV called on the faithful to defend the Christian East from the Ottomans. When the Hungarians took Niš and Sofia that summer, Christians throughout the Balkans took up arms against the Ottomans. Western arms and money poured in to support the rebellion of the Albanian chief Iskander Beg. The Ottoman sultanate was in the throes of an internal crisis, and the liberation of the entire Balkans seemed a possibility. In August 1444, 20,000 crusaders assembled under King Ladislas of Hungary and Janos Hunyadi. A western fleet sailed for the Dardanelles, but was unable to prevent the sultan Murad II crossing the Bosporus to defeat the Hungarians at Varna.

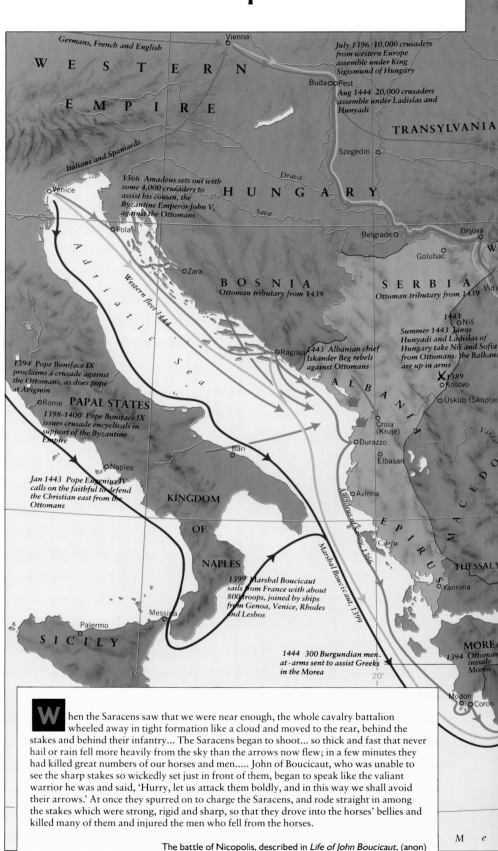

Germans, French and English

July 1396 10,000 crusaders from western Europe assemble under King Sigismund of Hungary

Aug 1444 20,000 crusaders assemble under Ladislas and Hunyadi

WESTERN EMPIRE

TRANSYLVANIA

Italians and Spaniards

1366 Amadeus sets out with some 4,000 crusaders to assist his cousin, the Byzantine Emperor John V, against the Ottomans

HUNGARY

Szegedin

Drava

Sava

Belgrade

Orsova

Golubac

BOSNIA
Ottoman tributary from 1439

SERBIA
Ottoman tributary from 1439

Western fleet 1444

Zara

Ragusa

1443 Albanian chief Iskander Beg rebels against Ottomans

1443
Niš
Summer 1443 János Hunyadi and Ladislas of Hungary take Niš and Sofia from Ottomans: the Balkans are up in arms

1389
Kosovo

Üsküb (Skoplje)

1394 Pope Boniface IX proclaims a crusade against the Ottomans, as does pope at Avignon

Rome PAPAL STATES

ALBANIA

Croia (Krujë)

1398-1400 Pope Boniface IX issues crusade encyclicals in support of the Byzantine Empire

Durazzo

Elbasan

Bari

MACEDONIA

Naples

Jan 1443 Pope Eugenius IV calls on the faithful to defend the Christian east from the Ottomans

Avlona

EPIRUS

Corfu

KINGDOM

OF

NAPLES

1399 Marshal Boucicaut sails from France with about 800 troops, joined by ships from Genoa, Venice, Rhodes and Lesbos

Messina

Palermo

SICILY

THESSALY

Yannina

1444 300 Burgundian men-at-arms sent to assist Greeks in the Morea

1394 Ottomans invade Morea

MOREA

Modon

Coron

> hen the Saracens saw that we were near enough, the whole cavalry battalion wheeled away in tight formation like a cloud and moved to the rear, behind the stakes and behind their infantry... The Saracens began to shoot... so thick and fast that never hail or rain fell more heavily from the sky than the arrows now flew; in a few minutes they had killed great numbers of our horses and men..... John of Boucicaut, who was unable to see the sharp stakes so wickedly set just in front of them, began to speak like the valiant warrior he was and said, 'Hurry, let us attack them boldly, and in this way we shall avoid their arrows.' At once they spurred on to charge the Saracens, and rode straight in among the stakes which were strong, rigid and sharp, so that they drove into the horses' bellies and killed many of them and injured the men who fell from the horses.

The battle of Nicopolis, described in *Life of John Boucicaut*, (anon)

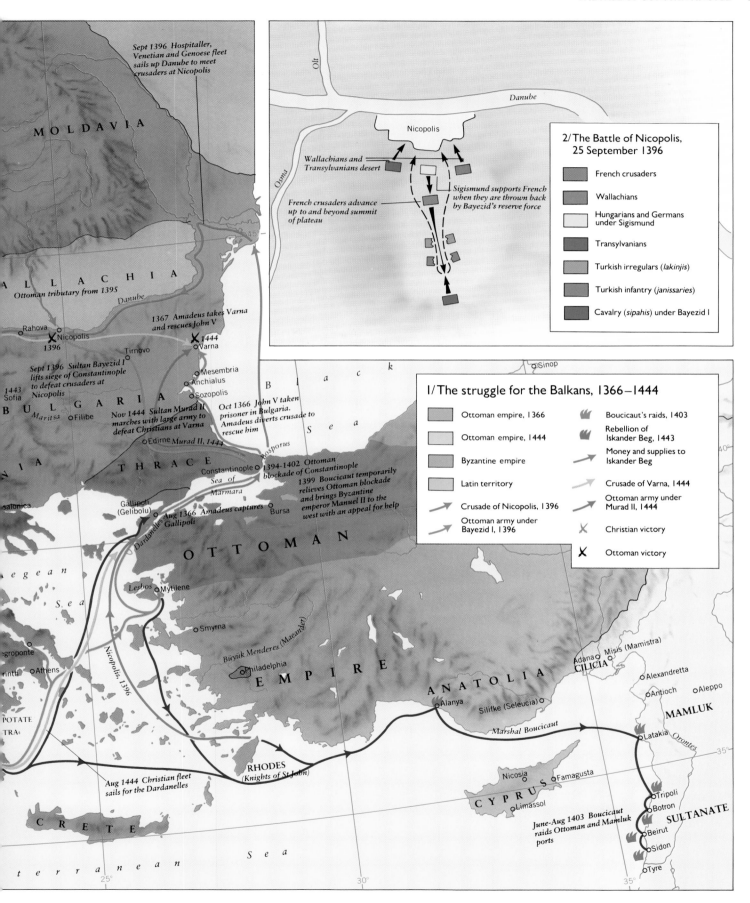

Sept 1396 Hospitaller, Venetian and Genoese fleet sails up Danube to meet crusaders at Nicopolis

2/ The Battle of Nicopolis, 25 September 1396

Wallachians and Transylvanians desert

French crusaders advance up to and beyond summit of plateau

Sigismund supports French when they are thrown back by Bayezid's reserve force

- French crusaders
- Wallachians
- Hungarians and Germans under Sigismund
- Transylvanians
- Turkish irregulars (*lakinjis*)
- Turkish infantry (*janissaries*)
- Cavalry (*sipahis*) under Bayezid I

1367 Amadeus takes Varna and rescues John V

Ottoman tributary from 1395

1396 Nicopolis

1444 Varna

Sept 1396 Sultan Bayezid I lifts siege of Constantinople to defeat crusaders at Nicopolis

1443 Sofia

Nov 1444 Sultan Murad II marches with large army to defeat Christians at Varna

Oct 1366 John V taken prisoner in Bulgaria. Amadeus diverts crusade to rescue him

Edirne Murad II, 1443

1394-1402 Ottoman blockade of Constantinople
1399 Boucicaut temporarily relieves Ottoman blockade and brings Byzantine emperor Manuel II to the west with an appeal for help

Constantinople

Sea of Marmara

Aug 1366 Amadeus captures Gallipoli

Bursa

1/ The struggle for the Balkans, 1366–1444

- Ottoman empire, 1366
- Ottoman empire, 1444
- Byzantine empire
- Latin territory
- Crusade of Nicopolis, 1396
- Ottoman army under Bayezid I, 1396
- Boucicaut's raids, 1403
- Rebellion of Iskander Beg, 1443
- Money and supplies to Iskander Beg
- Crusade of Varna, 1444
- Ottoman army under Murad II, 1444
- Christian victory
- Ottoman victory

Nicopolis 1396

Aug 1444 Christian fleet sails for the Dardanelles

RHODES (Knights of St John)

June-Aug 1403 Boucicaut raids Ottoman and Mamluk ports

Marshal Boucicaut

MAMLUK

SULTANATE

The New Islamic Empire

The fall of Constantinople in 1453 spelt the end of the old order in Europe and the Near East. The Ottomans were now poised to strike deep into Christian heartlands.

The Sultan Mehmet II, 'the Conqueror', devoted his career to incessant military activity. Within two years of his accession, his cannons had breached the thousand-year-old walls of Constantinople and brought about the final extinction of the Byzantine empire. The city was promptly rebuilt and repopulated to become the capital of an Islamic empire.

The remnants of the medieval Byzantine and Islamic state systems in the Balkans and Asia Minor soon succumbed. In Albania, resistance lasted until 1478. But an attempt to wrest Belgrade from the Hungarians in 1456 ended in disaster (▶*page 152*), and a Turkish bridgehead in Italy and a siege of Rhodes were abandoned on the sultan's death in 1481 (▶*page 136*).

Mehmet's successor, Bayezid II, was hamstrung by the fact that his brother Jem was held as a hostage in the West. In spite of the conquest of the important commercial ports of Kilia and Akkerman in 1484, the sultan achieved little in his wars with Poland (1497-1499) and Venice (1499-1503). By 1500, the stability of the Ottoman state was seriously threatened by the rise to power of the militantly Shi'i Safavid order in Iran and the resulting Shi'i unrest in Asia Minor.

Civil war broke out between Bayezid II and his sons for possession of the throne. With the death of Bayezid in 1512 and the ascendancy of his most able son Selim I, the rhythm of incessant campaign and conquest began again. After defeating the Safavids at Çaldiran and occupying their capital Tabriz in 1514, Selim eliminated the threat of a Safavid-Mamluk alliance by conquering the Mamluk sultanate in Egypt. The old Muslim lands of Syria and Egypt, and the Holy Places of Islam, Mecca and Medina, thus passed into Ottoman hands.

With the accession of Selim's only son, Suleyman I 'The Magnificent' in 1520, the reins of the Ottoman counter-crusade were taken up once more. In the first campaigns of his reign, Suleyman concluded two of the three great pieces of unfinished business from the reign of the Conqueror by seizing Belgrade in 1521 and Rhodes in 1522. The way was now open for the Ottomans to ex-

tend their naval power into the Mediterranean and their land forces into Hungary. In 1526, Suleyman destroyed the Hungarian kingdom at the Battle of Mohács. This brought the Ottomans into direct conflict with the Habsburgs (▶*page 164*), initiating what was perhaps the greatest religious and imperial struggle of early modern history and, in another sense, the last era of the crusading movement.

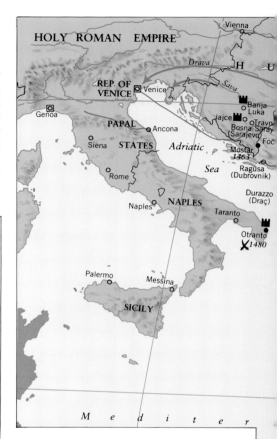

He also gave instructions for a palace to be built on the promontory where the ancient city of Constantinople juts into the sea, which was to be greater and more wonderful than any previous one in its grace, size, perfection and charm... It was his purpose to make Constantinople the most powerful and self-sufficient city in all respects, enjoying its previous level of attainment in terms of power, wealth, reputation, sciences, arts and all other affairs and fine accomplishments, and in the quality of the buildings and monuments set up for the public good.

Kritovoulos describes Mehmet II's restoration of Constantinople

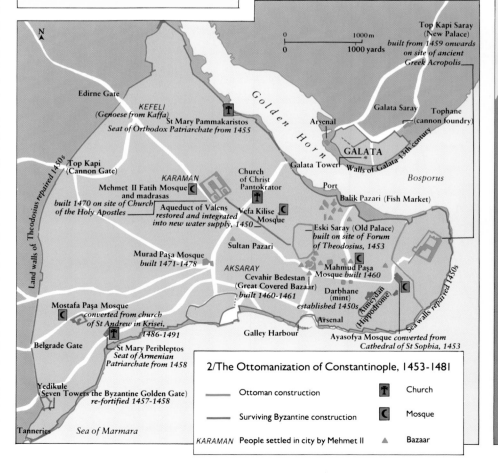

2/The Ottomanization of Constantinople, 1453-1481

—— Ottoman construction

—— Surviving Byzantine construction

KARAMAN People settled in city by Mehmet II

✝ Church

C Mosque

▲ Bazaar

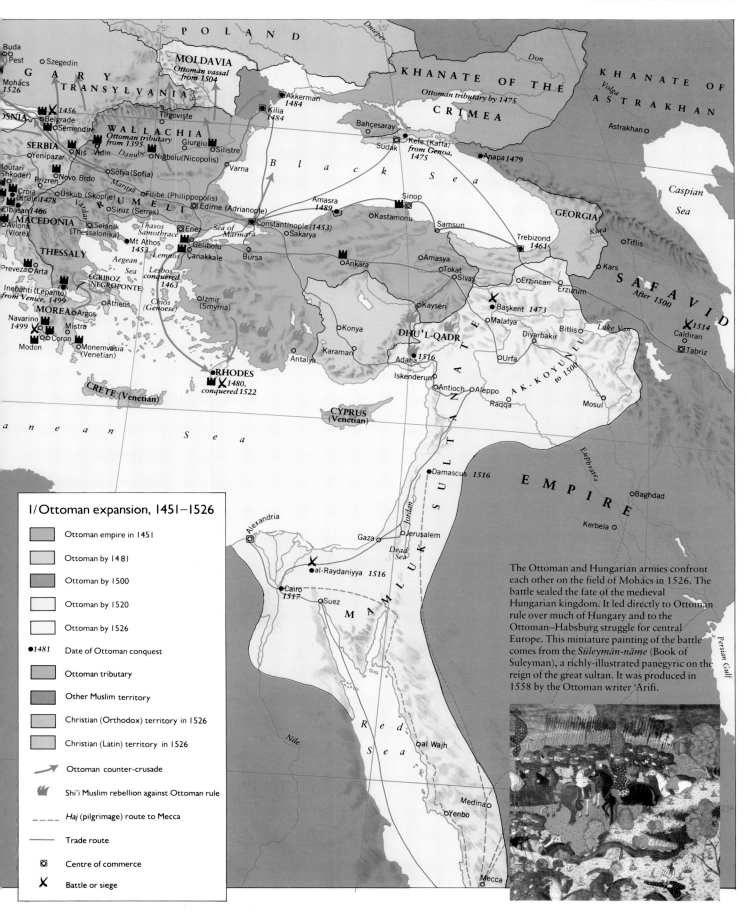

I/Ottoman expansion, 1451–1526

- Ottoman empire in 1451
- Ottoman by 1481
- Ottoman by 1500
- Ottoman by 1520
- Ottoman by 1526
- •1481 Date of Ottoman conquest
- Ottoman tributary
- Other Muslim territory
- Christian (Orthodox) territory in 1526
- Christian (Latin) territory in 1526
- → Ottoman counter-crusade
- Shi'i Muslim rebellion against Ottoman rule
- - - - Haj (pilgrimage) route to Mecca
- — Trade route
- ◎ Centre of commerce
- ✕ Battle or siege

The Ottoman and Hungarian armies confront each other on the field of Mohács in 1526. The battle sealed the fate of the medieval Hungarian kingdom. It led directly to Ottoman rule over much of Hungary and to the Ottoman–Habsburg struggle for central Europe. This miniature painting of the battle comes from the *Süleymān-nāme* (Book of Suleyman), a richly-illustrated panegyric on the reign of the great sultan. It was produced in 1558 by the Ottoman writer 'Arifi.

Map labels

POLAND

MOLDAVIA *Ottoman vassal from 1504*

KHANATE OF THE CRIMEA
Ottoman tributary by 1475

KHANATE OF ASTRAKHAN

Buda
Pest
Szegedin
Mohács 1526
TRANSYLVANIA
Tîrgovişte
Akkerman 1484
Kilia 1484
Don
Astrakhan
Volga

GARY
X 1456
Belgrade
Semendire
WALLACHIA *Ottoman tributary from 1395*
Giurgiu
Nigbolu (Nicopolis)
Silistre
Bahçesaray
Kefe (Kaffa) *from Genoa, 1475*
Sudak
Anapa 1479

SERBIA
Yenipazar
Niš
Vidin
Danube
Sofya (Sofia)
Varna
Black Sea
Caspian Sea

Boutari (Shkodër)
Prizren
Novo Brdo
Maritsa
Filibe (Philippopolis)
Üsküb (Skopje)
Edirne (Adrianople)
Amasra 1489
Sinop
GEORGIA
Kira
Tiflis

Croia (Kruje) 1478
Elbasan 1466
R U M E L I
Siruz (Serres)
Vardar
Constantinople (1453)
Sakarya
Kastamonu
Samsun
Trebizond 1461
Kars

MACEDONIA
Avlona (Vlorë)
Selanik (Thessalonika)
Thasos Samothrace
Enez
Mt Athos 1453
Gelibolu
Lemnos
Çanakkale
Sea of Marmara
Bursa
Ankara
Amasya
Tokat
Sivas
Erzincan
Erzurum
After 1500
SAFAVID

THESSALY
Aegean Sea
Lesbos *conquered 1463*
Başkent 1473
Malatya
Bitlis
Lake Van
X 1514
Caldiran
Tabriz

EGRIBOZ (NEGROPONTE)
Inebahti (Lepanto) *from Venice, 1499*
Preveza
Arta
Chios (Genoese)
Izmir (Smyrna)
Kayseri
Konya
DHU'L-QADR
Urfa
AK-KOYUNLU *to 1500*
Mosul

MOREA
Navarino 1499
Mistra
Argos
Athens
Antalya
Karaman
Adana 1516
Iskenderun
Antioch
Aleppo
Raqqa

Modon
Coron
Monemvasia (Venetian)
RHODES *1480, conquered 1522*

CRETE (Venetian)

CYPRUS (Venetian)

Mediterranean Sea

Alexandria
Gaza
Jerusalem
Dead Sea
Jordan
Damascus 1516
S U L T A N A T E
E M P I R E
Baghdad
Kerbela
Euphrates

al-Raydaniyya 1516
Cairo 1517
Suez
M A M L U K
Nile
Red Sea
al Wajh
Medina
Yenbo
Mecca

Persian Gulf

The Defence of Belgrade

As the inexorable advance of the Ottoman empire approached Belgrade, János Hunyadi and the preacher St John of Capistrano summoned up a last-ditch Christian resistance.

Shortly after the fall of Constantinople in 1453 (▶ *page 150*), Pope Nicholas V issued a letter calling for a crusade against the Ottomans. Enthusiasm for a crusade was low, with the Christian states preoccupied with quarrels among themselves, but the princes eventually agreed to gather troops in response to the urgent pleas of the emperor's ambassador Æneas Sylvius (later Pope Pius II), and John of Capistrano, the holy Minorite friar of the Observance.

In June 1455, Capistrano set off for the Hungarian diet in Győr, where János Hunyadi was preparing an offensive against the Turks. Hunyadi and Capistrano believed that, with Western aid, it would be possible to drive the Ottomans out of Europe and to recover Constantinople, perhaps even Jerusalem. Capistrano spent the following months in a long preaching tour in western Hungary and Transylvania, ending in Buda in January 1456. Here the Cardinal Carvajal presented Capistrano with a papal commission to preach the crusade and a crucifix blessed by the Pope. In April, the news arrived that the Sultan Mehmet II was marching towards Hungary with a large army. While Cardinal Carvajal attempted to raise troops in the West, Hunyadi threw himself into military preparations, and Capistrano preached the crusade in southern Hungary, bearing the papal crucifix on his breast and carrying a banner adorned with the cross.

> T he crusaders took no heed of Hunyadi's command, but rushing upon the enemy, they put themselves in grave danger. But I, the least of your Holiness's servants, when from the walls I was unable to recall them, went down into the battlefield, and running to and fro, I called them back at first, then encouraged them, and drew them up in order, so they would not be surrounded by the enemy. Finally the Lord, who can bring deliverance to a few as well as to many, mercifully gave us the victory and caused the flight of the Turks' huge army, and our men got possession of all their cannon and diabolical machines wherewith they thought to make all Christendom subject to themselves.
>
> *St John of Capistrano describes the victory at Belgrade to the pope*

As the Ottomans approached Belgrade, Hunyadi, with very few trained troops, summoned Capistrano with as many crusaders as he could gather. About 40,000 had pledged themselves in Hungary alone, and 27,000 had accepted the cross from the hands of John of Capistrano. Many of these only reached Belgrade after the battle, but Hunyadi's troops and the crusaders, with their war cry of 'Jesus! Jesus! Jesus!', succeeded in breaking the siege of Belgrade, routing the much larger Ottoman army, and halting the Ottoman drive into Hungary. But Hunyadi and Capistrano both died of the plague soon after the battle, and the dreams of a great crusading movement turning the Ottomans out of Europe dissipated.

A somewhat fanciful contemporary view of Belgrade at the time of the siege, 1456. Ships weighted with sand and rocks were released into the current to crash into the Ottoman galleys. Hunyadi's troops followed in river vessels, scattering the Turkish fleet.

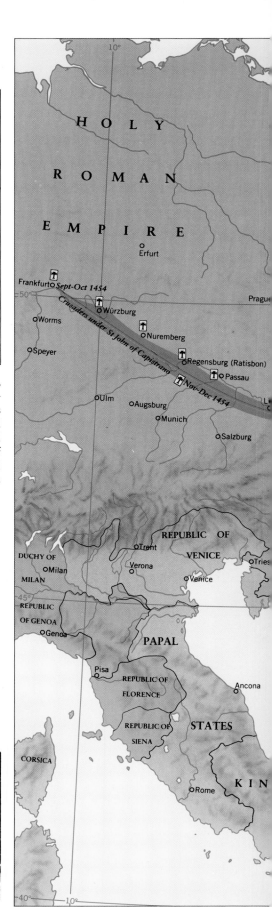

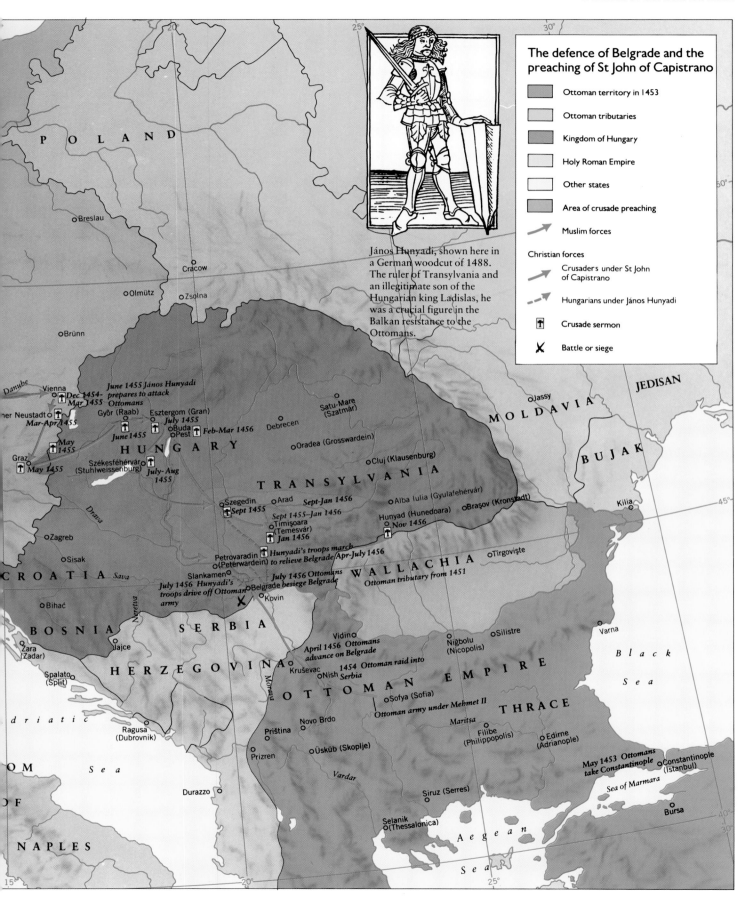

The defence of Belgrade and the
preaching of St John of Capistrano

	Ottoman territory in 1453
	Ottoman tributaries
	Kingdom of Hungary
	Holy Roman Empire
	Other states
	Area of crusade preaching
→	Muslim forces
	Christian forces
→	Crusaders under St John of Capistrano
⇢	Hungarians under János Hunyadi
✝	Crusade sermon
✗	Battle or siege

János Hunyadi, shown here in
a German woodcut of 1488.
The ruler of Transylvania and
an illegitimate son of the
Hungarian king Ladislas, he
was a crucial figure in the
Balkan resistance to the
Ottomans.

POLAND

Breslau

Cracow

Olmütz   Zsolna

Brünn

Danube

Vienna   June 1455 János Hunyadi
Dec 1454–   prepares to attack
Mar 1455   Ottomans
ner Neustadt   Győr (Raab)   Esztergom (Gran)
Mar–Apr 1455   July 1455
May   June 1455   Buda   Feb–Mar 1456
1455   Pest
Graz   Székesfehérvár   HUNGARY
May 1455   (Stuhlweissenburg)   July–Aug
1455

Zagreb   Drava

Sisak

CROATIA   Sava

Bihać   Nereva

BOSNIA   SERBIA

Zara
(Zadar)

Spalato   HERZEGOVINA
(Split)

Ragusa
(Dubrovnik)

driatic

OM   Sea

OF   Durazzo

NAPLES

Satu-Mare
(Szatmár)

Debrecen

Oradea (Grosswardein)

Cluj (Klausenburg)

TRANSYLVANIA

Szegedin   Arad   Sept–Jan 1456
Sept 1455   Sept 1455–Jan 1456   Alba Iulia (Gyulafehérvár)
Timișoara   Hunyad (Hunedoara)   Brașov (Kronstadt)
(Temesvár)   Nov 1456
Jan 1456

Petrovaradin   Hunyadi's troops march
(Peterwardein)   to relieve Belgrade Apr–July 1456   WALLACHIA   Tîrgoviște
Slankamen   July 1456 Ottomans   Ottoman tributary from 1451
July 1456 Hunyadi's   Belgrade besiege Belgrade
troops drive off Ottoman   Kovin
army

Vidin   Nigbolu   Silistre   Varna
April 1456 Ottomans   (Nicopolis)
advance on Belgrade   Black
Kruševac   1454 Ottoman raid into   Sea
Niš   Serbia
OTTOMAN   EMPIRE   THRACE
Sofya (Sofia)
Novo Brdo   Ottoman army under Mehmet II   Maritsa
Priština   Filibe   Edirne
(Philippopolis)   (Adrianople)
Prizren   Üsküb (Skoplje)
May 1453 Ottomans   Constantinople
take Constantinople   (İstanbul)
Vardar
Siruz (Serres)   Sea of Marmara
Durazzo   Bursa

Selanik
(Thessalonica)

Aegean

Sea

JEDISAN

Jassy

MOLDAVIA

BUJAK

Kilia

MORAVA

Part 4
THE LAST CRUSADERS

A century after the siege of Belgrade, Christians were again engaged in a heroic defence against the Ottomans. By 23 June 1565, the eve of the feast of St John, the fort of St Elmo, across the waters of the Grand Harbour from the main positions of the Hospitaller Knights of St John on Malta, had become an unrecognizable jumble of masonry. Since 24 May it had been under almost constant bombardment and attack by a huge Turkish army. Some six to seven thousand shots a day had been directed at it; and it was described as being 'like a volcano in eruption, spouting fire and smoke'. Waves of assault had overwhelmed its outer works. It had been kept going by regular reinforcement from small parties of men, some of them volunteers, despatched under cover of darkness across the Grand Harbour by the Grand Master, Jean Parisot de la Valette, who as a young brother had fought in the second Turkish siege of Rhodes. But now the strength of Turkish firepower directed at the harbour waters meant that the garrison was isolated.

During the previous night it had become clear that the Turks were massing for the final storm. 'The poor ones of St Elmo,' wrote an eyewitness across the water, 'having seen that our attempt to send them help had failed, prepared themselves to die in the service of Jesus Christ'. The two brother priests in the fort heard the confessions of the less than 100 surviving defenders. They hid the precious vessels in the chapel under the floor and they set fire to a pile of tapestries, pictures and furniture so that they could not be desecrated. Then, as a last gesture, they began to ring the chapel bell. At first light the garrison prepared for the end. In a breach was placed two chairs, on which the senior commanders, the elderly brother knight Juan de Guaras and a Spanish captain

called de Miranda, both terribly wounded, were seated with drawn swords in their hands. The fort was finally overwhelmed after an hour of assault from every side, but it had already contributed to Malta's eventual salvation by holding out for so long. The Hospitallers had lost 1,500 men in it, 120 of whom were members of the Order. The Turks had probably lost 8,000; they had perhaps sacrificed as many as 30,000 before they finally withdrew from the island on 8 September, the feast of the Nativity of the Blessed Virgin Mary. Of the Hospitaller garrison of 9,000 at the start of the siege, only about 600 were still capable of bearing arms. Nearly 250 Knights of St John had been killed; those that survived were nearly all wounded. The news of the Turks' defeat caused rejoicing throughout Catholic Europe and even in Protestant England, where a form of thanksgiving was composed to be used in the churches three times a week for six weeks.

Two hundred and thirty-three years later, on 13 June 1798, Napoleon Bonaparte, in command of a French expeditionary force destined for Egypt, landed on Malta. The island, the most heavily fortified in the Mediterranean, surrendered to the French forces after a day of desultory and sporadic fighting. Of the 332 brother knights on the island, 50 were too old or ill to fight. The plans for defence were obsolete: they had not been revised for over 30 years. For nearly a century the guns had only been used to fire ceremonial rounds. The powder was rotten, the shot was bad. The frightened troops were officered by men who had not bothered to learn Maltese. Senior command was in the hands of ancient knights who held it because of seniority rather than ability. 'Malta,' wrote Napoleon, 'could not withstand a bombardment of twenty-four hours; the place certainly possessed immense physical means of resistance, but no moral strength whatever.' The effect of this disaster on the Order was catastrophic. A party of brother knights deposed the Grand Master, Ferdinand von Hompesch, and elected in his place Tsar Paul I of Russia, who was not Catholic or celibate, or a professed brother, but was certainly mad. The Order found itself split into fragments, despised and distrusted. In 1802 the treaty of Amiens gave Malta back to it, but the island had been seized two years earlier by the British and in 1814 the treaty of Paris recognized the British occupation.

Memorial tablet to Fra' François de Tressemanes Chastueil Brunet in the Hospitallers' conventual church, now co-cathedral, in Valletta. This is one of 375 marble tablets which carpet the floor, making it the mausoleum of chivalry.

If the spirited defence of Malta in 1565 demonstrates that crusading was still a powerful ideal, the pathetic surrender of the island in 1798 illustrates its collapse. By the late 18th century crusading had become an object of scorn to enlightened, educated, reasonable men, who could see in its history only fanaticism, folly, extravagance and impoverishment. Crusading passed out of the currency of everyday thought so completely that its more recent history was forgotten; indeed it is only in the last 20 years that its strength and adaptability in the 16th and 17th centuries has been rediscovered. What had happened? How could a movement with such a genuinely popular appeal in the past have faded out of existence?

The threat to Christendom from Islam had evaporated. Everywhere in the 18th-century Muslim world there was a decline and retreat, and the idea that the Turks now posed a threat to the heartlands of Europe was no longer credible. To survive, Christian holy war needed the just cause provided by an enemy who was seen to be aggressive; indeed one of the weaknesses of the crusading movement throughout its history was the tendency for it to be only reactive. Although according to canonists' interpretation of the just cause, it was not absolutely necessary for the initiative to lie in the enemy's hands, the enthusiasm of the laity, on whom the movement depended, responded in practice only to disaster or a clearly perceived threat. With the lowering of the temperature in Christian relations with Muslims, the naval operations of the Order of St John began to slacken. In the 16th and 17th centuries its war galleys had actively scoured the Mediterranean for Muslim shipping; even as late as the period 1722-1741 its ships of the line, which after 1700 had begun to replace the galleys, accounted for a significant haul of Muslim vessels. But by the middle of the 18th century the fleet was becoming more decorative than operational.

This was echoed in the brothers' lifestyle. In the city of Valletta, planned and built on the peninsula along which the bitter attacks on Fort St Elmo had been launched in 1565, the Knights of Malta, as the Hospitaller brothers were now called, had abandoned the principle of monastic enclosure which had prevailed on Rhodes and their conventual buildings were scattered throughout the town. At first these were austere and functional, but by the middle of the 18th century they were extravagantly decorated and comfortably furnished. The asceticism of a religious order had to a large extent given way to the tone of a smart, rather backward military academy. The historian

An 18th-century Hospitaller galley. Rowed by slaves, the galley was officered by young brother knights. They carried out raids against Muslim shipping before returning to Europe to manage commanderies on their Order's behalf.

Roderick Cavaliero paints a compelling picture of Hospitaller Valletta at this time:

'A society managed entirely by elderly staff officers – which is an adequate description of 18th-century Malta – undoubtedly lacked a certain elasticity and suffered from defects of imagination. Dullness was the keynote of life in the island. The tone set at the top was of mild urbanity with a meticulous and fussy insistence on discipline and precedence.'

It is not surprising that the highest ambition of many brother knights, once they had completed their *caravans*, or service in the Order's navy, was to retire as commanders to the life of country gentlemen on the Order's estates in western Europe.

Another feature of the 18th century was the decay of many of the political and social institutions which had survived since the Middle Ages and had helped to mould the *anciens régimes*. Their sudden collapse in the face of the French Revolution and the advance of the revolutionary armies across Europe suggests that their hearts had already been eaten away. The Order of St John on Malta had proved itself incapable of internal reform – in the sense of spiritual rebirth as a religious order – even in the aftermath of the reforming Council of Trent, while many of the elements underpinning it no longer had the appeal they once had. A third of Europe had become Protestant. Chivalry was now an empty show.

And nobility and knighthood were maintained only by privilege, since military and social worth and economic wealth no longer justified them.

Christian holy war, moreover, could thrive only when there was general agreement that violence could be positive. From the late 16th century onwards, the idea gradually gained currency that violence was negative in the sense that it was intrinsically evil. It could be justifed only as the lesser of evils and as a means of the restoration of a status quo that had been disturbed by aggression or injury. As the Dutch jurist Grotius put it:

'We mean to enquire whether any war can be just, and then what is just in war. For law in this case means simply what is just; and that in a sense negative rather than affirmative, namely that that is lawful which is not unjust.'

This was a far cry from the ringing calls to arms of St Bernard of Clairvaux and Pope Innocent III.

At the same time there was no longer any association of the intentions of Christ with a universal Christian political order, which had been such a feature of central medieval thought. Crusading leagues had been, as we have seen, responses to the emergence of nation states, the existence of which contradicted the notion of a single 'Christian Republic', but for a long time – at least well into the 16th century – everyone seems to have kept up the fiction that such a political order co-existed with the reality of the sovereign powers. By the 18th century the fiction could no longer be maintained, and from being perceived as politically committed, Christ was now believed to be politically neutral, an objective judge before whom a plethora of independent states stood in more or less equality.

Crusading needed the idea of a morally neutral violence which took colouring from the intentions of the perpetrator and a politically committed Christ whose plans for mankind would be frustrated unless military action was taken against his opponents. It is not, therefore, surprising that by 1798 crusading had disappeared from the scene or that the Order of St John on Malta was in danger of becoming an archaic irrelevance.

Even 19th-century romanticism could not

Members of St John Ambulance, familiar in Britain by their regular attendance at sporting events. They constitute one of two major charities of the Most Venerable Order of St John, the other being an ophthalmic hospital in Jerusalem.

breathe life into the corpse of crusading, but this does not mean that the movement's last representatives died with it. The Hospitallers of St John, after a few decades of confusion, renewed themselves by reverting to their first task of caring for the sick and the poor. Now based in Rome, they transformed their Order from the 1850s onwards into a major humanitarian organization. A similar development took place in England, where the non-Catholic Order of St John, founded by French Knights of Malta, began to engage vigorously in medical work from the 1860s and in 1872 began the activity which was to lead to the establishment of St John Ambulance, now to be found throughout the British Commonwealth.

The contempt of the 18th-century rationalists survived into the 20th century, a late expression of it being the magnificent words with which in the 1950s Sir Steven Runciman ended his influential history of the crusades:

'The Holy War itself was nothing more than a long act of intolerance in the name of God, which is a sin against the Holy Ghost.'

Until 30 years ago very few historians were prepared to believe that crusaders acted from ideal-

Christian Liberation

Christian Liberation draws on an interpretation of scripture and an acceptance of some of the tenets of Marxism. It has at its heart a belief that mankind has been subjected to a long historical process, a march away from injustice and alienation to the ultimate goal of salvation. The cause of poverty and injustice is sin. Freedom, on the other hand, involves true love of God and neighbour. It is believed that liberation is a salvatory process and is one in which Christ is intimately involved. He is perceived not only to be present in the course of liberation; he also makes a gift to us of liberation. 'The fullness of liberation – a free gift from Christ – is communion with God and with other men.' (Gustavo Gutiérrez).

The course of liberation is seen to be manifesting itself especially in the underdeveloped or oppressed regions of the world,

where there is a struggle to build just societies in which men and women can live in dignity as brothers and sisters, in control of their own destinies. The process of liberation is, therefore, a political one and it is clear that in Liberation ethics Christ has returned to his medieval role as a leader committed to a particular political cause. The owners of the means of production, the oppressors, are said to be standing in the way of liberation by resisting the just demands of the oppressed. There is, therefore, among the supporters of Liberation a conviction that the world is engaged in a class struggle. They are convinced that it is the duty of Christians and the Church to align themselves with the oppressed. In doing so they will be showing love for the oppressors, as well as for the oppressed:

'Universal love is that which in solidarity with the oppressed seeks also to liberate the oppressors from their own power, from their ambition and from their selfishness. "Love for those who live in a condition of objective sin demands that we struggle to liberate them from it. The liberation of the poor and the liberation of the rich are achieved simultaneously." One loves the oppressors by liberating them from their inhuman condition as oppressors, by liberating them from themselves.' (Gustavo Gutiérrez, quoting Giulio Girardi)

There are plenty of upholders of Christian Liberation who do not promote violence. But it is easy for the more militant to point out that the oppressors of the poor, putting up barriers in the way of Christ's

intentions in the historical process, will not be defeated except by the use of force; in this case, of course, by rebellion rather than by war. So they justify violence in the name of Christ and fraternal love. The enemy may be different, but the basic theology is similar to that which underpinned crusading; and there are other echoes of crusading thought. For instance, participation in revolution is perceived to be a moral imperative: 'The Catholic who is not a revolutionary is living in mortal sin.' And the dead can occasionally be treated as martyrs: one Catholic priest who resigned his orders, joined a guerrilla band and was killed in 1966, was placed among 'the purest, the most noble, the most authentic exponents and martyrs of the new Christianity.'

ism. Indeed the notion was so abhorrent to them that they were prepared to look anywhere but in that direction when trying to explain the reasons why so many took the cross; hence the fashion for discussing the motives of crusaders in economic or colonial terms. But even as Runciman was writing his magnificent peroration the world around him was changing. The development of combat psychiatry was leading everyone to reconsider the performance and reactions of men under stress and to distinguish between motives for recruitment and behaviour in combat zones. There had been a revival of interest in the ideology of war in the 1930s. After 1945 this interest was fuelled by discussion about obedience to *legitimate authority*, made topical by the prosecution of German leaders in the Nuremberg Trials, and debates about the criterion of *right intention*, inspired by the issue of nuclear deterrence and 'proportionality'.

More important than these, however, has been the re-emergence since the 1960s in Islam, Judaism and Christianity of justifications of positive violence. As far as Christianity is concerned, the Liberation movement has steadily gained ground and has given birth to a militant wing which has been prominent in Latin America. In a world in which there is again being preached a sophisticated and well-grounded theology which can underly theories of positive force and in which sincere and intelligent contemporaries are justifying or engaging in acts of violence in the name of Christ, it is no longer possible for historians to treat the crusaders simply as greedy imperialists or uncomprehending barbarians.

The reappearance of justifications of positive force in three great world religions poses serious questions. Will the concepts remain the preserve of small minorities or will they grow? Are we witnessing a temporary reversion, in response to particular pressures, to historically outdated convictions or is this a prelude to a return to the norm?

Whatever our views, the fact remains that the study of the crusades, the most popular and long-lasting expression of Christian holy war, is directly relevant to our attitude to the world around us. Whether we like it or not, we can only come to terms with what is happening now and seek to influence the course of events by understanding the history of Christian violence.

The Reformation

The Reformation split Christian Europe and weakened the crusading movement. But crusading ideas were present in several of the religious wars that followed.

A crusade was, by definition, a religious war authorized by the pope. Although Protestant leaders were not opposed to religious warfare as such, and some thinkers even proposed Protestant versions of crusading, crusading itself was anathema to Protestants. A large part of northern Europe was therefore removed from the orbit of crusading and, since the Protestants were also opposed to monasticism, they destroyed the Military Orders in the territories under their control.

For Catholics, Protestantism was a heresy; crusading had been used to combat heresy before (▶ *page 76 and 130*), and the response to the Reformation was in part a crusading one. The Council of Trent in 1544 specifically linked the 'removal of religious discord' with a crusade against the infidel, and crusading elements were to surface as late as the Thirty Years' War (1618-1648).

England seems to have been a particular focus for crusading schemes. The English rebels against Henry VIII in the Pilgrimage of Grace (1536-1537) deliberately adopted badges of Christ's Five Wounds which had been worn on crusade in North Africa. English Catholic exiles such as Cardinal Reginald Pole called for a crusade against Henry VIII, and in the reign of Elizabeth I an exiled Catholic freebooter, Thomas Stukeley, was granted indulgences in 1575 to undertake an invasion of Ireland. Although Stukeley diverted his troops to fight with King Sebastian of Portugal in Morocco (▶ *page 162*) a Catholic force under James Fitz-Maurice FitzGerald and Nicholas Saunders landed in Ireland a year later. This quickly foundered, but the crusading rhetoric which had surrounded it was resurrected a decade later for the Spanish Armada.

Pope Sixtus V allowed King Philip II of Spain to collect crusade taxes and apparently granted crusade indulgences to the Armada. The blessing of the Armada's banner on 25 April 1588 at Lisbon was full of crusade imagery, reminiscent of a similar ceremony before the departure of the fleet for Lepanto in 1571 (▶ *page 164*). The plan was to sail a large fleet of 130 ships from Spain to rendezvous at Dunkirk with the duke of Parma, the Spanish commander in the Netherlands, and escort his army in its barges across the Channel. The Armada, under an inexperienced admiral, the duke of Medina Sidonia, reached Calais on 6th August, shadowed by the English fleet. Its formation was then broken by fire-ships sailed into the port by the English. A change in the weather prevented the Armada coming in close to shore and then blew the hapless fleet northwards to be destroyed on the hostile coasts of western Scotland and Ireland.

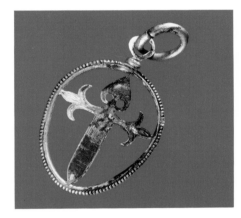

The Cross of the Order of Santiago of Compostela (above), belonging to Don Alonso de Leira, an Armada commander who drowned on the return voyage off Ireland. The cross is in the form of a lily-sword, symbol of the Order's patron, St James.

The Badge of Five Wounds depicting the Five Wounds of Christ (below), worn by English rebels during the Pilgrimage of Grace. The crusading associations are clear. Lord Darcy, a rebel leader, had used the badges on an expedition against the Moors in 1511. He was later asked whether the rebels 'who wore them were told they were Christ's Soldiers'.

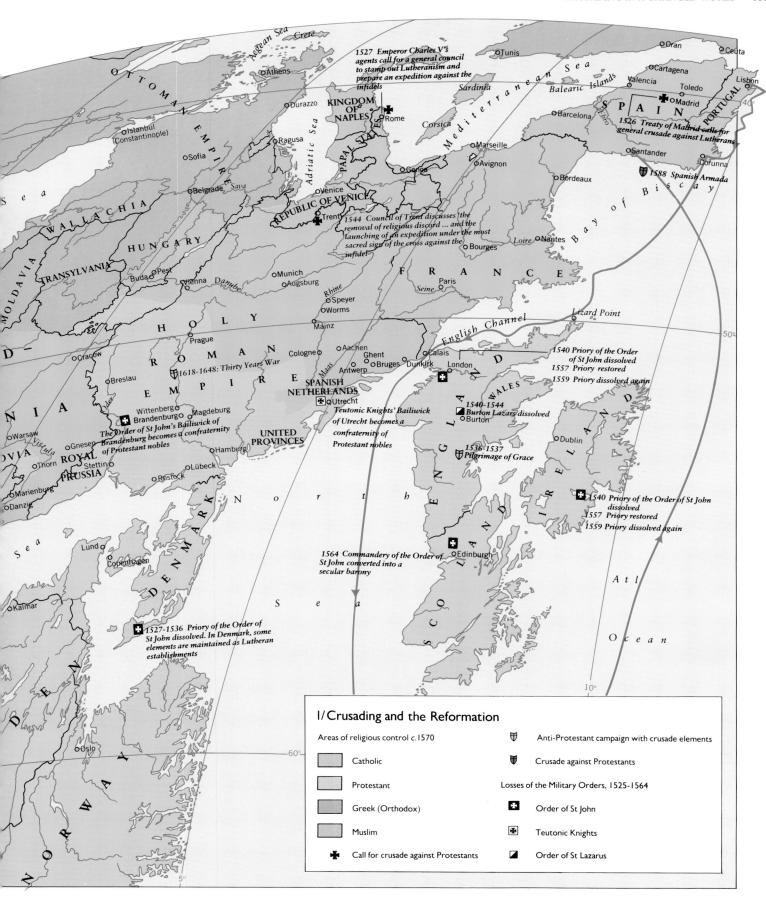

1527 Emperor Charles V's agents call for a general council to stamp out Lutheranism and prepare an expedition against the infidels

1526 Treaty of Madrid calls for general crusade against Lutherans

1588 Spanish Armada

1544 Council of Trent discusses the removal of religious discord ... and the launching of an expedition under the most sacred sign of the cross against the infidel

1540 Priory of the Order of St John dissolved
1557 Priory restored
1559 Priory dissolved again

1540–1544 Burton Lazars dissolved

1536–1537 Pilgrimage of Grace

1540 Priory of the Order of St John dissolved
1557 Priory restored
1559 Priory dissolved again

Teutonic Knights' Bailiwick of Utrecht becomes a confraternity of Protestant nobles

The Order of St John's Bailiwick of Brandenburg becomes a confraternity of Protestant nobles

1618–1648: Thirty Years War

1564 Commandery of the Order of St John converted into a secular barony

1527–1536 Priory of the Order of St John dissolved. In Denmark, some elements are maintained as Lutheran establishments

I/Crusading and the Reformation

Areas of religious control c.1570

- Catholic
- Protestant
- Greek (Orthodox)
- Muslim
- Call for crusade against Protestants

- Anti-Protestant campaign with crusade elements
- Crusade against Protestants

Losses of the Military Orders, 1525–1564
- Order of St John
- Teutonic Knights
- Order of St Lazarus

Crusades to North Africa

After the conquest of Granada, the rulers of Spain attempted to push their war against the Muslims onwards into North Africa itself.

With Granada in Christian hands (▶ *page 126*), its Muslim inhabitants experienced a brief period of toleration only: in 1502, Ferdinand and Isabella decreed that they and all Muslims in Castile must accept baptism or be exiled. The same choice was extended to Muslims in Aragon in 1525. This policy left Spain with a discontented and unassimilable minority of some 300,000 baptised Muslims (*moriscos*) along its vulnerable Mediterranean coast, where they could help the North African corsairs who constantly raided Spain and Italy for booty and slaves.

To destroy the corsair bases, Isabella and her adviser Cardinal Cisneros decided to extend the Reconquest into North Africa. They established a series of bridgeheads: Melilla (1497), Mers al-Kabir (1505), Oran (1509) and Vélez de la Gomera, Bougie, Peñón d'Argel and Tripoli (1508-1510). But neither Isabella's husband Ferdinand nor his successor Charles V would invest enough resources to consolidate these victories, and control was lost to corsairs such as the brothers Aruj and Khair al-Din Barbarossa. Aruj was killed in 1518, but Khair al-Din went on to lead raids as far afield as Italy.

The Ottoman empire, meanwhile, was expanding up the Danube and westward into North Africa, where many of the corsairs acted as its agents. Its fleet, which already dominated the eastern Mediterranean, now hoped to dominate the western. Charles V tried to block its advance by establishing the Order of St John on Malta and in Tripoli in 1530 (▶ *page 168*), and by capturing bases such as Cherchell (1520) and Hunayn (1531). In 1535 he organized an expedition to recapture Tunis from Khair al-Din Barbarossa, who had taken it the year before. A crusade was preached; indulgences were given; and Pope Paul III sent ships and money. Despite the success of this expedition, Charles was overwhelmed by his European commitments and eventually lost most of his North African ports.

His successor Philip II took the corsair base of Jerba in 1560, but the Ottomans besieged the Christians in the town, and most died or were taken prisoner. Philip only just managed to raise the Turkish siege of Malta in 1565 and was extremely lucky to suppress a *morisco* uprising in the Alpujarras mountains without serious Turkish intervention (1568-1571). But in 1571, in alliance with Venice and the papacy, he destroyed the Turkish fleet at Lepanto (▶ *page 164*), ending Ottoman expansion into the western Mediterranean.

Portugal, meanwhile, had been attempting to dominate the Atlantic coast of Morocco. In 1578, King Sebastian decided to lead a large expedition himself. A romantic but incompetent crusader, he was defeated and killed, together with many of his nobles, at Alcazarquivir. This left Portugal and its colonies to be inherited by Philip II in 1580; the Spanish king then turned his attention away from the Mediterranean crusades and towards the Atlantic.

T he Spanish had steadfastly defended the fortress over a period of three months or more. Nearly all their supplies had run out and they had given up hope of being relieved. But by far the worst of the torments under that scorching sun was thirst. There was one cistern – and it was a large one – full of water, but it could not cater for the needs of such a large number of people. So a daily ration of water was measured out for everyone: just enough to prevent him dying of thirst. Many supplemented this with a mixture of sea water from which the salt had been removed by distillation – luckily there was an alchemist there who knew how to do this – but this supply did not reach everyone. Many people lay stretched out on the ground dying; one single word escaped from their gaping mouths – 'water!'. If someone took pity on them he would sprinkle a little water into their mouths. They would then get up and stand for a while, then sit down until the benefit of the water wore off, when they again collapsed; in the end, parched with thirst, they expired.

Ghiselin de Busbecq describes the sufferings of the crusaders at Jerba, 1560

Atlantic Ocean

Bay of Biscay

PORTUGAL

SPAIN

Duero

Madrid

Tagus

Toledo

Lisbon

Guadiana

Guadalquivir

Lagos

Seville

King Sebastian's crusade, 1578

ALPUJARRAS

Cádiz

Gibraltar   Málaga 1540   1497

Alcazarseguer
Tangier   Ceuta

Arzila   1508   1522   1564

Graciosa   Mers el-Kebir Hunayn

Alcazarquivir   Vélez de la Gomera   Melilla

1578   Tlemcen

Azemmour   Fez   Atlas Mountains   Moulouya

SULTANATE

Mazagan

Safi

Atlas

OF

Marrakesh

Santa Cruz de Aguer (Agadir)

Massa

MOROCCO

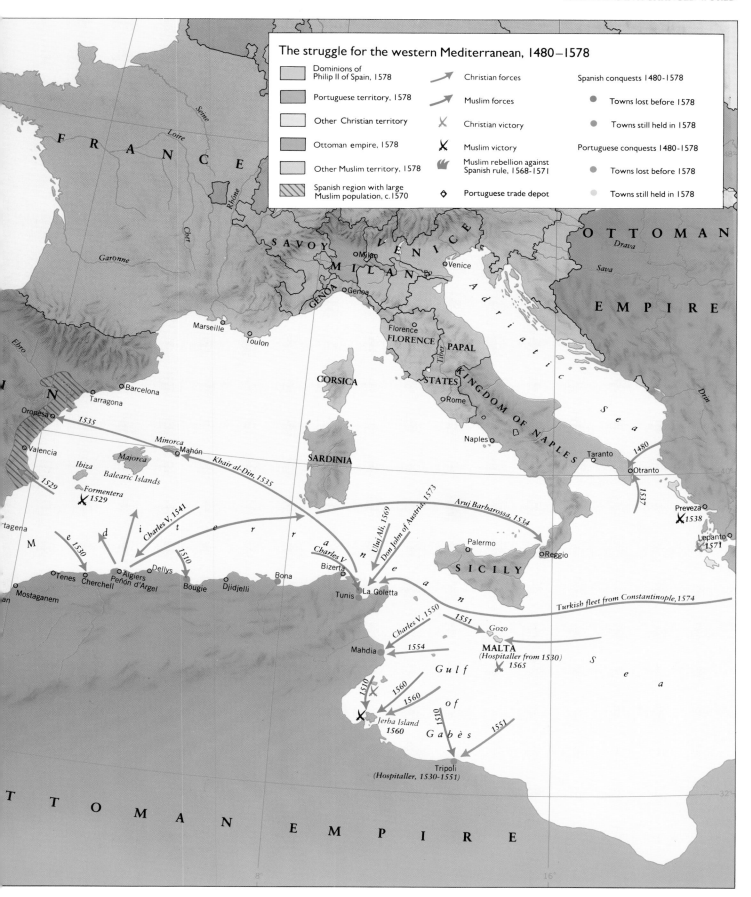

The struggle for the western Mediterranean, 1480–1578

Dominions of
Philip II of Spain, 1578

Portuguese territory, 1578

Other Christian territory

Ottoman empire, 1578

Other Muslim territory, 1578

Spanish region with large
Muslim population, c.1570

Christian forces

Muslim forces

Christian victory

Muslim victory

Muslim rebellion against
Spanish rule, 1568–1571

Portuguese trade depot

Spanish conquests 1480–1578

Towns lost before 1578

Towns still held in 1578

Portuguese conquests 1480–1578

Towns lost before 1578

Towns still held in 1578

FRANCE

Seine

Loire

Cher

Garonne

Rhône

Ebro

SAVOY

VENICE

MILAN

Milan

GENOA

Genoa

Venice

Po

OTTOMAN

Drava

Sava

EMPIRE

Marseille

Toulon

Florence

FLORENCE

PAPAL

STATES

Tiber

Rome

A
d
r
i
a
t
i
c

S
e
a

Drin

KINGDOM OF NAPLES

CORSICA

SARDINIA

Barcelona

Tarragona

Oropesa   1535

Valencia

1529

Ibiza

Majorca

Balearic Islands

Minorca

Mahón

Khair al-Din, 1535

Formentera
1529

Cartagena

M

e 1530

d

i

t

e

r

r

a

Charles V, 1541

1510

Tenes

Cherchell

Algiers

Peñon d'Argel

Dellys

Bougie

Djidjelli

Bona

Bizerta

Tunis

La Goletta

Mostaganem

Charles V
1510

Ului Ali, 1569

Don John of Austria, 1573

Aruj Barbarossa, 1534

n

Naples

Taranto

Otranto   1480

1537

Preveza
1538

Lepanto
1571

Palermo

Reggio

SICILY

e

a

n

S

e

a

Turkish fleet from Constantinople, 1574

Charles V, 1550

1551

1554

Gozo

MALTA
(Hospitaller from 1530)
1565

Gulf

of

Gabès

1510

1560

1560

1510

1551

Mahdia

Jerba Island
1560

Tripoli
(Hospitaller, 1530–1551)

OTTOMAN   EMPIRE

The Ottoman Advance

Distracted by their European rivalries, the Christian powers were unable to withstand the advance of the Ottoman empire into central Europe and the Aegean.

With the accession of the dynamic sultan Suleyman the Magnificent in 1520, the Ottomans posed a renewed threat to Christendom both in the Mediterranean and on the long central European frontier. By 1526, they had reached Mohács, and King Louis of Hungary was killed in the battle for the city (▶page 150). Sweeping through Hungary and Croatia, Suleyman besieged Vienna in 1529, and only there was his advance checked.

Austria stood directly in the line of Ottoman advance; for its Habsburg rulers, crusading ideas were intimately linked to the defence of their own lands, for which they claimed the title 'Bulwark of Christendom'. In the 16th and 17th centuries a series of crusading popes attempted to unite Christian forces around the Habsburgs. It was rarely possible, however, to overcome the mutual suspicions that existed among the European princes for long. The Holy League of 1537-1540 allied the pope, the Emperor Charles V and the republic of Venice; but it fell apart after the Ottoman forces defeated a Christian fleet led by Andrea Doria at Preveza.

Suleyman died on campaign during the Christian defence of Sziget in 1566, and the Ottoman threat appeared briefly to subside. Pope Pius V tried to rouse a crusade, but found little response. Only when the Ottomans invaded the Venetian island of Cyprus in 1570 did Venice, Spain and the papacy unite in a new Holy League. Shortly after the fall of Famagusta in 1571, a united Christian fleet under the command of Don John of Austria defeated the Ottomans at Lepanto. The Christian victory raised great hopes but had little practical effect because of differences among the allies: Don John's visions of liberating the Holy Land faded as Venice made a separate peace with the Ottoman government and the League collapsed.

War smouldered on in the Balkans and central Europe from 1593 to 1606. The papacy and the Habsburgs called for uprisings of Balkan Christians against the infidel. Michael the Brave, prince of Wallachia, briefly succeeded in routing the Ottoman forces sent against them. But it was containment rather than crusade that halted Ottoman expansion, when a series of border

fortresses was constructed from Transylvania to the Adriatic coast. Crusading enthusiasm was reawakened in 1663, when Spain, the papacy, the German states and even France sent aid to halt a new Ottoman incursion into Hungary; but after the Christian victory at St Gotthard, a hasty peace was made, allowing the Habsburg emperor Leopold to turn his attention to a threat from the French.

In 1645, the onus shifted once again to the Aegean possessions of Venice. That year, the Ottomans attacked Candia in Crete, initiating a war that was to continue for the next 24 years. The besieged walls of Candia attracted Christian soldiers anxious to fight for Christendom; both individuals and official contingents streamed in from all over Europe. The Venetian fleet, supplemented by ships provided by the papacy and the Hospitallers (▶page 168), won several naval victories; but Venice was finally forced to surrender Crete in 1669.

The Ottoman empire also expanded to the north, forcing the Poles to cede Podolia in 1672. Although the Polish King Jan Sobieski defeated the Turks at Khotin the following year, he was unable to recapture the lost province.

> **T**his morning the galley of the magnificent Onfrè Giustiniano arrived with much firing of cannon, dragging Turkish ensigns through the water and bringing the best possible news that this most serene republic of Venice, and indeed the whole of Christendom could receive: the total rout and ruin of the whole Turkish fleet, which had taken place on Sunday 7 October, at about the third hour of the day.
>
> **Venice reports the Christian victory at Lepanto, 1571**

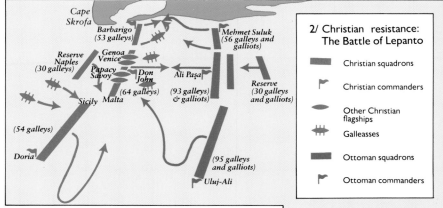

2/ Christian resistance: The Battle of Lepanto

- Christian squadrons
- Christian commanders
- Other Christian flagships
- Galleasses
- Ottoman squadrons
- Ottoman commanders

I/ The Ottoman advance, 1521–1672

- Ottoman territory by 1521
- Ottoman territory by 1606
- Annexed by Ottomans in 1664
- Annexed by Ottomans in 1672
- Ottoman tributaries
- Venetian territory
- ✗ Ottoman victory
- ✗ Christian victory
- ⚑ Border fort

Lublin

25°

Kiev

Zhitomir

P O L A N D

P O D O L I A

Conquered by Ottomans 1672

Khotin
1673

Tokaj

Satu Mare
(Szatmár)

Debrecen

K H A N A T E
O F   T H E   C R I M E A
Ottoman tributary from 1478

JEDISAN
*Conquered by Ottomans
1526*

M O L D A V I A

Iaşi

Odessa

Kherson

✗1664
Oradea
(Grosswardein,
Nagyvárad)

Cluj (Kolozsvár)

Ottoman tributary

BUJAK
*Conquered by Ottomans
1538*

Akkerman

CRIMEA

T R A N S Y L V A N I A
Ottoman tributary from 1541

Yevpatoriya

Kaffa

Timişoara (Temesvár)

✗1552

W A L L A C H I A
Ottoman tributary from 1541

Bucharest

Călugăreni
1595

Danube

Vidin

Nicopolis

B l a c k

S e a

Niš

B U L G A R I A

Sofia

Varna

A detail from Giorgio Vasari's painting of the
Battle of Lepanto. The Christian victory was
commemorated in every kind of literary, musical
and graphic medium. Allegories of Lepanto were
particularly popular, but even realistic depictions
of the battle like Vasari's, often stressed the role of
divine intervention on the Christian side.

O T T O M A N

MACEDONIA

T H R A C E

Edirne
(Adrianople)

Constantinople

Thessalonica

THESSALY

E M P I R E

Dardanelles

1656 ✗

A e g e a n

Scyros ✗
1538

S e a

Smyrna (Izmir)

Adana

Tarsus

✗1571
Lepanto

Chios

1566 ✗
1566

✗ Samos
1550

Antioch (Antakya)

G R E E C E

Andros

Tenos
(Tinos)

Nauplia ✗
MOREA 1540

Naxos

Bodrum

✗1540
Malvasia
(Monemvasia)

Cerigo (Kithira)

✗1522
Rhodes

Nicosia ✗
1570

✗ Famagusta
1571

Cyprus

M e d i t e r r a n e a n

Candia (Iraklion)

Crete ✗1669

S e a

Tokaj

Szent... 1596

The Siege of Vienna and the Holy League

As the Ottoman forces reached the gates of Vienna in 1683, the Christian states temporarily sank their differences in a Holy League to repel the invasion.

Rebellion in Habsburg Hungary gave the Ottomans a pretext for refusing to renew a truce which was due to expire in 1682. Once again an Ottoman army assembled to attack Vienna. It was only as this army was advancing that the Habsburg emperor Leopold was able to negotiate aid from Bavaria, Saxony, other smaller German states and, most importantly, from Poland, where Jan Sobieski's Catholic faith and national interests combined to ensure his participation in the defence of Vienna. The city was under siege for three months before the allied armies arrived to put the Ottoman forces to flight.

Pope Innocent XI, who had organized considerable financial subsidies for the relief of Vienna, attempted to bring the Christian powers together in a league to oppose the Ottomans. His efforts had little diplomatic effect until the immediate threat had passed, but in March 1684 a Holy League consisting of the Habsburg empire, Poland and Venice was created under papal sponsorship. Leopold compromised with France to secure his western borders, and the allied forces devoted their full attention to driving back the Ottomans. The Poles and the Cossacks fought in Bessarabia and Moldavia. In Hungary and Serbia, first Buda fell to imperial forces (1686), and then Belgrade (1688). The Venetians recovered the Morea, aided by papal, Tuscan and Maltese galleys and troops hired from Hanover, while Slav irregulars seized extensive territories in Dalmatia.

These advances were halted, however, when Louis XIV resumed hostilities in the west in 1688. This indirect encouragement to the Ottomans earned the French king the sobriquet of 'Most Christian Turk'. A successful Ottoman counter-offensive re-took Belgrade in 1690. It was only in 1697, when the imperial forces could once again be devoted to the eastern front, that the Ottoman army was entirely routed at the battle of Senta. The Peace of Karlowitz in 1699 confirmed the return to Christendom of major Ottoman possessions in central Europe and Greece.

The Ottomans were unwilling to concede these losses for long. In 1710 they made war on the Russian tsar Peter the Great, who had

captured Azov after joining the Holy League in 1686. Peter entered this war as a champion of the Balkan Christians. As he set out for Moldavia from Moscow – the 'Third Rome' — the tsar adopted the banner of Constantine the Great: a cross with the inscription 'In this sign we conquer'. But without the expected Balkan-wide Christian uprising, he was forced to admit defeat in 1711 on the river Prut.

The Ottomans then returned to war with the republic of Venice in 1715. Profiting from the dissatisfaction of the Orthodox Greek inhabitants with Venetian rule, they quickly reoccupied the Morea and Venice's Aegean islands. In 1716 the Austrians intervened on behalf of Venice, crushing an Ottoman army at Peterwardein in southern Hungary and retaking Belgrade. By this time the Venetians, too, were beginning to mark victories against the Ottomans, beating off an attack on Corfu and making gains on the mainland.

In spite of these successes, the emperor, once again distracted by hostilities in the west, accepted the Peace of Passarowitz in 1718. Though Venice retained its Ionian islands and some new territory in Dalmatia and on the Greek mainland, it was forced to relinquish the Morea, the islands of Aegina and Tenos, and its last fortresses on Crete. The Habsburgs were now the predominant Christian power in the Balkans.

An English broadsheet of 1684, one of many issued in connection with the siege of Vienna. It includes an attack on 'the most Christian monarch' Louis XIV of France, whose foreign policy had taken advantage of the Ottoman invasion of the empire.

2/ The Christian allies in Central Europe and Greece, 1684–1718

- Christian allies, 1718
- Christian gains by Treaty of Karlowitz, 1699
- Christian gains by Treaty of Passarowitz, 1718
- Ottoman empire, 1718
- Ottoman gains by Treaty of Passarowitz, 1718
- ✗ Christian victory
- ✗ Ottoman victory

1/The attack on Vienna, 1683
Christian territory
Ottoman territory
Ottoman troops
Ottoman vassals
Imperial German troops
Polish troops
BRUNSWICK-LÜNEBURG
BRANDENBURG
Hanover
ELECTORATE OF SAXONY
Dresden
HOLY ROMAN EMPIRE
Würzburg
FRANCONIA
WÜRTTEMBERG
Regensburg
Ulm
BAVARIA
SWABIA
Munich
Passau
Prague
Krems
Tulln
Nikolsburg
Vienna
HABSBURG LANDS
Györ (Raab)
Buda
Székesfehérvár (Stuhlweissenburg)
HUNGARY
POLAND
Warsaw
Częstochowa
Cracow
GALICIA
Lemberg (Lwów)
VOLHYNIA
PODOLIA
BESSARABIA
JEDISAN
MOLDAVIA
TRANSYLVANIA
OTTOMAN EMPIRE
Brăila
Osijek
Belgrade
WALLACHIA
BOSNIA
SERBIA
Niš
BULGARIA
Varna
MONTENEGRO
REPUBLIC OF RAGUSA
Adriatic Sea
Black Sea
Edirne (Adrianople)
Constantinople
Bari
KINGDOM OF NAPLES
ALBANIA
Yannina (Ianina)
GREECE
Ionian Islands
Aegean Sea
Mediterranean Sea
MOREA
10°
15°
20°
25°
30°
50°
45°
40°
PODOLIA
Ceded to Poland 1699
Dniester
Jassy
MOLDAVIA
Stănileşti 1711
CHIA
Bucharest
Danube
Black Sea
THRACE
Constantinople
Rhodes
Chios
nalonga
45°
40°
50°

The Final Outpost

The 250 years the Hospitallers spent on Malta saw the Order decline from a militant crusading brotherhood into an indolent and impotent anachronism.

When the Ottomans captured Rhodes in 1522 (▶ *page 136*) the surviving Hospitallers retreated to an itinerant exile in Italy. The emperor Charles V decided to use the Order to defend his Mediterranean empire, and in 1530 the brethren reluctantly occupied Tripoli in North Africa and the small islands of Malta and Gozo. The sea castle of Sant'Angelo in the Grand Harbour and its suburb of Birgu became the Hospital's Maltese headquarters, but only limited efforts were made to fortify them and 1551 the Turks totally devastated Gozo and recaptured Tripoli (▶ *page 162*). In 1565 the Ottomans besieged Malta itself, but disagreements and delays among their leaders allowed the Grand Master Jean de la Valette, veteran of the final siege of Rhodes, to organize an effective and heroic defence. The Turks had to operate through the summer heat at the end of lengthy lines of communication, while García de Toledo, the viceroy at Palermo, led the Spanish fleet to the rescue. The Turks fled,

leaving the Knights to enjoy colossal public acclaim.

After the siege the knights were committed to Malta. They moved their headquarters to the new city of Valletta, around which ever more extensive stone defences were endlessly constructed. Birgu, renamed Vittoriosa, and the villages opposite Valletta were surrounded by the powerful Cottonera lines. The Order's galley fleet was strengthened and took part in the Christian triumph at Lepanto in 1571 (▶ *page 164*) and in many other campaigns. The Knights also harassed Turkish shipping in a form of licensed piracy, the *corso*, which brought them fluctuating profits for over two centuries. The harbour and its quarantine facilities developed into a major emporium; Maltese commerce and agriculture, both based on cotton, were encouraged and the population rose rapidly.

The island became the well-adorned seat of a prosperous court and cosmopolitan culture, and the Order an aristocratic, if comparatively benevolent despotism. By the late 18th century, the Knights had lost their military-religious function and were corrupted by wealth and tainted with freemasonry. The European priories on which Malta still partly depended, had dwindled; some were destroyed by the Reformation, others just stopped sending men and money. When the French national assembly confiscated the Hospital's estates in 1792 the end was in sight. In 1798 Napoleon arrived to expel the Knights, who offered no resistance, from this last outpost of crusading.

I do not believe that music ever sounded so sweet to human ears as the peal of our bells did to ours on that eighth day of September – the day of the Nativity of Our Lady. For the last three months they had only been struck to give the alarm signal, but now the Grand Master ordered them to be rung at the hour when the reveille was usually sounded. During the morning they rang for the pontifical high mass which was celebrated with great solemnity in thanksgiving to Our Lord God and to His Holy Mother, for the mercy they had shown us.

Francisco Balbi di Corregio describes the end of the siege of Malta, 1565

Philip of Vendôme (1655-1727), illegitimate great-grandson of Henry IV of France, and Grand Prior of the Knights of Malta of France from 1681. After a series of court scandals, Vendôme was exiled by Louis XIV. He became Captain-General of the Galleys in Malta and was involved in the Order's re-fortification projects.

I/Hospitaller naval operations in the Mediterranean

- Christian territory, c.1740
- Muslim territory, c.1740
- → Muslim corsair routes
- ▲ Major Hospitaller operation
- ✗ Battle or siege

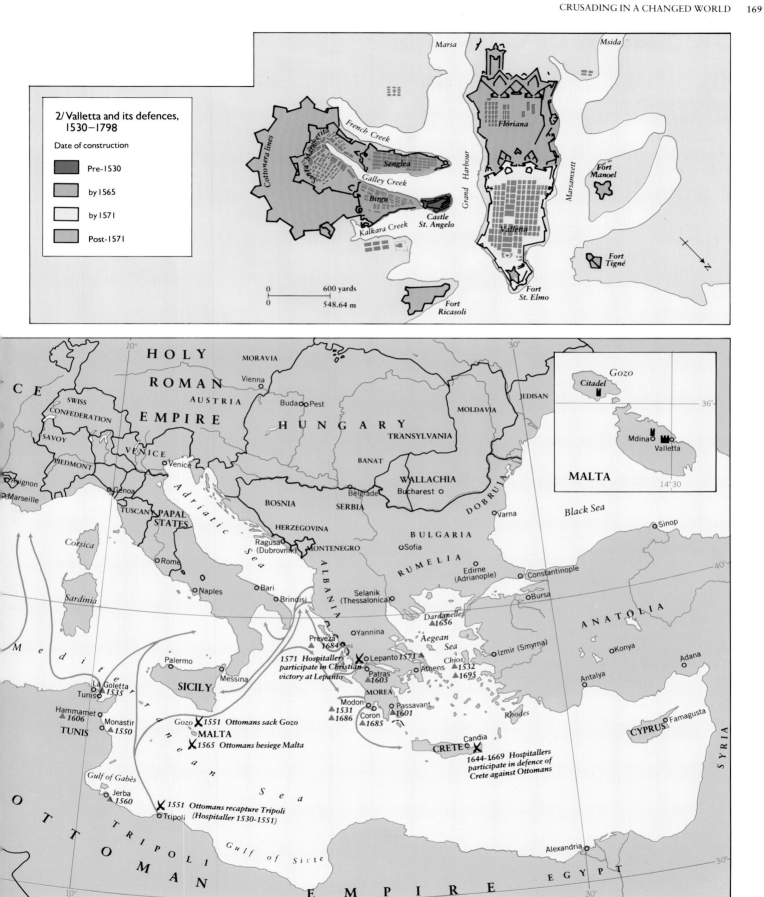

2/ Valletta and its defences, 1530–1798

Date of construction

- Pre-1530
- by 1565
- by 1571
- Post-1571

Marsa

Msida

French Creek

Floriana

Senglea

Galley Creek

Birgu

Cottonera lines

Santa Margherita

Kalkara Creek

Castle St. Angelo

Fort Manoel

Grand Harbour

Marsamxett

Valletta

Fort Tigné

0 — 600 yards
0 — 548.64 m

Fort Ricasoli

Fort St. Elmo

N

HOLY ROMAN EMPIRE

MORAVIA

Vienna

AUSTRIA

Buda Pest

HUNGARY

MOLDAVIA

TRANSYLVANIA

BANAT

SWISS CONFEDERATION

SAVOY

VENICE

PIEDMONT

Venice

WALLACHIA

Bucharest

Belgrade

BOSNIA

SERBIA

JEDISAN

Avignon

Marseille

Genoa

TUSCANY

PAPAL STATES

Adriatic Sea

Rome

Corsica

Sardinia

HERZEGOVINA

Ragusa (Dubrovnik)

MONTENEGRO

ALBANIA

BULGARIA

Sofia

RUMELIA

DOBRUJA

Varna

Black Sea

Sinop

Gozo

Citadel

36°

Mdina

Valletta

MALTA

14° 30

Naples

Bari

Brindisi

Yannina

Preveza 1684

Selanik (Thessalonica)

Edirne (Adrianople)

Constantinople

Bursa

ANATOLIA

40°

1571 Hospitallers participate in Christian victory at Lepanto

Lepanto 1571

Patras 1603

Athens

MOREA

Aegean Sea

Chios 1532 1695

Dardanelles 1656

Izmir (Smyrna)

Konya

Adana

Palermo

Messina

SICILY

Modon 1531 1686

Coron 1685

Passavant 1601

Rhodes

Antalya

La Goletta 1535

Tunis

Gozo 1551 Ottomans sack Gozo

MALTA

1565 Ottomans besiege Malta

Candia

CRETE

1644–1669 Hospitallers participate in defence of Crete against Ottomans

CYPRUS

Famagusta

SYRIA

Hammamet 1606

Monastir 1550

TUNIS

Jerba 1560

Gulf of Gabès

1551 Ottomans recapture Tripoli (Hospitaller 1530–1551)

Tripoli

TRIPOLI

Gulf of Sirte

OTTOMAN EMPIRE

EGYPT

Alexandria

Mediterranean Sea

30°

10°

30°

The Shadow of Crusading

The memory of crusading passed quickly from the minds of Europeans; but something which was around for so long could not fail to leave its mark on the modern world.

Crusading was first and foremost a religious movement, and it is in religion that its shadow can be found. Although the liberation fighters of Latin America, Asia and Africa seem scarcely aware of it, the theology of Christian violence that underpins their movements is similar to that which inspired thinking crusaders. Echoes of a crusading ethos also linger in the Baltic states, the Balkans, Spain and Spanish America, where Christian rule was carved by war: the *cruzada* (privileges linked to a crusade tax) was only abolished in the diocese of Pueblo, Colorado, in 1945.

Still with us are the indulgence, which developed with crusading; income tax, which was introduced to meet the needs of crusaders; and the Franciscan guardianship of the holy places, confirmed by the papacy in 1342 when it was becoming clear that Christendom was unlikely to reconquer the Holy Land. So are a plethora of religious, military and chivalric orders with crusading origins. The titular bishops, now employed by Rome on special missions, date back to the Muslim reconquests in the 12th century, which exiled a host of prelates from their dioceses (▶*page 104*).

The Maronites, the chief indigenous Christian group in the county of Tripoli and now in the state of Lebanon, were persuaded in around 1181 to enter into religious union with Rome. Resisting Islam in their mountain fastnesses, the Maronites looked back on the period of Latin occupation as a golden age, and it is impossible to understand their fierce independence today without reference to their history.

After the loss of Malta (▶*page 168*), the Order of the Hospital of St John gradually came to terms with an existence in which it had to concentrate entirely on its first ideal, the care of the sick poor. It is still recognized as a sovereign entity in international law, and has its headquarters in Rome. Three other Orders of St John, in Germany, Sweden and the Netherlands, descend from a Hospitaller province which survived the Reformation as a Protestant order. In England, the Most Venerable Order of St John came into exis-

tence in the 1820s when French knights of Malta were trying to raise a military force to help the Greek independence fighters and conquer an island as a new headquarters. These non-Catholic Orders of St John are not, of course, orders of the church, but they are recognized orders of chivalry. They and the Order of Malta have between them more than 50,000 members and are responsible for major charitable enterprises.

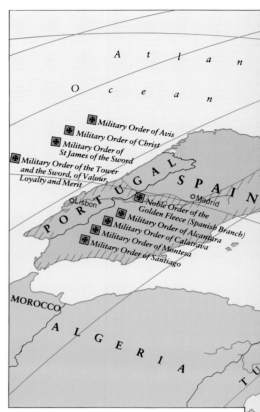

His Most Eminent Highness Fra' Andrew Bertie, the first English Grand Master of the Order of the Hospital of St John since the 13th century. His red uniform is directly descended from the 13th-century red surcoat granted to the Hospitaller Knights by the Pope.

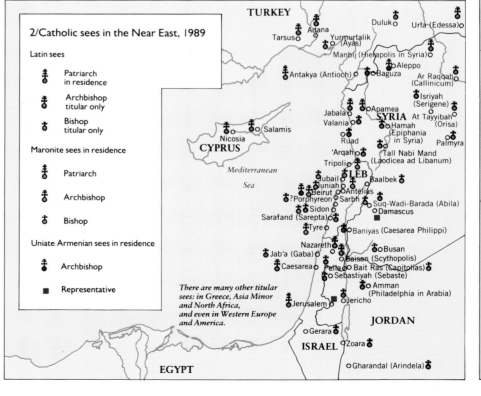

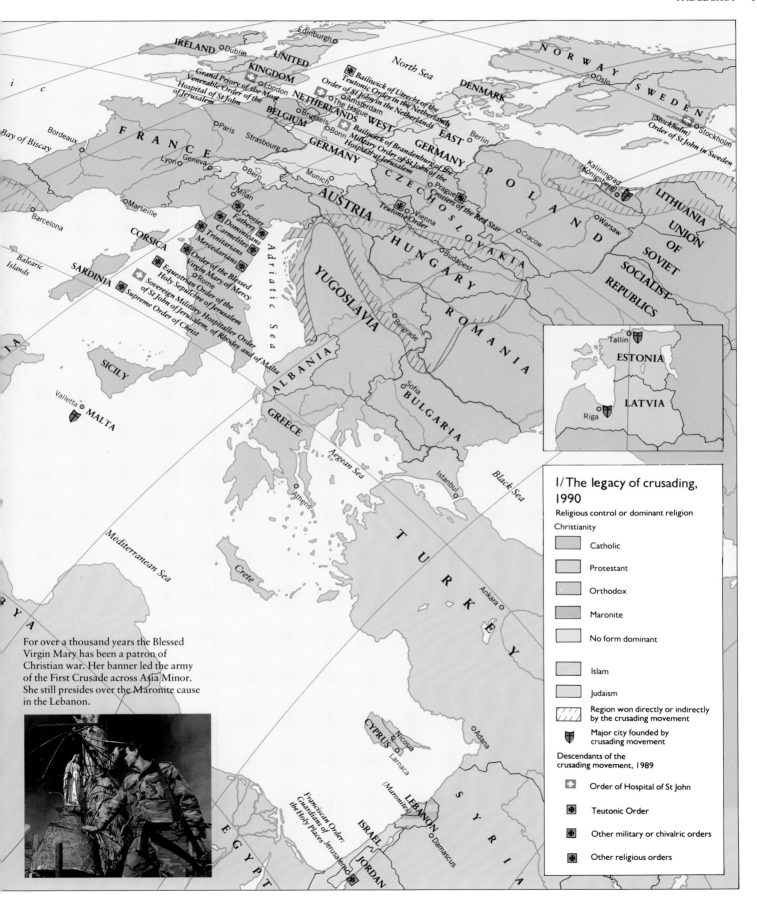

For over a thousand years the Blessed
Virgin Mary has been a patron of
Christian war. Her banner led the army
of the First Crusade across Asia Minor.
She still presides over the Maronite cause
in the Lebanon.

**I/The legacy of crusading,
1990**

Religious control or dominant religion

Christianity

Catholic

Protestant

Orthodox

Maronite

No form dominant

Islam

Judaism

Region won directly or indirectly
by the crusading movement

Major city founded by
crusading movement

Descendants of the
crusading movement, 1989

Order of Hospital of St John

Teutonic Order

Other military or chivalric orders

Other religious orders

Grand Priory of the Most
Venerable Order of the
Hospital of St John
of Jerusalem

Bailiwick of Utrecht of the
Teutonic Order in the Netherlands
Order of St John in the Netherlands

Bailiwick of Brandenburg of the
Military Order of St John of the
Hospital of Jerusalem

Order of St John in Sweden

Crosiers of the Red Star

Teutonic Order

Crosier
Fathers
Dominicans
Carmelites
Trinitarians
Mercedarians
Order of the Blessed
Virgin Mary of Mercy
Equestrian Order of the
Holy Sepulchre of Jerusalem
Sovereign Military Hospitaller Order
of St John of Jerusalem, of Rhodes and of Malta
Supreme Order of Christ

Franciscan Order:
Guardians of
the Holy Places Jerusalem

BIBLIOGRAPHY

GENERAL
N. J. Housley, *The Avignon Papacy and the Crusades, 1305-1378*, 1986
H. E. Mayer, *The Crusades*, 2nd ed. 1988
J. S. C. Riley-Smith, *The Crusades. A Short History*, 1987
S. Runciman, *A History of the Crusades*, 3 vols, 1951-54
K. M. Setton (ed-in-chief), *A History of the Crusades*, 2nd ed., 5 vols to date, 1969-
K. M. Setton, *The Papacy and the Levant, 1204-1571*, 4 vols, 1976-84

COLLECTIONS OF TRANSLATED SOURCES
E. Hallam *Chronicles of the Crusades*, 1989
L. and J. S. C. Riley-Smith *The Crusades: Idea and Reality, 1095-1274*, 1981

IDEAS OF CRUSADING
J. A. Brundage, *Medieval Canon Law and the Crusade*, 1969
C. Erdmann, *The Origin of the Idea of the Crusade*, 1977
B. Z. Kedar, *Crusade and Mission*, 1984
J. S. C. Riley-Smith, *What were the Crusades?* 1977
F. H. Russell, *The Just War in the Middle Ages*, 1975
E. Siberry, *Criticism of Crusading 1095-1274*, 1985

THE HOME FRONT
W. C. Jordan, *Louis IX and the Challenge of the Crusade*, 1979
S. Lloyd, *English Society and the Crusade 1216-1307*, 1988
C. Tyerman, *England and the Crusades 1095-1588*, 1988

CRUSADES TO THE EAST AND NORTH AFRICA
J. M. Powell, *Anatomy of a Crusade, 1213-1221*, 1986
D. E. Queller, *The Fourth Crusade*, 1978
J. S. C. Riley-Smith, *The First Crusade and the Idea of Crusading*, 1986

THE CRUSADER SETTLEMENTS IN THE EAST
E. Ashtor, *Levant Trade in the Later Middle Ages*, 1983
M. Benvenisti, *The Crusaders in the Holy Land*, 1970
T. S. R. Boase (ed), *The Cilician Kingdom of Armenia*, 1978
H. Buchthal, *Miniature Painting in the Latin Kingdom of Jerusalem*, 1957
N. Cheetham, *Medieval Greece*, 1981
P. W. Edbury and J. G. Rowe, *William of Tyre*, 1988
J. Folda, *Crusader Manuscript Illumination at Saint Jean d'Acre, 1275-1291*, 1976
B. Hamilton, *The Latin Church in the Crusader States: The secular church*, 1980
G. F. Hill, *A History of Cyprus*, vols. 2-3, 1948
D. M. Metcalf, *Coinage of the Crusades and the Latin East*, 1983

W. Müller-Wiener, *Castles of the Crusaders*, 1966
J. Prawer, *The Latin Kingdom of Jerusalem*, 1972
J. Prawer, *Crusader Institutions*, 1980
D. Pringle, *The Red Tower*, 1986
J. H. Pryor, *Geography, Technology and War: Studies in the maritime history of the Mediterranean 649-1571*, 1988
J. Pritchard, *The Latin Kingdom of Jerusalem*, 2 vols, 1979
J. S. C. Riley-Smith, *The Feudal Nobility and the Kingdom of Jerusalem*, 1973
R. C. Smail, *Crusading Warfare 1097-1193*, 1956
S. Tibble, *Monarchy and Lordships in the Latin Kingdom of Jerusalem*, 1989

MUSLIMS AND MONGOLS
C. Cahen, *Pre-Ottoman Turkey*, 1968
M. G. S. Hodgson, *The Order of Assassins*, 1955
P. M. Holt, *The Age of the Crusades: The Near East from the eleventh century to 1517*, 1986
R. S. Humphreys, *From Saladin to the Mongols: The Ayyubids in Damascus 1193-1260*, 1977
H. Inalcik, *The Ottoman Empire*, 1973
R. Irwin, *The Middle East in the Middle Ages: The early Mamluk Sultanate 1250-1382*, 1986
M. C. Lyons and D. E. P. Jackson, *Saladin*, 1982
D. O. Morgan, *The Mongols*, 1986

CRUSADES IN EUROPE
R. I. Burns, *The Crusader Kingdom of Valencia*, 2 vols, 1967
E. Christiansen, *The Northern Crusades*, 1980
N. J. Housley, *The Italian Crusades*, 1982
D. W. Lomax, *The Reconquest of Spain*, 1978

THE MILITARY ORDERS
M. Barber, *The Trial of the Templars*, 1978
M. Burleigh, *Prussian Society and the German Order*, 1984 (for the Teutonic Knights, see also Christiansen, *The Northern Crusades* and Housley, *The Avignon Papacy*, both listed above.)
R. Cavaliero, *The Last of the Crusaders*, 1960
A. J. Forey, *The Templars in the Corona de Aragon*, 1973
A. Hoppen, *The Fortification of Malta by the Order of St John, 1530-1798*, 1979
J. Q. Hughes, *The Building of Malta during the Period of the Knights of St John of Jerusalem, 1530-1798*, 1956
A. T. Luttrell, *The Hospitallers in Cyprus, Rhodes, Greece and the West, 1291-1440*, 1978 A.T. Luttrell, *Latin Greece, the Hospitallers and the Crusades, 1291-1400*, 1982
J. F. O'Callaghan, *The Spanish Military Order of Calatrava and its Affiliates*, 1975
J. S. C. Riley-Smith, *The Knights of St John in Jerusalem and Cyprus, c.1050-1310*, 1967

Catholic Church Government

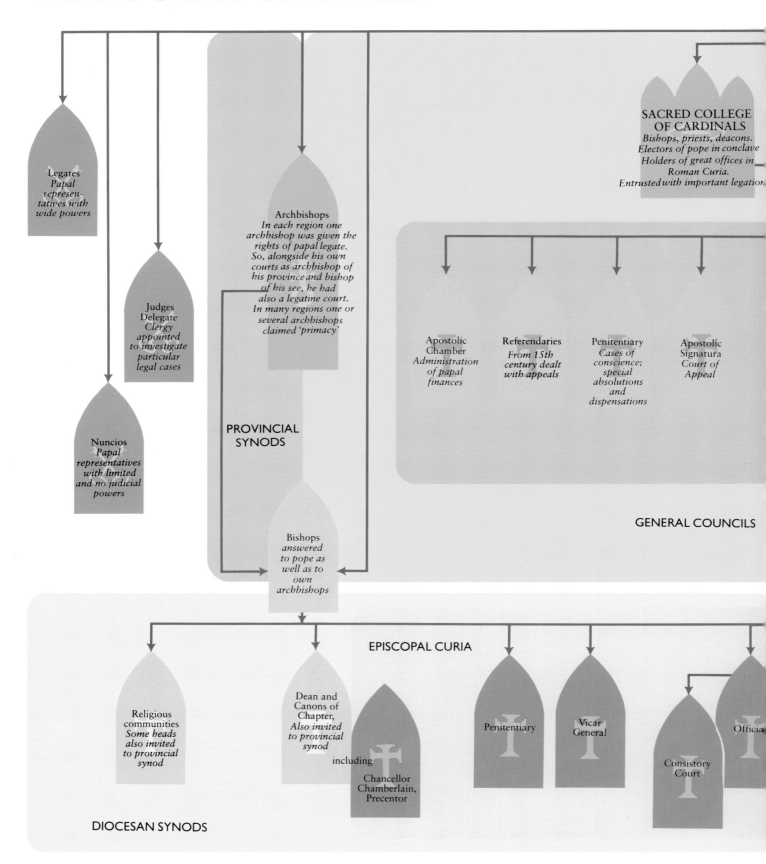

Legates
Papal representatives with wide powers

Judges Delegate
Clergy appointed to investigate particular legal cases

Nuncios
Papal representatives with limited and no judicial powers

Archbishops
In each region one archbishop was given the rights of papal legate. So, alongside his own courts as archbishop of his province and bishop of his see, he had also a legatine court. In many regions one or several archbishops claimed 'primacy'

PROVINCIAL SYNODS

SACRED COLLEGE OF CARDINALS
Bishops, priests, deacons. Electors of pope in conclave. Holders of great offices in Roman Curia. Entrusted with important legation

Apostolic Chamber
Administration of papal finances

Referendaries
From 15th century dealt with appeals

Penitentiary
Cases of conscience; special absolutions and dispensations

Apostolic Signatura
Court of Appeal

GENERAL COUNCILS

Bishops
answered to pope as well as to own archbishops

EPISCOPAL CURIA

Religious communities
Some heads also invited to provincial synod

Dean and Canons of Chapter,
Also invited to provincial synod

including

Chancellor Chamberlain, Precentor

Penitentiary

Vicar General

Official

Consistory Court

DIOCESAN SYNODS

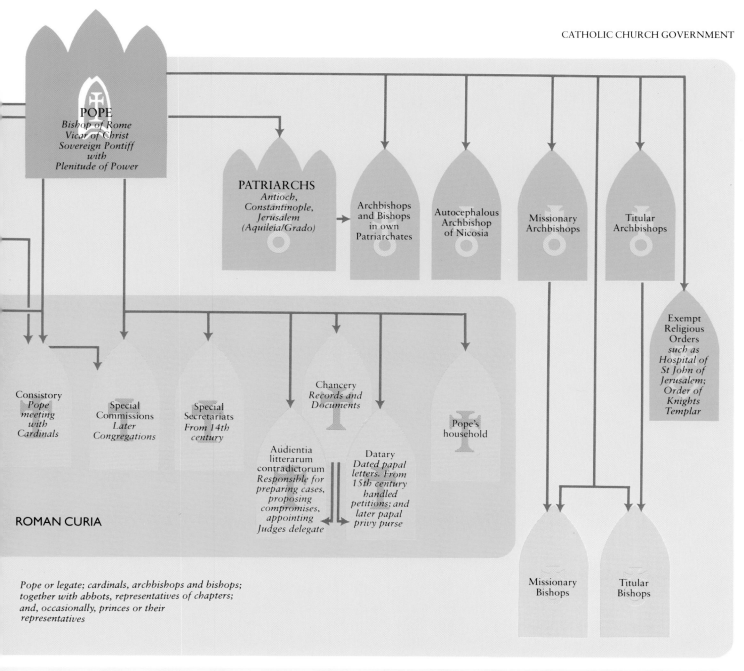

POPE
Bishop of Rome
Vicar of Christ
Sovereign Pontiff
with
Plenitude of Power

PATRIARCHS
Antioch,
Constantinople,
Jerusalem
(Aquileia/Grado)

Archbishops and Bishops in own Patriarchates

Autocephalous Archbishop of Nicosia

Missionary Archbishops

Titular Archbishops

Exempt Religious Orders *such as Hospital of St John of Jerusalem; Order of Knights Templar*

Consistory
Pope meeting with Cardinals

Special Commissions
Later Congregations

Special Secretariats
From 14th century

Chancery
Records and Documents

Audientia litterarum contradictorum
Responsible for preparing cases, proposing compromises, appointing Judges delegate

Datary
Dated papal letters. From 15th century handled petitions; and later papal privy purse

Pope's household

ROMAN CURIA

Pope or legate; cardinals, archbishops and bishops; together with abbots, representatives of chapters; and, occasionally, princes or their representatives

Missionary Bishops

Titular Bishops

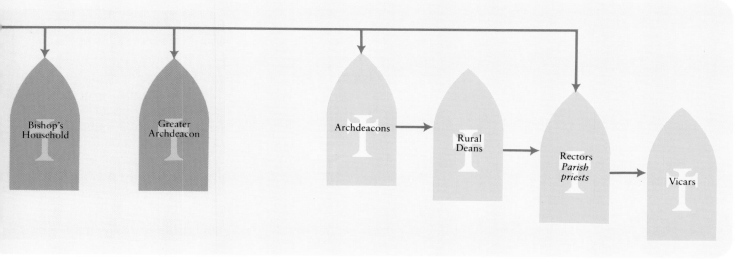

Bishop's Household

Greater Archdeacon

Archdeacons

Rural Deans

Rectors
Parish priests

Vicars

GLOSSARY

'**Abbasids** The family of Sunni caliphs in Iraq and Baghdad, 749-1258, and in Cairo, 1261-1517, who were descended from the Prophet Muhammad's uncle al-'Abbas.

Almohads The successors to the Almoravids as religio-political leaders in North-West Africa and Spain, 1130-1269.

Almoravids Berber rulers, arising in a religious movement and dominating North-West Africa and Spain, 1056-1147.

Apanage Land granted for maintenance of king's younger child or widow.

Armenian Church An independent Church, founded in the 4th century, which was regarded as Monophysite, although it was not in full communion with the Monophysites. In the late 1190s a minority of Armenians accepted union with the Catholic Church.

Assassins Extremist Shi'is, using religious assassination as a weapon. Founded by Hasan-i Sabbah, who, when the Fatimid movement was doctrinally split in 1094, recognized Nizar, the dead caliph's eldest son, as heir. Hasan had already settled at Alamut in northern Iran; another centre was established in Syria. Alamut was taken by the Mongols in 1256 and the last Syrian stronghold fell to the Egyptian Mamluks in 1273.

Assize The usual word in the kingdom of Jerusalem for a law, issued by the king after taking counsel.

Atabeg A Turkish military commander appointed as tutor-guardian to a Seljuk prince.

Auberge A hostel. In the Order of St John of Jerusalem the enclosed building or buildings in which the brother knights serving in the central Convent resided.

Aydin A Turkish emirate in western Asia Minor, which included Smyrna and under Umur Bey (d.1348) played an important rôle in Aegean naval affairs.

Ayyubids The descendants of Saladin's father and rulers of Saladin's empire in Egypt, Syria and the Yemen from 1169 to the later 13th century, although one branch remained in existence until the end of the 15th century.

Bailli A title, involving representative executive powers, with a wide variety of uses in the Latin East, accorded to men who were local officials and also administrators in the Military Orders and governors of the kingdom of Jerusalem when the king was a minor or was absent.

Byzantine empire The direct heir of the eastern Roman empire, ruled from Constantinople until its fall to the Ottomans in 1453.

Caliph Title of the supreme head of the Muslim community, the Imam, as successor or vice-regent of the Prophet Muhammad. By the 11th century the temporal authority of the caliphate had declined with the delegation of power to officials and the emergence of rival caliphates in Spain and Egypt.

Canon law The law of the Church.

Carmelites Members of a Mendicant Order of friars, originating in a group of hermits living on Mt Carmel in Palestine, who were given a Rule in the early 13th century.

Castellan An officer of the crown or of a lord with responsibilities as garrison commander in a fortress; or the lord of a lordship of moderate size, centred on a castle.

Chaghatai Khanate Chaghatai, Chinggis Khan's second son, was given lands in Transoxiana, Semireche and eastern Turkestan. The real founder of the khanate was Chaghatai's grandson Alughu, who seized Khwarazm, western Turkestan and Afghanistan: these became the nucleus of the khanate. Although the family were overthrown in the 14th century by Timur, an eastern branch persisted until the 17th century.

Cilician Armenia Armenians, fleeing from the Turkish advance in the second half of the 11th century, settled in Cilicia and established lordships there. In 1198 the Armenian ruler of Cilicia accepted a crown from the western emperor.

Collachium An area of the city of Rhodes, walled off from the rest of the town, where the rules of monastic enclosure were followed by the Hospitaller brothers.

Constable A military title; in the kingdom of Jerusalem it was given to the crown's chief military officer.

Convent Any religious community, male or female. The central convent of the Hospitallers, for instance, was the headquarters where the Master resided.

Danishmends Two dynasties in central and eastern Asia Minor, c.1071-1178, founded by Danishmend, a *ghazi* who established himself at the expense of the Seljuks of Rum.

Dhimmi The religions of the 'People of Scripture' – Jews, Christians and Sabaeans (interpreted to included Zoroastrians) – were tolerated in a Muslim state. The *dhimmis* had to pay a poll tax, were distinguished in certain ways, including dress, and suffered certain legal disabilities.

Domain See Royal Domain.

Dominicans Mendicant friars and members of the Order of Preachers, founded by St Dominic in the early 13th century.

Dragoman Dragomans in the kingdom of Jerusalem were minor local officials, perhaps representing the legal rights of landlords in relation to their villages.

Emir A military commander; also used as the title of the possessor of a lordship.

Excommunication A judicial sanction at the disposal of the Church. It involved expulsion from the Church and the denial of the sacraments; and the faithful were technically forbidden to have any dealings with an excommunicate.

Fatimids The family of Shi'i caliphs in North Africa, Egypt and Syria, 909-1171, claiming descent from Fatima, the daughter of the Prophet Muhammad and the wife of the fourth caliph 'Ali.

Feudalism From the point of view of economics, a system based on the provision of services in return for upkeep or property. In law, a system of contracts, in each of which one party, the lord, promised protection and maintenance, while the other, the vassal, promised loyalty and services. In terms of landholding, a system in which tenancies, in the form of fiefs, were more prevalent than freeholds. A feudal society was one in which dependent feudal relationships prevailed.

Fief Given by the lord in consequence of his obligation to provide maintenance under the feudal contract. It could take the form of land, but also of an annual income or even of upkeep in his household.

Franciscans Mendicant friars, members of the Order of Friars Minor, founded by St Francis in the early 13th century.

Franks Originally a barbarian people who invaded the Roman empire in the 5th century. By the central Middle Ages the name was given to all those living in northern and central France and in neighbouring French-speaking imperial territories such as Lorraine. By extension it was used by the people of the eastern Mediterranean region to describe all crusaders and settlers.

Germiyan A Turkish emirate in western Asia Minor.

Ghibellines Parties in 13th- and 14th-century Italian cities traditionally opposed to the Italian policies of the popes and associated with imperial policies. The name is a corruption of Waiblingen, the battle-cry of the Staufen faction in Germany.

Golden Horde The khans (1226-1502) were descendants of Jochi, Chinggis's eldest son, who had been given western Siberia and the Kipchak Steppe. Jochi's sons Batu and Orda founded the Blue Horde in southern Russia (nucleus of the Golden Horde) and the White Horde in western Siberia respectively. The two groups were united in the 14th century.

Great Khanate The nucleus of the Mongol empire in Mongolia and northern China, ruled by Chinggis and his descendants through Ögödei, his third son, 1206-1368. The Great Khans survived in Mongolia until the 17th century.

Guelfs Parties in 13th- and 14th- century Italian cities which traditionally supported the Italian politics of the popes. Their name stemmed from that of the Welfs, a German dynasty which rivalled the Staufen.

Hafsids The rulers of Tunisia and eastern Algeria 1228-1574, and descendants of Shaikh Abu-Hafs 'Umar, a general of the Almohads.

Haj The pilgrimage to Mecca. Every adult Muslim is required to perform the Haj at least once, provided he or she is able to do so.

Hammadids A branch of the Berber Zirid dynasty

ruling central north-west Africa, 1015-1152, until conquered by the Almohads.

Hanseatic League An association of merchants with the support of their cities, comprising all the north German and Rhineland trading centres. In the 14th century it dominated Baltic and North Sea commerce.

High Court of Jerusalem The king (or his representative) and all vassals who had entered into a feudal contract with him. After the 1160s they could include rear-vassals, who were obliged to contract with the king as well as with their immediate lords.

Holy Roman empire See Western empire.

Homage The ceremony of entering into a feudal contract. A vassal made homage to his lord.

Hospitallers Members of the Order of the Hospital of St John of Jerusalem.

Hussites Czech nationalists and reformers, the followers of Jan Hus (burned for heresy 1415), who demanded communion in both kinds, the reform of the clergy, secular jurisdiction in the case of morals, freedom of preaching and an investigation into the temporal possessions of the Church.

Ilkhanate Iran, Iraq, the Caucasus and Anatolia under the rule of the Mongol descendants of Chinggis's grandson Hülegü, 1256-1353.

Interdict A judicial sanction at the disposal of the Church, involving the withdrawal of the services of the clergy and of the sacraments from a defined region.

Ismailis See Assassins.

Jacobite Church A Syrian Monophysite Church, taking its name from Jacob Baradaeus, who had organized the Syrian Monophysites into an independent Church in the 6th century.

Karasi A Turkish emirate in north-western Asia Minor.

Latin The language of the Catholic rite; and, by extension, used of all western Europeans.

March Frontier territory.

Marinids Berber successors to the territories of the Almohads in north-west Africa in the 13th century. They tried to rebuild the Almohad empire and, inspired by the Jihad, to reconquer Spain. The dynasty ruled Morocco until 1465; a collateral branch of the family took over until extinguished in 1549.

Maronites Apparently they took their name from the monastery of St Maro near Apamea. They adopted Monotheletism in the 7th century and so became separated from the Orthodox Church. Were displaced and withdrew to the Lebanon mountains in the 10th century. In c.1181 they were persuaded to enter into full union with Rome and formed the first uniate Church.

Marshal Military official, a subordinate of the constable, from whom he held his office in fief in the kingdom of Jerusalem. He was particularly concerned with cavalry.

Menteşe A Turkish emirate in western Asia Minor.

Monophysites Christians who believe that Christ has only one nature, the divine, as opposed to the Catholic/Orthodox belief that he has two, being both God and Man.

Monotheletes Christians who believe that Christ has only one will.

Nizaris See Assassins.

Orthodox Church The Eastern or Greek Church, comprising the Greek patriarchates of Constantinople, Antioch, Alexandria and Jerusalem, which in practice recognized the seniority of the patriarchs of Constantinople and in the Middle Ages looked to the Byzantine emperors for protection; and Churches, such as those in Georgia, Bulgaria, Romania, Serbia and Russia, which are in communion with it.

Ottoman empire The empire established in Asia Minor, the Balkans, the Arab lands and North Africa by the descendants of Osman (died c.1324). The dynasty remained in power until 1924.

Patriarchates Originally three, then five major areas of Church government being subject to the patriarchs of Rome (the pope), Alexandria, Antioch, Constantinople and Jerusalem. Under each patriarch there are hierarchies of archbishops and bishops. In the western Church a few archbishops have also been given the title of patriarch.

Priory A monastic officer without the full independence of an abbot. The Hospitaller priors ruled provinces of the Order, subject to the Master and their Order's General Chapter.

Rays A transliteration of ra'is, an Arabic title for an officer with authority over a community, who acted as intermediary between government and governed. In Latin Palestine and Syria the title was given to several officials, and particularly to village headmen.

Rear-vassal The vassal of a vassal, with at least one

intermediate lord between him and the chief lord.

Royal Domain The personal estates of the king, some of which were granted out to minor vassals.

St Lazarus, Order of A Military and Hospitaller Order founded in the first half of the 12th century, particularly to care for lepers, who by the 13th century could become brother knights.

St Thomas of Acre, Order of An English Order in the East, founded in the 1190s, which became a Military Order in the late 1220s. It settled in England in the 14th century.

Saladin Tithe A tax on income and capital (a tenth of income and the value of movable goods) levied in 1188 in England and France for the crusade.

Saruhan A Turkish emirate in western Asia Minor.

Schism A division, creating disunity in the Church.

Scribe In Latin Palestine and Syria this title (a translation from an Arabic equivalent) was given to minor officials engaged in the collection of revenue.

Seljuks. 1) Great Seljuks The descendants of Tughril I, who conquered Iran and Iraq in the name of Sunni orthodoxy. The Seljuk sultans ruled on the 'Abbasid caliphs' behalf, 1055-1194.
2) Seljuks of Rum The son of a Seljuk chieftain, who had rebelled against the Seljuk sultan, settled at Nicaea in Asia Minor *c*.1077. The capital of Rum was later Konya (Iconium). The sultanate became a tributary of the Mongols in 1243 and was occupied by the Mongols in 1307.

Seneschal The chief officer of the crown in the kingdom of Jerusalem. He presided over the High Court in the king's absence. He was head of the financial administration and he had supervision of royal fortresses.

Shi'a (Shi'i) A general name for a large group of Muslim sects, all of which recognize 'Ali as the legitimate caliph after the death of the Prophet Muhammad. They are to be distinguished from the orthodox Sunni.

Sultan A title first used by the Seljuks, implying executive power under the caliph. Sultans, therefore, could be paramount kings.

Sunna The theory and practice of orthodox Islam, followed by most Muslims.

Sunni One of the main two divisions of Islam, split over the question of succession to the Prophet Muhammad. For Sunnis, the majority of Muslims, religious authority lies in the consensus of the community reinforcing the holy law.

Taifa kingdoms The Spanish Ummayyad caliphate of Córdoba was extinguished in 1031 and Moorish Spain fragmented into these political units, of varying size, ruled by local dynasties.

Tekke A Turkish emirate in south-western Asia Minor.

Tenant-in-Chief An immediate vassal of the king.

Titular bishop In the Catholic Church a true bishop in all things except his rights of residence and jurisdiction, because in the vast majority of cases his diocese lies outside Catholic, and perhaps Christian control.

Troubadours Poets from Languedoc and Provence – the equivalents are *trouveres* in northern France and *minnesingern* in Germany – who composed songs, especially *cansos*, love songs, and *sirventes*, moral or political songs.

Turcopoles In the Latin East these were either native cavalry or European mercenaries using native equipment.

Uniate Churches Churches of the eastern rite in full communion with Rome while preserving their own rites, ceremonies canon law and bishops; with no religious superior other than the pope.

Vassal The inferior in a feudal contract, bound by loyalty to his lord to whom he owed services and from whom he held a fief as a tenant.

Vows Canon law concerning Christian vows developed at the same time as the crusading movement. Vows came to be defined as deliberate commitments made to God to do, or not to do, certain acts. They could be simple (informal and unenforceable) or solemn, general (mandatory for all) or special, necessary (in that they were needed for salvation) or voluntary, pure or conditional. The crusade vow was usually solemn, always special and voluntary, and often conditional.

Wazir A chief minister, exercising civil authority on behalf of the caliph or sultan.

Wends A group of pagan Slavonic peoples who occupied the Baltic coast from the bay of Kiel to the Vistula.

Western empire The inheritor of a revival of the western Roman empire by the papacy and Charlemagne in 800. Called the Holy Roman empire from 1158, although this term is not customarily used by historians until the late medieval and early modern periods.

INDEX

The index includes only those places which are annotated on the maps, have a keyed symbol, or are mentioned in the text. Names added for locational purposes are not indexed. Variant names and spellings are given in brackets, and separately cross-referenced. Places are located by reference to the state in which they now lie (except Israel and Jordan) or by island groups or sea areas. References are narrowed down as necessary by location as N(orth), W(est), C(entral), etc. Where any page contains two or more numbered maps, these are distinguished by a number after an oblique stroke: 97/2, for example, refers to map 2 on page 97.

The index also includes personal and other proper names mentioned in the text. References to names occurring only in the text are distinguished by t after the page number.

Abbreviations			
a/c also called	Chin Chinese	Heb Hebrew	n/c now called
Alb Albanian	Cz Czech	Hung Hungarian	n/s now spelled
anc ancient	Dut Dutch	Ital Italian	Per Persian
Ar Arabic	Eng English	Lat Latin	Pol Polish
Arm Armenian	Est Estonian	Latv Latvian	Port Portuguese
a/s also spelled	Finn Finnish	Lith Lithuanian	Rom Romanian
bibl biblical	form formerly	Mac Macedonian	Russ Russian
Bulg Bulgarian	Fr French	med medieval	S Cr Serbo-Croat
Cat Catalan	Ger German	MGr Modern Greek	Sp Spanish
	Gr Greek		Turk Turkish

Aalst (Fr Alost) Flanders crusader family 28
al-'Abbasa N Egypt Mamluk victory 108/2
Abbasids Muslim dynasty 26t
Abbeville NE France 125
Abergavenny S Wales crusade sermon 88/2
Abila see Suq-Wadi-Barada
Åbo (Finn Turku) SW Finland bishopric 75
Abu Qubais W Syria Hospitaller castle 53/1; tribute to Military Orders 107
Accabara C Palestine 102/2
Acciaiuoli, Nerio Lord of Corinth 138-139
Acco see Acre
Aceca C Spain castle 54
Achaea, principality of S Greece Latin state 87; Hospitaller intervention 137; Angevin control 139; Neapolitan suzerainty 141
Acre (Bibl Acco, Lat Ptolemais, Med St Jean d'Acre, Ar 'Akka, Heb 'Akko) N Palestine Christian conquest 55/1; royal domain 37/1; monastery 43; council of 1148 51; Templar castle and hospital 53/1; 57; falls to Saladin 61/1; captured in Third Crusade 63; Fifth Crusade 95; fortified by Louis IX 97; arrival of Frederick II 98/3; John of Beirut 99; Mediterranean trade 101/1; spice trade 101/3; extent of territory 102/2; plan of city 102-103; bishopric 104; headquarters of Hospitallers 107; taken by Mamluks 114t
Acrocorinth (Gr Akrokorinthos) C Greece Latin base 87; Latin activity 139
Adalia (anc Attalia, Turk Antalya) S Anatolia crusaders embark for Syria 51; Mediterranean trade 133; occupied by crusading league 141; taken by Peter I 143; conquered by Ottomans 147
Adana W Turkey Latin see 170
al-'Adiliyah N Egypt Fifth Crusade 95/2
al-'Adil Sayf al-Din (a/c Saphadin) Ayyubid sultan 108/2
Adramyttium (Turk Edremit) NW Turkey battle 141
Adrianople (Turk Edirne) NW Turkey Third Crusade 63; conquered by Ottomans 147; Ottoman commercial centre 151
Adummim C Palestine places of pilgrimage 42
Aegean Sea routes 137; Turkish raids 147
Aegium see Vostitsa
Afamiyah see Apamea
al-Afdal Egyptian general First Crusade 31
al-Afdal 'Ali, prince of Damascus 108/3
Africa trade 100/1, 2
Africa, West gold fields 100/2

Agadir see Santa Cruz de Aguer
Agde SW France ecclesiastical lordship 76/2
Agen SW France crusade against the Cathars 76/2; Templar house 125
Agridi N Cyprus taken by John of Beirut 99
'Aidhab battle see 'Aydhab
Aigues-Mortes S France Shepherds' crusades 83; crusades of St Louis 93,97
Aila (Ar al-'Aqaban) S Jordan Latin castle 57
'Ain Jalut see 'Ayn Jalut
Ainstable N England crusader landholding 89
Aintab (Turk Gaziantep) SE Turkey castle 35/2
Aix-en-Provence SE France Templar house 125
Aiyion see Vostitsa
Ajlun C Transjordan Muslim castle 57
Akçehisar see Croia
'Akka see Acre
'Akkar SW Syria Latin castle 57; falls to Saladin 61/1; see also Gibelcar
Akkerman (Russ Belgorod Dnestrovskiy, Rom Cetatea Alba) SW Russia trade 101/1; conquered by Ottomans 151
'Akko see Acre
Ak-Koyunlu (a/s Aq-Qoyunlu) tribal group of SE Turkey conquered by Ottomans 147, 151
Akova Latin activity 139
Akrokorinthos see Acrocorinth
Alamut N Iran Assassin stronghold 27; Assassins defeated by Mongols 113
Alange W Spain castle 55; battle 73
Alanya see Alaya
Alarcón C Spain castle 54
Alarcos C Spain battle 72-73
Alaşehir see Philadelphia
Alaya (med Scandelore or Candeloro, Turk Alanya) S Turkey Byzantine castle 57; emirate 141/2; raided by Peter I 143; conquered by Ottomans 147; raided by Boucicaut 149
Albania revolt against Ottomans 130; 147; conquered by Ottomans 147
Albara (Ar al-Barah) W Syria bishopric 104
Albelda N Spain battle 32
Albert, bishop of Riga 74t
Albert, duke of Austria Hussite crusades 131/1
Albi SW France crusades against the Cathars 76/2; Templar house 125
Albufeira S Portugal castle 55
Alcácer S Portugal castle 54; convent 55
Alcalá de los Gazules S Spain castle 55
Alcanadre N Spain Templar property 124
Alcañiz NE Spain castle 54; convent 55
Alcántara W Spain castle 33/1, 73; Military Order property 54t; convent 55

Alcántara, Order of W Spain granted Templar property 124; castles in S Spain 127/2
Alcaraz C Spain Christian advance 73
Alcaudete S Spain castle 55; S Spain battle 127/4
Alcázar de San Juan C Spain castle 55
Alcazarquivir (Ar Al-Qasr al-Kabir) N Morocco Portuguese conquest 162
Alconétar N Morocco Portuguese conquest 162
Alconétar W Spain castle 55; Templar property 124
Alcoraz NE Spain battle 33/1
Aledo SE Spain castle 55; SE Spain Santiago castle 127/2
Aleppo (Ar Halab) N Syria early trade 27; Muslim castle 57; taken by Zangi 59; spice trade 101/3; Ayyubid capital 109; Mamluk capital 108/2; Timur's invasion 146/2; Uniate Armenian see 170
Al'es S France Templar house 125
Alexander Nevsky, Prince defeat of Teutonic Knights 75
Alexandretta (Turk Iskenderun) S Turkey Christian conquest 35/1; Latin castle 57; trade 135
Alexandria N Egypt early trade 26; besieged by crusaders 57; Muslim fort 97/2; Mediterranean trade 101/1, 3; trade embargo 133; sacked by Peter I 143; Ottoman commercial centre 151
Alexius I Byzantine emperor 21
Alexius III Byzantine emperor 84t
Alexius IV Byzantine emperor 84t
Alexius V Byzantine emperor 84t
Alfambra NE Spain castle 54, 55
Alfonso I of Aragon 34t
Alfonso IV of Portugal battle of Salado river 126t
Alfonso VI of Leon 32t
Alfonso VII of Leon 32t
Alfonso VII of Castile Second Crusade 48t, 49
Alfonso VIII of Castile 54t, 72t
Alfonso IX of Leon 72t
Alfonso X of Leon 72t
Alfonso XI of Castile battle of River Salado 126t
Algeciras S Spain recaptured by Christians 127/2
Alger see Algiers
Algeria Spanish opposition to Ottoman advance 163
Alghero NW Sardinia Mediterranean trade 133
Algiers (Fr Alger) Algeria Mediterranean trade 132; Spanish attack 163; Hospitaller operation against Ottomans 169/1
Alguaire NE Spain Military Order property 55
Alhama S Spain battle 127/3
Alhambra C Spain castle 55
Alhándega N Spain battle 32
Alicante Mediterranean trade 132
Aljubarrota C Portugal battle 145
Aljustrel S Portugal castle 55
Almada S Portugal castle 54, 55
Almadén C Spain castle 55
Almagro C Spain castle 55
Almalyk (med Armalech) C Asia Franciscan bishopric 105
Almeida N Portugal John of Gaunt's crusade 144/3
Almería S Spain captured by Alfonso VII 49, 73, 127; Mediterranean trade 100/1, 132
Almoguera C Spain castle 54, 55
Almohad empire S Spain and NW Africa

struggle against Christian forces 33, 54, 72; Mediterranean trade 100/1
Almoravid empire S Spain and NW Africa 29; First Crusade 30; Second Crusade 49; overthrown by Almohads 72t
Almyros see Halmyros
Alnmouth N England crusader landholding 89
Alnwick N England crusader landholding 89
Alost see Aalst
Alp Arslan Seljuk sultan 26t, 27
Alphonse of Poitiers 92t
Alphonso Jordan, count of Toulouse Second Crusade 48t, 49, 50
Alpujarras mountains of S Spain Muslim rebellion 162
Althaus N Poland Teutonic Knights 129
Amadeus of Savoy crusade in support of Constantinople 148
Amalfi C Italy Mediterranean trade 100/1
Amanus Mountains NW Syria Templar control 53/2
Amasra N Turkey Genoese trading centre 147; conquered by Ottomans 151
Amfissa see Salona
Amida Ayyubid capital 109
Amiens NE France popular crusades 83; St Louis's Crusade 93
Amisus (Turk Samsun) N Turkey Dominican bishopric 105
Amman (Bibl Rabbath-ammon, Lat Philadelphia) C Transjordan Templar castle 53/1; Latin castle 57; Latin see 170
Ammochostos see Famagusta
Amoudain S Turkey fort of Teutonic Knights 107
Amphissa see Salona
Amposta NE Spain convent 55
Amposta NE Spain Hospitaller castellany (province) 90/1
Amuda S Turkey Armenian castle 57
Amwas see Emmaus
Anafeh see Nephin
Anamour (Turk Anamur) S Turkey Byzantine castle 57; raided by Peter I 143
Anapa see Mappa
Anavarza (a/c Anazarba, anc Anazarbus) S Turkey Armenian castle 57
Anazarba, Anazarbus see Anavarza
Ancenis NW France Templar house 125
Anchialus E Bulgaria crusades in support of Constantinople 149
Ancona NE Italy Mediterranean trade 100/1; Mediterranean trade 133
Ancona, March of papal state 79/1
Ancre C Palestine 102/2
Andalucia region of S Spain Muslims expelled 72t
Andravida (a/c Andreville M Gr Andravidha) W Greece Villehardouin court 87
Andreville see Andravida
Andrew, king of Hungary Fifth Crusade 94-95
Andújar S Spain raided by Muslims 127/2
Angers NW France crusader recruiting centre 29
Angevin dynasty supremacy in S Italy 78-79
Angora see Ankara
Angoulême W France Templar house 125
Anjou region of NW France recruiting for St Louis's Crusade 93
Ankara (med Angora) battle 146/2; conquered by Ottomans 147
Anna E Spain castle 55
Annaba see Bona
an-Nasiriyah see Nazareth

ACKNOWLEDGEMENTS

PICTURE CREDITS

21 12th-century sculpture of a pilgrim and his wife. Photo: Conway Library, Courtauld Institute of Art, London.
26 Friday Mosque, Isfahan. Photo: Ancient Art and Architecture Collection, London.
28 Pope Urban II at Cluny, from 'Book of Offices and Chronicon Cluniacense' Bibliothèque Nationale, Paris. MS lat. 17716 fol 91r. Photo: Edimedia, Paris.
32 Great Mosque of Córdoba. Photo: Arxiu Mas, Barcelona.
36 Ivory cover of 'Queen Melisende's Psalter'. British Library. EG 1139.
39 Arched street in Caesarea, Israel. Photograph by Denys Pringle. Seals of Walter Garnier and Evremar of Chocques. Drawings after originals in Archives of Order of St John of Jerusalem.
42 12th-century pilgrim, photograph taken from Paul Henri Michel *Les Fresques de Tavant* Paris, Editions du Chêne 1944. Photo: British Library.
44 12th-century map of Jerusalem: Bibliothèque royale Albert 1er, Bruxelles: MS 9823-9824 fol 157.
47 Crosses carved by pilgrims in Jerusalem. Photograph by Jane Taylor. Photo: Sonia Halliday, Stoke Mandeville.
52 Templar seal c. 1202. Drawing after original in British Museum. Seal of Hospitaller Master Cast of Murolles c.1170. Drawing after original in archives of Order of St John of Jerusalem, Malta.
55 Church of Vera Cruz near Segovia. Photo: Arxiu Mas, Barcelona.
56 Ditch at castle of Saone. Photo: A.F. Kersting, London.
58 Two pages from koran. Photo from Keir Collection, England.
65 Two 13th-century tiles from Chertsey Abbey. British Museum, Pottery Catalogue 30-31.
67 Fresco of Pope Innocent III at Priory of Subiaco, Italy. Photo: Scala, Florence.
70 Crusader from 13th-century psalter from Westminster Abbey. British Library: MS Royal 2A XXII fol. 220.
72 Almohad banner from Las Huelgas convent in Burgos. Photo: Arxiu Mas, Barcelona.
73 Fresco in the Palacio Real Mayor, Barcelona.
78 North Italian stone relief. Victoria and Albert Museum, London.
82 14th-century English peasants. Miniature from *Luttrell Psalter*, British Library: MS ADD 42130.
88 Holy Sepulchre chapel, Winchester cathedral. Photograph by John Crook for Dean and Chapter of Winchester.
91 Crypt of 12th-century church of Hospitaller priory at Clerkenwell. Photo: Library of Museum of Order of St John.
92 Louis IX with Blanche of Castile, from 'Bible Abrègé' M240 f 8. Pierpont Morgan Library New York 1990. (1) denier parisis, (2) denier tournois, (3) gros tournois. Drawings of coins found in most major collections.
94 Fighting at Damietta, from Matthew Paris, 'Historia Maiora'. Reproduced by permission of The Master and Fellows of Corpus Christi College, Cambridge. MS 16 f54v.
96 Louis IX of France rides towards Damietta. Bibliothèque Nationale, Paris. MS Ir 2628 f328.
101 (1) Florence gold florin, British Museum C311, (2) Genoa gold florin, British Museum C309, (3) Venice gold ducat, British Museum C313.
105 Catholic and Oriental Bishops. Miniature from 'Latin Kingdom of Jerusalem'. Bibliothèque Nationale, Paris. MS fr 2628 f323.
106 Krak des Chevaliers. Photo: Aerofilms Ltd. London.
108 Citadel of Aleppo. Photo: A.F. Kersting, London.
110 Three Mamluk officers. Drawing by Mansueti. Windsor Castle: RLO82. Royal Library copyright 1990 Her Majesty the Queen.
112 Portrait said to be of Hülegü Khan. British Museum 9-17 130.
114 Gothic marble doorway from Acre. Photo: A.F. Kersting.

117 Luther of Brunswick, drawn from a memorial effigy in Kaliningrad Cathedral, USSR.
119 Knight representing city of Prato, c.1335-40. British Museum MS Royal 6E IX fol 24.
122 Crusader galley. Reproduced by permission of Bodleian Library, Oxford. MS Tanner 190 fol 20.
124 Execution of Jacques de Molay, miniature from 'Chroniques de France'. British Library, MS Royal 20 C.VII fol 48.
126 Coat of arms of United Kingdom of Spain, a woodcut from Garcia's *Peregrina Sevilla* 1498.
128 Castle and palace of Marienburg. Photo: Museum of Zamkowe at Malborke, Poland.
129 Teutonic knight drawn from original in Manessa Codex, Heidelberg University.
130 Hussite wagon fortress. Photograph taken from H.Toman, *Husitske Valechictvi* Prague 1898. Photo: British Library.
133 Portolan map. British Library. MS Add. 25691.
134 Catholic cathedral, Famagusta ,and Hospitaller castle. Photos: Richard Cleave.
136 Fra' Alberto Arringhieri by Pinturicchio, Duomo, Siena. Photo: Scala, Florence.
138 Tower at Markopoulo, photograph by Peter Lock, York; two helmets (top two illustrations are same helmet) from National Historical Museum, Athens. Photo: Catherine Norman, London.
140 Coronation of Pope Clement VI. Miniature from 'Cronaca Villani' MS Chigi Lviii.296, fol. 214v. Vatican Library.
142 Silver gros of King Peter I. British Museum C660.
143 Abbey of Praemonstratensian Order, Bellapaïs, Cyprus. Photo: Richard Cleave.
144 Papal Palace, Avignon. Photo: Ancient Art and Architecture Collection, London.
146 Mehmet II by Gentile Bellini c.1481. National Gallery, London.
151 Battle of Mohács in 1526. Photo: Ancient Art and Architecture Collection, London.
152 Belgrade in 1456, from Johannes de Turocz, *Chronica Hungarorum*, Augsburg 1488.
153 János Hunyadi, from Johannes de Turocz, *Chronica Hungarorum*, Augsburg 1488.
156 Memorial tablet from the Cathedral in Valletta. Photo: Library of Museum of Order of St John.
157 Gallery of Grand Master Emmanuel Pinto 1741-1743. Watercolour. National Gallery of Malta. Photo: Library of Museum of Order of St John.
158 Members of St John Ambulance Brigade. Photograph by Bob Komar, courtesy of St John Ambulance.
160 Cross of Order of Santiago of Compostela. Ulster Museum, Belfast; badge of Five Wounds, embroidery on crimson silk velvet in gold, coloured threads, Arundel Castle, reproduced by permission of Baroness Herries.
165 Battle of Lepanto by Giorgio Vasari. Vatican Museum. Photo: Scala, Florence.
166 Broadsheet, printed in England, 1684.
168 Philip of Vendôme, attributed to Jean Raoux. Photo: Library of Museum of Order of St John.
169 His Most Eminent Highness Fra' Andrew Bertie. Photo: Grand Magistry SMOM, Rome. Maronite Soldier in Lebanon. Photograph by Karim Daher. Photo: SSP/Gamma.

QUOTATIONS

26 Fulcher of Chartres in *Historia Hierosolymitana* trans. L. and J. Riley-Smith, *The Crusades: Idea and Reality, 1095 -1274*, London, Edward Arnold 1981, p.41.
28 *Cartulaire de l'abbaye de Saint-Père de Chartres*, ed. B.E.C. Guérard, Paris 1840. vol. II, pp.428-9.
30 Raymond of Aguilers, *Historia*, trans. L. Riley-Smith.
32 Pope Calixtus II, trans. L. and J. Riley-Smith, *op. cit.* p.74.
38 Fulcher of Chartres in *Historia Hierosolymitana* trans. L. Riley-Smith.
40 Theodoric, trans. A. Stewart in R.G. Musto, *Guide to*

the Holy Land, 2nd ed., New York, Italica Press 1986.
50 Eudes of Deuil in *De profectione Ludovici VII in Orientem*, trans. L. Riley-Smith.
52 St Bernard of Clairvaux, *De laude novae militiae*, trans. L. and J. Riley-Smith, *op. cit.* p.102.
54 Archbishop of Toledo, Rodrigo Jiménez de Rada, *De rebus Hispaniae*, book VII, ch. 27.
57 William of Tyre, *Chronicon*, trans. L. Riley-Smith.
58 Cf. *Encyclopaedia of Islam* 1st and 2nd editions, s.v. Djihad; Rudolph Peters, *Islam and Colonialism: The doctrine of jihad in modern history*, The Hague 1979, ch. 2, 'The classical doctrine of jihad'.
60 Ibn al-Athir in *Universal History*, trans. M.C. Lyons and D.E.P. Jackson, *Saladin* Cambridge, Cambridge University Press 1982, p. 263.
64 Ambroise, *L'Estoire de la guerre sainte*, trans. M.J. Hubert, *The Crusade of Richard Lion-Heart*, New York, Columbia University Press 1941, p. 260.
74 Henry of Livonia, *Chronicon*, trans. L. Riley-Smith.
80 Humbert of Romans, trans. L. and J. Riley-Smith, *op. cit.* pp.104-15.
82 Matthew Paris, *Historia Maiora*, trans. L. and J. Riley-Smith, *op. cit.* pp.140-1.
84 Gunther of Pairis, trans. L. and J. Riley-Smith, *op. cit.* pp.172-3.
86 *The Chronicle of the Morea*, trans. H.E. Lurier, *Crusaders as Conquerors*, New York, Columbia University Press 1964.
92 'Por joie avoir perfite en paradis', anon, trans. L. and J. Riley-Smith, *op. cit.* pp.157-8.
102 The Templar of Tyre, *Gestes des Chiprois*, trans. L. Riley-Smith.
104 James of Vitry, trans. L. Riley-Smith.
107 *De constructione castri Saphet*, trans. L. Riley-Smith.
113 John of Plano Carpini, trans. by a nun of Stanbrook Abbey, in *The Mongol Mission* ed. C. Dawson, London, Sheed and Ward 1955.
114 Abu' l-Fida, trans. P.M. Holt, *The Memoirs of a Syrian Prince*, Wiesbaden, Franz Steiner Verlag 1983, pp.16-17.
122 Marino Sanudo, trans. in E. Hallam, *Chronicles of the Crusades*, London, Guild Publishing 1989, p. 292.
128 d'Oronville in *Chronique du Bon Duc Loys de Bourbon*, trans. M. Keen, *Chivalry*, New Haven, Yale University Press 1984, p.173.
130 Cardinal Henry Beaufort, trans. in Hallam, *op. cit.* p.309.
134 Ludolph of Sudheim, *De insula Cypro*, trans. in Hallam, *op. cit.*, p.293.
142 Petrarch, trans. in Hallam, *op.cit.* p.297.
148 *Life of John Boucicaut*, anon, trans. in Hallam, *op.cit.* p.302.
150 Kritovoulos, trans. in Hallam, *op cit.* p.329.
152 K. M. Setton, *The Papacy and the Levant*, American Philosophical Society 1976-84, vol. 2, pp.182-3.
162 Ogier Ghiselin de Busbecq, trans. L. Riley-Smith.
168 Francisco Balbi di Corregio, trans. H.A. Balbi, *The Siege of Malta*, p.163, in Capt. O.F. Golloher and Dr H. C. Ole Postook, Copenhagen, Bagsvaerd, 1961.

OTHER ACKNOWLEDGEMENTS
Dr Michael Angold, University of Edinburgh; Dr Lindy Grant, Courtauld Institute of Art, University of London; Dr Julian Raby, The Oriental Institute, Oxford University; Louise Riley-Smith, 5 Claremont Road, Windsor, Berkshire SL4 3AX; Pamela Willis, Curator, and other staff of the Order of St John, St John's Gate, London EC1.

the busy woman's
home spa book

the busy woman's home spa book

Liz Wilde

with photography by Daniel Farmer

RYLAND
PETERS
& SMALL
LONDON NEW YORK

DESIGNER *Sonya Nathoo*
SENIOR EDITOR *Clare Double*
PICTURE RESEARCH *Tracy Ogino*
PRODUCTION *Sheila Smith*
ART DIRECTOR *Gabriella Le Grazie*
PUBLISHING DIRECTOR *Alison Starling*

ILLUSTRATIONS *Javier Joaquin*

First published in the United States in 2005 by
Ryland Peters & Small
519 Broadway, 5th Floor, New York, NY 10012
www.rylandpeters.com

10 9 8 7 6 5 4 3 2 1

Library of Congress Cataloging-in-Publication Data
Wilde, Liz.
The busy woman's home spa book / Liz Wilde ; with
photography by Daniel Farmer.
p. cm.
Includes index.
ISBN 1-84172-974-4
1. Beauty, Personal. 2. Women--Health and hygiene. I.
Title.
RA778.W536 2005
646.7'042--dc22
2005005309

Printed and bound in China.

Neither the author nor the publisher can be held
responsible for any claim arising out of the use or
misuse of suggestions made in this book. If you are
in any doubt about your health, please consult your
doctor before making any changes to your usual
well-being and dietary regime. Essential oils are very
powerful and potentially toxic if used too liberally.
Please follow the advice given and never use the
oils neat on bare skin, unless advised otherwise.

contents

are you too busy to be beautiful?

We all have the same 1,440 minutes in a day we've always had, yet the most common complaint today is that we're all too busy. New technology has been invented to save us time (two-minute e-mails versus ten-minute phone conversations), but rather than using our saved time to do less, we cram even more into our rescued moments.

If time is flying, then you're the pilot. When you're too busy, something has to go—and it's usually you. To illustrate how important you are, hold up your hand. Now, imagine your fingers represent the various parts you play during the day: employee, partner, mother, nursemaid, friend. Your palm represents the real you. If you shut one of your fingers in the car door (while trying to do three things at once, perhaps?), the finger gets a splint, but the rest of your roles can carry on regardless. But imagine if you injure your palm. Suddenly your whole hand is useless, as your palm controls all your fingers.

The most important choice we can make in life is what we make important. Spending time on the things that make us feel good inside and out (rather than setting ourselves a to-do list with no end) is one of the best ways we can create a life we love. And it will not only benefit the way you look and feel about yourself, but the way you interact with everyone else around you.

Spa vacations and day spas have never been so popular. As our lives hit breakneck speed, me-time has never been so precious, and the appeal of spas is that they force us to take a step back. These luxury havens allow you to do little more than relax by the pool between treatments that unknot your shoulders and massage your cares away. Unfortunately, this blissful experience comes at a (high) price, but you can give yourself the gift of free time in your own home every day at little or no cost at all.

To live your best life, you need to be in good health, both mentally and physically. Well-being and happiness are holistic processes. The Greek word *holis* means "whole" and is based on the idea that mind and body have a natural balance reached by paying attention to every area of your life— which means that to look good, you also have to feel good. Improving your well-being feels great, but first you have to decide you're worth looking after.

Years ago, beauty and health were considered two very different things. But as our lives become more frantic, we're looking increasingly toward Eastern healing practices to help us cope with Western stress. We now know that practicing yoga not only eases our bodies of tension, but clears our skin and brightens our eyes. Beauty is an inside job. You can spend a fortune on the most expensive face cream, but if you're still living your life at high speed with no time for yourself, that cream will do little more than sit on your skin as you race through the day.

This book will tell you how to incorporate beauty and self-care rituals into your day, whether you have an hour to spare or just five minutes. From stress-busting facials to stress-relieving stretches. From feel-good food to look-good makeup techniques. Everything in this book is designed to make you look and feel better. There are also lots of easy-to-make home recipes (no more than two ingredients required—guaranteed), so you don't even have to buy new beauty products. And as it's estimated that up to 60 percent of what we put on our skin ends up in the bloodstream, making your own cosmetics is the only way to know what you're absorbing.

Try everything and see what you most enjoy. You need to love these self-care rituals enough to want to spend time boosting your body and mind health every day. We're hard-wired to do things that please us, so the more enjoyable your me-time activities, the more likely you'll stick with them for life.

But what if you're reading this convinced you don't have any spare time for yourself? We may insist we're slaves to our schedules, but we all have more choice than we realize over how we use what time we have. You control your time, not the other way around, so start using it to nurture you, not exhaust you. How many hours this week have you spent on activities that have no meaning to you? Try this simple exercise:

LIST ALL THE WAYS *YOU* MISUSE YOUR TIME

TV watching, e-mail checking, complaining, phone gossiping, net surfing, excessive shopping, worrying…
What could you cut back on? Perhaps you only need to shop once a week? Check e-mails twice a day? Only watch programs you're interested in? Start focusing on the good stuff in your life rather than what's not working?

LIST ALL THE WAYS *OTHER PEOPLE* MISUSE YOUR TIME

Meetings at work, waiting in traffic, listening to friends' problems, constant interruptions from colleagues, running errands for family members…
What changes need to be made to lighten your load? What can you stop doing? What can you delegate or outsource? Who do you need to say no to? Where do you need to tell the truth?
Now, subtract two things you're currently doing that you don't enjoy, and add two things that will make you look and feel fantastic. It's that simple.

The consequences of constantly racing against the clock include everything from skin problems to low immunity. So if you can't slow down, look at your thoughts. If you believe you can only be successful by being busy, you will always fill your days with tasks and chores. Who said everyone else was more important than you? We live in a culture that tells us relaxing is the equivalent of being lazy, so we cram our lives full of activity. But relaxing is not the same as collapsing—it's simply time to refuel.

It's so much easier to be positive about life when you're looking after yourself—whether that's pampering your face, feeding your body, or simply starting and ending each day doing things that make you look and feel good. So decide today to put aside time for the feel-good habits and rituals in this book. Lifting your spirits works like a natural facelift—the better you look after yourself, the better you look. Isn't it time you started taking *very* good care of yourself?

creating a haven

The most luxurious treatment in the world won't relax your body and unwind your mind if you have to rush for the phone halfway through. To get the best possible results from all your pampering treats and rituals, you need to give yourself a break from the outside world and create a special place in your home.

Your bathroom is perfect as you can lock the door, but if yours is less than luxurious, find another place to pamper and just use the bathroom for its water supply. You'll know you've got the mood right when just walking into your haven makes you feel better. The trick is to indulge your senses for an overall feeling of well-being. Here's what you'll find in top spas, all of which you can copy to bring that feeling of relaxed calm into your own home. Finally, don't rush, and turn off the bell on your phone before you begin.

LIGHTING
This must be subtle to relax your eyes (and mind). Many of us spend our days under fluorescent strip lighting, which can leave you feeling tired and headachy. For the most calming lighting, invest in full-spectrum bulbs that simulate natural daylight. Or go one better—turn off the main light and surround yourself with candles (they also work a treat at hiding outdated bathroom fixtures!).

SOUND
No spa experience is complete without soothing music to ease your mind. Listening to music you love can improve your mood no matter how nasty the day has been. High frequencies stimulate your central nervous system, so choose mellow sounds or go classical.

TEMPERATURE
You want this to be warm and comforting. Too cold and you won't relax, too warm and you'll feel stifled.

SCENT
If you're using a diffuser, pour a little water into the saucer and let it warm up first before adding your favorite oils (the scent will last longer). Or create your own diffusers by adding a few drops of essential oil to small bowls of water and placing them near radiators. Scented candles look luxurious, but you can get the same effect by using plain (much cheaper) ones. Light the wick, allow a puddle of wax to collect around the top, and then carefully sprinkle on a few drops of oil—the melted wax will be the perfect temperature to release the aroma. Scented flowers can also change the mood of a room from practical to pampering (and they feel like a wonderful treat).

COMFORT
Most spas are scattered with cushions for comfortable lounging—an easy effect to imitate. You could also put up photographs of people you love, or objects you've collected that have a special meaning to you. The minute you step into your haven, your memory will respond to the stimulus and go straight back to that happy time, creating an instant feel-good mood.

the healing power of color

Color has been used to heal as far back as Egyptian times, when patients would sit in different areas of a room constructed so the sun's rays were broken up into the seven colors of the spectrum. Modern research shows that you can seriously affect your mood by surrounding yourself with the right colors. Here's what a trip to Home Depot could do for you and your haven.

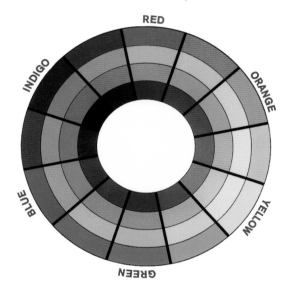

If you combine primary colors (red, yellow, and blue), secondary colors (violet, orange, and green) appear between them. The inner rings show the colors with added white (tints), gray (tones), and black (shades).

COLOR	WHAT IT DOES	WHAT IT HELPS
BLUE	Calms nerves, relaxes and quietens your mind.	Insomnia, depression.
RED	Raises body temperature. Stimulates mental energy.	Aches and pains, poor circulation.
YELLOW	Encourages optimism. Boosts confidence.	Depression, digestive problems.
ORANGE	Inspires joy. Eases loneliness.	Lethargy, detoxing.
GREEN	Aids meditation. Eases anger and frustration.	Exhaustion, headaches.
INDIGO	Stimulates imagination. Promotes optimism.	Weak immune system, negativity.

host your own spa party

Once you realize how beneficial the therapies, treatments, and rituals in this book can be, you may want to share them with your friends.

Spa parties are the latest way for the A-list to get together without a complexion-wrecking hangover in the morning. They may go to a $1,000-a-night spa, but you could just as easily host your own spa party at home. Throw a theme-based bash (energy-boosting, detoxing, rejuvenating), or replace the usual wine bar with your living room to celebrate an event (birthday, engagement, promotion). Spa parties work perfectly for any get-together, from a baby shower to a post-vacation photo exchange. Ask each of your friends to bring a homemade or purchased treatment, plus a towel, and bathrobe and slippers if they really want to recreate the spa experience. Whisk up some fresh juice or brew a pot of green tea, and prepare recipes beforehand (keep them in the fridge) for stress-free hosting. After all, isn't that the point?

look fabulous

five ways to look better instantly

When you want an instant lift, use these quick tips to improve your looks—starting with the best natural image-booster, a smile.

1 SMILE

Everyone looks better when they're smiling, and a smile also enhances your immunity by improving your mood. Nothing to smile about? At bedtime, list all the things that have made you happy during the day. Most of us are naturally negative, so we have to train ourselves to look on the bright side, but it's worth it. Studies have shown that being optimistic can actually add seven and a half years to your life!

2 IMPROVE YOUR POSTURE

Slouching not only looks unattractive, it causes muscle tension in the neck, shoulders, and back due to the extra effort needed to support the head. It actually takes much less energy to stand up straight with your head held high resting on the top of your spine. Imagine a piece of string pulling you up from the top of your head so your neck, head, and spine are all in a straight line, then relax your shoulders. Congratulations—you've just lost five pounds.

3 LAUGH

Laughter reduces the stress hormones in your body, so you instantly feel less tense. After a good laugh your blood pressure drops, muscle tension decreases, and your breathing slows down—all of which make you look far more relaxed and attractive to others.

4 MAKE EYE CONTACT

Looking into the other person's eyes for longer than three seconds as you're talking sends out the subconscious sign that you're honest and confident. Plus you're interested in their reaction to you, which is very attractive.

5 TAKE THAT FROWN OFF YOUR FACE

Not only will your forehead be smoother, you'll be healthier, too. Studies have found that being worry-free reduces your levels of a chemical linked to heart disease, diabetes, and cancer. So stop worrying about what you can't control. Worry never solved a problem, and 90 percent of what we worry about never happens anyway—so it's a complete waste of your time.

Everyone looks better when they're smiling, and a smile also enhances your immunity by improving your mood.

six needle-free steps to great skin

There's no need to spend $100 on face cream—or $1,000 on collagen injections—to improve your skin. Here's what any skin specialist will tell you.

1 ALWAYS WEAR A SUNSCREEN

It's estimated that around 80 percent of skin aging is due to sun damage, which means that the majority of wrinkles and other signs of skin aging such as pigmentation don't have to happen at all. The fact is that, far from a tan being healthy, your skin's darkened tone is its immediate reaction to the damage you've just inflicted on it. The good news is that, even after years of sun-worshipping, getting serious about sun protection can significantly improve your skin's condition. So even if baby oil used to be your sunscreen of choice, it's never too late to reach for that factor 15 (at least) and 25 (in hot sun). Reapply regularly to keep the level of protection up. And a word of warning about sunscreens in makeup. Some studies say these sunscreens can all but disappear after a few hours on your face, so always use a separate sunscreen underneath.

2 GET PLENTY OF SLEEP

You'll not only feel better, you'll look better, too. That's because while you're snoozing your body is working hard to regenerate from the stresses of the day. It does this by secreting growth hormones responsible for restoring cells and rebuilding skin, which is why too many late nights will show up on your face in dark circles and dull-as-ditchwater skin. Fact: if you want to like what you see in the mirror every morning, treat yourself to regular early nights. Many skin experts also recommend you sleep bare-faced so your skin has a chance to rebalance itself during the night. If you have skin problems, you may want to try this, although the initial tightness takes a little getting used to.

3 EXERCISE REGULARLY

Any activity that increases your circulation will bring blood and nutrients to your skin. You don't have to go to aerobics classes; this includes brisk walking, cycling, swimming, yoga, even dancing (and sex).

When your heart rate increases, oxygen surges to every cell in your body, helping each one to grow faster. The result is an increase in collagen production, meaning stronger and smoother skin. Plus, any form of exercise is a proven stress-buster, and we all know what stress can do to your skin. If possible, clean your face before exercise to stop sweat from being blocked in your pores.

4 STOP SMOKING

If the health warnings aren't enough, perhaps vanity will help you kick the habit. The skin of a smoker is likely to look sallow and develop more blackheads than a non-smoker's. Why? Because smoking destroys the vitamin C that keeps the collagen fibers attached to your skin, causing pores to become dilated. Add to this the fact that the skin of a smoker takes longer to heal (the reason some plastic surgeons refuse to operate on smokers), and it's no wonder most skin experts can spot a smoker at twenty paces.

5 EAT WELL

It's no surprise that good nutrition improves your overall appearance, but certain foods are particularly beneficial to your skin. Step forward antioxidants such as healing lycopene, which is even known to reduce sunburn. Find it in watermelon and tomatoes (lycopene is best absorbed when consumed in cooked tomato products, rather than those eaten raw). Carrots and mangos are also a great source of the powerful antioxidant betacarotene, the plant form of vitamin A. When you're at the supermarket, make your shopping basket an intensely colorful one (including dark-green, red, and orange foods) for the best variety of skin-enhancing nutrients. (See over the page for more beauty superfoods.)

6 DRINK LOTS OF WATER

Water is needed to flush out toxins, hydrate your skin, and help all the nutrients you eat do their job. Many of us are in a permanent state of dehydration without realizing it. A good way to tell if you're not drinking enough fluid (and we don't mean coffee or alcohol) is to check the color of your urine. If it's any darker than pale yellow, you need to step up your intake. Two quarts of water a day will do the job no face cream can, either bottled (which also provides minerals such as calcium, magnesium, and potassium), mixed with fruit juice, or in herbal teas. Remember: by the time you feel thirsty, your body's cells are already in serious need of hydration, so drink little and often during the day. And spray your face with water between cleansing and moisturizing to lock in more moisture (but blot before applying moisturizer, or you'll dilute the benefits).

beauty superfoods

Good-for-you food not only keeps your body healthy, it also gives you clear skin, glossy hair, and bright eyes. Here's what the experts agree should be a large part of your life.

FATTY FISH such as salmon, mackerel, and sardines are the best source of essential fatty acids (EFAs, including omega-3), and should be eaten at least three times a week. Our bodies can't produce these naturally, so we depend entirely on our diet to supply them. EFAs are the building blocks of membranes around and within cells, making them vitally important for keeping skin, hair, and nails in good condition.

FRUIT AND VEGETABLES (raw or cooked) contain age-protecting antioxidants and should be eaten every day. If you'd rather not eat a cocktail of unspecified chemicals (and who would?), go for organic, which means no artificial fertilizers, pesticides, or herbicides have been used in crop growing. And choose fresh over canned, as canned versions may contain salt and sugar (if in doubt, look on the label).

GREEN TEA contains some of the most powerful antioxidants available, and its benefits include boosting your immune system and even helping prevent tooth decay. Compounds called polyphenols also protect skin cells by helping eliminate free radicals, and green tea has been linked to skin cell rejuvenation. Not surprisingly, it's the world's second most popular drink.

LIVE NATURAL YOGURT is a great source of protein and calcium, plus its beneficial bacteria help keep your digestive system healthy. Sheep's and goat's milk yogurt is easier to digest than yogurt made from cow's milk. Buy it in small quantities as the levels of friendly bacteria decrease the longer they spend in the fridge.

WATER is the best beautifier around. About two-thirds of our bodies are made up of water, so it's no surprise we need around two quarts a day to keep us topped up. And a hydrated body will have more energy and softer, plumper skin. Drink between meals, or you'll flush away the nutrients in your food, and choose pure still water over (potentially bloating) sparkling every time.

CARBOHYDRATES have had a bad press, but whole-grain versions are bursting with protein, healthy fat, vitamins, and minerals. Whole grain means the nutrients are intact (refined flours have been stripped of healthy germ and bran). Look for the word "whole" when buying bread, rice, oats, and pasta (beware food that's simply a nice brown shade—it could be added food coloring). Why the fuss? These complex carbs are digested slowly in your body to provide plenty of energy, plus the fiber keeps your digestion healthy.

Steaming your face not only opens pores to release impurities missed during your regular cleanse, it also plumps up your skin to soften fine lines. A steam on a bad face day will shrink under-eye puffiness, and added herbs or essential oils in the water will soothe your mind.

treat yourself:

steam facial

I Boil a kettle or pan of water and pour it into a large bowl. Either sprinkle in a handful of dried herbs (use chamomile to soothe and peppermint to stimulate), or add a couple of drops of your favorite essential oil. To decongest sinus passages or ease cold symptoms, use a few drops of eucalyptus essential oil.

2 Let the water cool just a little (you want it to be hot but not scalding), drape a large towel over your head so it traps all the steam, and lean your face over the bowl (at least 8 inches (20 cm) away). Protect the delicate skin around your eyes by first applying a thin film of moisturizer.

3 Stay steaming for ten minutes maximum, taking deep breaths through your nose.

4 Press in any moisture left on your skin with a washcloth, or wipe with a mild toner. Apply a light moisturizer and relax with a cup of green tea, or hot water with a few squirts of lemon added, to complete the detox process.

IF YOU HAVE TEN MINUTES MORE
□ Follow your steam with a clay-based face mask to draw out the very last impurities left in your warm, open pores.
□ Treat your hair to a conditioning mask at the same time, as the heat will encourage any product to sink right into the hair shaft.

Warning: Be wary if you suffer from red veins: steaming could make them worse. Limit your steam to five minutes and make the water warm, not hot.

facial exercises

Tight facial muscles can cause everything from headaches and biting problems (teeth clenching or nighttime grinding) to neck pain and facial puffiness. Method Putkisto exercises for the face will retrain these muscles and loosen tension.

Practice the sequence opposite two to three times a week for three or four weeks and you'll see an improvement in skin condition, a disappearing double chin, and brighter eyes. The exercises will also help ease headaches, sinus and biting problems, release upper body tension, and even improve your voice! Before you start, make sure your face and hands are clean, and don't force or strain the facial muscles.

TEST YOUR TENSION

Place your fingertips on your temples and bite, and you'll feel how your biting muscles reach all the way into your hairline at eye level. To test how loose these muscles are, relax your jaw and all the muscles around your mouth. If you can fit three fingers between your teeth, the muscles are in a good condition. Sadly, for many of us our mouths hardly open at all.

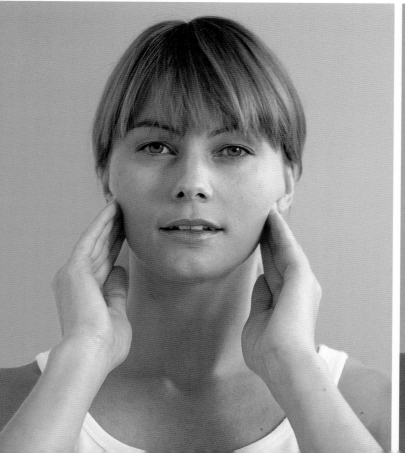

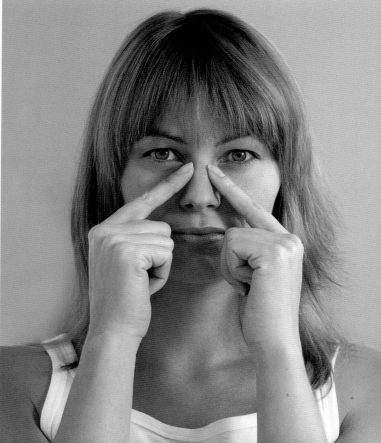

1 HORSESHOE MASSAGE

To increase lymph flow, helping remove toxins from your body. Use a very light touch. Beginning at the back of your neck, slide your fingertips around your neck and pause between your collarbones. Press firmly down toward your breastbone. Repeat twice.

2 COOL DOWN YOUR TEMPLES

Refreshes the eyes, relaxes the cheeks and jaw, and eases headaches. Use a firm touch. Place your fingers on the lowest part of your temples. Slide your fingertips straight up, following the temples. At the same time, move your upper jaw and upper lip down, creating a stretch. Repeat 5–8 times.

3 NOSE QUARTET (FOUR PRESSURES)

Centerline Pressure

This will relax the back of the neck. Place the tip of both your middle or index fingers on the inside of your eyebrows. Find this point by following the arch of the browbone, starting from the bridge of your nose. Lift the inside corner of your eyebrows slightly and press. Take your time—count to five.

The next pressures activate muscles around your nose and open the sinuses, making it easier to breathe.

Bridge of the Nose Circle (illustrated near left)

Move your fingertips downward, toward the bridge of your nose. Keep repeating a small circular movement, first pressing toward the bridge of the nose and then releasing. Repeat 5–8 times.

Double Nostril Pressure

Move your fingertips to the tip of your nose, with one finger on each side of your nostrils. Press very firmly toward your upper teeth, count to five, and release. This may feel painful, so relax and keep breathing.

Single Nose Pressure

Place one fingertip directly below your septum, aiming for the point where the nose begins. Press toward the center of your upper lip and count to five.

4 PICK UP YOUR BITING MUSCLES (illustrated far left)

This relaxes the strong biting muscles and releases tension in the neck and back. Place your fingertips on the corner of your jaw and slide them underneath the jawbone. Lift the muscles up and over the corner of the jaw and massage them with a circular movement. Pause, then stretch them by opening the jaw slowly against the muscles underneath your fingertips. Begin from the outer jaw and move toward the center.

5 BRIGHTEN YOUR EYES (TWO PRESSURES)

Both these exercises will increase circulation to the eye muscles, relax your neck, and brighten your eyes.

Teardrop Pressure 1

Using a light touch, place your fingertips underneath your lower eyelid at the point where the lowest part of your eyeball is located, and close your eyes.
□ Breathe slowly and focus on relaxing the muscles around and behind your eyes.
□ Lift the lids gently upward and relax your eyeball against your fingertips. Count to five.
□ Tilt your chin toward your chest and move your fingertips to the outer corners of your lower eyelids.
□ Increasing the pressure slightly, press the eyeball gently inward and relax your eyes even more.

Teardrop Pressure 2

Tilt your chin toward your chest and move your fingertips toward the outer corners of your eyelids. Press gently inward, relax, and breathe normally.

Finish by doing the Horseshoe Massage five times.

relaxing face and neck massage

These simple moves will relax the muscles in your face and neck (not to mention the rest of you), and boost blood circulation to nourish your skin. Tie your hair away and smooth on either a moisturizer or facial oil before you begin.

IF YOU'VE GOT TWO MINUTES

I Get your circulation going by tapping your face using light, quick movements. Using the pads of your first two fingers, work out along your jawline to each ear, then tap up from the sides of your mouth to your inner eye, and from your nose out along your cheekbones (this also helps blocked sinuses).

2 To finish, tap from the bridge of your nose out across your eyebrows to your temples. Repeat the whole sequence six times.

IF YOU'VE GOT FIVE MINUTES

I Start at your temples and massage in a counterclockwise direction using the first two fingers of each hand.

2 Beginning just below your eyebrows at the bridge of your nose, use your middle finger to press up slowly and gently along your eyebrows as far as your temples.

3 Using the pads of your first two fingers, tap all around your eyes, working from the bridge of your nose, up and around.

4 Lean your elbows on a table and place your chin in the cup of your hands with your fingers resting on your cheekbones. Starting either side of your nostrils, gently press your cheekbones using your middle finger. Hold each press for 30 seconds and repeat all the way to your ears.

5 Release the tension in your jaw by using the first two fingers of each hand to massage the joint (where the upper and lower jaws meet), in big circles working up toward the ear.

6 Placing your thumb on one side of your throat and your fingers on the other, massage in circular movements up and down.

7 Rest your right elbow in your left hand and, using your hand as support, grasp the muscles all along your left shoulder. Repeat on the other side.

8 Finish by gently pressing your first two fingers just under the bone at the base of your skull either side of your spine. Lean back onto your fingers and then work in gentle circular movements down each side of your neck.

Make your own massage oil for this 30-minute relaxing facial. Pour jojoba, almond, or grapeseed oil into your palm and add one drop of lavender, vetiver, or frankincense oil to aid relaxation.

treat yourself:

de-stress facial

I Before you begin, prepare your skin by holding a warm cloth to your face. Fill a basin with hot water, add a few drops of lavender essential oil, dunk a washcloth, and wring out before pressing it onto your skin for a few minutes.

2 This massage will take around ten minutes. Repeat the movements three times each, flowing them together, and breathe deeply to inhale the oil's healing aroma.
□ Starting on your chest, work in crisscross movements from shoulder to shoulder.
□ Slide your fingers up your neck and, in one movement, bring them up over your chin, around the bridge of your nose, across your eyebrows, under your eyes and around to finish at your temples.
□ From your jaw, sweep hands up over your cheeks to your ears.
□ To ease tension, sweep across your forehead from side to side, using slightly more pressure. Then, using your first two fingers, use scissor movements across your forehead followed by more outward sweeping to smooth your skin.
□ Hook your middle fingers just underneath your eyebrows either side of the bridge of your nose and press and release all around your eye socket.
□ Drop down so you're now either side of your nostrils, and press and release to unblock sinuses and help you breathe more easily.
□ Finish with the second movement, sweeping from your neck to your temples.

3 Now your skin's ready for a mask. Mature skins love a chopped-up avocado. Leave on for ten minutes or, if time is tight, use the avocado stone to massage the mask into your skin before rinsing with warm water. Sensitive faces love runny honey as it helps bind moisture to the skin. Leave on for ten minutes and relax.

4 After rinsing, pat on moisturizer (don't rub) and do as little as possible!

(easy) natural remedies for tired and puffy eyes

The eye area is the most delicate on your face, as the skin there has few oil glands and so dries up quicker than the rest of you.

USE AN EYE CREAM OR GEL (better for sensitive skin) morning and night as part of your daily routine, patting (not rubbing) around your eye, and for a quick pre-makeup pick-me-up keep one in the fridge.

IF YOU WORK AT A COMPUTER all day, you could buy an anti-glare screen to cut down on dust attracted by static, which can aggravate tired eyes.

JUST ABOUT ANYTHING COOL will soothe tired eyes and shrink under-eye bags. A couple of cold potato or cucumber slices are the classic solution for irritated eyes, or wrap an ice cube in plastic wrap and stroke over the eye area. Alternatively, keep two stainless-steel spoons in the fridge and place them over your eyes for five minutes at the end of a long day.

CHAMOMILE is soothing and reduces inflammation. Steep two chamomile teabags in boiling water for five minutes, and let them cool right down before placing over your eyes for ten minutes. Or steep a chamomile teabag in boiling water for five minutes, remove and allow the tea to cool before adding half a cup of rosewater (to tone and tighten the skin). Soak two cotton balls in the mixture and place over eyelids for ten minutes. Two chamomile teabags will ease sore eyes after exposure to extreme weather.

THE FATS IN MILK have an anti-inflammatory effect. Soak two cotton balls in a mixture of half cold whole milk and half ice-cold water. Place them over your eyes and lie back for ten minutes.

GREEN TEA contains anti-inflammatory polyphenols which, used cold, reduce swelling, plus green tea is a great wrinkle-fighting antioxidant. Moisten two green teabags with water, chill in the fridge for five minutes, and then place over your eyes for ten.

□ Eye drops that promise to whiten your eyes contain a vasoconstrictor that shrinks the blood vessels, temporarily brightening the whites of your eyes. Use occasionally for instant results on the go, but choose one of the natural solutions opposite for a regular rescue remedy.

□ When all else fails, try a favorite makeup artist's trick. Apply a smudge of silver eyeshadow right at the inner corner of each eye—used on sleepy supermodels by makeup artists everywhere to brighten post-long-haul-flight eyes.

DIY DE-PUFFER MASSAGE

□ Swelling is caused by a buildup of toxins and excess fluid, and you can stimulate your lymphatic system to flush them away. Press gently along your eyebrow and around the eye socket with your middle finger. Then press the point at the inside corners of your brows on each side of your nose, and finish by lightly pressing both your temples.

□ Another quick eye wake-up is to tap lightly all over lids with your first two fingers. Perfect as a midday rescue as you won't smudge your makeup.

Just about anything cool will soothe tired eyes. Cold potato or cucumber slices are the classic solution.

(easy) natural remedies for your face

FACIAL SCRUBS
(Warning: Avoid these if your skin's sensitive.)

□ Make your skin glow by adding a handful of oatmeal or sugar to your usual cleanser and gently massaging it onto your skin in circular movements before rinsing well with warm water. Or add ground brown sugar to warm milk (a natural mild exfoliator), and let the mixture cool to room temperature before massaging it on. Rinse well as before.

□ To scrub greasy skin, mix a handful of sunflower seeds (oil absorbing) with two teaspoons of apple sauce, gently massage onto your skin and leave for five minutes.

MOISTURIZERS
Massage in with sweeping upward strokes.

□ For a nourishing night treat on dry skins, pour two tablespoons of jojoba oil (extra nourishing) into a small lidded jar and add seven drops of your favorite essential oil. Shake well and apply a few drops to your face and neck before bedtime.

□ For a non-greasy, healing treat on problem skins, put two tablespoons of aloe vera gel (antibacterial and anti-inflammatory) in a bowl, and add seven drops of your favorite essential oil. Blend together with a fork and pour into a small lidded jar to use day and night.

Mash one half of an avocado and mix with a dribble of vegetable oil (sunflower and sesame are soothing) before smoothing on.

FACE MASKS
(Leave all the following on for five minutes unless otherwise stated.)

□ Smooth honey onto your neck and face and leave for about 15 minutes until it's dry, then rinse with warm water. Or mash up a ripe banana with honey and leave for 20 minutes (especially good for wrinkles).

□ Mash one half of an avocado and mix with a dribble of vegetable oil (sunflower and sesame are soothing for sensitive skins) before smoothing on.

□ Mashed strawberries are great for mopping up greasy skins, while mashed ripe papaya will exfoliate, tone, and tighten. For a moisturizing mask, mash one banana into an egg yolk, spread it over your face, and rinse with lukewarm water.

□ Natural yogurt contains lactic acid, which works as a gentle exfoliator. Smooth on and rinse off with cool water.

□ Eat the fruit and use the skins instead. Papaya, watermelon, or banana skins placed over your face will refresh and stimulate dull, dehydrated skin.

□ To absorb excess oil and remove dead skin cells from greasy skin, mix two teaspoons of natural yogurt with half a teaspoon of cosmetic clay (buy this at health and natural food stores). Apply evenly to your face, avoiding the eye area, and leave for 15 minutes before rinsing with warm water.

□ Mash up a ripe tomato, smooth over your face, and leave for 15 minutes before rinsing off with warm water (best for oily skins).

The following facial is designed to lift your face and your spirits, using homemade recipes that won't cost you a fortune.

treat yourself:

facelift facial

I Cleanse your skin with cucumber toner, wiped off with cotton. To make, chop up half a cucumber (leave the skin on, but discard the seeds), liquidize in a blender, and pour into a spray bottle to keep in the fridge.

2 Make a face mask with egg white to tighten and firm dull skin. Beat it thoroughly and use your fingers to apply all over your face, avoiding the eye area. Leave for ten minutes to set, and rinse with plenty of lukewarm water.

3 Transform a basic moisturizer (aqueous cream works well) into an uplifting treat with essential oils. Scoop into the palm of your hand and add one drop of a citrus oil like lemon or bitter orange. Apply with upward movements to work against gravity and then use your fingertips in quick taps to stimulate your skin. Press around the eyes (avoid near the tear duct as this can cause puffiness), and finish with gentle pinching movements along the jawline, working toward your ears.

4 Leave ten minutes before applying makeup so your skin can absorb moisture.

MORE INSTANT PICK-ME-UPS

□ Add two tablespoons of runny honey to a pint of warm water and squeeze in the juice of half a lemon. Pour the mixture into an ice cube tray and freeze. On feel-bad mornings wipe a cube over your skin for a nourishing pick-me-up.

□ Soak a cloth in cold-as-you-can-take-it water and lay it over your face for two minutes. For added zing, add a few drops of peppermint essential oil to the water.

Protect your skin by wearing a
good moisturizer and keep your
environment skin-friendly by
upping the humidity.

busy day skincare solutions

Many skin stresses are caused by doing too much (or the wrong thing), so you may find you need to cut back on your routine to help your skin rebalance itself. You can use these simple solutions every day—no matter how busy you are.

SENSITIVE

Over 60 percent of us believe we have sensitive skin, and the problem seems to be getting worse. Blame it on pollution, more complicated skincare ingredients, lifestyle, or genetics, the golden rule with sensitive skin is to keep it simple. Which means less time spent fussing, less heat, less friction, fewer ingredients, and fewer products. Many sensitive skin problems are cumulative, meaning you can use the same ingredient for years, and only then have a sudden reaction against it. Unfortunately, this often means your skin is now sensitized, so the reaction will happen every time you use the ingredient in future.

◻ Build up your skin's defenses from within by drinking two quarts of water a day. Protect it by wearing a good moisturizer and keep your environment skin-friendly by upping the humidity in your home and office (well-watered plants will do the trick).

◻ If your skin's being reactive, go back to basics and introduce extra products one at a time so you can monitor any problems. Start with a very gentle cotton/tissue off cleanser and work from there. Take advantage of tester samples in stores (if you can't see any, ask) and try a small amount on the corner of your face or behind your ear. Wait at least 24 hours to check for any redness or change in skin texture before buying a big size.

◻ Sensitive skins don't like chemical sunscreens, so look for mineral sunscreen ingredients like zinc oxide and titanium dioxide, which sit on the surface without irritation. Other ingredients your skin may not take to include sodium lauryl/laureth sulfate, petrolatum, and paraffinum liquidum (a name for mineral oil). Make use of the ingredients listing to check before you buy. And remember: even though a product says "allergy tested," it could still cause you a problem.

OILY

We were once encouraged to use strong antibacterial washes and toners that smelled similar to alcohol. But far from making greasy skins less oily, all they did was strip away surface oil, encouraging skin to make more in compensation. Nowadays, skin experts agree that a gentle approach is best.

□ Use a gentle foaming cleanser no more than twice a day. Over-cleaning will get those oil glands pumping.

□ Ditch harsh toner for a splash of lukewarm water or alcohol-free witch hazel or orange flower water.

□ For a natural degreaser, squeeze a little neat lemon juice onto a cotton ball and wipe over oily areas (just don't go in the sun afterward).

□ Your skin's best friend is a "non-comedogenic" moisturizer. These are oil-free, so won't block up your pores with more grease, causing potential breakouts. Also look for a non-comedogenic sunscreen, preferably a gel-based formula designed for facial use.

□ If you regularly get spots in the same place, they could be caused by hormonal changes inside your body (we're three times more likely to suffer skin problems just before a period), or by a bad habit. Common breakout inducers include constantly touching your face (formaldehyde and toluene in some nail polishes—check the label—are also known skin enemies), tucking a dirty phone under your chin, and not cleaning the bridge of your glasses.

DRY/MATURE

As the name suggests, dry skin is low in moisture, making it look thin and papery. Thinner skin shows redness more easily and can feel tight and sore. The obvious answer is to slather on a rich moisturizer, but dry skin benefits from your working on the inside, too.

□ Omega-3 and -6 fatty acids are essential to moisturize your skin from within. Take them as a supplement or as cold-pressed organic oils poured over salads (much better-tasting than mayonnaise).

□ As with sensitive skin, keep your atmosphere moist with plenty of misted plants and bowls of water near radiators. And hydrate from the inside with lots of pure, still water. As a rule, for every caffeinated drink, you need to down double its volume in water.

□ Avoid wash-off foaming cleansers (anything that bubbles contains a detergent), and switch to a creamy one you remove with cotton or a soft cloth.

□ Most toners are a no-no for dry or mature skin types, but if you want something to give you that squeaky-clean feeling after cleansing, choose a gentle soothing rosewater toner, or simply splash your face with cool water.

□ Which moisturizer to use? Go by this simple rule. If your skin isn't soft to the touch after you've applied moisturizer, you're not using a rich enough product. Don't be afraid to apply a double helping on your drier areas. Just let the first one sink in before applying the second.

□ Dry skins have more dead skin cells sitting on the surface, so exfoliate regularly (but not more than twice a week). Use gentle circular movements and choose a moisturizing product (for a homemade option, mix a handful of sesame seeds with a scoop of runny honey).

COMBINATION

If you haven't time to use two different products on your face (and who has?), look for skincare that calls itself "balancing," which will take both your skin types into account. Or simply apply less moisturizer on your greasy areas and more on the bits of you that are dry.

professional makeup lesson

I Foundation or tinted moisturizer always comes before concealer or you end up wiping away your clever camouflage. Apply tinted moisturizer by squeezing a quarter-sized amount into your (clean) palm, and rubbing your hands together before smoothing over your face. Foundation takes a little more work as you want to build the coverage up gradually. Squeeze two drops onto a cosmetic sponge and then press and blend onto your face just where you need it. The harder you press, the more will come out of the sponge, so go easy at first.

EXTRA TIP Don't apply tinted moisturizer or foundation under your eyes, where it will crease, or over your top lip, where it accentuates fine hairs. Also beware of getting color in your eyebrows and hairline—mistakes can be wiped away with a damp cotton swab.

2 Light-reflecting liquid concealers disguise under-eye shadows; cream compacts or sticks camouflage blemishes. Either way, you'll get best results with a brush. For under-eye shadows, apply a tiny amount of liquid where the darkness is (it won't work if you use it all over), and then blend with a brush. For blemishes and broken capillaries, apply cream concealer with a brush and blend by pressing with your middle finger.

EXTRA TIP If your shadows are particularly dark, apply concealer, brush on a little powder, and then apply another layer of concealer just over the darkest area.

3 Never use powder all over your face. For a natural look, you want a little shine to show through, so just apply with a large brush to the T-zone and any areas where you've worked a camouflage miracle. **EXTRA TIP** If too much shine breaks through, don't apply more powder as the buildup will look caked. Instead, spray your face with water and then blot gently with a tissue.

4 Eyeliner along your top lids will define eyes and make lashes look thicker. This technique may sound tricky, but after a few practice runs you'll be drawing like a pro. Spray a dark powder eyeshadow with a little water and, using a flat-edged brush, look at yourself straight in the mirror and press the brush through your lashes (the line will come out just at the base of your lashes). Start at the outside corner and work along the top lid right into the inner corner. Once the powder dries, it will stay put without smudging.

EXTRA TIP Leaving your lower lid eyeliner-free helps lift the eyes (although kohl along the inner rims looks dramatic for evenings).

5 The easiest and most flattering eyeshadows to wear are liquid to powder formulas. They're foolproof to apply (all over the lid and just into the socket), never look overdone, and dry to give a long-lasting result. Most come with a sponge for two-second application, or you can smooth it on with a finger. **EXTRA TIP** If you're not a fan of color, use a neutral shade to hide any redness on your eyelid.

6 When applying mascara, zigzag the brush as you work up your lashes, as this separates the hairs while coloring them. Concentrate on your outer lashes for the most eye-widening effect.

EXTRA TIP Avoid mascara on lower lashes as it can drag your eyes down (and end up on your skin later).

7 Your blusher color should be near your natural color you turn when flushed. Use a large brush and light strokes to apply it over the apples of your cheeks (the fatty part), blending away to your hairline.
EXTRA TIP Even if you're using a cream blusher, apply with a large brush and you'll find it goes on much more evenly.

8 Whatever lip product you're using, leave lip liner until last, as there's nothing worse than the rest of your color rubbing off, leaving an obvious outline behind. If you're using a lip gloss, apply the gloss first and then line your lips over the top. For lipstick days, first smooth on a lip balm, then apply lipstick over the top with a brush and finally go around the edges with a pencil.
EXTRA TIP To make your lips stand out or to strengthen a weak lip line, use a fine brush to draw a line of concealer around your whole lip area before blending the edges away.

WHAT ANY MAKEUP ARTIST WILL TELL YOU

☐ Spend the most on your foundation. You can cut corners on other products, but foundation is worth spending money on. The only way to buy the right color is to test it in natural light, so take a compact mirror with you when foundation shopping. Apply colors to your jawline or just between your eyebrows before nipping outside to look in the mirror. The shade that disappears into your skin is the one to buy.

☐ Beauty makeovers in department stores are no longer done by counter staff with little training. In fact, choose a brand known for specializing in makeup, and you'll have your makeover done by a professional makeup artist. Most of these lessons last around 45 minutes and need to be pre-booked (unless you visit at a quiet time). Expect to pay between $25 and $50, which is always redeemable against any products you buy. And there's no need to save your new skills for best. Tell the makeup artist how much time you have in the morning and she can adapt the look to suit.

☐ Use brushes for the best results. This may add two minutes to your makeup routine, but adds two hours to your makeup's staying power. Some professionals use a short, fat brush to put on foundation—great for applying exactly where you want it, and no need to wash your hands (or sponge) afterward. Stroke in the direction of hair growth to avoid accentuating them.

☐ Most makeup artists wouldn't consider applying their art to an unprepared surface, and use a makeup primer. These clear liquids go on before foundation and after (or instead of) moisturizer. Think of it as applying undercoat to a wall before painting color over the top. The shade goes on better, looks fresher, and lasts longer—and your makeup will, too.

how to look younger by tomorrow

1 A shot of pink blusher can make you look ten years younger. Cream blush is best as it blends well. But don't apply it where you did when you were 18. As we age, our faces lose fatty tissue, meaning it's much more flattering to apply blusher toward the center of your face on the apples of your cheeks rather than along your cheekbones.

2 Eyelash curlers are a must for young-looking eyes. For most flattering results, use the double squeeze method. Before applying mascara, hold the curler close to your upper eyelash roots and squeeze for 5–10 seconds. Release, move the curler halfway along your lashes and squeeze again for five seconds.

3 We lose color from our faces as we age. Too-dark hair emphasizes wrinkles, under-eye shadows, and saggy skin, so consider having highlights or lowlights to lift your overall color a few shades lighter (and perhaps disguise the first signs of gray).

4 Lips lose some fullness with age, but you can create the illusion of it without resorting to collagen. Dot pearly highlighter on the center of your lower lip and just inside the Cupid's bow of your upper lip. Every time the light catches it, your lips will look larger.

5 Get bangs. Most hairdressers agree that bangs are instantly de-aging, but avoid heavy styles, which only suit teenagers. What you want is a longer, feathery fringe that sweeps over any furrows on your forehead, but allows a little flattering light through.

6 Droopy eyelids are a classic sign of aging. To make any droop recede with makeup, hold a mirror at a 45-degree angle below eye level and tilt your head back so you can see the whole eye area. Apply a light eyeshadow shade to the lid and browbone, then using a slanted contour eyeshadow brush, apply a darker shade to the entire crease area in an arc.

7 You can always tell someone's age (even facelifted celebs) by their hands. To plump up weather-beaten skin, slather on hand cream before slipping on your dishwashing gloves, and the warmth of the water will encourage your skin to drink up the moisture. In summer, apply factor 15 sunscreen to the backs of your hands, and hide veins or sun spots with fake tan.

8 Your neck's another age giveaway because the skin there has fewer fat cells than your face, making it prone to dryness. Add constant movement and neglect (how often do you moisturize your neck?), and fine lines are the inevitable result. Get into the habit of including neck and chest in your daily skincare regime, and apply your moisturizer in gravity-defying upward strokes for an instant lifting effect.

what makeup can do for you

Makeup was invented for days when you're looking and feeling less than your best. You can look sunkissed (when you haven't left the office in two weeks) or well rested (when you've been up with a teething baby). The trick, as always, is in the application.

I To wake up tired skin in seconds, apply blusher on the apples of your cheeks (to find the right place, simply smile at yourself in the mirror) and finish your face with lipstick.

2 Light-reflecting makeup is a lifesaver as it bounces light off your face to minimize imperfections, brighten dark areas, and give your skin an instant glow. Look like you've had eight hours' sleep (when you've only had five) by brushing on a light-reflecting liquid concealer in the following places:

□ under your eyes, blending just along the dark area
□ on either side of the bridge of your nose at the inside corner of your eyes
□ at the outer corners of your eyes over any redness.

3 Get glowing skin on even your dullest days with a complexion enhancer. These creams, lotions, and powders (look for the words "illuminating" or "brightening" in the title) are designed to give the impression of radiant skin. Don't apply all over your face, or the effect will be more greasy than glowing. Just use on the ridge of your browbone, the tops of cheekbones, and along your jawline. Apply with a brush after your foundation or tinted moisturizer and go easy, as a little goes a long way.

4 Get a healthy color with the help of a bronzing powder or gel. To warm up your skin, apply the bronzer just where the sun would naturally hit your face (forehead, nose, temples, cheeks, and chin). But beware of using a bronzer when you're tired, as brown can also drag you down.

To wake up tired skin in seconds, apply blusher on the apples of your cheeks and finish your face with lipstick.

5 Give yourself instant cheekbones by sweeping bronzing powder just under your cheekbones with a medium-sized brush (suck in your cheeks to find the right spot), followed by a brush of highlighting powder just above.

6 Brighten the whites of your eyes by using a white kohl pencil along the inside rim. But avoid brilliant whites (they look great in pictures, not so natural in real life) and choose an off-white, cream, or slightly blue-white for a softer effect.

7 Make your teeth look whiter with lipstick shades that contrast with yellow. That means avoiding anything with a yellow or orange undertone, such as coral and some browns, and going for colors with a cool tone such as shades of berry and burgundy, plus blue-based reds and pinks.

8 Bring out the color of your eyes by choosing the right eyeshadow shade, and it's not always the one you'd expect. Surprisingly, blue eyeshadow won't bring out the blue in your gray or blue eyes—orangey brown will do that. Warm eggplant shades will enhance the green in hazel eyes, and darker colors are most flattering on light-colored eyes. And steer clear of brown if your eyes are the same shade—what you need is a blue or green to add color.

9 Use bronzing powder to disguise a double chin— apply just under the chin and blend well.

10 Alter the size of your eyes with shading. For small eyes, use a pale shadow all over, with a slightly darker one along the socket line and a dab of white shadow on the browbone to widen. Large eyes suit a darker matte shade on lids, blended into the socket line.

21 (fast) great grooming tips

1 Plump and smooth your lips by exfoliating them with a child's toothbrush (more gentle than one made for adults). Twice a week, apply a little lip balm and brush horizontally for a minute. Not only will you slough off dry skin, the brushing will also stimulate blood flow, giving you that just-been-kissed look.

2 Apply fake tan to your face, and your eyes and teeth will look instantly brighter. Moisturize well first, or mix a little of your moisturizer in with the self-tan to make sure the color's diluted for not-too-dark results. Fake aficionados remove earrings first to avoid white marks, and smooth petroleum jelly through brows to stop staining. Avoid dotting the product directly onto your face, or you could end up with brown circles where the tan has grabbed on before you've had a chance to blend. Instead, apply a little tan to your hands, rub your palms together, and smooth over your face in a thin layer.

3 If your fake-tan color develops with streaks, rub them with half a lemon to bleach the brown away.

4 For days when you're feeling pale and gaunt, apply your blusher (any shade of pink will look fresh and natural) over your brows close to your hairline, and then add a little on your browbones to give warmth to your eyes. And don't be scared of applying too much. Professional makeup artists tone down too-bright blusher with a layer of neutral powder over the top. Or you can invest in a lilac-toned powder, which will revive tired, sallow skin. Apply it sparingly over cheeks, chin, nose, and forehead for instant radiance.

5 Remove shine instantly with oil-blotting sheets. Just don't rub. The idea is to press them onto your skin, or they'll remove your makeup, too.

6 Make close-set eyes seem farther apart by dotting concealer onto the inner corners of your lids, extending to the dark shadowy under-eye area on either side of your nose, and blending well.

7 During the night your tongue works like a sponge, holding onto all kinds of bacteria and toxins. Mouthwashes will do a cosmetic job of freshening your breath, but much better is a morning tongue-scraping session to remove all these nasties and make sure your mouth stays fresh all day. You can buy a special tongue scraper from drugstores or simply use a spoon (whatever you use, rinse well before and after).

8 When blow-drying, don't make the mistake of trying to style your hair from wet. You're just wasting precious time. Instead, tip your head upside down and ruffle your hair through with your fingers, while rough-drying it approximately 80 percent dry (this also gives great root lift). Turn your head the right way up and start using a brush with your dryer pointing downward to smooth the cuticles on the surface. Hair experts prefer to use nylon bristle brushes, as natural bristles can cause static and make your hair fly away. Style the front of your hair first as that's what everyone sees (plus it dries fastest), and then carry on working through the sides and back if you've got time. Finally, finish with a quick blast of cold air to set your style.

9 Stop lipstick from getting on your teeth by following this model's tip. Pucker up as if you're about to give someone a kiss, then pop your first finger in your mouth and pull it out again. Any excess color on the inside of your lips will come off on your finger, not in 20 minutes on your teeth.

IO Never use a pencil to emphasize your brows—powder gives a much more natural finish. Invest in a stiff, angled eyebrow brush and, starting at the inside corner working out, use light strokes to deposit the color on the eyebrow hairs rather than the skin itself.

II Groomed brows smarten up your whole face, and accentuating the natural arch also gives your eyes a natural lift. The highest point of each brow should line up with the outer edge of your iris, and the most flattering brows start just above the inner corner of the eye, extending as far as possible at the outer edges. Tweeze after a bath or shower when your pores are open, or dab on some teething or mouth ulcer gel to numb the area. It's a myth that you can only pluck from underneath—stray hairs on top of your brows look just as messy. But go slowly, as brows grow back less quickly than other body hair (expect to wait six weeks before you can try again).

I2 Use a clean mascara wand (wipe a finished one in eye makeup remover, wash and dry) to brush brows up and along. Or invest in clear mascara to set your just-groomed brows in place.

I3 There's no substitute for a good trim, but when heated styling tools or home colorants have left you with split ends, try this quick-fix trick. Take a section of hair, twist it tightly so all the little ends stick out, and snip off the split ones with sharp scissors.

14 Stuck without your full makeup kit? Then get creative. A little blusher or pinky/purple eyeshadow can do the work of lipstick. Brush on and then seal with a coat of lip balm. And if you're caught short with a spot and no concealer, the residue around the top of your foundation bottle is the perfect consistency for covering blemishes, and exactly the right skin tone to go totally unnoticed.

15 Make facial hair invisible with bleach. Invest in a home-bleaching kit especially formulated for the face and leave the mixture on for ten minutes before rinsing (do a patch test first to check for sensitivity). Not only will your hairs look less obvious, the bleach will soften their texture, too.

16 Before waxing, be kind to yourself by placing a warm washcloth on the area to open the pores and reduce pain. Smooth on the strip and, taking a deep breath, hold the skin taut (the secret of getting all the hairs in one swipe), and pull off fast as you breathe out. Regular waxing will make the regrowth finer and eventually actually stop hair from growing, so at least you won't have to do it forever.

17 Make the most of a less-than-ample cleavage with a good bra and a little clever shading. Choose a natural matte blusher that's not too far from your own skin tone and apply with a large brush between your breasts in a curved Y shape. Follow with a little highlighter along the top of your breasts to emphasize their (bra-enhanced) fullness.

18 For an instant skin soother, drench a cotton pad in rosewater and swipe it over your face a few times. Orange flower water works well too, and is perfect for super-sensitive skins.

19 No time to wait around for nail polish to dry (and who has)? Then buff your nails to a healthy pink shine instead, using a buffing file. The friction of buffing also stimulates blood flow, encouraging nails to grow faster. A word of warning: Never buff without first applying a nail oil or cream. Without it, buffing can literally take the top layer off your nails, weakening them in double-quick time. Simply smooth on your product and buff in a sideways motion for 30 seconds a nail (no longer).

20 The best time to push back your cuticles is straight after a bath or shower, when the skin is soft. The quickest method? Use the pointed edge of a towel. Two minutes tops.

21 Every time you apply lip balm, rub a little into your cuticles to keep them soft and pliable.

(easy) natural remedies for your hair

CONDITIONERS

Heat-styling sessions and sun exposure damage hair. Little wonder the cuticles on the surface are left sticking out in all directions, resulting in dull-looking hair as the outer layer no longer reflects light. Combing through one of these deep conditioners (with a wide-tooth comb) will smooth the surface so light can bounce off it again. Treat your hair weekly if it's damaged, or two-weekly if you have normal hair, and leave it to dry naturally as often as possible.

□ Mayonnaise is the perfect conditioner for dry hair. Smooth on, massage in, and then cover your head with plastic wrap to encourage the mayonnaise to sink in. Rinse off with lukewarm water to avoid curdling. For more heavy-duty moisturizing, mix mayonnaise with half an avocado and massage into hair. Cover your head and leave for 20 minutes before rinsing. Follow with one shampoo and condition as normal.

□ Olive oil is the classic deep treatment for dehydrated hair. Massage two teaspoons of oil over your hair and cover with a lightweight shower cap (the sort you find in hotel bathrooms). Leave overnight for extra-soft results, or for 20–30 minutes. To remove, apply shampoo before rinsing, then shampoo again as normal. You can make this treatment extra luxurious by adding 3–4 drops of your favorite essential oil.

□ Mash together half a banana with two tablespoons of coconut milk. Massage through your hair and leave for ten minutes before washing off with lukewarm water.

NATURAL RINSES

□ To remove styling product buildup from dull hair, add half a cup of white vinegar to a jug of boiling water, let it cool, and use as a second (lather-free) shampoo.

□ Use mint tea as a final rinse to give greasy hair shine.

□ One tablespoon of vinegar in a pint of warm water will ease tangles in dry and chemically treated hair.

□ Give limp hair volume by using cola as a final rinse.

body and mind cleansing

Both showers and baths are seriously therapeutic. In a shower, the water on your skin gives the same feeling as a massage, while a bath makes you feel cocooned due to being weightless in the warm water.

Ever wondered why a long, luxurious bath is all you can think about after a hard day? That's because, just like flotation, bathing also has a beneficial effect on the neurochemicals in your brain, encouraging the release of feel-good endorphins. The result is an almost instant reduction in stress levels.

Showering has a similar restorative effect, as cleansing your body can literally feel like you're scrubbing off the stresses of the day. When we feel clean on the outside, we're more likely to feel clean on the inside—think of it as washing your cares down the drain.

Bathing rituals have been a part of pampering since ancient times (remember Cleopatra and her modesty-preserving milk bath?). What they knew even back then was that bathing can be so much more than just skin washing. Add your favorite essential oils to the water, and it turns into a healing experience for both mind and body. See opposite for some essential oil suggestions.

Used in conjunction with warm water, the therapeutic benefits of essential oils are increased, because heat encourages capillaries to come to the surface of your skin so the oil can be absorbed straight into your bloodstream. Add no more than six drops in total and soak for 20 minutes (any longer and you'll dehydrate and emerge prunelike). Don't make the water too hot; 97–100°F (36–38°C) is ideal. Add the oils after your bath water has run so the vapors don't escape in the steam. Sprinkle oils at the faucet end and agitate the water well before stepping in, as some essential oils (especially citrus) may sting the skin if they are not properly dispersed.

You can also benefit from essential oils in your shower. Simply sprinkle six drops over the shower floor, and as the warm water hits they'll disperse and diffuse into the steam.

See pages 66–67 for more natural bath additives.

Ten Top Oils For Relaxing

Chamomile · Lavender · Neroli · Rose · Mandarin · Vetivert
Sweet Marjoram · Clary Sage · Frankincense · Lemongrass

Ten Top Oils For Energizing

Grapefruit · Bergamot · Eucalyptus · Orange · Peppermint
Juniper · Fennel · Rosemary · Geranium · Lemon

water therapy

Water therapy has been used to cure health problems since ancient Greek, Roman, and Celtic times. Now popular in spas everywhere, it's easy (and free) to do yourself at home.

A FREEZING COLD SHOWER is the best way to start your day, as it will instantly wake you up and stimulate every part of your body—including your brain. Stay under for 30 seconds to one minute before switching the dial back to warm.

TRY HOME THERMOTHERAPY by alternating warm water with cold for 30 seconds each. Cold on the body sends blood to your organs, while warm brings it rushing back to the muscles, adding up to a serious boost for your circulation and immune system.

TO BRIGHTEN A TIRED COMPLEXION aim a gentle cold shower at your face, working in circular movements, and pat dry with your hands.

IMPROVE THE APPEARANCE OF CELLULITE by using a high-pressure shower head on your legs and bottom. Work toward the heart to encourage toxin drainage.

TRY A LITTLE REFLEXOLOGY Lie back in warm water with two tennis balls resting on the end of the bath under your feet. Rotate them, gripping and releasing with your toes to stimulate nerve endings in your feet. With 72,000 per foot, you're guaranteed to hit the spot.

THALASSOTHERAPY is spa treatments using sea water and seaweed. Minerals present in sea water are similar to those in the body, meaning they are easy to absorb through your skin. Benefits include increased energy and better circulation. Invest in a sea bath product (see page 124) and follow this five-step treatment:
1 Relax in a not-too-hot bath (the minerals and trace elements in your sea product will raise the temperature a few degrees for extra penetration).
2 Shower without soap to leave maximum minerals on your skin (only half have been absorbed so far).
3 Rest for 20 minutes wrapped in a terrycloth robe so the remaining trace elements can sink in.
4 Shower with soap to remove any bath residue.
5 Grit your teeth and turn the water to cold, as this tightens pores and locks in the treatment benefits.

shortcut to smooth skin

Nothing smooths your skin faster than a good scrub. Whisk dull-looking dead skin away and the skin underneath is much softer. The drier your skin, the more often you need to scrub—up to three times a week. But all of us could do with a regular removal of rough skin on areas like feet and elbows. If your moisturizer won't rub in, chances are dry skin is acting as a block to the lotion, so needs to be scrubbed away. Always exfoliate on damp skin in the bath or shower. Massage firmly up your legs and down your arms. Then work in large circles over your stomach and around your breasts, finishing with sweeping strokes over your shoulders.

Pick the scrub option that suits the time you have.

ONE MINUTE
For the quickest option, choose an exfoliating soap bar to use in the bath or shower. But look for the word "gentle" as bodies don't like sharp, scratchy bits (no matter how natural they sound). Or press a handful of oats onto your usual bar of soap to make a no-cost alternative.

TWO MINUTES
Body puffs and exfoliating mitts are next in line. Body puffs are more gentle so suit sensitive skins, and also score marks for encouraging the weakest wash into a luxurious lather. Exfoliating mitts give a more intense scrub experience. They take seconds to slip on dry— and a few more to take off when wet. Just lather with your usual soap or gel and get to work.

FIVE MINUTES
For the softest, most luxurious scrub, treat yourself to a moisturizing mixture. These are usually either sugar or salt added to an oil base, which makes them very easy to do yourself at home. For a simple scrub, mix a handful of coarse sea salt with a teaspoon of any vegetable oil or runny honey, and massage onto damp skin before rinsing off thoroughly. Sensitive skin will prefer a handful of brown sugar mixed with oil or honey, as the effect is slightly less abrasive.

BATH OPTION
If you prefer to scrub in the bath, simply add a cup of sea salt to your water and scrub as you clean.

cellulite solutions that work

Pudgy thighs may be a common curse, but there's plenty you can do to improve the look of your lower half without spending a fortune on treatments.

1 EAT AND DRINK YOURSELF SMOOTHER

The aim is to boost circulation and also strengthen the collagen fibers in your skin responsible for elasticity (meaning lumps and bumps are less noticeable below the surface). Fruit and vegetables will do just that as they're rich in antioxidants and vitamin C, so eat at least five portions a day. Dehydration is another reason circulation becomes sluggish, so drink two quarts of water a day to help flush out toxins.

2 BRUSH AWAY THOSE BUMPS

Without doubt, one of the best ways to improve the look of dimply thighs and bottom is by brushing your skin. The type of body brush you use is unimportant; it's the way you do it that counts. Sweeping strokes on dry skin in the direction of your heart will stimulate the skin and the lymph nodes underneath. Start on your legs, working up to your bottom, daily before your bath or shower.

3 KNEAD YOUR KNOBBLES (BUT NOT TOO HARD)

Massage will help break down and disperse the fatty cells below your skin's surface, and you don't need to spend a fortune on cellulite creams to get results. Make your own dimple-buster with one tablespoon of carrier oil (any vegetable oil from your kitchen cupboard will do), plus two drops of cypress essential oil (to stimulate) and two drops of juniper essential oil (a diuretic). Smooth on daily and then gently pinch and roll sections of your less-than-perfect flesh between fingers and thumb.

4 BURN OFF YOUR FAT

There's no escaping it. Any form of cardiovascular exercise will encourage your body to burn fat and tone up flabby muscles, plus it boosts circulation. For best results, choose activities that target your legs and bottom, such as cycling, fast walking, and running. Studies also show that bouncing on a mini-trampoline not only gives good cardio (without putting stress on your joints), but also helps boost your lymphatic system (the one responsible for getting rid of toxins). Do it daily for at least five minutes for best effects.

Sweeping strokes in the direction of your heart will stimulate the skin and the lymph nodes underneath.

five ways to a flatter stomach

1 Avoid foods that cause bloating, such as beans, lentils, mushrooms, onions, wheat, and all carbonated drinks. You want to be eating plenty of easily digestible food such as plain bio yogurt, eggs, and oats, plus leafy salads rather than root vegetables. It's also a good idea to peel the skin off fruit, as it can be hard to digest, causing the dreaded gas. Talking of gas, high-fiber foods are also bad news for flat stomachs, so if you've got a tight dress to fit into, limit (or cut out) your high-fiber intake 24 hours before your big night.

2 Even if you eat the most easily digestible food, if you shovel it down, you'll still end up with a big belly. A major cause of bloating is eating too fast, or eating when you're stressed. And beware of talking non-stop at mealtimes as you'll be taking in gulps of air between mouthfuls that go straight to your stomach. So calm down, chew slowly, and concentrate on the food in front of you. And don't leave it too long between meals—the reason why most of us eat too fast is because we're so hungry.

3 Both pilates and yoga have a move that involves contracting your stomach so it remains drawn in during exercise. Easy to do any time, it's a great invisible stomach-muscle strengthener. Breathe in and pull up all the way from your pelvic floor muscles to your lower abdomen (imagine you're trying to stop yourself mid-flow on the toilet). The area above your navel should continue to move freely as you breathe. Hold this upward, inward contraction for 10–20 breaths—and repeat whenever you remember.

4 You may not have time for a hundred sit-ups a day as boasted by some six-pack-owning celebrities, but you actually get better results doing fewer high-quality crunches than lots of tired, out-of-breath ones. The trick is to target your stomach from different angles so you're using all your muscles, not just the same ones over and over again. To strengthen your entire stomach area, try the following.

□ Lie on the floor with your hands by your ears and legs straight up in the air. Tighten your abdominals, breathe out, and curl your shoulders off the floor, being careful not to pull on your neck. At the same time, bring your legs and pelvis toward your ribcage, using your lower abdominals to lift you (not the swing of your legs). Inhale, lower, and repeat ten times.

□ In the same position, tighten your abdominals, breathe out, and raise your right shoulder and elbow up toward the outside of your left thigh. At the same time, bend your left knee and bring your thigh toward your ribcage, again using your abdominals to do the work. Inhale, lower, and repeat on each side ten times.

5 If you suffer from bloating, pinpoint potential problem foods by keeping a record for a week of what you eat and how you feel 45–60 minutes afterward. Nutritionists believe that one in three of us may have a food intolerance, and simply by avoiding the problem you can reduce any bloating dramatically. Common bloat-causers include starchy foods such as potatoes, wheat, grains, and yeast. Alternatively, visit a nutritionist for a food intolerance test.

(easy) natural remedies for your body

□ The natural bleach in lemon will lighten red skin on your elbows and heels. Cut a lemon in half crosswise, squeeze out the juice, and rest your elbows or heels in each half for ten minutes.

□ Olive oil is contained in many prestige beauty products, so why not use it in its purest form straight from the bottle? Smooth on after a bath or shower and it will lock the moisture into your skin.

□ Add 4–5 drops of essential oil to a tablespoon of light olive oil (or any vegetable oil in your kitchen cupboard) to make a rich moisturizer with extra healing properties. Lavender is perfect for use before bedtime and also helps heal blemishes. Mandarin oil works well on stretch marks as it speeds up cell regeneration, and citrus oils such as grapefruit or lemon will wake you up in the morning.

□ Empty the contents of a vitamin E oil capsule and mix with a few drops of olive oil before massaging into your cuticles to encourage healthy new growth.

□ To soothe dry skin and eczema, put a handful of uncooked oatmeal in a large cotton handkerchief, hold all four corners together, and let your bath water run through it. The milky water it produces is a great softener and healer for sore and irritated skin.

☐ Lie down with a cold compress to relieve headaches. Add a few drops of either peppermint (for tension headaches) or rosemary and eucalyptus (for blocked sinuses) to a bowl of cold water. Swirl a facecloth around in the water and loosely wring out. Lie down comfortably and place the cloth over your forehead for ten minutes, refreshing it in the water as it warms.

☐ A teaspoon of anti-inflammatory sesame oil will soothe tired, stressed muscles at the end of the day. Or add a teaspoon of clove oil (a natural astringent with mild anesthetic properties) to a teaspoon of sesame oil and massage into sore feet at the end of the day.

☐ As another pick-me-up for tired feet, add four drops of peppermint oil (stimulating) to two tablespoons of aloe vera gel (non-greasy, anti-inflammatory), and mix together with a fork before massaging into your feet.

☐ Spa body wrap treatments are popular for detoxifying the body, plus they tone and tighten skin, improving the look of cellulite. Do it yourself at home by adding a cup of sea salt to four cups of boiling water. Stir until dissolved and add two cups of cosmetic clay (available from health and natural food stores). Mix and let it cool for 10–15 minutes while you take a warm shower to open your pores. Then dip gauze strips (bandages will do) into the mixture one at a time and wrap firmly (but comfortably) around problem areas. Relax for an hour before removing and jumping in a lukewarm bath.

☐ Other natural bath additives to help skin conditions are a cup of wine vinegar to soothe dry skin, a cup of powdered skimmed milk to moisturize all skin types (very Cleopatra), and a cup of epsom salts to soothe sore muscles at the end of the day.

15-minute manicure

Who has time for weekly manicures? Luckily this one lasts for up two weeks. The secret? It's all in the way you apply your polish.

I Most importantly, you need to get your nail shape right. It should reflect your cuticle shape, so if the base of your nails are square, you want your free edge to be, too. Getting an even result is hard to do on yourself, so check when you've finished by turning your hand around. With palm facing toward you, look to see if the free edges of your nails are straight. If they look uneven, finish shaping from this angle. And avoid filing down the sides—simply use one light stroke to clean up any snags and prevent splitting.

2 Before you work on the other hand, massage cuticle oil into the nails you're just filed.

3 Place both hands in warm water and soak them for five minutes.

4 Tap your nails on a towel to remove excess water and then, using an orange stick wrapped in cotton and dipped in oil, push back the cuticles on each hand.

5 Smooth on your favorite hand cream and then copy these reflexology massage movements.

□ Starting at your wrist, with your thumb underneath and four fingers on top, gently squeeze and release up to your elbow.

□ Using sideways movements in one direction only, stroke over the top of each hand.

□ Press all around each palm using the thumb of your opposite hand.

□ Interlock fingers and then press into the knuckles of each hand with the fingertips of your opposite hand (this improves flexibility).

□ Gently pull each finger using the thumb and first finger of your opposite hand.

6 Dip a facecloth in cold water and rub the nails clean until they squeak.

7 Apply base coat and then two coats of polish. Forget the old three-stroke rule. The more strokes you use to apply your polish, the longer-lasting the result. Take your brush out of the front of the bottle so the side loaded with polish is facing away from you and ready to paint. For the first coat, don't worry about streaks—just make a base. Start by spreading the bristles out at the cuticle (there should be a tiny gap between color and cuticle) and then run the brush up the nail in one clean sweep. On the second coat, keep stroking until all the air bubbles are out and the surface is perfectly flat.

8 The slower you paint on your color, the less likely it is to chip. For the same reason, don't attempt to dry your nails under the heat of a hairdryer; this dehydrates the polish, shrinking the edges and causing it to chip.

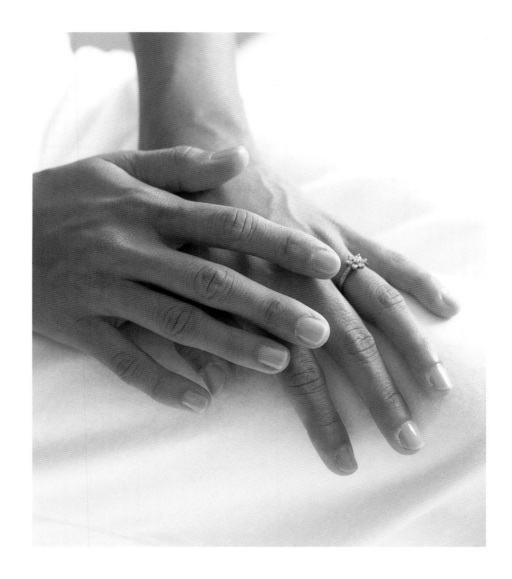

9 After ten minutes, smooth a drop of oil over each nail to protect your polish from knocks and dust while it dries completely.

10 Top coat wears off before base coat, so replace it every two days. Not only will your color look like new, your manicure will last twice as long, too.

Your nail shape should reflect your cuticle shape, so if the base of your nails are square, you want your free edge to be square, too.

15-minute pedicure

Toenails come in for less grief than fingernails so you can expect
a pedicure to last longer. But up to two months? Now that is a luxury.

1 Place your feet in tepid water (hot water will make them swell) and add a squirt of liquid soap to cleanse. If your skin's dry, sprinkle in two tablespoons of baby-milk powder, which will loosen hard skin. Or add a few drops of eucalyptus essential oil to freshen up smelly feet.

2 Take out your left foot and, using a ceramic foot file (a pumice collects oil and loses its sharpness), get to work on hard skin. File across rather than up and down your foot so you don't risk removing good skin.

3 Trim toenails straight across with a nail cutter and then file to smooth the edges.

4 Massage oil into your cuticles and then use a body exfoliator (see pages 60–61 for do-it-yourself recipes) all over your foot to smooth away leftover dirt and dead skin cells.

5 Place your left foot back in the water and repeat on your right one.

6 Use a cotton-covered orange stick to push back cuticles and clean underneath the nails. Then buff the surface of your toenails to smooth ridges and remove any discoloring.

7 Massage in a cooling cream (don't use anything too slippery) and then blot away any excess.

8 To reduce swelling and wake up your feet for a night out, wipe an ice cube all over them until it melts.

9 Squeak the nails with a facecloth soaked in cold water in preparation for painting.

10 Twist a strip of toilet paper and weave it through your toes to separate them (far easier to walk in than foam toe dividers). Apply a base coat and then two coats of color. Follow the painting technique described for a manicure (see previous page) and remember to reapply your top coat every two days for the longest-lasting pedicure you've ever had. No time to wait for your polish to dry before putting on shoes? After ten minutes, smooth a drop of oil over each nail and then wrap plastic film around your feet to protect the color without smudging it.

NIGHTTIME NAIL TREAT
For a homemade heated hand and foot treatment, place a pair of cotton gloves and socks on a warm radiator. Before going to bed, massage a teaspoon of olive oil into your skin and then slip them on. The heat will encourage the oil to penetrate deeply as you sleep.

MAINTAIN YOUR MANICURE
Before doing anything dirty, run your nails over a bar of soap. When you've finished, wash your hands, and any dirt will come away with the impacted soap (and won't need digging out, which can damage nails).

21 instant rescue remedies

For when you're *looking* less than your best.

1 Woken up with flat hair and no time to wash? Simply hang your head upside down and rub your scalp all over using your fingertips (this is also great for headaches). Or mist with a little water, twist your hair into a high knot and secure with a clip or scrunchie. Wait an hour before shaking out and you'll have volume aplenty.

2 To beat morning frizz, again mist your hair with water and then smooth a tiny amount of serum between your palms (any more than a nickel-sized squirt is too much). Scrunch the curls back into your hair with your hands.

3 If you've woken up with a spot that's crying out to be squeezed (you can see the white sebum under the skin), then minimize damage for the rest of the day by opening your pores first. Either squeeze after a bath or shower, or hold a hot cloth over your face for five minutes. Wash your hands and wrap a tissue around the tips of your index fingers before squeezing gently. You want the spot to pop within seconds or the redness caused by your squeezing will look worse than the spot itself. Either way, dab on a little tea tree oil to guard against infection and then apply a concealer containing salicylic acid, an ingredient that's proven to clear blemishes and smooth skin.

4 An emergency tip for flaky lips. Press a piece of tape onto wet lips, gently remove, and the flakes will come away, too. Follow with a healthy dollop of lip balm to soften your lips.

5 Soothe redness due to heat or hormones by soaking a facecloth in ice-cold water, wringing out and placing over your face for five minutes.

6 To calm a red spot, place an ice cube over the top to cool the inflammation instantly. Another quick fix: dip a cotton swab in hot water and then neat tea tree oil before holding it over your spot for 30 seconds.

7 Celebrities use it, and so do makeup artists when they're making up a less-than-super model. A tiny amount of hemorrhoid cream applied onto the orbital bone below your eye will shrink under-eye bags instantly. But save this emergency measure for when you really need it.

8 Give dull skin instant energy by splashing with warm and then cold water. Repeat five times to boost circulation and bring color back to your cheeks.

9 Transform frizz into perfect ringlets by taking chunky sections, smoothing on a little molding mud or putty (the tacky-textured styling gunk that doesn't dry) and then twisting each section around your finger. And if you've only got five minutes just do the outer layer—it's the only bit everyone sees anyway.

10 When your hair needs a wash but you don't have time, just wash and blow-dry the front. Section off a triangle at the front and carefully lather and rinse before styling. This is the part that gets greasy faster, and what everyone notices about you first.

II When last night's excess is still with you in the morning, start the day with a cup of hot water and a slice or squeeze of lemon to support your overworked liver. Follow with some deep breathing (see pages 106–107) to oxygenate your skin, and splash your face with cold water to wake up your mind and calm any redness. Ashtray hair can be sweetened by spraying some scent into the air and walking through the mist (shut your eyes). Drink a quart of water by lunchtime, and you should be feeling almost human.

I2 Running late? A tinted moisturizer or concealer plus mascara and lip color is all you really need.

I3 If you regularly wake in the morning with marks on your face, switch your cotton pillowcase for a satin or silk one. Dermatologists can actually tell which side of your face you sleep on by the lines left by your pillow, so minimize the damage by sleeping on something silky-smooth.

I4 Woken up with flaking lips? Never try to apply lipstick over the top as it just accentuates the problem. Instead, try this makeup artist's trick. Use tweezers to peel away the loose flakes of skin gently and then apply a generous layer of lip balm. Leave to soak in before lining your lips and then filling in with lipstick.

15 To banish a canker sore by the following day, apply neat peppermint, chamomile, or lavender essential oils with a cotton swab every 30 minutes (outside the mouth only).

16 Shrink under-eye bags with a spot of do-it-yourself lymph drainage massage. Lie down and, using the pads of your fingers, gently press under your eyes from your nose out to the sides of your face to remove excess fluid. Repeat five times.

17 No time for fuss? Ice-cold water splashed over your face is guaranteed to get your circulation going on a bad morning and bring a youthful blush to your cheeks (however, avoid this treatment if you suffer from broken veins).

18 Dry skin may be due to a moisture-sucking atmosphere. If you feel flaky, try putting bowls of water by all your radiators and surround yourself with well-watered, regularly misted plants.

19 If you have a shiny nose and forehead, invest in a T-zone control gel to wear alone or under makeup. These products contain powder particles that absorb oil to leave you shine-free all day. Or carry oil-absorbing blotting sheets, to dab on during the day.

20 To calm static and create shine, rub a fabric softening sheet over the surface of your hair.

21 If you have open pores, don't use moisturizer on your problem areas. They'll instantly look less obvious.

feel fabulous

healthy habits

A great way to feel in charge of a frantic life is to set up what you want to happen each day. That means creating and including activities that will improve the quality of your life.

The only rule is that these habits must be enjoyable, so you'll want to do them no matter how hectic your day. Make each one something you love, but which you might normally forget to do because of all the other chores that take up your time. The habits that work best are ones that boost your well-being. That might mean adding something new (like only eating organic), or ditching something that you recognize does nothing for you (like watching four hours of TV a night). We all have habits we're not aware of that cause us stress, and the more you can replace these with healthy habits, the better your life will be. The object is to look after yourself very well—extreme self-care is the best habit of all.

WHAT COULD YOU DO EVERY DAY THAT WOULD MAKE YOU FEEL GOOD?

The rules are simple. Make your habits

☐ simple and easy
☐ things that give you energy
☐ things you want to do (not think you should do).

And feel free to change them whenever you like. Remember: you're in charge of your own life, so it's up to you to make it enjoyable.

IDEAS FOR FEEL-GOOD HEALTHY HABITS

☐ Ten minutes of meditation, or simply sit quietly.
☐ Drink herbal tea instead of coffee.
☐ Do ten minutes of slow, deep breathing.
☐ Be in bed by 11 P.M.
☐ Use essential oils in some way.
☐ Take your vitamins.
☐ Indulge in a ten-minute self-massage.
☐ Limit your TV watching to an hour.
☐ Do ten minutes of yoga or stretching.
☐ Allow time to read things you really enjoy.
☐ Only eat foods that give you energy.
☐ Be kind to one person.
☐ Make yourself a fresh juice in the morning.
☐ Spend an hour playing with your children.
☐ Make a decision based on your intuition.
☐ Talk to a friend who makes you laugh.
☐ Play music you love.
☐ Have a hug or kiss.
☐ Go for a ten-minute walk in the park.

Now, over to you…

We all have habits we're not aware of that cause us stress, and the more you can replace these with healthy habits, the better your life will be.

why getting out is good for you

The benefits of nature are both physical and mental. Plants cleanse our air, taking the carbon dioxide we exhale and turning it into oxygen for us to inhale. No surprise then that plant-filled spaces are instantly relaxing and provide a peaceful escape from our otherwise high-tech day.

And the sheer size of nature can help put human problems in perspective. Many behavioral experts believe it's impossible to feel depressed when you're gazing up at the expanse of a bright blue sky.

GET OUTSIDE AND SPEND TIME WITH NATURE

Lie on your back in the park at lunchtime and watch the clouds. It won't matter how many people are around you, you'll feel instantly alone. Watching water is also very calming, so sit by a river or stream and

concentrate your mind on its movement. Nature can also benefit your well-being when you're indoors, so place plants around your home and in your office. Research has found they absorb common pollutants such as formaldehyde, and because plants pump out water, they'll also help counteract low humidity caused by air-conditioning and central heating.

THE SUN (IN MODERATION) IS GOOD FOR YOU

Vitamin D is formed on our skins by direct sunlight. A 15-minute walk in sunlight every day during summer is all you need to store enough vitamin D to take you through winter. Our immune systems rely on vitamin D to help prevent infections, plus it's necessary for calcium absorption in the gut. Calcium not only gives you healthy bones and teeth, but helps release the feel-good hormone serotonin, which boosts your mood and helps you sleep. It also has a calming effect on the nervous system, which is why we always feel positive after sun exposure. Although you can get your vitamin D fix in other ways (from foods such as fortified cereals, oily fish, egg yolk, cheese, and butter), the vitamin D your body makes from ultraviolet rays is the most effective. So, as many of us work and live in high-rise cities where sunlight is getting harder to find, counteract a lack of light by spending more time in open spaces (even on overcast days), and increase your consumption of vitamin D-rich foods as the days get darker.

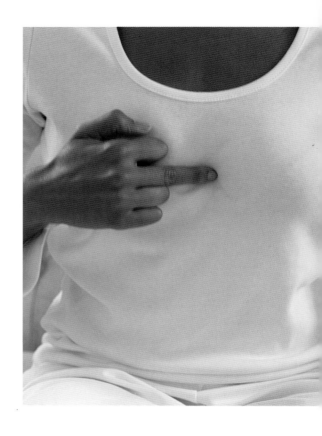

self-help acupressure

Acupressure, part of Chinese medicine, has been used for thousands of years to ease minor ailments. Like acupuncture, it works on the idea that health problems are caused by blockages of energy in the body. By releasing the block, energy can move freely again. But, while acupuncture uses fine needles, acupressure works by simple fingertip pressure. If you're pregnant, consult a qualified practitioner before treating yourself.

Do-it-yourself acupressure is easy to practice any time, anywhere. Simply apply steady, firm pressure, using the tip of your middle finger, to the acupressure point related to your problem. Hold your finger at a right angle to the surface of your skin (if you have long nails, you could use your knuckle instead). If

you're not sure you've hit the right spot, probe until you feel a sore sensation—the pressure should feel slightly uncomfortable. Hold each pressure for 20 seconds, release for 10, and then press for another 20 seconds. Repeat up to six times, plus a couple of times over the next few hours until your symptoms ease.

STRESS

Find the point between two tendons on your inner arm, about three finger widths from the wrist crease (see far left). Clench your fist so you can see the tendons, and relax it again before applying pressure with the middle finger of your opposite hand. Repeat both sides.

ENERGY BOOST

This point is at the tip of each finger either side of the nail. Take the top of your pinky finger between the index finger and thumb of the other hand and squeeze firmly. Hold for a few seconds. Repeat on each finger.

TEMPLE AND EYE HEADACHES

The pressure point is between the first and second toes. With your thumb and index finger (thumb on top), press gently into the webbing of your foot. Then gently squeeze the inside of the big toe just below the nail, but softly as this may feel sore.

ANXIETY

The anxiety point lies on the center of the breastbone three thumb widths up from the base of the bone (see center left). Apply firm pressure.

TENSION HEADACHES

The point lies on the top of your hand at the center of the fleshy part between your thumb and index finger (see center right). Repeat on both hands.

EXHAUSTION

To combat exhaustion, find the point four finger widths below your kneecap at the outside of your shinbone (see above right). Repeat on the other side.

TIRED EYES

This pressure point lies on top of your foot two finger widths from the joint between your big and second toes. Repeat on the other side.

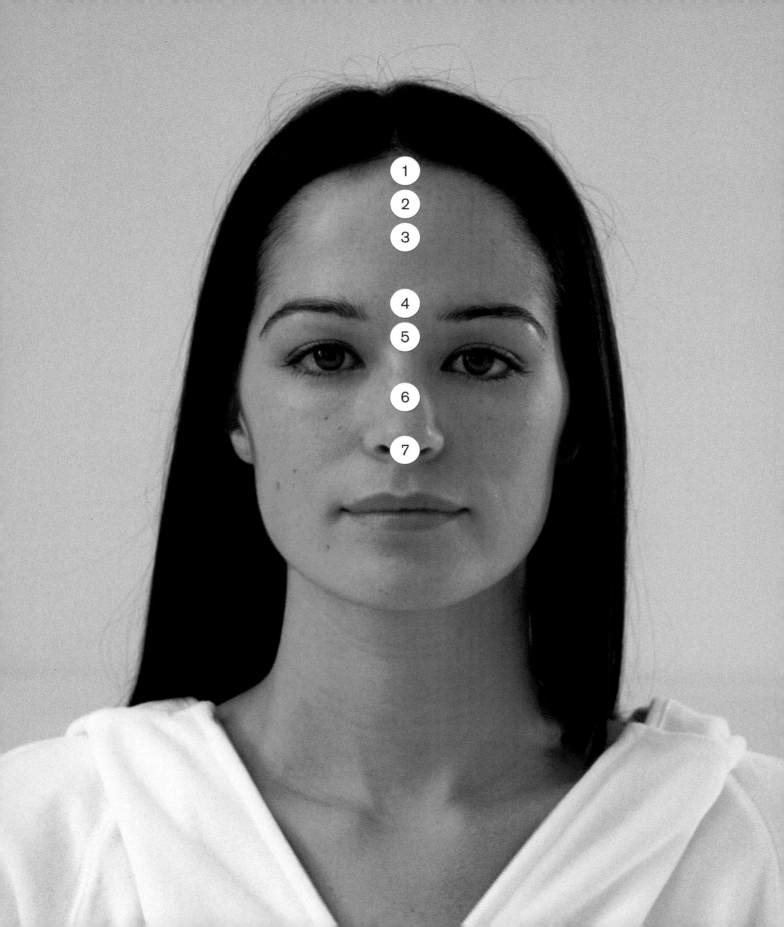

face reflexology

Face reflexology works more quickly and effectively than traditional foot reflexology because it activates your brain waves. A treatment stimulates the bloodstream and entire nervous system, while giving you a serious sense of relaxation. Using acupuncture points corresponding to nerve endings, it's also simple to do on yourself at home.

This sequence will relax and rebalance you after a busy day. There are seven points to massage. Apply medium pressure and work *very* slowly and rhythmically.

1 Lie down for best results, or sit in a comfortable chair. Take a few deep breaths before you begin.

2 Starting on the first reflexology point just under your hairline (1), use your middle finger to circle around the point eight times. The movement needs to be calm and your working hand and shoulder relaxed. To divert your mind from busy thoughts, concentrate on an image of each point as you massage around it. Then circle in the opposite direction eight times.

3 Drop down one finger width and massage the second reflexology point (2) eight times in each direction. Remember to keep your shoulder and hand relaxed and the movements very slow.

4 Drop down one more finger width and massage the third point (3) eight times in each direction.

5 There's a small gap between the third and fourth points (4); drop down another finger width to find the fifth point (5). Massage eight times in each direction.

6 The sixth point (6) is at the soft part of your nose about halfway down, and the seventh (7) is on the tip of your nose. Massage eight times in each direction.

FACE MAPPING
Reflexologists believe that each part of your body relates to a corresponding area on your face. Putting pressure on these points is said to unblock the internal flow of energy within the related part of your body, releasing stress and toxins. Another way to make use of reflexology is to learn how to read your face so you can pick up slight imbalances in your body before they become a problem.

□ Between your eyebrows relates to your liver. Too many nights out drinking alcohol can cause spots here.

□ Problems such as broken veins on your nose can mean your cardiovascular system is under stress.

□ Your cheeks are related to your lungs, and irritation or spots here are linked to too much diary in your diet.

□ Around your chin is related to your reproductive system and hormones, the reason so many women suffer spots here during their period.

do-it-yourself body massage

Massage has been a part of healing for thousands of years (the oldest known massage book was written in 3000 B.C.). This is no surprise—massage encourages the release of endorphins that reduce pain and produce a feeling of calm, strengthens the immune system, improves breathing patterns, and boosts skin.

Before you begin the following sequence, take a few deep breaths, and as you do, cup both palms over your closed eyes. Relax your neck and shoulders and stay in this position for two minutes. (It's also perfect for taking a break during a stressful day.) Repeat each movement five times, and each time you apply pressure, breathe out. The key to self-massage is to work *very* slowly to relax your mind and body. Keep your eyes closed when possible and breathe deeply.

I SCALP
Using the fingers of both hands, apply firm static pressure, making very slow circles. Spread your fingers wide and, rather than slide them over your skin, think of "moving" the scalp gently over your skull.

2 TEMPLES
With hands and wrists relaxed, press firmly into the soft part of your temples with your middle three fingers (where you will feel a pulse). Follow with little circles, keeping the movements slow and relaxed.

3 JAW
With your fingers around the back of your head, press your thumbs into the corners of your jaw. The right spot is around the middle of the ear in the soft part just under your cheekbones (if you move your jaw

from side to side, you will feel the joint under your thumb). Relax your jaw and apply pressure into the muscle with your thumb, keeping the rest of your hands relaxed.

4 SHOULDERS
Use the middle finger of each hand to apply pressure into the sore spot of the opposite shoulder. Press very slowly as you breathe out and follow with small circles.

5 HAND
Make small, firm circles with your thumb in the center of your opposite palm. Then grasp one finger from the base, keep firm pressure, and pull straight out toward the fingertips. When you're about to slide off, squeeze the fingertip for five seconds before you release.

6 FEET
In a sitting position, hold one foot. Using both thumbs, "walk" along the center of the sole firmly and slowly.

7 LOWER BACK
In a standing position, using the fingers of both hands, massage any sore areas along the spine (don't come up too high or you'll put strain on your shoulders). Then hold flat hands on both sides of your spine and rub vigorously up and down to warm the whole area.

yoga moves for busy bodies

Most of us think of winding down as lying on the sofa watching TV, but deep relaxation is better achieved through gentle movement. That's because, as we stretch, our muscles release any tension that would otherwise stop us from feeling completely relaxed.

Yoga is the perfect wind-down exercise as it combines controlled breath (the body's natural tranquilizer) with movement, which calms your mind while energizing your body. The poses are designed to work every single muscle and joint, plus they also stimulate your digestive, nervous, and cardiovascular systems. The

breath is deep and always through your nose. As a general rule, you inhale as you lift and exhale during downward movements. A feel-good addition is to smile gently as you inhale, as this not only allows the air to swirl around the back of your throat, but also works in the same way as the inner smile technique (see page 116). Most importantly, never hold your breath and keep it gentle—if you can't breathe freely, you're pushing yourself too far.

ALL YOU NEED

☐ An empty stomach—don't eat for at least one hour beforehand (wait two hours after a heavy meal).

☐ Comfortable clothing and bare feet.

IF YOU ONLY HAVE FIVE MINUTES IN THE MORNING

◄ STOMACH LIFT

This abdominal toner is the way yogis start their day and must be done on an empty stomach. Stand with your feet shoulder width apart and your knees slightly bent. With your hands resting on your thighs, inhale deeply and then drop your body forward as you exhale completely (until your lungs are empty of air). Holding your breath, come up to the starting position and pull up your stomach muscles as if you were trying to touch your spine with your navel. Hold for a count of three, release, and repeat.

CORPSE POSE

Begin and end any yoga sequence by lying flat on the floor with your arms a little away from your sides and your chin tucked slightly toward your chest to lengthen your neck. Imagine your spine relaxing into the floor, close your eyes, and focus on breathing in and out through your nose. This is a wonderful way to end your day as it allows your heartbeat to return to normal while circulating fresh air through your body.

IF YOU HAVE LONGER

OVERHEAD STRETCH

From the Corpse Pose, stretch your spine by bringing your arms above your head and interlocking your fingers. Inhale and stretch your arms toward the wall behind you. On the next inhalation, stretch your toes toward the opposite wall to stretch your whole body.

CHEST HUG

Ease a stiff back by bringing your knees toward your chest and holding on just below them. Inhale, and on the exhale bring your knees a little closer to your chest. Repeat five times.

▼ BACK LIFT

To soothe backache (and tone your bottom), bend your knees with feet flat on the floor, hip width apart and close to your body. Arms are by your sides with palms flat—your fingertips should almost touch your heels. Inhale, and on the exhale, lift your spine off the floor, tilting your pelvic bone and rolling up vertebra by vertebra. Keep your chin slightly tucked in and your shoulders on the floor so you feel your chest open. Take five gentle breaths and roll back the same way.

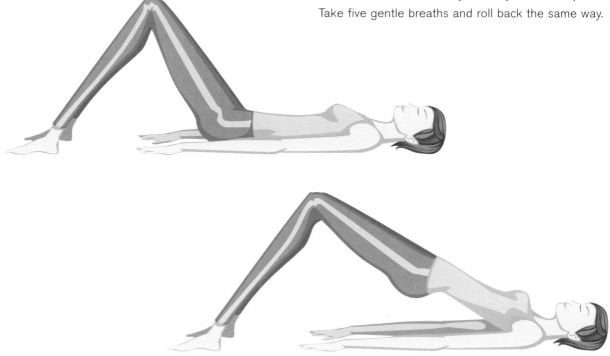

HAMSTRING STRETCH ▶

Improve flexibility in the back of your legs by coming up
to a sitting position with both legs straight out in front of you.
Inhale, lift your spine, and reach your hands straight up above
you. Exhale and bend forward from the hips (not the waist),
placing your hands as far down your legs as you can. Soften
your knees slightly, relax, and hold for five gentle breaths.

KNEE TWIST

To relieve tightness in the lower back, lie down with
your arms out to the sides and palms flat on the floor.
Inhale, and on the exhale take both knees over to the
right, keeping your shoulders on the floor and turning
your head to the left. Take five gentle breaths, come
up on an inhale, exhale and repeat on the other side.

THE CAT

Great for strengthening the spine and easing backache.
Start on all fours with hands below your shoulders
and knees below your hips. Inhale, and relax your back
down into its natural curve with your head lifted. Then
exhale, drop your head, and curl your back up. Repeat
five times, keeping the movements slow and gentle.

▲ SITTING TWIST

This pose will improve the flexibility in your back and spine while toning your waist. Begin as for the Hamstring Stretch, sitting tall with your legs out in front of you. Lift your right foot over your left thigh so that your foot is flat on the floor just above your knee and place your right hand behind your back. Inhale and lengthen your spine, bringing your left hand over the outside of your right knee. Exhale, and slowly turn your head over your right shoulder, twisting your entire upper body in the same direction. Continue to breathe gently five times and then slowly turn back and repeat the Sitting Twist on the other side.

HIP STRETCH

Perfect for anyone who spends their day sitting at a desk, this will ease tension in the hips and tone your buttocks. From a kneeling position, take your right leg forward, placing your foot directly under your knee. With your fingers resting on the floor to steady your balance, inhale, and on the exhale press forward and down gently until you feel a stretch in your left hip. Make sure your right knee is still directly over your ankle and hold the pose for five breaths before repeating on the other side.

AFTER STRETCHING

Finish by relaxing into Corpse Pose, staying there for at least five minutes (ten is better!).

Reminder: If you have any health problems or are pregnant, please consult your doctor before beginning any new exercise routine.

no time to exercise?

First, let's look at what you're missing. All exercise (whether it's serious boot camp aerobics or more gentle yoga stretching) will do the following.

- ☐ Increase your heartbeat.
- ☐ Give you more energy.
- ☐ Lower blood pressure.
- ☐ Ease back pain by strengthening stomach muscles.
- ☐ Release toxins and tension.
- ☐ Improve your memory.
- ☐ Lower your cholesterol.
- ☐ Tone and tighten muscles.
- ☐ Calm your mind.

- ☐ Improve your breathing.
- ☐ Strengthen your body.
- ☐ Help you sleep better.
- ☐ Improve your skin's condition.
- ☐ Make you look and feel younger.

And research shows that exercise also makes you live longer, so by exercising you're actually *making* time rather than wasting it.

IF YOU HAVEN'T GOT TIME TO VISIT THE GYM, BRING THE GYM TO YOU

There's no need to invest in an expensive gym membership or home exercise equipment. Experts say it's not the twice-weekly run on a treadmill that brings the most benefits, but daily activity. A good recommendation is to walk 10,000 steps a day (about an hour and a quarter). This may sound a lot, but the little things add up: include using stairs instead of the elevator (approx 500 steps), 30 minutes of housework (1,500), and 30 minutes of lunchtime shopping (2,000) and you're almost halfway there.

Most importantly, include activities in your life that you enjoy and that also benefit your body—it's the only way you're going to want to keep on doing them. And while we're on the subject, sex burns on average 200 calories a session and also increases endorphins that make your hair, eyes, and skin shine. What more excuse do you need?

HOW TO MOVE MORE EVERY DAY

□ Buy a basket for your bike and cycle to the shops.
□ Park your car at the farthest corner of the lot, or three streets from work.
□ Ditch the car and walk whenever you can.
□ Take the stairs to the restroom three floors down.
□ Put all your remote controls in a drawer so you have to move off the couch once in a while.
□ Play with your children (or a friend's children).
□ Never use the elevator, and walk up escalators.

□ Take a ten-minute walk after lunch, and a 20-minute walk after dinner (weather permitting).
□ Get off the bus or train one stop early and walk the remainder of the way.
□ Walk your dog once more every day (or borrow your neighbors'—they'll be glad of the help).
□ Give the office cafeteria a miss and walk to a deli ten minutes away.
□ Get out in the garden at the weekend—weeding and pruning count as aerobic exercise.
□ Go out dancing or take up salsa or swing.
□ Volunteer to mow the lawn or wash the dishes (wearing dishwashing gloves, of course).

Include activities that you enjoy and that also benefit your body—it's the only way you're going to want to keep on doing them.

stretches for instant stress relief (without leaving your chair)

Tension in your body can be caused by both physical and mental stress. You may be sitting in the same position all day, or it may be your excessive workload that's sending your shoulders ear-ward. Keyboard users are also prone to soreness in the back, neck, and shoulders, not to mention eye strain.

These stiff-muscle-busters are the perfect 3:00 pick-me-up, but they'll also feel great any time you feel sore after sitting for long periods of time. The stretches marked with an asterisk (*) are particularly good for releasing the tight muscles that cause tension headaches. Do them all in sequence, or if you've only got a few minutes, choose the ones that target your area of tension.

CHEST STRETCH

Interlock your fingers behind your back, keeping your arms as straight as possible. Inhale, and as you exhale open your chest and pull back your shoulders. Hold for three breaths, relax, and repeat three times. (Do this standing up if your chair has a high back.)

NECK STRETCH*

Interlock your fingers behind your head with your elbows pointing out to the sides. Inhale, and as you exhale, drop your chin to your chest and bring your elbows together in front of your face. Hold for three breaths, lift up, and repeat three times.

▼ NECK SIDE STRETCH*

Inhale, and on the exhale slowly stretch your head down to one side, feeling a pull on the opposite side. Come up on the inhale. Repeat three times each side.

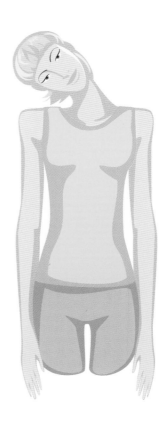

SHOULDER ROLLS

Place your hands on your shoulders with your elbows pointing straight out to the sides. Keeping your shoulders relaxed, breathe deeply as you move your elbows back and around in three large circles. Repeat in the opposite direction.

SHOULDER STRETCH

Interlock your fingers and stretch your arms up in the air over your head. Relax your shoulders, inhale, and then as you exhale look toward your hands and stretch. Hold each stretch for three breaths, release, and repeat three times.

UPPER BACK STRETCH

Interlock your fingers with your arms straight out in front of you and your head relaxed forward. Inhale, and as you exhale, push your arms out with palms facing away from you until you feel a stretch. Hold for three breaths, relax, and repeat three times.

▼ BACK STRETCH

Making sure you have room in front of you, inhale, and as you exhale, bend forward from the waist, relaxing your head down. Take hold of your ankles, inhale, and on the exhale gently arch your back to increase the stretch. Hold for five breaths before coming up.

BACK TWIST

Sitting tall in your chair, slowly twist to the right from your hips so your chest faces to the side. Hold the back of the chair with your hand to help you stretch (but don't strain), and look over your right shoulder. Hold for three breaths and repeat on the other side.

▼ CALF STRETCH

Sit upright in your chair and lift your left leg straight out in front of you. Slowly flex and point your toe three times on each side.

FOREARM STRETCH

Lift and stretch your arms straight out to the sides. Slowly flex and extend your hands five times, feeling the pull on the upper and lower forearms as you go.

EYE STRETCH

Without moving your neck, look up to the ceiling. Now imagine you're watching a moving clock and follow the hand clockwise from twelve o'clock to one o'clock and then all the way around back to twelve. Repeat counterclockwise. Finish by rubbing your palms together to generate heat and cupping them over your closed eyes as you breathe deeply for five breaths.

FACE STRETCH*

You may want to do this when no one's watching! Inhale, and squeeze your face up tight, then as you exhale, open your eyes and mouth as wide as possible and stick out your tongue (try to reach your chin!). Now exhale with force, making an "ahh" sound. Repeat three times.

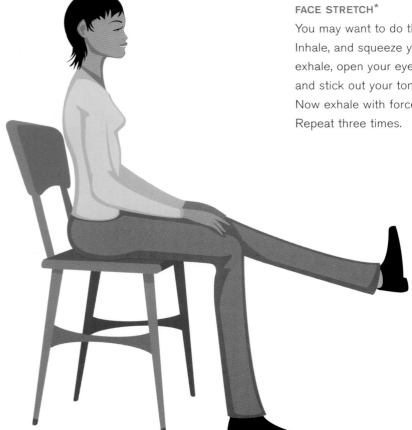

FULL ARM STRETCH

Take your right arm behind your back and bend it up, then take your left arm over your shoulder so your hands can clasp together behind your back (if you can't take hold of your hand, then try to touch your fingers). Breathe deeply as you hold the stretch for five breaths.

HIP STRETCH

Bend your right leg up in front of you and hold your knee with your right hand. Take your left hand and hold your right foot, keeping the ankle straight and in line with your lower leg. Straighten your spine to lift up through your waist and gently rock the right leg from side to side, feeling the stretch in your right hip (be very gentle, as this is an intense stretch). Hold for five deep breaths and repeat on the opposite side.

▼ FULL BODY STRETCH

Sit upright as before with your hands clasped loosely behind your back. Drop your head toward your chest so your back is rounded, and lift your left leg straight out in front of you. Inhale, flex your foot, and as you exhale, move your body gently forward to increase the stretch. Hold for five breaths, release, and repeat the sequence with the right leg.

aromatherapy to help you through your day

Our noses work like a direct passage to the brain. The moment we smell a fragrance that reminds us of a positive memory, we experience the same good feelings again.

Natural scents go one better, as they affect the mind and body no matter what memories are associated with them. That makes essential oils some of the most powerful mood-altering substances available—and they're legal! Buy 100 percent pure oils and store in a cool, dry place.

WAYS TO SURROUND YOURSELF WITH SCENT

□ Place ceramic ring diffusers above light bulbs in your home and office, or add a few drops of oil directly to the bulb. As it heats up, the aroma will be released.

□ Invest in a small diffuser designed to slot into the lighter socket in your car.

□ Sprinkle oils onto your linen, the corner of a carpet, or your pillow at night (there's actually no oil in essential oils, so they won't stain fabric).

□ Add five drops to your bath water or shower floor, or sprinkle onto a wet washcloth and rub over your body.

□ Burn scented candles or a diffuser in your office and home (clean diffusers with a little vodka between oils to neutralize any leftover aroma).

□ Add a few drops of oil to the water compartment of your iron and the steam will scent your clothes.

□ Make up massage blends (five drops to a tablespoon of vegetable oil) for a rich moisturizing treat.

□ As essential oils come in tiny bottles, they're easy to use on the go. Sprinkle onto a handkerchief or simply sniff straight from the bottle.

HERE'S WHAT WILL HIT THE SPOT

☐ Get going in the morning with orange, lemon, lime, or grapefruit essential oils, all guaranteed to clear the fuzz from the night before. For weekend mornings when you want to wake up gradually, lavender is perfect.

☐ If you're driving long-distance, using rosemary oil in a car diffuser will aid concentration and help you get to your destination safely, with less stress. Lavender will soothe road-rage nerves without sending you to sleep.

☐ Give yourself a wake-up call at work with cedarwood or peppermint. Again, if it's concentration you're lacking, rosemary will get you back on track. Sprinkle two drops on a handkerchief, lay it over the top of your computer, and the gentle heat will diffuse the oil into your space.

☐ Keep going at midday with a blast of peppermint oil to revive a tired mind. Peppermint is also good before an important meeting as it soothes and calms nerves. If you're suffering from low spirits, eucalyptus will lift you up, and stressed-out days will seem a little less frantic after smelling orange essential oil.

☐ Slow down at night by surrounding yourself with the scent of relaxing jasmine. If you're wanting to create a sensual atmosphere, sandalwood and ylang ylang are renowned aphrodisiacs and also smell very romantic.

☐ Prepare yourself for bed by adding chamomile or lavender oil to your bath water—perfect for tired bodies and minds. Sprinkle lavender on your pillow to insure a good night's sleep (it stimulates the part of your brain responsible for regulating sleep patterns), but use sparingly, as a too-strong aroma will have the opposite effect. If you've got a cold choose eucalyptus instead: it will aid your breathing in the night.

chill-out techniques

Too busy to breathe? Take a few minutes out of your
busy schedule to practice one of these relaxation tricks.

IF YOU'VE GOT TWO MINUTES

A big stretch will loosen up tense muscles, and
lengthening your spine not only feels fantastic, it also
creates space, enabling you to breathe more deeply.
Lie on your back with your arms stretched out over
your head. Interlock your fingers, point your toes,
take a big breath in, and stretch your arms and legs
away from you. Hold for a few seconds, relax, and
repeat three times.

Singing and humming relieve stress as they cause
relaxing vibrations in your throat. Hum to yourself
when you start to feel stressed, and after a busy day,
turn up your car radio and sing all the way home.

IF YOU'VE GOT FIVE MINUTES

You don't need to be in a calming environment to
meditate effectively. Simply zone out by watching
something repetitive like washing in a machine or
traffic from a bus window. Just soften your focus
and detach your thoughts for a while—you may be
surprised where they go when you let them wander.

Shiatsu massage works on your body's meridians
to influence the energy flowing through you. To find
your stress-relief point, slide your thumb between the
bones leading away from your middle and ring fingers
until you reach the center of your palm. Breathe in and
press your thumb into this point as you slowly breathe
out (if you've hit the right spot, you'll feel a dull ache).
For best results, press and hold six times on each hand.

Yogis relax into child's pose, as it calms and tones
the nervous system while gently stretching the neck,
shoulders, and spine. Kneel on the floor with your
arms by your sides, and bend forward until your
forehead is gently resting on the floor and your hands
are resting by your feet. Inhale and exhale as you feel
your breath slow and your body completely relax. Bliss.

The next time you feel stressed, laugh. Laughter
releases endorphins into your brain (the ones you
usually have to exercise to get), which reduce levels
of the stress hormone cortisol, relax tense muscles,
and boost your immune system. The average adult
laughs only 17 times a day (compared to 300 times
as a child), so do what it takes to lighten up. Phone
a witty friend, recall a funny memory, or share a joke.

IF YOU CAN SPARE TEN MINUTES

Progressive muscle relaxation is the most thorough
way to relax your body. Lie on the floor and, starting
with each foot, clench your toes tight for five seconds
before letting your foot go floppy. Next lift each leg
off the floor and hold for five seconds before gently
dropping it down. Repeat the tensing and relaxing
process all the way up your body, concentrating on
different muscles every time. Clench your bottom hard
and release, make a fist, lift each arm off the floor in
turn, and tense your shoulders up to your ears. When
you reach your face, close your eyes tightly, then open
your mouth wide, stick out your tongue, and make
a loud "ahh" sound. Spend at least five minutes in this

super-relaxed state, feeling the full weight of your body heavy on the floor.

With new technology providing ever-increasing ways to communicate, most of us are reaching attention overload, which is why it's important to do absolutely nothing once in a while. Go to any comfortable, quiet spot: your couch, your car, or a café, and simply watch your mind do its thing. Don't judge what comes up, just be aware of all the activity. Detaching yourself in this way frees your mind from the fear that stops you from seeing things clearly—this is the reason why solutions to previously unsolvable problems can come up when you least expect them.

detox without trying

You don't need to live on lettuce leaves to feel the benefits of a spa detox. Read on for the real-life way.

DITCH THE LATTE AND START YOUR DAY WITH A GLASS OF HOT WATER AND LEMON

Just a few squeezes of lemon in a cup of hot water will have a cleansing effect on your liver, unlike coffee, which puts extra stress on your body by encouraging your adrenal glands to work harder. The result is an increased heart rate and slower digestion, neither of which encourage a mellow start to the day.

EAT ORGANIC FRUIT AND VEGETABLES

The best way to reduce exposure to toxic substances is to buy organic. Not only does organic farming keep the air and soil clean, but fruit and vegetables not treated with pesticides are also much more nutritious. They may be more expensive, but absorbing all those extra nutrients is so much better for your health. If you can't buy organic, take the outer layer off by peeling or scraping, so you know you've at least got rid of surface chemicals.

DON'T IGNORE WHAT YOU PUT ON YOUR SKIN

Up to 60 percent of any substance applied to your skin is absorbed, so if you're eating organic it makes perfect sense to buy organic skincare and makeup, too. You may experience an initial skin breakout, but this is just your skin's way of cleansing itself of chemicals, so give it time to adjust. Look for brands that contain plant-based ingredients and organic essential oils, plus natural preservatives (if any). For guaranteed good-for-you beauty products, look for certified organic products.

DRINK YOUR WATER FROM A GLASS, NOT AN OLD PLASTIC BOTTLE

Once a bottle is opened, bacteria enter the top, and by refilling it you're letting the bacteria multiply. And don't leave a half-empty bottle on your desk without a lid, as bacteria are attracted to the oxygen in the water.

LET PLANTS (NOT YOU) ABSORB COMPUTER RADIATION

Computers emit energy-sapping electromagnetic radiation, so no wonder sitting in front of one all day can leave you feeling drained. Luckily, studies have shown that placing a plant by your screen can actually reduce tiredness as the plant, rather than you, absorbs the electromagnetic excess.

SWITCH TO ORGANIC DAIRY AND MEAT PRODUCTS, TOO

The average farm animal is fed growth enhancers plus food supplements of animal origin, which contain a high level of pollutants. Organic meat and dairy products come from livestock fed their natural diet, which means a far lower level of chemicals.

BEWARE OF CHEMICALS WHILE COOKING

You may think an alfresco barbecue is healthy, but that burned kabob could contain potentially harmful oxidants. Also beware burning your food in non-stick pans, as they emit chemicals known as PFCs when overheated. And if you use a microwave, let your food stand for a few minutes before you eat it, as the energy created during microwave cooking can affect your blood and immune systems.

easy ways to eat better

Gone are the days when spa food meant spartan. What you will find at spas are plenty of the following, plus "mindful" eating: attending to your meal rather than eating in front of the TV.

START A NEW HABIT OF ALWAYS EATING AT THE TABLE
Light a candle and play soothing music to make it a feel-good ritual. Eat slowly and chew well so you really notice how your meal tastes. And wait ten minutes before helping yourself to another portion—your stomach needs this long to register how full it feels.

EAT FOODS AS CLOSE TO THEIR NATURAL STATE AS POSSIBLE FOR THE MOST HEALTHFUL DIET
That means plenty of whole grains (rather than their processed white equivalents), plus fresh fruit and vegetables. What needs to go, or be limited, are convenience foods such as ready meals, fast food, chips, cakes, and cookies. Give your body a spa-type break by going on a mini detox for the weekend. This not only makes you feel lighter and more energized, it also improves the condition of your skin and hair. Cut out meat, dairy products, convenience foods, wheat, salt, sugar, caffeinated drinks, and alcohol for two days. Beware side effects like headaches and sugar cravings as your body eliminates toxins. (The worse you feel, the more you probably need it.)

DRINK FRESH FRUIT AND VEGETABLE JUICES
It's a quick way to pack extra vitamins and minerals into your diet, and can count as one of your daily portions of fruit and vegetables. For best results and flavour, make your own at home using a blender or electric juicer. There's no magic formula here. Just combine your favorite fruit and vegetables and see what works best—soft vegetables like tomatoes and cucumber are the easiest to juice. Wash all produce first and drink immediately, as freshly squeezed juice doesn't keep for long (proof that making your own is so much better for you than the purchased variety).

USE HEALTH-PROMOTING HERBS, OILS, AND SPICES TO LIVEN UP YOUR MEALS
Try not to rely on salt and sugar (the secret behind those tasty TV dinners) to flavor your food. Add garlic to stir-fries for its immunity-boosting properties; it's antibacterial and antiviral, so helps fight off infection. Fry with sesame oil, which contains essential fatty acids to keep your heart healthy. And add finely chopped chili pepper to your food to aid digestion, help fight colds, and warm your body on a cold night.

STIR-FRY OR STEAM YOUR FOOD IN A WOK
This will retain most of its nutrients. The large surface area of the base allows heat to spread quickly, which means food cooks quickly without losing important goodness, or taste. Both couldn't be easier. To stir-fry, cut food into bite-sized pieces and use just enough oil to coat the inside of the wok—never use butter. Steaming is even healthier as it involves no extra fat and preserves most of the water-soluble vitamins that boiling takes away. Invest in some bamboo steamers to place above the simmering water. Don't pack your food too tightly or the steam won't be able to circulate evenly, and replace water with freshly boiled.

Juices are a quick way to pack extra vitamins and minerals into your diet, and can count as one of your daily portions of fruit and vegetables.

just a perfect day

Looking after yourself—all day—not only makes you feel great, it also boosts your self-esteem, because you're treating yourself like someone who's *worth* looking after.

RISE AND SHINE

Take a few minutes to think positively about the day ahead. The minute your eyes open, ask yourself: What is today's exciting thing? Having at least one thing to look forward to sets an optimistic tone for the rest of the day. If life seems aimless, ask yourself: For what or whom am I getting up today? Take control of your life by deciding where to place your attention that day.

Still in bed, practice some energizing deep breaths. Most of the time we breathe shallowly, but breathing more deeply brings a rich supply of oxygen to the blood. This energizes your body, leaving you more clear-headed for the day ahead. Imagine your lungs are divided into three sections: lower, middle, and upper. One complete breath in fills each section with air; one complete breath out leaves you feeling empty.

1 With hands resting on your abdomen, feel it rise as you inhale deeply through your nose, drawing air into the lower part of your lungs.

2 Move your hands to rest just below your ribs, and without pausing continue your inhalation, feeling a smaller rise under your hands.

3 Cross your arms and place your fingers just below your collarbone as you continue your inhalation, drawing air into the upper part of your lungs. Again, your collarbones should rise slightly.

4 Pause for a few seconds and then exhale slowly from the upper, middle, and lower part of your lungs, until you feel completely empty of air. Repeat five times with your arms resting by your sides.

You may have to wake up 30 minutes earlier than normal, but making time for the things you enjoy can change the entire course of your day. What start to the day usually means you have a good one?

□ Playing your favorite CD while dressing?
□ Sprinkling essential oils in the shower?
□ Eating an energy-packed breakfast?
□ Taking a walk or going for a swim?
□ Wearing your best underwear?

Even simple changes such as waking up to a relaxing CD rather than a nerve-jarring alarm can make all the difference to your morning.

LUNCHTIME LAW

Whatever your workload, always eat lunch away from your desk. If your body's eating and your mind's working, you're completely out of balance. Plus you won't even notice what you've put in your mouth—a waste of a good meal. After lunch, take a ten-minute walk outside to encourage your body to digest the food you've just eaten. Studies show that gentle exercise after eating burns up serious calories, plus the fresh air will clear your mind for the afternoon.

MIDDAY RESCUES

This is the time when aromatherapy oils can make the difference between a wasted afternoon and a productive one. A few drops of an energizing citrus oil such as lemon, lime, orange, mandarin, or bergamot on a handkerchief is all you need for a post-lunch pick-me-up (see pages 98–99 for more ideas).

If you find yourself stressed out, nervous, or angry, practice some alternate nostril breathing. By inhaling through one nostril and exhaling through the other, you'll balance your body and soothe your nervous system. Repeat the following at least five times or until your anxiety fades.

1 Close your right nostril with your right thumb and inhale deeply through your left nostril.

2 Hold for a few seconds, then close your left nostril with the middle finger of your right hand, release your thumb, and exhale through your right nostril.

3 Without moving your middle finger, inhale deeply through your right nostril.

4 Hold for a few seconds, close your right nostril with your thumb, and then release your left nostril before exhaling.

EVENING KICKBACKS

If you have trouble switching off after a hard day, literally scrub off your stress in the shower. Visualize your worries being washed down the drain as you go to work with your loofah or massage mitt. Change into some feel-good clothes (choose natural fibers such as cotton, linen, silk, wool, or cashmere) and you'll feel refreshed and ready for relaxation.

Slowing down at the end of a busy day is not being lazy, it's essential for a good night's sleep and to prepare yourself for the next day. Of course, some day's-end activities are more nurturing than others. Spending the evening flipping TV channels may feel relaxing, but if you try to sleep immediately afterward, your mind will still be busy and your body tense. Instead, set aside at least an hour before bedtime for some quiet pampering time.

Never end the day with a head full of unfinished tasks and chores. Rather than add to your neverending to-do list, change your perspective with a "done" list instead. Write down all the things you've achieved during the day and go to bed with a sense of achievement, not stress.

The best position to sleep in is on your side, as it encourages deep breathing through your nostrils, rather than the shallow breathing through your mouth (and snoring) you do when lying on your back. Most of us sleep with too many pillows, which can cause neck strain. Instead, use only one pillow and tuck it right into your neck to make sure your head and spine stay in alignment.

a quiet life

Silence is golden—and elusive. From the minute your alarm goes off, your head is filled with noise. Music blaring, people shouting, car alarms wailing, even your partner snoring. No wonder silence is so hard to find, which makes it all the more important to experience a few moments of tranquility every day.

It's hard to be productive with a racing mind, but when your mind's quiet, you can focus on what you're doing while still being able to see the whole picture. You can learn how to slow down and enjoy a state of internal silence by practicing the following techniques.

MEDITATION simply means concentrating on a mantra to replace your normal internal chatter while breathing deeply. This replaces stress with deep relaxation. Long-term benefits include clear thinking plus greater tolerance and decreased irritability, which not surprisingly leads to improved relationships and a feeling of happiness and well-being. The technique involves sitting comfortably (on the sofa, in a park, or even on a train) for 15–20 minutes with your eyes closed, silently repeating a mantra. Your breathing slows down as your mind experiences an inner silence while being wide awake. Bliss? Not far from it. For the first few times, choose a quiet place where you won't be interrupted (unplug the phone) and turn down the lights/close the blinds. Make sure you're comfortable and then start to imagine each part of your body relaxing. Begin with your scalp and work down to your toes, all the while thinking a two-syllable mantra (anything works: try "feel-good," "re-lax," or "me-time"). Concentrate on your breathing, and when thoughts break through the calm just let them come and go.

After 15 minutes, open your eyes and sit quietly for a few minutes before getting up and on with your day.

VISUALIZATION was devised by a radiotherapist who became convinced that patients' minds could be used to heal their bodies. Studies show that visualization encourages activity in the right side of your brain, which produces positive thoughts and energy. All you need is your imagination. If you want to relax, simply visualize a place that you find calming and peaceful. It could be an open meadow or wide lake (nature automatically regenerates the heart), or somewhere you associate with happy times (a beach or even your childhood bedroom). Whatever you choose, picture the scene in detail—the color of the sea, the sound of the waves, the smell of suntan lotion, the feel of sand under your feet. Once you've built up a vivid picture, you'll be able to recreate it quickly in times of need. Visualization can also be used to promote good health (look inside yourself and imagine your internal organs smiling at you), or to calm apprehensive thoughts about the future (you can imagine yourself acting the part while knowing no harm will come to you). However you use it, visualization works like a mini mind vacation. Simply find somewhere quiet to sit comfortably, be aware of your posture and breathing, and keep your feet on the ground to feel centered during your head trip.

stress strategies

In today's busy world, the following two mind games can
make all the difference between surviving and thriving.

ONE MINUTE THAT COULD SAVE YOUR DAY
You don't need 20 minutes to meditate. You can turn
a stressful situation into a one-minute mini-meditation.

1 Terrified you're going to ruin your presentation?
Paranoid about office politics? Just sad for no reason?
Avoid your mind's doom-and-gloom spiral: "If I blow
this I'll lose my job," and so on. Take a deep slow breath
and observe *exactly* how you're thinking and feeling.

2 Now breathe out and put those observations
into words: "I'm scared because I haven't done enough
research," or "I messed up my last presentation—why
should this one be any different?"

3 Keep breathing deeply as you put your fears into words. Simply by acknowledging exactly what's going on, you can do something practical or at the very least shift your perspective. Fear is simply an energy, and you can choose to use it to your advantage.

☐ What can you find out in the next hour that will help you feel more confident? Who can help you with this last-minute research? What can you learn from this experience so you never let it happen again?

☐ Maybe you're much better prepared than last time? Maybe you're more experienced? Perhaps your audience is less intimidating? Perhaps you know your subject better? Just looking at what else could be possible can change your mindset and make you feel so much more positive about the challenge ahead.

ONE SENTENCE THAT CAN SAVE YOUR SANITY

The word *mantra* means "mind tool" in Sanskrit, and the right one can stop the most stressed mind in its tracks. You already have many mantras in your head, and you're probably not even aware of them.

☐ "I always ruin things."
☐ "I can't be alone."
☐ "It never works out for me."

Your brain works by repetition, so the longer a thought stays there, the stronger it will be. No surprise, then, that eventually that thought becomes an automatic reaction every time you hit hard times. Guess what? If you think it never works out for you, it rarely will.

So what could you invent to replace that self-defeating phrase? You want to make a concrete contradiction, not just an airy positive platitude.

So "It never works out for me" can't be replaced with a Pollyanna-ish "Life is wonderful"—your mind's too smart for that. Far more powerful is a mantra that can be supported with hard evidence. "I will survive, I always do" puts you in control, if not of what happens in your life, then at least of how you deal with it. Next, write down the evidence to back it up—all the times when things didn't go your way, but you got through it and came out the other side a stronger person.

INSPIRATION TO INVENT YOUR OWN MANTRA

☐ "If I'm facing in the right direction, all I have to do is just keep going."
☐ "I know no matter how bad this feels, it will pass."
☐ "What doesn't kill me makes me stronger."
☐ "There is always a solution."

The next time life speeds up, repeat your chosen phrase in your head. You may be surprised by how much quicker your panicky mind slows down again.

indulge your senses

When you're busy, it's easy to forget there's more to you than just practical thoughts and actions. To nurture yourself completely, you have to get in touch with all your five pleasure senses.

These get forgotten in times of stress, when shallow breathing stops you from smelling what's around you, and eating on the run stops you from tasting fully what you put in your mouth. But sensory deprivation is one route to madness, so it's no wonder that fully indulging your senses feels so relaxing.

What gives you pleasure is unique, so start off by making a list of what you love.

I LOVE...
I love the taste of…
I love the smell of…
I love the sight of…
I love the sound of…
I love the touch of…

Stress stops us from appreciating the simple things in life, so it may take a while to come up with more than the obvious. You'll probably be quick to write "chocolate cake" down under taste, but you need to go deeper to find your true sensory pleasures. Perhaps the taste of your child's skin? Or your partner as you kiss him goodnight? Feeding yourself foods that make you feel good (rather than uncomfortable and bloated) is a treat for your taste buds as well as your body. And making meals a pleasure by eating slowly will indulge your senses far more than shoveling food down at your desk. Read on for more inspiration.

SMELL
Surround yourself with scents that calm you down or lift you up, depending on what you need. Burn essential oils at your desk, or sprinkle them in your bath water or on your pillow at night (turn to pages 98–99 for more ideas). Take a trip around a perfume department and hunt out scents that bring back happy memories. Perhaps there's one that reminds you of your teenage party years, or a brand your mother used when you were young. Wearing them now will have an instant effect on your mood, whether it's giving you that excited feeling before a night out or making you feel safe and secure.

SIGHT
Do your surroundings please you? When was the last time you really noticed what you live with every day? Perhaps your bedroom needs painting, or the curtains in your living room are threadbare. If your workplace is a depressing sight first thing in the morning, take in photos from home or buy a plant for your desk. If you spend your days in an office, get out into green spaces at lunchtime for an instant feel-good effect.

SOUND
What music gives you a warm feeling? Dig out your old records and make up compilations to play in your car. And it's not just music that soothes us. Does the sound of a particular friend's voice make you feel

supported? Would the tinkling of a wind chime on your porch relax you (or drive you and your neighbors mad)? The sounds of nature are always soothing, so invest in a CD of water, waves, or wind rustling through the trees to play after a hard day.

TOUCH

Do the clothes you wear feel great against your skin, or do they have scratchy seams and uncomfortable zippers? Do you sleep on good-quality cotton sheets, or rough old polyester ones? Do you take the time to massage body lotion into your skin after bathing or just rub yourself down with a rough towel? Do you give yourself (or someone else) a hug every day? Many of us are desperately touch-deprived, so let your friends and family know you care by regularly showing them affection.

Include as many sensory pleasures in your day as possible, particularly when you're scared, sad, or bored. Wear your favorite perfume to the dentist, or a cashmere sweater when visiting your difficult mother-in-law. You'll enjoy every moment just a little bit more.

mood improvers

Our bodies are set up for happiness. We get a natural rush of endorphins (feel-good chemical messengers) when laughing, doing physical exercise, being with people we love, or feeling completely relaxed. But we can manufacture the same response by *remembering* an experience that recreates positive emotions.

MAKE YOUR OWN ENDORPHINS

It's easy. Start off relaxed and just think of a happy thought: your partner doing something special for you, your friend showing how much she cared. Then make this thought more and more vivid in your mind until you begin feeling the good vibes you experienced when it took place. Indulge in the sensation until you become aware of which parts of your body feel good. Do you have a tingle in your stomach or a warm glow in your heart? Hold that feeling and really pay attention to it. You want to be able to conjure up the same sensation again and again, particularly when what's going on around you may not be so positive.

Go all Julie Andrews and make a list of your favorite things. These can be things people have said to you or done for you, or simple pleasures such as stroking your cat. Now you have a list of the happy thoughts and memories that you can call on when you want to experience an endorphin rush any time, anywhere.

SPONTANEOUS SMILE INDUCERS

Smiling is a very serious business—it releases tension and promotes a feeling of total well-being.

For a few days, observe what makes you smile spontaneously. We're talking a genuine smile, not the socially acceptable one you put on when meeting someone new. A genuine smile lifts your spirits. What events, situations, and people produce your inner (and perhaps outer) smile? Make a note of every smile sighting until you have a list of spontaneous smile inducers. Then treat yourself to at least two a day. Remember: these are things that make you feel good, not things you think *should* make you feel good. If the very thought of going to the gym makes you smile, put it on your list. If not, it's never going to be one of your spontaneous smilers—however much you want it to be.

PRACTICE YOUR OWN INNER SMILE

As an alternative to endorphin-fueled mood improvers, you can recreate a smiley feeling with an inner smile.

1 Start by sitting comfortably. You can do this anywhere—on the bus, at work, or stuck in traffic.
2 Allow a smile to come into your eyes. Then let it spread to the rest of your face so the corners of your mouth turn up slightly.
3 Now smile into any part of your body that's tense and feel it begin to relax.
4 Next, smile into any part of your body that feels good and thank it for keeping you healthy.
5 Last, smile into the parts of your life that are working and allow yourself to feel grateful—for a work project that's going well, a nurturing friendship, or a home that makes you feel relaxed and secure.

20 instant rescue remedies

For when you're *feeling* less than your best.

1 Sore, tired feet love a warm foot bath with either a handful of epsom salts or five drops of peppermint essential oil added. Finish with a shot of cold water from the shower to reduce any puffiness before drying thoroughly.

2 When you hit a tired spell, ditch the coffee and instead drink two glasses of pure water quickly. Follow with a ten-minute walk outside, which will stimulate your heart, lungs, muscles, and mind.

3 Alcohol lowers your body's supply of vitamins B and C, so rather than drinking water the morning after make yourself a juice for a far more potent hangover cure. Top marks go to a carrot or celery and apple combination, which will help rebalance your body. And give yourself a better chance of recovery by taking the detoxing herb milk thistle before and after drinking. It works by helping your liver process alcohol, so reducing the effects of any hangover the next day.

4 When times are tough, it's even more important to connect with the people you love. So no matter how busy you are, make time to see and speak to those closest to you. Knowing you are cared about puts even the worst day into perspective.

5 If your skin's prone to flushing in hot atmospheres, drink a cup of hot peppermint tea, which will instantly cool down your system.

6 Don't even think about starting the day with a bagel or white toast (both refined carbohydrates) when you're feeling less than energetic. What you need are complex carbs (preferably uncooked ones) such as granola, with a bit of protein for slow, sustained energy throughout the day.

7 To override a midday or mid-afternoon energy slump, eat a slice of avocado on whole-wheat toast or a small handful of nuts or seeds for a steady, long-lasting high.

8 New ideas come from a fresh mind, so when you're stuck, take a break for five minutes or longer. Gaze out of the window and let your mind wander, or go for a walk and let the fresh air blow through your brain. By the time you return, you'll be thinking far more calmly and clearly.

9 Release the tension in a tight, stressed jaw by biting into a crunchy apple. Apples are also the perfect way to freshen breath on the go, as they cause your mouth to step up saliva production, breaking down food particles that may be causing bad breath.

IO When you have trouble sleeping, eat a small portion of starchy food such as a piece of whole-wheat bread with fruit preserves before bedtime. But avoid butter or margarine, as fat will interfere with the sedative effect.

II For a quick energy boost, grate a small spoonful of fresh ginger into a mug of hot water. The same mixture can also be used as a hot compress for lower back ache. Dip a washcloth in the water, wring out, and hold over the problem area (avoid if you're pregnant).

I2 Ease winter cold and cough symptoms with a cup of parsley tea. Boil one bunch of parsley in a small saucepan of water, pour the mixture into a cup, and drink before you eat. You can also soothe congestion by massaging your chest with five drops of eucalyptus oil mixed with one tablespoon of vegetable oil.

I3 Never wait until you feel lousy to take echinacea. The time to start is when you first feel you're coming down with something. And don't be tempted to take it long term, as studies show that echinacea loses its immunity-boosting powers if your body gets too accustomed on the effects.

I4 Tell yourself you'll have a good day and you probably will. Research shows that people who think good things will happen to them are usually right, so next time your mind takes a negative turn, ask yourself what more positive outcome could be possible. We make our own thoughts, so we may as well make them optimistic.

I5 If a busy mind is waking you at 2A.M., keep a notebook by your bed and write down any problems, insights, or solutions. With your head clear you'll be much more likely to fall straight back to sleep, and you can deal with things far better in the morning.

16 When you're feeling low in energy, eat foods rich in vitamin B, which is required for the production of energy. These include fruit, vegetables, seeds, nuts, whole grains, and fish. Bananas are also a great energy boost due to their high concentration of natural sugar, which produces a slow, steady shot in the arm. And rather than three large meals a day, eat smaller meals more often to sustain you.

17 Tense, stressed headache? Gently press your first two fingers just under the bone at the base of your skull either side of your spine. Lean back onto your fingers and then work in gentle circular movements down each side of your neck, spending a little longer on tender areas.

18 Another headache cure. Soak your feet for ten minutes in a bowl of warm water mixed with a teaspoon of cayenne pepper, as the heat will draw blood away from your head and ease the pain. Foods that heal headaches are salty, so try eating a couple of olives in brine. If after a few minutes this doesn't help, quickly drink two glasses of cool water.

19 Book your next time off from work, even if you're not going away on vacation. Just knowing you will have time to relax then will help you to keep going when life feels out of control. Even if you've only managed to clear one day, plan to do something you'll really enjoy—no chores allowed.

20 Determine what parts of your day make you the most stressed (for example, sitting in traffic, doing housework, answering e-mails), and then work out a way to lessen your irritation (solutions could be listening to books on tape, getting a cleaner, only responding to mail that really needs a reply).

ten ways to look after yourself when you're busy

1 GIVE YOURSELF THE FIRST TEN PERCENT
You can only look after others if you first take care of yourself properly.

2 INVEST IN YOURSELF
Whether that means me-time, great-quality food, or new experiences.

3 TAKE THE PHONE OFF THE HOOK AFTER DINNER
You don't have to be available to others 24 hours a day, seven days a week.

4 GET A GOOD NIGHT'S SLEEP
The average adult needs eight hours' sleep a day, so improve your chances of deep rest with a good-quality mattress and pillows.

5 SURROUND YOURSELF WITH "UP" PEOPLE
Your environment has a profound effect on you, so make sure the people you spend most time with are supportive.

6 PRACTICE DO-ANYWHERE DE-STRESS STRATEGIES
For example, take three deep breaths while rubbing the insides of your palms to improve blood supply and stimulate circulation.

7 ONLY DO ONE THING AT A TIME
It's OK to do two things at once, but only as long as you don't need to do either of them very well.

8 KEEP THINGS IN PERSPECTIVE
In times of stress, it's important to stop and admit that what you're facing is actually more annoying than life-threatening.

9 HAVE A SENSE OF HUMOR
Laughter reduces stress hormone levels, so find something to lighten your mood every day.

10 DO WHAT MEANS THE MOST TO YOU
Figure out what brings you the most joy and make it your mission to find time for that every day of your life.

last word

If you want to see what your thoughts were like yesterday, look at your body today. If you want to see what your body will be like tomorrow, look at your thoughts today.

OLD INDIAN SAYING

useful addresses

RETAILERS

Aveda
866 823 1425
for stores
www.aveda.com

Barneys New York
660 Madison Avenue
New York NY 10021
212 826 8900
www.barneys.com

Bath & Body Works
800 395 1001 for stores
www.bathandbody
    works.com

Crabtree & Evelyn
800 272 2873 for stores
www.crabtree-evelyn.com

Crate & Barrel
650 Madison Avenue
New York, NY 10022
800 967 6696 for stores
www.crateandbarrel.com

**Giorgio Armani
Cosmetics**
www.giorgioarmani.com

Green People
www.greenpeople.co.uk

Laura Mercier Cosmetics
www.lauramercier.com

Origins
www.origins.com

Sephora
2103 Broadway
New York, NY 10023
212 362 1500
www.sephora.com

INFORMATION

**American Massage
Therapy Association**
500 Davis Street,
Suite 900
Evanston, IL 60201
847 864 0123
www.amtamassage.org
Help with finding a
massage therapist
near you.

**National Acupuncture and
Oriental Medicine Alliance**
6405 43rd Avenue Ct.
NW, Suite B
Gig Harbor, WA 98335
253 851 6896
www.acuall.org

Information on
complementary and
alternative medicine
and on finding a
practitioner near you.

**National Women's Health
Resource Center**
157 Broad Street,
Suite 315
Red Bank, NJ 07701
877 986 9472
www.healthywomen.org
Information resource
designed to encourage
women to pursue healthy
lifestyles.

OTHER RESOURCES

Calmia
52–54 Marylebone
High Street
London W1U 5HR
+44 845 0092450
www.calmia.com
Holistic lifestyle store and
inner beauty day spa.

Chelsea Nail Studio
5 Pond Place
London SW3 6QR
+44 20 7225 3889

Method Putkisto Institute
56 Derby Road
London SW14 7DP
To order the Method
Putkisto Face School
video, DVD, or manual
call +44 20 8878 7384
www.methodputkisto.com
See pages 26–27.

Phytomer
Call +44 1753 856836
for stockists and
mail order
www.phytomer.com
Sea water and seaweed
products.

Also available from
The Beauty Room
www.thebeautyroom.com

Pure Massage
3–5 Vanston Place
London SW6 1AY
+44 20 7381 8100
www.puremassage.uk.com
Body and face massages,
also Introduction to
Massage Course.

index

acknowledgments

Many thanks to The Method Putkisto Face School (see pages 26–27); Tracy Hemmings at Calmia Inner Beauty Day Spa, who devised the de-stress facial (page 30) and facelift facial (page 36); Virginie Espil at Laura Mercier, Harrods, and Sheila Toofaneeram at Giorgio Armani, Harvey Nichols, London (see pages 48–49); Robyn Opie at the Chelsea Nail Studio (see pages 68–71); and Beata Aleksandrowicz at Pure Massage (see pages 84–87).

The author would like to thank all her wonderful friends and family.
Visit Liz Wilde's website at www.wildelifecoaching.com for information about her online programs, one-to-one coaching, and to subscribe to her free Monthly Motivator Mail.

picture credits

Photography by Daniel Farmer unless otherwise stated.
a=above, b=below, r=right, l=left, c=center

Page 14 © The Color Wheel Company (www.colorwheelco.com); **David Montgomery** endpapers, 23al, 24, 30al inset & background, 36–37l, 40–41, 49 background, 53, 59, 61c & b, 73, 98–99, 102, 112, 114–115l & ar, 119, 124–127; **Dan Duchars** 3, 30r inset, 44–45, 51, 62, 75r, 79 inset, 107, 109, 113; **Alan Williams** 4–5 / Alannah Weston's house in London designed by Stickland Coombe Architecture; **Jan Baldwin** 13 / Angela and David Coxon's family home in Kent, 61a, 80 / the Meiré family home, designed by Marc Meiré; **Debi Treloar** 15ar, 21, 57, 63, 105bl & r; **Chris Everard** 18–20, 75c, 81, 92; **Nicky Dowey** 22 & 23bl; **Martin Brigdale** 23ar; **William Lingwood** 23br; **Andrew Wood** 60, 75l; **Ian Wallace** 74r; **Tom Leighton** 79 background, 115br; **Simon Upton** 105al; **Polly Wreford** 123, 128.

Stickland Coombe Architecture 258 Lavender Hill, London SW11 1LJ, UK t. +44 20 7924 1699 www.sticklandandcoombe.com Pages 4–5
Angela Southwell Interior Design t. +44 1732 763246 angsouthwell@hotmail.com Page 13
Also featured in this home: Maybury tropical rustic furniture and accessories (www.mayburydesign.co.uk)